SELECTED WRITINGS ❦ SAMUEL JOHNSON

Selected Writings ❦ Samuel Johnson

Edited by Peter Martin

The Belknap Press of Harvard University Press

Cambridge, Massachusetts · London, England

2009

Library of Congress Cataloging-in-Publication Data

Johnson, Samuel, 1709–1784.
[Selections. 2009]
Samuel Johnson : selected writings / edited by Peter Martin.
p.   cm.
Includes bibliographical references.
ISBN 978-0-674-03585-0 (cloth : alk. paper)
I. Martin, Peter, 1940–   II. Title.
PR3522.M25 2009
828′.609—dc22   2009011802

Contents

Note on the Text

This text has been prepared for the general reader. Its aim is to introduce readers to the wisdom and great pleasures of Samuel Johnson's writing.

My text has been sourced from the 1825 Oxford edition of *The Works of Samuel Johnson,* and I have also consulted several contemporary and modern editions. I have modernized Johnson's spelling and punctuation, except in poetry and the titles of works.

The standard scholarly edition of Johnson's works remains the Yale Edition (still in progress).

Introduction

With its persistent and aggressive demands for our attention from the blogosphere to the media to the bookshops, our age appears to have urgent need of what Samuel Johnson (1709–1784) has to say in his essays. The world distracts us endlessly with stimuli, making it easy to focus on its allurements and forget Johnson's admonitions to look within. He encourages us to take a good hard look at ourselves, to think about who we are, how we are responding to the world around us, how we have arrived where we are, and where we are heading. "Time and again, in whatever direction we go, we meet Johnson returning on the way back," one critic has said.[1] Written over the course of some thirty-five years, Johnson's many essays—psychological, literary, political, social, ethical, and religious—make him one of the greatest moralists in the literature of English-speaking nations. From Johnson's Enlightenment era to the present day, his writings have taken their place as an iconic part of national cultures and private lives.

Johnson's contemporaries recognized the power and depth of his essays, especially in the periodical the *Rambler*, even if some complained of his bleak view of human nature and his penetrating but unsparing exploration of pride and egotism in human behavior. "I have never complied with temporary curiosity," he wrote in his last *Rambler* essay, "nor enabled my readers to discuss the topic of the day." His strengths lay elsewhere. The essayist and poet Catherine Talbot remarked to Elizabeth Carter, Johnson's young intellectual friend and protégé, that his essays "seem to flow from his heart, and from a heart amiable and delicate to a great degree."[2] He was proposing to dive deep into human egotism and the complex texture of morality where he thought any man (especially he) was bound to feel naked and be found wanting.

John Ruskin, himself one of the greatest English essayists of the nineteenth century and a powerful social reformer in his day, wrote that before embarking on a family journey his father would carefully slip into a bag "four little volumes" of Johnson's *Rambler* and *Idler* moral essays because they contained "more substantial literary nourishment than could be, from any other author, packed into so portable [a] compass. . . . I at once and forever recognized in him a man entirely sincere, and infallibly wise in the view and estimate he gave of the common questions, business, and ways of the world. . . . No other writer could have secured me, as he did, against all chance of being misled by my own sanguine and metaphysical temperament. He taught me to measure life, and distrust fortune. . . . he saved me forever from false thoughts and futile speculations." More recently, the playwright Samuel Beckett remarked, "it's Johnson, always Johnson, who is with me. And if I follow any tradition, it is his." Beckett was thinking more of Johnson's private, melancholic, tormented life than his periodical essays, but many of the essays are emanations and reflections, as Shakespeare put it, of "that perilous stuff/Which weighs upon the heart." In his acceptance speech for the Nobel Prize in Literature in 1995, Seamus Heaney acknowledged the *Rambler*'s durable appeal: "the mind still longs to repose in what Samuel Johnson once called with superb confidence 'the stability of truth.'" On American soil, Henry Adams drew inspiration from Johnson's moral essays for his own essays or "useful reflections" on human nature in the *Gazette of the United States* in 1790–1791. And the poet and physician Oliver Wendell Holmes relished Johnson's wit and humaneness in his "Breakfast Table" series of essays in the mid-nineteenth century. Harold Bloom, one of the world's greatest modern critics, announced, "I worship Johnson," and he called him his critical hero: "Johnson deserves all the indulgences that can be granted, because he was greatly good as well as great-hearted. A more humane critic has never existed, nor one who demonstrates quite so well the true value of the highest literature for life."

The list seems endless. Indeed, it is remarkable how Johnson, perhaps more than any other English author except Shakespeare, is almost a pre-occupation, even an obsession, in the minds of authors, critics, religious thinkers, social commentators, and politicians—a prolific and seemingly omniscient reference point and moral authority where judgment, acute and often uncomfortable insight, and common sense are called for. To read the moral essays is to touch the heart of Johnson. "We are perpetu-ally moralists, but we are geometricians only by chance," wrote Johnson in his "Life of Milton."[3]

At a time when we seem determined to destroy our planet through ig-norance, war, and abuse of each other, Johnson's essays speak to us today as powerfully and perhaps even more urgently than they did for his own readers. And yet that universality in his writings may appear surprising in light of the circumstances in which he wrote them. Why is it that in spite of their context of illness, melancholia, and vitriolic anger directed against the oppressiveness of a society that had thwarted him repeatedly, not to mention relentless deadlines imposed by the nature of the periodical es-say, the essays are timeless? One answer is that they are timeless precisely because they are the fruits, the distillation, of a life "diseased" from birth, through adolescence and young manhood and into early professional life by sickness, failure, shattered hopes, and the shades of poverty. Adversity had dogged his footsteps for years but had paradoxically opened his bril-liant scholarly and philosophical mind into a larger wisdom of insight, hard realism, and far-reaching irony. His agonies—which must not be understated—not philosophical leisure and detachment, helped create his moral voice. In the moral essays his vantage point is not that of a preacher from a pulpit but of a human being talking to other humans, en-couraging them with an understanding and assurance that we are all to-gether in the same boat, grappling with similar problems, linked to each other by the human predicament. He does not take us into the labyrinths of abstruse philosophy but grounds his reflections on human nature with immediacy so we can use them in our lives to avoid self-delusion, pride, pretentiousness, and other forms of egotism, moving us toward an appre-ciation of what human nature really is. As he wrote in the famous Preface to his edition of *Shakespeare*, "nothing can please many and please long but just representations of general nature." Twenty-first-century readers can feel this Johnsonian humanity at least as palpably as have readers during the previous two and a half centuries. It is what powers his essays and makes them so accessible.

There is Christianity in Johnson's moral probing, but it is mainly implied, seeming at times to be almost an afterthought. Instead of admonishing at the outset what virtues, Christian or otherwise, should be guiding human thought and behavior, he begins a typical moral essay by portraying people, behaviors, motivations, and situations with a cool, reasoning realism, often an angry and biting one at that. His method is to proceed in terms of how people deceive and delude themselves out of vanity, greed, pride, ignorance, and ambition. This is conventionally the literary instinct of a satirist like Jonathan Swift (of whom Johnson was very critical because he "show[s] the age involved in darkness, and shade[s] the picture with sullen emulation"), but instead of making such targets ends in themselves, with reductive severity his emphasis is on what should be avoided in personal and social behavior if people are to achieve the sorts of lives that will make them happy. He penetrates the subtleties of self-delusion, persisting in his analysis of human motivations until they are starkly and even brutally clear, in order to discover and demonstrate the roots of unhappiness, disappointment, false hope, and misery. His readers take note and privately resolve to think and behave better than his characters have. It is all done with compassion and practical reference to the real lives people lead and the conditions in which from time to time we all find ourselves, many of which Johnson portrays as comic and pitiful and all of which he renders with psychological precision.

This tercentenary selection of Johnson's writings is not representative of the wide range of his literary output and achievement. Missing are, among others, Johnson the poet, dramatist, journalist, and writer on travel and religion. The selection offers a *portion* of Johnson—Johnson the moralist and critic—and at its center is a generous offering of the periodical essays published in the *Rambler* (1750–1752), *Adventurer* (1753–1754), and *Idler* (1758–1760). For convenience these are grouped in the following categories: morality, behavior, and psychology; society and manners; biography and autobiography; literature and authorship; death; and politics. Also included are excerpts from several of the *Lives of the Poets* (Johnson's greatest critical achievement), and the Prefaces to the *Dictionary* and his edition of *Shakespeare*. It is well to remember that when Johnson writes criticism, it is experiential criticism. He illustrates, as Harold Bloom has put it, that this literary art "joins itself to the ancient genre of wisdom writing," and that "the authority of criticism as a literary genre depends upon the human wisdom of the critic." Literary criticism, adds Bloom—in a phrase that has a certain Johnsonian ring to it—is "the wisdom of interpretation and the interpretation of wisdom."[4] As such, it is at home in a selection that focuses on Johnson the moralist. Included here is also *Rasselas* (1759), his philosophical tale or moral fable, because it should be seen as a coda to a decade of great moral outpouring. Together, these works—allied in their literary, social, and moral concerns— are the ones likeliest to speak to readers today.

The *Rambler*

By 1750, the year in which the essays in the *Rambler* began to appear, Johnson had already been struggling in London for thirteen years to make a name for himself with his writing and earn enough money from it to pluck himself and his wife, Tetty, from near-poverty. He had experienced only a small measure of success: his well-received *London: A Poem* (published anonymously in 1738 but eventually known as his), his sensational *Account of the Life of Mr. Richard Savage* in 1744 (also anonymous), and his brilliant satiric poem *The Vanity of Human Wishes* in 1749, the first work to appear under his own name and his finest poetic effort. His journalistic work for the *Gentleman's Magazine*, mainly from 1738 to 1745, together with some biographical and scholarly labor (much of it abortive), had brought him attention within the London publishing world (but not within the wider public) and won him a contract in 1746 to write the *Dictionary of the English Language*, but by 1750 he was still little known and poor. Moreover, his work on the *Dictionary* had recently stuttered to a virtual standstill owing to a crisis in his methods, and he was suffering from melancholia, loneliness, and marital troubles.

Published twice weekly for two years, the *Rambler* offered him a lifeline. Although the essays appeared anonymously, it was not long before friends like the actor David Garrick, the novelist Samuel Richardson, and others familiar with his sonorous rhythms and elegant, balanced syntax transmitting an air of authority and dignity caught on that he was the author. Richardson wrote to Edward Cave, the founder and editor of the famous *Gentleman's Magazine,* "There is but one man, I think, that could write them," to which Cave replied, "Mr. Johnson is the *Great Rambler,* being, as you observe, the only man who can furnish two such papers in a week, besides his other great business."[5] His name was soon on everyone's lips. The money was welcome and it was steady work that gave him a chance to escape from his study and through his prose interact with the public immediately and regularly. The relentless deadlines also forced him to conquer (at least momentarily) his natural indolence. In the last essay (number 208), he wrote poignantly of the pains of composition: "He that condemns himself to compose on a stated day will often bring to his task an attention dissipated, a memory embarrassed, an imagination overwhelmed, a mind distracted with anxieties, a body languishing with disease." Nonetheless, he added, "Whatever shall be the final sentence of mankind, I have at least endeavoured to deserve their kindness. I have laboured to refine our language to grammatical purity, and to clear it from colloquial barbarisms, licentious idioms, and irregular combinations." As for the "professedly serious" essays, by which he meant those on explicitly moral themes as well as those involving sketches or portraits that turn on lessons of human behavior, he wrote, "I . . . look back on this part of my work with pleasure, which no blame or praise of man shall diminish or augment. I shall never envy the honours which wit and learning obtain in any other cause, if I can be numbered among the writers who have given ardour to virtue, and confidence to truth." To the end of his days, he was prouder of the *Rambler* than of anything else he ever wrote: while his other writings were "wine and water," "my Rambler is pure wine." With its reflections on the human predicament, it is the most personal and psychologically charged body of prose he ever wrote.

A prevailing undercurrent in the essays is anger against the Establishment and power elites that perpetuate egotism, venality, stupidity, destructive discrimination, and cruelty in society. His indignation is often irrepressible, rising from a lifetime of festering social wounds. In the last number he declared proudly, "I have seen the meteors of fashion rise and fall, without any attempt to add a moment to their duration. . . . I did not feel much dejection from the want of popularity." Tempered by a focus on reconciliation, community, and moral regeneration, the essays nonetheless abound with stridency, disdainful accounts of inhumane social institutions and attitudes, and character sketches of people in ludicrous and tragic pursuit of pitiful and vain illusions. His subjects and literary forms include, among others, allegory and fictional narratives, parables, biography, literary criticism, the world of learning and authorship, reading, education, patronage, poverty, and social reform regarding prisons, orphanages, prostitutes, slavery, capital punishment, religion, law and government, parental tyranny, women, and marriage. There is a seemingly endless parade of moral topics—among them envy, happiness, thirst for riches, idleness, procrastination, vanity, sorrow and grief, melancholia, fear, false hope, piety, fame, death, self-knowledge, overuse of the imagination, friendship, age, economy, pride, humor, shortness of life, complacency, reputation, and adversity. In its cumulative comprehensiveness, the *Rambler* has been described as Johnson's most representative single work chiefly because of its direct applicability to the human condition, to what Hamlet invoked as "the glory, jest, and riddle of the world."

The *Adventurer*

It is no mere coincidence that Johnson published his last *Rambler* essay on March 14, 1752, just three days before his wife Tetty's death. His grief was so profound and life-altering that he could not bring himself to write any more of them. His friend and biographer William Shaw wrote that in the weeks and months following, "study disgusted him, and the books of all kinds were equally insipid."[6] Several months before her death he had roused himself again to begin serious work on the *Dictionary*, but now that also faltered briefly, even in the garret of his house in Gough Square where he could manage to get some work done because it was less haunted by painful memories of her. By November 1752, however, the wheels began to turn again and he was able to help his friend John Hawkesworth establish a new twice-weekly periodical, the *Adventurer,* which helped him take his mind off his grief and relieve the *Dictionary* drudgery. The intention was to appeal to a wider audience than the *Rambler* had done by including not only essays about grave moral issues but also, in Johnson's words, lighter "pieces of the imagination, pictures of life." It was agreed that Hawkesworth would write forty-six and Johnson and his friend Joseph Warton twenty-three each, although Johnson ended up writing twenty-nine, all anonymous (signed with a "T"). He was reticent about owning up to them, but neither the "T" nor his style fooled several of his friends, such as Elizabeth Carter, who wrote, "I discern Mr. Johnson . . . as evidently as if I saw him through the keyhole with the pen in his hand."[7] He might have written more essays had it not been for the growing demands of the *Dictionary* and his reluctance to "condemn himself to compose on a stated day." The intervals between his essays averaged from one to seven days. The periodical lasted for 140 numbers, Johnson's last essay (number 138) appearing on March 2, 1754.

With its relative lightness and greater diversity, the *Adventurer* proved to be a bigger commercial success than the *Rambler.* Johnson wrote his essays with larger brush strokes for more casual readers, but he was still intensely indignant and often bleak in exposing human flaws and vices. He covered many of the same subjects and themes as in the *Rambler,* focusing especially on vanity and its dangers: flattery, learning, lying, retirement, egocentricity, complacency, happiness, and the pride of thinking of ourselves as somehow exempt from the rules and realities that bind the rest of mankind. Especially interesting are those themes that may be taken as autobiographical—for example, life as a warfare in which one must fight the good fight, the scars and doubts of authorship, and his courageous admission in his penultimate paper (number 137), "That the world has grown apparently better, since the publication of the *Adventurer,* I have not observed; but am willing to think that many have been affected by single sentiments." In his last essay he spoke of the suffering inherent in authorship: "Composition is, for the most part, an effort of slow diligence and steady perseverance, to which the mind is dragged by necessity or resolution, and from which the attention is every moment starting to more delightful amusements."

Preface to the *Dictionary*

If ever there was a large writing project on which Johnson worked that for a variety of reasons he strongly felt was a desperate grind and drudgery, a monumental emotional and spiritual challenge that threatened at times to defeat him, it was the *Dictionary*. A lexicographer was "doomed only to remove rubbish and clear obstructions from the paths of learning and genius," he wrote in the Preface. Nonetheless, his raw courage enabled him to overcome obstacles that might well have caused despair in others and impelled them to fly from the clutches of lexicography forever. The group of booksellers who had contracted with him for the *Dictionary* back in 1746 had become so exasperated by his delays that by late 1752 they were clamoring for him to complete the work. He had little choice but to knuckle down, writing a prayer in November of that year asking God to help him "shun sloth and negligence."[8] For the next two years in "anxious diligence" he worked astonishingly fast to complete it, and his labors were finally crowned when it was published on April 15, 1755.

His strategy for the Preface was conventional enough in that it is an *apologia* for what he had done, a way of anticipating and deflecting criticism. But it is also a remarkably honest and moving personal revelation. He wrote of "the gloom of solitude" during the long nine years he had had this albatross around his neck. At first he had visions "of the hours which I should revel away in feasts of literature . . . and the triumph with which I should display my acquisitions to mankind." Life, as distinct from art, had awakened him rudely to the realization that "these were the dreams of a poet doomed at last to wake a lexicographer. . . . much of my life has been lost under the pressure of disease; much has been trifled away. . . . a whole life cannot be spent upon syntax and etymology." Unaided for the most part, he had pushed on through treacherous lexicographical waters, "not in the soft obscurities of retirement, or under the shelter of academic bowers, but amidst inconvenience and distraction, in sickness and sorrow."

That said, the Preface is not predominantly introspective and melancholic. Most of it is an authoritative and intellectually penetrating explanation of his theory and practice. He considers English in a sociolinguistic context. Initially, in his *Plan of a Dictionary of the English Language* from 1747—a publicity move in which he presented himself and staked out his territory at the same time as he specified his methods and principles—he stated that he intended "a dictionary by which the pronunciation of our language may be fixed, and its attainment facilitated; by which its purity may be preserved, its use ascertained, and its duration lengthened." In other words, his dictionary would prescribe what was right and wrong in current usage. By the time he wrote the Preface, after almost nine years of work, he had changed his mind. His *Dictionary* describes, not prescribes, usage. Not only grammar and spelling, but also the choices and definitions of words, including everyday words, are determined by how people actually use the language in a civilized society, not by what academies or authorities dictate from within the rarefied regions of lexicography. If a word has become obsolete, it should be allowed to fade: "what makes a word obsolete, more than general agreement to forbear it? And how shall it be continued, when it conveys an offensive idea, or recalled again into the mouths of mankind, when it has once by disuse become unfamiliar, and by unfamiliarity unpleasing." While he did exercise discretion in drawing words from written rather than spoken English because of "the boundless chaos of a living speech" that was almost impossible to record, he put his case resoundingly and comprehensively in this passage: "When we see men grow old and die at a certain time one after another, from century to century, we laugh at the elixir that promises to prolong life to a thousand years; and with equal justice may the lexicographer be derided, who being able to produce no example of a nation that has preserved their words and phrases from mutability shall imagine that his dictionary can embalm his language, and secure it from corruption and decay, that it is in his power to change sublunary nature, or clear the world at once from folly, vanity, and affectation."

We can see the moralist in the character of the *Rambler* writing that passage: a nation that attempts to freeze its language is little less than barbaric; the authority rests in people, including its best writers—from whom Johnson drew well over one hundred thousand examples to illustrate usage. He also reminds the reader of his humanity as a lexicographer, just as he did in his moral essays. He has made mistakes and does not delude himself that everyone will applaud his achievement: "I may surely be contented without the praise of perfection, which, if I could obtain, in this gloom of solitude, what would it avail me? I have protracted my work till most of those whom I wished to please have sunk into the grave, and success and miscarriage are empty sounds: I therefore dismiss it with frigid tranquillity, having little to fear or hope from censure or from praise."[9]

The *Idler*

Many reviews of the *Dictionary* patriotically recognized the huge scale of Johnson's achievement for the glory of Britain. More than that, however, it was an embodiment of eighteenth century culture and ideas about language, and it became a standard work against which past and future dictionaries were measured. Recently, the historian Henry Hitchings has described it as "the most important British cultural monument of the eighteenth century."[10] It made Johnson famous overnight.

Four years later, Johnson embarked on the *Idler,* another outpouring of essays (weekly, though not all one hundred and three are his, between April 15, 1758, and April 5, 1760) featured on the front page of a new eight-page weekly gazette, the *Universal Chronicle.* Boswell noted that this time in order to attract more readers Johnson wrote the *Idler* essays with "less body and more spirit . . . more variety of real life, and greater facility of language" than the *Rambler* and *Adventurer* essays.[11] It is true the essays are shorter and with briefer sentences and an easier style; there are also many more on topical and less serious subjects such as sleep, memory, conversation, servants, bracelets, and advertising, although a good proportion do address morally significant issues, even if in a brisker manner than in the *Rambler.* There are essays, for example, on charity, history, slavery, debtors' prisons, hospitals, biography, idleness, false hope, the futility of forming "plans of life," the debilitating power of habits, and a variety of social and personal vanities. Literary criticism also comes in for greater scrutiny than in the earlier periodicals. Another major difference from the earlier series is that the character portraits are almost entirely positive and gentle, calculated to be immediately appealing to a contemporary reader. Perhaps of greatest value to the biographers of

Johnson are sixteen or so essays that are emotionally loaded with biographical and autobiographical themes, such as number 31 about Sober, a
man who wastes his life by deceiving himself through disguises of idleness, "a silent and peaceful quality that neither raises envy by ostentation, nor hatred by opposition." The concluding number (103) poignantly
dwells on how the "last" of anything forces the mind to reflect on the fi-
niteness of life.

Rasselas

While Johnson was in the middle of his *Idler* essays, his mother became
grievously ill and died in January 1759. To pay for her funeral, he wrote
his "little story book," *Rasselas,* more or less on the run. He told Joshua
Reynolds that he "composed it in the evenings of one week, sent it to the
press in portions as it was written, and had never since read it over."[12]
The book exploded from him. It was published anonymously in two volumes on April 20, 1759, though as before it was not long before the public
discovered he was its author.

It is an extended moral parable in the style of several oriental or eastern
tales he had written for the *Rambler,* notably about Seged, lord of Ethio-
pia and "the monarch of forty nations" (numbers 204 and 205), and one
he would write a year later for the *Idler* (number 101) about Omar, a
prominent politician in Baghdad who discovered that "terrestrial happiness is of short continuance" and that "it is of little use to form plans of
life." After about ten years of using the oriental philosophic tale to inculcate moral lessons, Johnson climaxes the literary type by deploying it
in a sustained narrative involving a young and hopeful prince, Rasselas,
and his sister Nekayah, who, although they have all their material desires
satisfied, feel bored, imprisoned, and shut off from life's variety in "the
happy valley" surrounded by mountains that was the ancient residence of
Abyssinian royalty. Rasselas spends a good deal of his time bemoaning
his isolation and stagnation—"discontent by degrees preyed upon him,
and he began to lose his thoughts in sadness." Under the tutelage and
guidance of Imlac, he and his sister finally escape from the valley through
the mountains, making their way to Cairo to find the "choice of life" they

are sure will bring them contentment. There they encounter numerous instances, several ludicrous and pitiful, of misguided efforts to find happiness and fulfillment.

It is a strongly cautionary tale that begins with this warning: "Ye who listen with credulity to the whispers of fancy, and pursue with eagerness the phantoms of hope; who expect that age will perform the promises of youth, and that the deficiencies of the present day will be supplied by the morrow; attend to the history of Rasselas, prince of Abyssinia." The tale then proceeds mostly through dialogue brimming with moral reflections and philosophical skepticism, with virtually no action to relieve it. It is a sobering journey for the prince and his sister, and at the end they return to Abyssinia wiser in the understanding that no single place or philosophy can shield human beings from the pain, suffering, disease, grief, disappointment, and sadness of life. Throw away "the encumbrance of precepts," Imlac demands. "Be not too hasty to trust, or to admire, the teachers of morality: they discourse like angels, but they live like men."

A prominent, autobiographical theme in the tale is madness—subtle and sometimes not so subtle gradations in mental imbalance such as Johnson had relentlessly examined in his moral essays. There is a sense of urgency and fear in his writing about it. "All power of fancy over reason is a degree of insanity," says Imlac; "it is not pronounced madness but when it comes ungovernable, and apparently influences speech or action." "Of the uncertainties of our present state," he adds, "the most dreadful and alarming is the uncertain continuance of reason." Johnson knew full well what he was talking about when he warned against the dangers of solitariness. The reader can almost feel him tremble when he has Imlac say, "When we are alone we are not always busy . . . the mind dances from scene to scene . . . Then fictions begin to operate as realities." The moment a man may dread at least as much as anything in life is "when solitude should deliver him to the tyranny of reflection." Grief, too (such as his own over Tetty's death), can sweep one toward melancholia and madness, as can guilt, religious or otherwise: "No disease of the imagination is so difficult to cure as that which is complicated with the dread of guilt: fancy and conscience then act interchangeably upon us, and so often shift their places, that the illusions of one are not distinguished from the dictates of the other. . . . For this reason the superstitious are often melancholy, and the melancholy almost always superstitious." The result is a devilish congregation of mental scorpions.

Nonetheless, *Rasselas* is not wholly bleak. Courage, piety, hope, compassion, and humor play a large part. Rasselas and Nekayah return home with rising hope, though subdued with the realization that they are never likely to obtain their desires. Indeed, the final chapter is titled "The Conclusion, in Which Nothing Is Concluded." The important thing is to keep moving. It is the "choice of eternity," not the "choice of life," that should govern our thoughts and actions and guide the conduct of our lives.

Preface to *Shakespeare*

On June 2, 1756, the year after he published his *Dictionary*, Johnson signed a contract with a group of booksellers for a new complete edition of Shakespeare's plays. He needed another major project for income and to keep himself from wasting too much time writing ephemera for magazines and prefaces and dedications for friends and booksellers that did him little material good. He agreed with the booksellers that he would produce the edition in eighteen months, but (as with the *Dictionary*) complications arising from his methods of dealing with the text, work on the *Idler,* his mother's death, and indolence aggravated by his melancholia conspired to block his progress for many years. His eight-volume edition did not appear until October 1765—almost a decade after he signed his contract. While textually the edition was not a major advance over previous Shakespeare editions published during the eighteenth century, Johnson did provide strikingly insightful glosses that have stood the test of time, and his edition did play an important part in the rise of patriotic Bardolatry climaxing in David Garrick's representation of the plays on the stage. But it is his Preface to the edition that is its great triumph.

The ground-breaking Preface, Johnson's most extended analysis of any writer, is another example of his sturdy common sense and brilliant, humanly anchored moral insight. It takes the reader into a more complex and discriminating critical study of literature than had ever before been attempted. He writes about Shakespeare's sublime imagination and his judgment of the poet's genius in representing the infinitely "mingled drama" of life on earth and his capacity to enter the human heart. The Preface resonates with Johnson's gratitude to Shakespeare for striking a chord with his own moral convictions and psyche, for projecting the realities of human nature with "common conversation and common occurrences." The characters in the plays are "the genuine progeny of common humanity, such as the world will always supply and observation will always find. His persons act and speak by the influence of those general passions and principles by which all minds are agitated, and the whole system of life is continued in motion." His drama is "the mirror of life" where one may read "human sentiments in human language, by scenes from which a hermit may estimate the transactions of the world, and a confessor predict the progress of the passions." The great Shakespearcan critic David Nichol Smith wrote in 1928 that "by common consent . . . [the Preface] is one of the greatest essays on Shakespeare that has ever been written."

Lives of the Poets

Early in 1777 Johnson was approached by a consortium of forty-two booksellers and six printers to write brief biographical sketches of and critical introductions to each poet in a large projected collection of British poetry. Such was his literary fame by then that "Johnson" was the name the booksellers wanted to appear at the head of the editions. As with the *Dictionary,* the project carried patriotic value for him since he felt "the chief glory of every people arises from its authors" and profoundly believed that England was Europe's "capital of litcrature." Soon after embarking on the *Lives of the Poets,* he decided that instead of settling for "little lives and little criticism" he would write long, substantial biographies, replete with critical observations and reflections on literature. Not all of the just over fifty "lives" he wrote turned out to be long or substantial, and many of the poets chosen by the booksellers for this odd collection were relatively obscure at the time, as they have remained since. Nor could he bring himself to do much research. Indeed, except for his *Account of the Life of Mr. Richard Savage* (Johnson knew Savage personally and had written his biography rather sensationally about thirty-five years earlier), these "lives" do not provide much biographical information. But many of them—including the ones that are excerpted here, those of Abraham Cowley, John Milton, Alexander Pope, William Collins, and Richard Savage—were at the time among the finest examples of literary biography and criticism ever written, and they show us Johnson at his critical best. He wrote them between 1777 and 1781, and they were first published separately in four volumes in 1781.

The critical commentary in them is still a feast today, full of acute and robust insights into the inventiveness and originality of poets and often the vicissitudes of life that conspired to determine poetic imagination and fame. His flexible and pragmatic compass guided him to consider whether poetry conforms to "truth" and nature, the centrality of life. His drive to establish his critical principles and then apply them quickly to the experiences of life constituted his powerful voice and stability as a critic. He searched for and tried to define genius: "Pope had . . . genius; a mind active, ambitious, and adventurous, always investigating, always aspiring; in its widest searches still longing to go forward, in its highest flights still wishing to be higher; always imagining something greater than it knows, always endeavouring more than it can do." In his "Life of Milton," he stated plainly, "The highest praise of genius is original invention," and that was the standard by which he measured the value and power of poetry. It was not literary theory or convention that impelled him: "To circumscribe poetry by a definition will only show the narrowness of the definer" ("Life of Pope"). His disdain for what he regarded as petty and frivolous critics is a constant theme: "To a thousand cavils one answer is sufficient; the purpose of a writer is to be read, and the criticism which would destroy the power of pleasing must be blown aside."

In this tercentenary year of Johnson's birth, it is our good fortune to be at least as close to Johnson, in a sympathetic and understanding relationship to him, as his readers have been in any previous era. Moreover, notwithstanding James Boswell's monumental biography of him, it has never been clearer that in order to get the measure of Johnson he must be read, not just read about. With his moral clarity and his strong reminders of how human beings are likely to misguide themselves or allow themselves to be manipulated by a legion of temptations and tempters, he has an uncanny ability to speak to the reader with unpretentious authority, like a man who has been through it all and knows what he is talking about. It is often an uncomfortable ride, which, instead of offering easy solutions and remedies, becomes a journey of self-discovery in inimitable prose and with fertile wit. This selection can do nothing more profitable than encourage a discovery or rediscovery of the writings of this great thinker.

SELECTED WRITINGS ❧ SAMUEL JOHNSON

PART I

Periodical Essays
(1750–1760)

Morality, Behavior, and Psychology

***Rambler* no. 2, March 24, 1750:**
The necessity and danger of looking into futurity

Stare loco nescit, pereunt vestigia mille
Ante fugam, absentemque ferit gravis ungula campum.

Statius, *Thebaid*, VI. 400–401

Th' impatient courser pants in ev'ry vein,
And pawing seems to beat the distant plain;
Hills, vales, and floods appear already crost,
And, ere he starts, a thousand steps are lost.

Alexander Pope

That the mind of man is never satisfied with the objects immediately before it, but is always breaking away from the present moment, and losing
itself in schemes of future felicity; and that we forget the proper use of the
time, now in our power, to provide for the enjoyment of that which, perhaps, may never be granted us, has been frequently remarked; and as this
practice is a commodious subject of raillery to the gay, and of declamation

3

to the serious, it has been ridiculed with all the pleasantry of wit, and exaggerated with all the amplifications of rhetoric. Every instance, by which its absurdity might appear most flagrant, has been studiously collected; it has been marked with every epithet of contempt, and all the tropes and figures have been called forth against it.

Censure is willingly indulged, because it always implies some superiority: men please themselves with imagining that they have made a deeper search, or wider survey, than others, and detected faults and follies which escape vulgar observation. And the pleasure of wantoning in common topics is so tempting to a writer, that he cannot easily resign it; a train of sentiments generally received enables him to shine without labour, and to conquer without a contest. It is so easy to laugh at the folly of him who lives only in idea, refuses immediate ease for distant pleasures, and, instead of enjoying the blessings of life, lets life glide away in preparations to enjoy them; it affords such opportunities of triumphant exultation, to exemplify the uncertainty of the human state, to rouse mortals from their dream and inform them of the silent celerity of time, that we may believe authors willing rather to transmit than examine so advantageous a principle, and more inclined to pursue a track so smooth and so flowery, than attentively to consider whether it leads to truth.

This quality of looking forward into futurity seems the unavoidable condition of a being whose motions are gradual and whose life is progressive: as his powers are limited, he must use means for the attainment of his ends, and intend first what he performs last; as by continual advances from his first stage of existence, he is perpetually varying the horizon of his prospects, he must always discover new motives of action, new excitements of fear, and allurements of desire.

The end therefore, which at present calls forth our efforts, will be found, when it is once gained, to be only one of the means to some remoter end. The natural flights of the human mind are not from pleasure to pleasure, but from hope to hope.

He that directs his steps to a certain point, must frequently turn his eyes to that place which he strives to reach; he that undergoes the fatigue of labour, must solace his weariness with the contemplation of its reward. In agriculture, one of the most simple and necessary employments, no man turns up the ground but because he thinks of the harvest, that harvest which blights may intercept, which inundations may sweep away, or which death or calamity may hinder him from reaping.

Yet, as few maxims are widely received or long retained but for some conformity with truth and nature, it must be confessed, that this caution against keeping our view too intent upon remote advantages is not without its propriety or usefulness, though it may have been recited with too much levity, or enforced with too little distinction; for, not to speak of that vehemence of desire which presses through right and wrong to its gratification, or that anxious inquietude which is justly chargeable with distrust of heaven, subjects too solemn for my present purpose; it frequently happens that, by indulging early the raptures of success, we forget the measures necessary to secure it, and suffer the imagination to riot in the fruition of some possible good, till the time of obtaining it has slipped away.

There would however be few enterprises of great labour or hazard undertaken if we had not the power of magnifying the advantages which we persuade ourselves to expect from them. When the knight of La Mancha gravely recounts to his companion the adventures by which he is to signalize himself in such a manner that he shall be summoned to the support of empires, solicited to accept the heiress of the crown which he has preserved, have honours and riches to scatter about him, and an island to bestow on his worthy squire,[1] very few readers, amidst their mirth or pity, can deny that they have admitted visions of the same kind; though they have not, perhaps, expected events equally strange, or by means equally inadequate. When we pity him, we reflect on our own disappointments; and when we laugh, our hearts inform us that he is not more ridiculous than ourselves, except that he tells what we have only thought.

The understanding of a man naturally sanguine, may, indeed, be easily vitiated by luxurious indulgence of hope, however necessary to the production of every thing great or excellent, as some plants are destroyed by too open exposure to that sun which gives life and beauty to the vegetable world.

Perhaps no class of the human species requires more to be cautioned against this anticipation of happiness, than those that aspire to the name of authors. A man of lively fancy no sooner finds a hint moving in his mind, than he makes momentaneous[2] excursions to the press, and to the world, and, with a little encouragement from flattery, pushes forward into future ages, and prognosticates the honours to be paid him, when envy is extinct, and faction forgotten, and those, whom partiality now suffers to obscure him, shall have given way to the triflers of as short duration as themselves.

Those who have proceeded so far as to appeal to the tribunal of succeeding times, are not likely to be cured of their infatuation; but all endeavours ought to be used for the prevention of a disease, for which, when it has attained its height, perhaps no remedy will be found in the gardens of philosophy, however she may boast her physic of the mind, her cathartics of vice, or lenitives of passion.

I shall, therefore, while I am yet but lightly touched with the symptoms of the writer's malady, endeavour to fortify myself against the infection, not without some weak hope, that my preservatives may extend their virtues to others, whose employment exposes them to the same danger:

> *Laudis amore tumes? Sunt certa piacula, quæ te*
> *Ter pure lecto poterunt recraere libello.*
>
> > Horace, *Epistles*, I.1. 36–37

> *Is fame your passion? Wisdom's pow'rful charm,*
> *If thrice read over, shall its force disarm.*
>
> > transl. Philip Francis

It is the sage advice of Epictetus, that a man should accustom himself often to think of what is most shocking and terrible, that by such reflections he may be preserved from too ardent wishes for seeming good, and from too much dejection in real evil.

There is nothing more dreadful to an author than neglect, compared with which reproach, hatred, and opposition, are names of happiness; yet this worst, this meanest fate, every one who dares to write has reason to fear.

> *I nunc, et versus tecum meditare canoros.*
>
> > Horace, *Epistles*, II.2.76

> *Go now, and meditate thy tuneful lays.*
>
> > transl. James Elphinston

It may not be unfit for him who makes a new entrance into the lettered world, so far to suspect his own powers, as to believe that he possibly may deserve neglect; that nature may not have qualified him much to enlarge or embellish knowledge, nor sent him forth entitled by indisputable superiority to regulate the conduct of the rest of mankind; that, though the world must be granted to be yet in ignorance, he is not destined to dispel the cloud, nor to shine out as one of the luminaries of life. For this suspicion, every catalogue of a library will furnish sufficient reason; as he will find it crowded with names of men, who, though now forgotten, were once no less enterprising or confident than himself, equally pleased with their own productions, equally caressed by their patrons, and flattered by their friends.

But though it should happen that an author is capable of excelling, yet his merit may pass without notice, huddled in the variety of things, and thrown into the general miscellany of life. He that endeavours after fame by writing, solicits the regard of a multitude fluctuating in pleasures, or immersed in business, without time for intellectual amusements; he appeals to judges prepossessed by passions, or corrupted by prejudices, which preclude their approbation of any new performance. Some are too indolent to read any thing, till its reputation is established; others too envious to promote that fame which gives them pain by its increase. What is new is opposed, because most are unwilling to be taught; and what is known is rejected, because it is not sufficiently considered that men more frequently require to be reminded than informed. The learned are afraid to declare their opinion early, lest they should put their reputation in hazard; the ignorant always imagine themselves giving some proof of delicacy, when they refuse to be pleased: and he that finds his way to reputation through all these obstructions, must acknowledge that he is indebted to other causes besides his industry, his learning, or his wit.

Rambler no. 5, April 3, 1750: A meditation on the spring

Et nunc omnis ager, nunc omnis parturit arbos,
Nunc frondent silvæ, nunc formosissimus annus.

Virgil, *Eclogues*, III. 56–57

Now ev'ry field, now ev'ry tree is green;
Now genial nature's fairest face is seen.

transl. Francis Elphinston

Every man is sufficiently discontented with some circumstances of his present state, to suffer his imagination to range more or less in quest of future happiness, and to fix upon some point of time in which, by the removal of the inconvenience which now perplexes him, or acquisition of the advantage which he at present wants, he shall find the condition of his life very much improved.

When this time, which is too often expected with great impatience, at last arrives, it generally comes without the blessing for which it was desired; but we solace ourselves with some new prospect, and press forward again with equal eagerness.

It is lucky for a man in whom this temper prevails when he turns his hopes upon things wholly out of his own power; since he forbears then to precipitate his affairs, for the sake of the great event that is to complete his felicity, and waits for the blissful hour with less neglect of the measures necessary to be taken in the mean time.

I have long known a person of this temper, who indulged his dream of happiness with less hurt to himself than such chimerical wishes commonly produce, and adjusted his scheme with such address, that his hopes were in full bloom three parts of the year, and in the other part never wholly blasted. Many, perhaps, would be desirous of learning by what means he procured to himself such a cheap and lasting satisfaction. It was gained by a constant practice of referring the removal of all his uneasiness to the coming of the next spring; if his health was impaired, the spring would restore it; if what he wanted was at a high price, it would fall its value in the spring.

The spring indeed did often come without any of these effects, but he was always certain that the next would be more propitious; nor was ever convinced, that the present spring would fail him before the middle of summer; for he always talked of the spring as coming till it was past, and when it was once past, every one agreed with him that it was coming.

By long converse with this man, I am, perhaps, brought to feel immoderate pleasure in the contemplation of this delightful season; but I have the satisfaction of finding many whom it can be no shame to resemble, infected with the same enthusiasm; for there is, I believe, scarce any poet of eminence who has not left some testimony of his fondness for the flowers, the zephyrs, and the warblers of the spring. Nor has the most luxuriant imagination been able to describe the serenity and happiness of the golden age, otherwise than by giving a perpetual spring as the highest reward of uncorrupted innocence.

There is, indeed, something inexpressibly pleasing in the annual renovation of the world, and the new display of the treasures of nature. The cold and darkness of winter, with the naked deformity of every object on which we turn our eyes, make us rejoice at the succeeding season, as well for what we have escaped as for what we may enjoy; and every budding flower, which a warm situation brings early to our view, is considered by us as a messenger to notify the approach of more joyous days.

The spring affords to a mind, so free from the disturbance of cares or passions as to be vacant to calm amusements, almost every thing that our present state makes us capable of enjoying. The variegated verdure of the fields and woods, the succession of grateful odours, the voice of pleasure pouring out its notes on every side, with the gladness apparently conceived by every animal, from the growth of his food, and the clemency of the weather, throw over the whole earth an air of gaiety, significantly expressed by the smile of nature.

Yet there are men to whom these scenes are able to give no delight, and who hurry away from all the varieties of rural beauty, to lose their hours and divert their thoughts by cards or assemblies, a tavern dinner, or the prattle of the day.

It may be laid down as a position which will seldom deceive, that when a man cannot bear his own company, there is something wrong. He must fly from himself, either because he feels a tediousness in life from the equipoise of an empty mind, which, having no tendency to one motion more than another, but as it is impelled by some external power, must always have recourse to foreign objects; or he must be afraid of the intrusion of some unpleasing ideas, and perhaps is struggling to escape from the remembrance of a loss, the fear of a calamity, or some other thought of greater horror.

Those whom sorrow incapacitates to enjoy the pleasures of contemplation, may properly apply to such diversions, provided they are innocent, as lay strong hold on the attention; and those, whom fear of any future affliction chains down to misery, must endeavour to obviate the danger.

My considerations shall, on this occasion, be turned on such as are burdensome to themselves merely because they want subjects for reflection, and to whom the volume of nature is thrown open without affording them pleasure or instruction, because they never learned to read the characters.

A French author has advanced this seeming paradox, that "very few men know how to take a walk"; and, indeed, it is true, that few know how to take a walk with a prospect of any other pleasure, than the same company would have afforded them at home.

There are animals that borrow their colour from the neighbouring body, and consequently vary their hue as they happen to change their place. In like manner it ought to be the endeavour of every man to derive his reflections from the objects about him; for it is to no purpose that he alters his position, if his attention continues fixed to the same point. The mind should be kept open to the access of every new idea, and so far disengaged from the predominance of particular thoughts, as easily to accommodate itself to occasional entertainment.

A man that has formed this habit of turning every new object to his entertainment, finds in the productions of nature an inexhaustible stock of materials upon which he can employ himself, without any temptations to envy or malevolence; faults, perhaps, seldom totally avoided by those whose judgment is much exercised upon the works of art. He has always a certain prospect of discovering new reasons for adoring the sovereign Author of the universe, and probable hopes of making some discovery of benefit to others, or of profit to himself. There is no doubt but many vegetables and animals have qualities that might be of great use, to the knowledge of which there is not required much force of penetration, or fatigue of study, but only frequent experiments, and close attention. What is said by the chemists of their darling mercury, is, perhaps, true of every body through the whole creation, that if a thousand lives should be spent upon it, all its properties would not be found out.

Mankind must necessarily be diversified by various tastes, since life affords and requires such multiplicity of employments, and a nation of naturalists is neither to be hoped, or desired; but it is surely not improper to point out a fresh amusement to those who languish in health, and repine in plenty, for want of some source of diversion that may be less easily exhausted, and to inform the multitudes of both sexes, who are burdened with every new day, that there are many shows which they have not seen.

He that enlarges his curiosity after the works of nature, demonstrably multiplies the inlets to happiness; and, therefore, the younger part of my readers, to whom I dedicate this vernal speculation, must excuse me for calling upon them, to make use at once of the spring of the year, and the spring of life; to acquire, while their minds may be yet impressed with new images, a love of innocent pleasures, and an ardour for useful knowledge; and to remember, that a blighted spring makes a barren year, and that the vernal flowers, however beautiful and gay, are only intended by nature as preparatives to autumnal fruits.

Rambler no. 8, April 14, 1750:
Regulating one's thoughts as they relate to past, present, and future

Patitur poenas peccandi sola voluntas;
Nam scelus intra se tacitum qui cogitat ullum,
Facti crimen habet.

Juvenal, *Satires,* XIII. 208–210

For he that but conceives a crime in thought,
Contracts the danger of an actual fault.

transl. Thomas Creech

If the most active and industrious of mankind was able, at the close of life, to recollect distinctly his past moments, and distribute them in a regular account, according to the manner in which they have been spent, it is scarcely to be imagined how few would be marked out to the mind, by any permanent or visible effects, how small a proportion his real action would bear to his seeming possibilities of action, how many chasms he would find of wide and continued vacuity, and how many interstitial spaces unfilled, even in the most tumultuous hurries of business, and the most eager vehemence of pursuit.

It is said by modern philosophers, that not only the great globes of matter are thinly scattered through the universe, but the hardest bodies are so porous, that, if all matter were compressed to perfect solidity, it might be contained in a cube of a few feet. In like manner, if all the employments of life were crowded into the time which it really occupied, perhaps a few weeks, days, or hours, would be sufficient for its accomplishment, so far as the mind was engaged in the performance. For such is the inequality of our corporeal to our intellectual faculties, that we contrive in minutes what we execute in years, and the soul often stands an idle spectator of the labour of the hands, and expedition of the feet.

For this reason the ancient generals often found themselves at leisure to pursue the study of philosophy in the camp; and Lucan, with historical veracity, makes Cæsar relate of himself that he noted the revolutions of the stars in the midst of preparations for battle.

> *Media inter proelia semper*
> *Stellarum, coelique plagis, superisque vacavi.*
> Lucan, *Pharsalia*, X. 185–186

> *Amid the storms of war, with curious eyes*
> *I trace the planets and survey the skies.*

That the soul always exerts her peculiar powers, with greater or less force, is very probable, though the common occasions of our present condition require but a small part of that incessant cogitation; and by the natural frame of our bodies, and general combination of the world, we are so frequently condemned to inactivity, that as through all our time we are thinking, so for a great part of our time we can only think.

Lest a power so restless should be either unprofitably or hurtfully employed, and the superfluities of intellect run to waste, it is no vain speculation to consider how we may govern our thoughts, restrain them from irregular motions, or confine them from boundless dissipation.

How the understanding is best conducted to the knowledge of science, by what steps it is to be led forwards in its pursuit, how it is to be cured of its defects, and habituated to new studies, has been the inquiry of many acute and learned men, whose observations I shall not either adopt or censure: my purpose being to consider the moral discipline of the mind, and to promote the increase of virtue rather than of learning.

This inquiry seems to have been neglected for want of remembering that all action has its origin in the mind, and that therefore to suffer the thoughts to be vitiated, is to poison the fountains of morality; irregular desires will produce licentious practices; what men allow themselves to wish they will soon believe, and will be at last incited to execute what they please themselves with contriving.

For this reason the casuists of the Romish church, who gain, by confession, great opportunities of knowing human nature, have generally determined that what it is a crime to do, it is a crime to think. Since by revolving with pleasure the facility, safety, or advantage of a wicked deed, a man soon begins to find his constancy relax, and his detestation soften; the happiness of success glittering before him withdraws his attention from the atrociousness of the guilt, and acts are at last confidently perpetrated, of which the first conception only crept into the mind, disguised in pleasing complications, and permitted rather than invited.

No man has ever been drawn to crimes by love or jealousy, envy or hatred, but he can tell how easily he might at first have repelled the temptation, how readily his mind would have obeyed a call to any other object, and how weak his passion has been after some casual avocation, till he has recalled it again to his heart, and revived the viper by too warm a fondness.

Such, therefore, is the importance of keeping reason a constant guard over imagination, that we have otherwise no security for our own virtue, but may corrupt our hearts in the most recluse solitude, with more pernicious and tyrannical appetites and wishes than the commerce of the world will generally produce; for we are easily shocked by crimes which appear at once in their full magnitude; but the gradual growth of our own wickedness, endeared by interest, and palliated by all the artifices of self-deceit, gives us time to form distinctions in our own favour, and reason by degrees submits to absurdity, as the eye is in time accommodated to darkness.

In this disease of the soul, it is of the utmost importance to apply remedies at the beginning; and therefore I shall endeavour to show what thoughts are to be rejected or improved, as they regard the past, present, or future; in hopes that some may be awakened to caution and vigilance, who, perhaps, indulge themselves in dangerous dreams, so much the more dangerous because, being yet only dreams, they are concluded innocent.

The recollection of the past is only useful by way of provision for the future; and, therefore, in reviewing all occurrences that fall under a religious consideration, it is proper that a man stop at the first thoughts, to remark how he was led thither, and why he continues the reflection. If he is dwelling with delight upon a stratagem of successful fraud, a night of licentious riot, or an intrigue of guilty pleasure, let him summon off his imagination as an unlawful pursuit, expel those passages from his remembrance, of which, though he cannot seriously approve them, the pleasure overpowers the guilt, and refer them to a future hour, when they may be considered with greater safety. Such an hour will certainly come; for the impressions of past pleasure are always lessening, but the sense of guilt, which respects futurity, continues the same.

The serious and impartial retrospect of our conduct, is indisputably necessary to the confirmation or recovery of virtue, and is, therefore, recommended under the name of self-examination, by divines, as the first act previous to repentance. It is indeed of so great use that without it we should always be to begin life, be seduced for ever by the same allurements, and misled by the same fallacies. But in order that we may not lose the advantage of our experience, we must endeavour to see every thing in its proper form, and excite in ourselves those sentiments which the great Author of nature has decreed the concomitants or followers of good and bad actions.

> Let not sleep (says Pythagoras) fall upon thy eyes till thou hast thrice reviewed the transactions of the past day. Where have I turned aside from rectitude? What have I been doing? What have I left undone, which I ought to have done? Begin thus from the first act, and proceed; and in conclusion, at the ill which thou hast done be troubled, and rejoice for the good.
>
> transl. of *Aurea Carmina*, ll. 40–44

Our thoughts on present things being determined by the objects before us, fall not under those indulgences or excursions which I am now considering. But I cannot forbear, under this head, to caution pious and tender minds, that are disturbed by the irruptions of wicked imaginations, against too great dejection, and too anxious alarms; for thoughts are only criminal when they are first chosen, and then voluntarily continued.

> *Evil into the mind of God or man*
> *May come and go, so unapprov'd, and leave*
> *No spot or stain behind.*
>   Milton, *Paradise Lost*, V. 117–119

In futurity chiefly are the snares lodged, by which the imagination is entangled. Futurity is the proper abode of hope and fear, with all their train and progeny of subordinate apprehensions and desires. In futurity, events and chances are yet floating at large, without apparent connection with their causes, and we therefore easily indulge the liberty of gratifying ourselves with a pleasing choice. To pick and cull among possible advantages is, as the civil law terms it, *in vacuum venire,* to take what belongs to nobody; but it has this hazard in it, that we shall be unwilling to quit what we have seized, though an owner should be found. It is easy to think on that which may be gained, till at last we resolve to gain it, and to image the happiness of particular conditions, till we can be easy in no other. We ought, at least, to let our desires fix upon nothing in another's power for the sake of our quiet, or in another's possession for the sake of our innocence. When a man finds himself led, though by a train of honest sentiments, to wish for that to which he has no right, he should start back as from a pitfall covered with flowers. He that fancies he should benefit the public more in a great station than the man that fills it, will in time imagine it an act of virtue to supplant him; and as opposition readily kindles into hatred, his eagerness to do that good, to which he is not called, will betray him to crimes, which in his original scheme were never purposed.

He therefore that would govern his actions by the laws of virtue, must regulate his thoughts by those of reason; he must keep guilt from the recesses of his heart, and remember that the pleasures of fancy, and the emotions of desire, are more dangerous as they are more hidden, since they escape the awe of observation, and operate equally in every situation, without the concurrence of external opportunities.

Rambler no. 28, June 23, 1750: The various arts of self-delusion

Illi mors gravis incubat,
Qui, notus nimis omnibus,
Ignotus moritur sibi.

Seneca, Thyestes, 401–403

To him, alas, to him, I fear,
The face of death will terrible appear,
Who in his life, flatt'ring his senseless pride,
By being known to all the world beside,
Does not himself, when he is dying know,
Nor what he is, nor whither he's to go.

transl. Abraham Cowley, "Of Solitude"

I have shown, in a late essay,[3] to what errors men are hourly betrayed by a mistaken opinion of their own powers, and a negligent inspection of their own character. But as I then confined my observations to common occurrences and familiar scenes, I think it proper to inquire, how far a nearer acquaintance with ourselves is necessary to our preservation from crimes as well as follies, and how much the attentive study of our own minds may contribute to secure to us the approbation of that Being, to whom we are accountable for our thoughts and our actions, and whose favour must finally constitute our total happiness.

If it be reasonable to estimate the difficulty of any enterprise by frequent miscarriages, it may justly be concluded that it is not easy for a man to know himself; for wheresoever we turn our view, we shall find almost all with whom we converse so nearly as to judge of their sentiments, indulging more favourable conceptions of their own virtue than they have been able to impress upon others, and congratulating themselves upon degrees of excellence which their fondest admirers cannot allow them to have attained.

Those representations of imaginary virtue are generally considered as arts of hypocrisy, and as snares laid for confidence and praise. But I believe the suspicion often unjust; those who thus propagate their own reputation, only extend the fraud by which they have been themselves deceived; for this failing is incident to numbers who seem to live without designs, competitions, or pursuits; it appears on occasions which promise no accession of honour or of profit, and to persons from whom very little is to be hoped or feared. It is, indeed, not easy to tell how far we may be blinded by the love of ourselves, when we reflect how much a secondary passion can cloud our judgment, and how few faults a man, in the first raptures of love, can discover in the person or conduct of his mistress.

To lay open all the sources from which error flows in upon him who contemplates his own character, would require more exact knowledge of the human heart, than, perhaps, the most acute and laborious observers have acquired. And since falsehood may be diversified without end, it is not unlikely that every man admits an imposture in some respect peculiar to himself, as his views have been accidentally directed, or his ideas particularly combined.

Some fallacies, however, there are, more frequently insidious, which it may, perhaps, not be useless to detect, because though they are gross they may be fatal, and because nothing but attention is necessary to defeat them.

One sophism by which men persuade themselves that they have those virtues which they really want, is formed by the substitution of single acts for habits. A miser who once relieved a friend from the danger of a prison, suffers his imagination to dwell for ever upon his own heroic generosity; he yields his heart up to indignation at those who are blind to merit, or insensible to misery, and who can please themselves with the enjoyment of that wealth which they never permit others to partake. From any censures of the world, or reproaches of his conscience, he has an appeal to action and to knowledge: and though his whole life is a course of rapacity and avarice, he concludes himself to be tender and liberal, because he has once performed an act of liberality and tenderness.

As a glass which magnifies objects by the approach of one end to the eye lessens them by the application of the other, so vices are extenuated by the inversion of that fallacy by which virtues are augmented. Those faults which we cannot conceal from our own notice, are considered, however frequent, not as habitual corruptions or settled practices, but as casual failures and single lapses. A man who has from year to year set his country to sale, either for the gratification of his ambition or resentment, confesses that the heat of party now and then betrays the severest virtue to measures that cannot be seriously defended. He that spends his days and nights in riot and debauchery, owns that his passions oftentimes overpower his resolutions. But each comforts himself that his faults are not without precedent, for the best and the wisest men have given way to the violence of sudden temptations.

There are men who always confound the praise of goodness with the practice, and who believe themselves mild and moderate, charitable and faithful, because they have exerted their eloquence in commendation of mildness, fidelity, and other virtues. This is an error almost universal among those that converse much with dependents, with such whose fear or interest disposes them to a seeming reverence for any declamation, however enthusiastic, and submission to any boast, however arrogant. Having none to recall their attention to their lives, they rate themselves by the goodness of their opinions, and forget how much more easily men may show their virtue in their talk than in their actions.

The tribe is likewise very numerous of those who regulate their lives, not by the standard of religion, but the measure of other men's virtue; who lull their own remorse with the remembrance of crimes more atrocious than their own, and seem to believe that they are not bad while another can be found worse.

For escaping these and a thousand other deceits, many expedients have been proposed. Some have recommended the frequent consultation of a wise friend, admitted to intimacy, and encouraged to sincerity.[4] But this appears a remedy by no means adapted to general use: for in order to secure the virtue of one, it pre-supposes more virtue in two than will generally be found. In the first, such a desire of rectitude and amendment, as may incline him to hear his own accusation from the mouth of him whom he esteems, and by whom, therefore, he will always hope that his faults are not discovered; and in the second, such zeal and honesty, as will make him content for his friend's advantage to lose his kindness.

A long life may be passed without finding a friend in whose understanding and virtue we can equally confide, and whose opinion we can value at once for its justness and sincerity. A weak man, however honest, is not qualified to judge. A man of the world, however penetrating, is not fit to counsel. Friends are often chosen for similitude of manners, and therefore each palliates the other's failing, because they are his own. Friends are tender, and unwilling to give pain, or they are interested, and fearful to offend.

These objections have inclined others to advise that he who would know himself, should consult his enemies, remember the reproaches that are vented to his face, and listen for the censures that are uttered in private. For his great business is to know his faults, and those malignity will discover, and resentment will reveal. But this precept may be often frustrated; for it seldom happens that rivals or opponents are suffered to come near enough to know our conduct with so much exactness as that conscience should allow and reflect the accusation. The charge of an enemy is often totally false, and commonly so mingled with falsehood, that the mind takes advantage from the failure of one part to discredit the rest, and never suffers any disturbance afterward from such partial reports.

Yet it seems that enemies have been always found by experience the most faithful monitors; for adversity has ever been considered as the state in which a man most easily becomes acquainted with himself, and this effect it must produce by withdrawing flatterers, whose business it is to hide our weaknesses from us, or by giving loose to malice, and licence to reproach; or at least by cutting off those pleasures which called us away from meditation on our own conduct, and repressing that pride which too easily persuades us that we merit whatever we enjoy.

Part of these benefits it is in every man's power to procure to himself, by assigning proper portions of his life to the examination of the rest, and by putting himself frequently in such a situation, by retirement and abstraction, as may weaken the influence of external objects. By this practice he may obtain the solitude of adversity without its melancholy, its instructions without its censures, and its sensibility without its perturbations.

The necessity of setting the world at a distance from us, when we are to take a survey of ourselves, has sent many from high stations to the severities of a monastic life: and, indeed, every man deeply engaged in business, if all regard to another state be not extinguished, must have the conviction, though perhaps not the resolution, of Valdesso, who, when he solicited Charles the Fifth to dismiss him, being asked, whether he retired upon disgust, answered that he laid down his commission for no other reason but because "there ought to be some time for sober reflection between the life of a soldier and his death."

There are few conditions which do not entangle us with sublunary hopes and fears, from which it is necessary to be at intervals disencumbered, that we may place ourselves in his presence who views effects in their causes, and actions in their motives; that we may, as Chillingworth expresses it, consider things as if there were no other beings in the world but God and ourselves; or, to use language yet more awful, "may commune with our own hearts, and be still."[5]

Death, says Seneca, falls heavy upon him who is too much known to others, and too little to himself; and Pontanus, a man celebrated among the early restorers of literature, thought the study of our own hearts of so much importance, that he has recommended it from his tomb. "Sum Joannes Jovianus Pontanus, quem amaverunt bonae musae, suspexerunt viri probi, honestaverunt reges domini; jam scis qui sim, vel qui potius fuerim; ego vero te, hospes, noscere in tenebris nequeo, sed teipsum ut noscas rogo." "I am Pontanus, beloved by the powers of literature, admired by men of worth, and dignified by the monarchs of the world. Thou knowest now who I am, or more properly who I was. For thee, stranger, I who am in darkness cannot know thee, but I entreat thee to know thyself."

I hope every reader of this paper will consider himself as engaged to the observation of a precept, which the wisdom and virtue of all ages have concurred to enforce: a precept, dictated by philosophers, inculcated by poets, and ratified by saints.

Rambler no. 29, June 26, 1750:
The dangers of overactive imagination in anticipating misfortunes

Prudens futuri temporis exitum
Caliginosa nocte premit deus,
   Ridetque, si mortalis ultra
    Fas trepidet

               Horace, *Odes*, III. 29. 29–32

But God has wisely hid from human sight
   The dark decrees of human fate,
And sown their seeds in depth of night;
He laughs at all the giddy turns of state,
When mortals search too soon, and fear too late.

John Dryden

There is nothing recommended with greater frequency among the gayer poets of antiquity, than the secure possession of the present hour, and the dismission[6] of all the cares which intrude upon our quiet, or hinder, by importunate perturbations, the enjoyment of those delights which our condition happens to set before us.

The ancient poets are, indeed, by no means unexceptionable teachers of morality; their precepts are to be always considered as the sallies of a genius, intent rather upon giving pleasure than instruction, eager to take every advantage of insinuation, and, provided the passions can be engaged on its side, very little solicitous about the suffrage of reason.

The darkness and uncertainty through which the heathens were compelled to wander in the pursuit of happiness, may, indeed, be alleged as an excuse for many of their seducing invitations to immediate enjoyment, which the moderns, by whom they have been imitated, have not to plead. It is no wonder that such as had no promise of another state should eagerly turn their thoughts upon the improvement of that which was before them; but surely those who are acquainted with the hopes and fears of eternity, might think it necessary to put some restraint upon their imagination, and reflect that by echoing the songs of the ancient bacchanals, and transmitting the maxims of past debauchery, they not only prove that they want invention, but virtue, and submit to the servility of imitation only to copy that of which the writer, if he was to live now, would often be ashamed.

Yet as the errors and follies of a great genius are seldom without some radiations of understanding, by which meaner minds may be enlightened, the incitements to pleasure are, in those authors, generally mingled with such reflections upon life as well deserve to be considered distinctly from the purposes for which they are produced, and to be treasured up as the settled conclusions of extensive observation, acute sagacity, and mature experience.

It is not without true judgment that on these occasions they often warn their readers against inquiries into futurity, and solicitude about events which lie hid in causes yet inactive, and which time has not brought forward into the view of reason. An idle and thoughtless resignation to chance, without any struggle against calamity, or endeavour after advantage, is indeed below the dignity of a reasonable being in whose power Providence has put a great part even of his present happiness; but it shows an equal ignorance of our proper sphere, to harass our thoughts with conjectures about things not yet in being. How can we regulate events of which we yet know not whether they will ever happen? And why should we think with painful anxiety about that on which our thoughts can have no influence?

It is a maxim commonly received, that a wise man is never surprised; and, perhaps, this exemption from astonishment may be imagined to proceed from such a prospect into futurity, as gave previous intimation of those evils which often fall unexpected upon others that have less foresight. But the truth is, that things to come, except when they approach very nearly, are equally hidden from men of all degrees of understanding; and if a wise man is not amazed at sudden occurrences, it is not that he has thought more, but less upon futurity. He never considered things not yet existing as the proper objects of his attention; he never indulged dreams till he was deceived by their phantoms, nor ever realized nonentities to his mind. He is not surprised, because he is not disappointed; and he escapes disappointment, because he never forms any expectations.

The concern about things to come, that is so justly censured, is not the result of those general reflections on the variableness of fortune, the uncertainty of life, and the universal insecurity of all human acquisitions, which must always be suggested by the view of the world; but such a desponding anticipation of misfortune, as fixes the mind upon scenes of gloom and melancholy, and makes fear predominate in every imagination.

Anxiety of this kind is nearly of the same nature with jealousy in love, and suspicion in the general commerce of life; a temper which keeps the man always in alarms; disposes him to judge of every thing in a manner that least favours his own quiet, fills him with perpetual stratagems of counteraction, wears him out in schemes to obviate evils which never threatened him, and, at length perhaps, contributes to the production of those mischiefs of which it had raised such dreadful apprehensions.

It has been usual in all ages for moralists to repress the swellings of vain hope by representations of the innumerable casualties to which life is subject, and by instances of the unexpected defeat of the wisest schemes of policy, and sudden subversions of the highest eminences of greatness. It has, perhaps, not been equally observed, that all these examples afford the proper antidote to fear as well as to hope, and may be applied with no less efficacy as consolations to the timorous, than as restraints to the proud.

Evil is uncertain in the same degree as good, and for the reason that we ought not to hope too securely, we ought not to fear with too much dejection. The state of the world is continually changing, and none can tell the result of the next vicissitude. Whatever is afloat in the stream of time, may, when it is very near us, be driven away by an accidental blast, which shall happen to cross the general course of the current. The sudden accidents by which the powerful are depressed, may fall upon those whose malice we fear; and the greatness by which we expect to be overborne, may become another proof of the false flatteries of fortune. Our enemies may become weak, or we grow strong before our encounter, or we may advance against each other without ever meeting. There are, indeed, natural evils which we can flatter ourselves with no hopes of escaping, and with little of delaying; but of the ills which are apprehended from human malignity, or the opposition of rival interests, we may always alleviate the terror by considering that our persecutors are weak and ignorant, and mortal like ourselves.

The misfortunes which arise from the concurrence of unhappy incidents should never be suffered to disturb us before they happen; because, if the breast be once laid open to the dread of mere possibilities of misery, life must be given a prey to dismal solicitude, and quiet must be lost for ever.

It is remarked by old [Luigi] Conaro, that it is absurd to be afraid of the natural dissolution of the body, because it must certainly happen, and can, by no caution or artifice, be avoided. Whether this sentiment be entirely just, I shall not examine; but certainly if it be improper to fear events which must happen, it is yet more evidently contrary to right reason to fear those which may never happen, and which, if they should come upon us, we cannot resist.

As we ought not to give way to fear, any more than indulgence to hope, because the objects both of fear and hope are yet uncertain, so we ought not to trust the representations of one more than of the other, because they are both equally fallacious; as hope enlarges happiness, fear aggravates calamity. It is generally allowed that no man ever found the happiness of possession proportionate to that expectation which incited his desire and invigorated his pursuit; nor has any man found the evils of life so formidable in reality as they were described to him by his own imagination: every species of distress brings with it some peculiar supports, some unforeseen means of resisting, or power of enduring. Taylor justly blames some pious persons who indulge their fancies too much, set themselves, by the force of imagination, in the place of the ancient martyrs and confessors, and question the validity of their own faith, because they shrink at the thoughts of flames and tortures. It is, says he, sufficient that you are able to encounter the temptations which now assault you; when God sends trials, he may send strength.[7]

All fear is in itself painful, and when it conduces not to safety is painful without use. Every consideration therefore, by which groundless terrors may be removed, adds something to human happiness. It is likewise not unworthy of remark that in proportion as our cares are employed upon the future they are abstracted from the present, from the only time which we can call our own, and of which if we neglect the apparent duties to make provision against visionary attacks, we shall certainly counteract our own purpose; for he, doubtless, mistakes his true interest who thinks that he can increase his safety, when he impairs his virtue.

Rambler no. 32, July 7, 1750: Vanity and irrationality of Stoicism

Of all the woes that load the mortal state,
Whate'er thy portion, mildly meet thy fate;
But ease it as thou can'st.

> Pythagoras, *Aurea Carmina*, II. 17–19;
> transl. James Elphinston

So large a part of human life passes in a state contrary to our natural desires, that one of the principal topics of moral instruction is the art of bearing calamities. And such is the certainty of evil, that it is the duty of every man to furnish his mind with those principles that may enable him to act under it with decency and propriety.

The sect of ancient philosophers that boasted to have carried this necessary science to the highest perfection were the stoics, or scholars of Zeno, whose wild enthusiastic virtue pretended to an exemption from the sensibilities of unenlightened mortals, and who proclaimed themselves exalted, by the doctrines of their sect, above the reach of those miseries which embitter life to the rest of the world. They therefore removed pain, poverty, loss of friends, exile, and violent death from the catalogue of evils; and passed, in their haughty style, a kind of irreversible decree, by which they forbad them to be counted any longer among the objects of terror or anxiety, or to give any disturbance to the tranquillity of a wise man.

This edict was, I think, not universally observed; for though one of the more resolute, when he was tortured by a violent disease, cried out, that let pain harass him to its utmost power, it should never force him to consider it as other than indifferent and neutral; yet all had not stubbornness to hold out against their senses: for a weaker pupil of Zeno is recorded to have confessed in the anguish of the gout, that "he now found pain to be an evil."

It may however be questioned, whether these philosophers can be very properly numbered among the teachers of patience; for if pain be not an evil, there seems no instruction requisite how it may be borne; and therefore, when they endeavour to arm their followers with arguments against it, they may be thought to have given up their first position. But such inconsistencies are to be expected from the greatest understandings, when they endeavour to grow eminent by singularity, and employ their strength in establishing opinions opposite to nature.

The controversy about the reality of external evils is now at an end. That life has many miseries, and that those miseries are, sometimes at least, equal to all the powers of fortitude, is now universally confessed; and therefore it is useful to consider not only how we may escape them, but by what means those which either the accidents of affairs or the infirmities of nature must bring upon us, may be mitigated and lightened, and how we may make those hours less wretched, which the condition of our present existence will not allow to be very happy.

The cure for the greatest part of human miseries is not radical, but palliative. Infelicity is involved in corporeal nature, and interwoven with our being; all attempts therefore to decline it wholly are useless and vain: the armies of pain send their arrows against us on every side, the choice is only between those which are more or less sharp, or tinged with poison of greater or less malignity; and the strongest armour which reason can supply will only blunt their points, but cannot repel them.

The great remedy which heaven has put in our hands is patience, by which, though we cannot lessen the torments of the body, we can in a great measure preserve the peace of the mind, and shall suffer only the natural and genuine force of an evil, without heightening its acrimony or prolonging its effects.

There is indeed nothing more unsuitable to the nature of man in any calamity than rage and turbulence, which, without examining whether they are not sometimes impious, are at least always offensive, and incline others rather to hate and despise than to pity and assist us. If what we suffer has been brought upon us by ourselves, it is observed by an ancient poet, that patience is eminently our duty, since no one should be angry at feeling that which he has deserved.

> *Leniter ex merito quicquid patiare ferendum est.*
> Ovid, *Heroides*, V. 7

> *Let pain deserv'd without complaint be borne.*

And surely, if we are conscious that we have not contributed to our own sufferings if punishment falls upon innocence, or disappointment happens to industry and prudence, patience, whether more necessary or not, is much easier, since our pain is then without aggravation, and we have not the bitterness of remorse to add to the asperity of misfortune.

In those evils which are allotted to us by Providence, such as deformity, privation of any of the senses, or old age, it is always to be remembered that impatience can have no present effect, but to deprive us of the consolations which our condition admits, by driving away from us those by whose conversation or advice we might be amused or helped; and that with regard to futurity it is yet less to be justified, since, without lessening the pain, it cuts off the hope of that reward which he, by whom it is inflicted, will confer upon them that bear it well.

In all evils which admit a remedy, impatience is to be avoided, because it wastes that time and attention in complaints, that, if properly applied, might remove the cause. [Vicomte de] Turenne, among the acknowledgments which he used to pay in conversation to the memory of those by whom he had been instructed in the art of war, mentioned one with honour, who taught him not to spend his time in regretting any mistake which he had made, but to set himself immediately and vigorously to repair it.

Patience and submission are very carefully to be distinguished from cowardice and indolence. We are not to repine, but we may lawfully struggle; for the calamities of life, like the necessities of nature, are calls to labour and exercises of diligence. When we feel any pressure of distress, we are not to conclude that we can only obey the will of heaven by languishing under it, any more than when we perceive the pain of thirst, we are to imagine that water is prohibited. Of misfortune it never can be certainly known whether, as proceeding from the hand of God, it is an act of favour or of punishment: but since all the ordinary dispensations of Providence are to be interpreted according to the general analogy of things, we may conclude that we have a right to remove one inconvenience as well as another; that we are only to take care lest we purchase ease with guilt; and that our Maker's purpose, whether of reward or severity, will be answered by the labours which he lays us under the necessity of performing.

This duty is not more difficult in any state than in diseases intensely painful, which may indeed suffer such exacerbations as seem to strain the powers of life to their utmost stretch, and leave very little of the attention vacant to precept or reproof. In this state the nature of man requires some indulgence, and every extravagance but impiety may be easily forgiven him. Yet, lest we should think ourselves too soon entitled to the mournful privileges of irresistible misery, it is proper to reflect that the utmost anguish which human wit can contrive, or human malice can inflict, has been borne with constancy; and that if the pains of disease be, as I believe they are, sometimes greater than those of artificial torture, they are therefore in their own nature shorter: the vital frame is quickly broken, the union between soul and body is for a time suspended by insensibility, and we soon cease to feel our maladies when they once become too violent to be borne. I think there is some reason for questioning whether the body and mind are not so proportioned, that the one can bear all that can be inflicted on the other, whether virtue cannot stand its ground as long as life, and whether a soul well principled will not be separated sooner than subdued.

In calamities which operate chiefly on our passions, such as diminution of fortune, loss of friends, or declension of character, the chief danger of impatience is upon the first attack, and many expedients have been contrived by which the blow may be broken. Of these the most general precept is not to take pleasure in any thing, of which it is not in our power to secure the possession to ourselves. This counsel, when we consider the enjoyment of any terrestrial advantage as opposite to a constant and habitual solicitude for future felicity, is undoubtedly just, and delivered by that authority which cannot be disputed, but in any other sense, is it not like advice, not to walk lest we should stumble, or not to see lest our eyes should light upon deformity? It seems to me reasonable to enjoy blessings with confidence, as well as to resign them with submission, and to hope for the continuance of good which we possess without insolence or voluptuousness, as for the restitution of that which we lose without despondency or murmurs.

The chief security against the fruitless anguish of impatience, must arise from frequent reflection on the wisdom and goodness of the God of nature, in whose hands are riches and poverty, honour and disgrace, pleasure and pain, and life and death. A settled conviction of the tendency of every thing to our good, and of the possibility of turning miseries into happiness, by receiving them rightly, will incline us to bless the name of the Lord, whether he gives or takes away.

Rambler no. 41, August 7, 1750: The uses of memory

Nulla recordanti lux est ingrata, gravisque,
  Nulla fuit cujus non meminisse velit.
Ampliat aetatis spatium sibi vir bonus, hoc est
  Vivere bis vitâ posse priore frui.

Martial, X. 23. 5–8

No day's remembrance shall the good regret,
Nor wish one bitter moment to forget:
They stretch the limits of this narrow span,
And, by enjoying, live past life again.

transl. Rev. Francis Lewis

So few of the hours of life are filled up with objects adequate to the mind of man, and so frequently are we in want of present pleasure or employment, that we are forced to have recourse every moment to the past and future for supplemental satisfactions, and relieve the vacuities of our being, by recollection of former passages, or anticipation of events to come.

I cannot but consider this necessity of searching on every side for matter on which the attention may be employed, as a strong proof of the superior and celestial nature of the soul of man. We have no reason to believe that other creatures have higher faculties, or more extensive capacities, than the preservation of themselves, or their species, requires; they seem always to be fully employed, or to be completely at ease without employment, to feel few intellectual miseries or pleasures, and to have no exuberance of understanding to lay out upon curiosity or caprice, but to have their minds exactly adapted to their bodies, with few other ideas than such as corporal pain or pleasure impresses upon them.

Of memory, which makes so large a part of the excellence of the human soul, and which has so much influence upon all its other powers, but a small portion has been allotted to the animal world. We do not find the grief with which the dams lament the loss of their young, proportionate to the tenderness with which they caress, the assiduity with which they feed, or the vehemence with which they defend them. Their regard for their offspring, when it is before their eyes, is not, in appearance, less than that of a human parent; but when it is taken away, it is very soon forgotten, and, after a short absence, if brought again, wholly disregarded.

That they have very little remembrance of any thing once out of the reach of their senses, and scarce any power of comparing the present with the past, and regulating their conclusions from experience, may be gathered from this, that their intellects are produced in their full perfection. The sparrow that was hatched last spring makes her first nest the ensuing season, of the same materials, and with the same art, as in any following year; and the hen conducts and shelters her first brood of chickens with all the prudence that she ever attains.

It has been asked by men who love to perplex any thing that is plain to common understandings, how reason differs from instinct; and Prior has with no great propriety made Solomon himself declare, that to distinguish them is "the fool's ignorance, and the pedant's pride."[8] To give an accurate answer to a question of which the terms are not completely understood is impossible; we do not know in what either reason or instinct consists, and therefore cannot tell with exactness how they differ; but surely he that contemplates a ship and a bird's nest will not be long without finding out that the idea of the one was impressed at once, and continued through all the progressive descents of the species, without variation or improvement; and that the other is the result of experiments compared with experiments, has grown, by accumulated observation, from less to greater excellence, and exhibits the collective knowledge of different ages and various professions.

Memory is the purveyor of reason, the power which places those images before the mind upon which the judgment is to be exercised, and which treasures up the determinations that are once passed as the rules of future action, or grounds of subsequent conclusions.

It is, indeed, the faculty of remembrance which may be said to place us in the class of moral agents. If we were to act only in consequence of some immediate impulse, and receive no direction from internal motives of choice, we should be pushed forward by an invincible fatality, without power or reason for the most part to prefer one thing to another, because we could make no comparison but of objects which might both happen to be present.

We owe to memory not only the increase of our knowledge and our progress in rational inquiries, but many other intellectual pleasures. Indeed, almost all that we can be said to enjoy is past or future; the present is in perpetual motion, leaves us as soon as it arrives, ceases to be present before its presence is well perceived, and is only known to have existed by the effects which it leaves behind. The greatest part of our ideas arises, therefore, from the view before or behind us, and we are happy or miserable according as we are affected by the survey of our life, or our prospect of future existence.

With regard to futurity, when events are at such a distance from us that we cannot take the whole concatenation into our view, we have generally power enough over our imagination to turn it upon pleasing scenes, and can promise ourselves riches, honours, and delights, without intermingling those vexations and anxieties, with which all human enjoyments are polluted. If fear breaks in on one side, and alarms us with dangers and disappointments, we can call in hope on the other, to solace us with rewards, and escapes, and victories; so that we are seldom without means of palliating remote evils, and can generally sooth ourselves to tranquillity, whenever any troublesome presage happens to attack us.

It is, therefore, I believe, much more common for the solitary and thoughtful to amuse themselves with schemes of the future, than reviews of the past. For the future is pliant and ductile, and will be easily moulded by a strong fancy into any form. But the images which memory presents are of a stubborn and intractable nature, the objects of remembrance have already existed, and left their signature behind them impressed upon the mind, so as to defy all attempts of rasure[9] or of change.

As the satisfactions, therefore, arising from memory are less arbitrary, they are more solid, and are, indeed, the only joys which we can call our own. Whatever we have once reposited,[10] as Dryden expresses it, "in the sacred treasure of the past," is out of the reach of accident or violence, nor can be lost either by our own weakness, or another's malice:

> *Non tamen irritum*
> *Quodcunque retro est efficiet; neque*
> *Diffinget, infectumque reddet*
> *Quod fugiens semel hora vexit.*
> Horace, Odes, III. 29. 45–48

> *Be fair or foul or rain or shine,*
> *The joys I have possess'd in spite of fate are mine.*
> *Not heav'n itself upon the past has pow'r,*
> *But what has been has been, and I have had my hour.*
> transl. John Dryden

There is certainly no greater happiness than to be able to look back on a life usefully and virtuously employed, to trace our own progress in existence by such tokens as excite neither shame nor sorrow. Life, in which nothing has been done or suffered to distinguish one day from another, is to him that has passed it as if it had never been, except that he is conscious how ill he has husbanded the great deposit of his Creator. Life, made memorable by crimes, and diversified through its several periods by wickedness, is indeed easily reviewed, but reviewed only with horror and remorse.

The great consideration which ought to influence us in the use of the present moment, is to arise from the effect which, as well or ill applied, it must have upon the time to come; for though its actual existence be inconceivably short, yet its effects are unlimited; and there is not the smallest point of time but may extend its consequences, either to our hurt or our advantage, through all eternity, and give us reason to remember it for ever, with anguish or exultation.

The time of life in which memory seems particularly to claim predominance over the other faculties of the mind, is our declining age. It has been remarked by former writers, that old men are generally narrative, and fall easily into recitals of past transactions, and accounts of persons known to them in their youth. When we approach the verge of the grave it is more eminently true;

> *Vitae summa brevis spem nos vetat inchoare longam.*
> Horace, *Odes,* I. 4.15

> *Life's span forbids thee to extend thy cares,*
>   *And stretch thy hopes beyond thy years.*
> transl. Thomas Creech

We have no longer any possibility of great vicissitudes in our favour; the changes which are to happen in the world will come too late for our accommodation; and those who have no hope before them, and to whom their present state is painful and irksome, must of necessity turn their thoughts back to try what retrospect will afford. It ought, therefore, to be the care of those who wish to pass the last hours with comfort, to lay up such a treasure of pleasing ideas as shall support the expenses of that time, which is to depend wholly upon the fund already acquired.

Petite hinc, juvenesque senesque
Finem animo certum, miserisque viatica canis.

Persius, Satires, V. 64–65

Seek here, ye young, the anchor of your mind;
Here, suff'ring age, a bless'd provision find.

transl. James Elphinston

In youth, however unhappy, we solace ourselves with the hope of better fortune, and however vicious, appease our consciences with intentions of repentance; but the time comes at last in which life has no more to promise, in which happiness can be drawn only from recollection, and virtue will be all that we can recollect with pleasure.

Rambler no. 47, August 28, 1750: Dealing with sorrow

Quamquam his solatiis acquiescam, debilitor & frangor eadem illa humanitate quae me, ut hoc ipsum permitterem, induxit, non ideo tamen velim durior fieri: nec ignoro alios hujusmodi casus nihil amplius vocare quam damnum; eoque sibi magnos homines & sapientes videri. Qui an magni sapientesque sint, nescio: homines non sunt. Hominis est enim affici dolore, sentire: resistere tamen, & solatia admittere; non solatiis non egere.

Pliny, Epistles, VIII. 16

These proceedings have afforded me some comfort in my distress; notwithstanding which, I am still dispirited and unhinged by the same motives of humanity that induced me to grant such indulgences. However, I by no means wish to become less susceptible of tenderness. I know these kind of misfortunes would be estimated by other persons only as common losses, and from such sensations they would conceive themselves great and wise men. I shall not determine either their greatness or their wisdom; but I am certain they have no humanity. It is the part of a man to be affected with grief; to feel sorrow, at the same time, that he is to resist it, and to admit of comfort.

transl. John Boyle, Earl of Orrery

Of the passions with which the mind of man is agitated, it may be observed, that they naturally hasten towards their own extinction, by inciting and quickening the attainment of their objects. Thus fear urges our flight, and desire animates our progress; and if there are some which perhaps may be indulged till they outgrow the good appropriated to their satisfaction, as it is frequently observed of avarice and ambition, yet their immediate tendency is to some means of happiness really existing, and generally within the prospect. The miser always imagines that there is a certain sum that will fill his heart to the brim; and every ambitious man, like king Pyrrhus, has an acquisition in his thoughts that is to terminate his labours, after which he shall pass the rest of his life in ease or gaiety, in repose or devotion.

Sorrow is perhaps the only affection of the breast that can be expected from this general remark, and it therefore deserves the particular attention of those who have assumed the arduous province of preserving the balance of the mental constitution. The other passions are diseases indeed, but they necessarily direct us to their proper cure. A man at once feels the pain and knows the medicine, to which he is carried with greater haste as the evil which requires it is more excruciating, and cures himself by unerring instinct, as the wounded stags of Crete are related by Ælian to have recourse to vulnerary herbs.[11] But for sorrow there is no remedy provided by nature; it is often occasioned by accidents irreparable, and dwells upon objects that have lost or changed their existence; it required what it cannot hope, that the laws of the universe should be repealed; that the dead should return, or the past should be recalled.

Sorrow is not that regret for negligence or error which may animate us to future care or activity, or that repentance of crimes for which, however irrevocable, our Creator has promised to accept it as an atonement; the pain which arises from these causes has very salutary effects, and is every hour extenuating itself by the reparation of those miscarriages that produce it. Sorrow is properly that state of the mind in which our desires are fixed upon the past, without looking forward to the future, an incessant wish that something were otherwise than it has been, a tormenting and harassing want of some enjoyment or possession which we have lost, which no endeavours can possibly regain. Into such anguish many have sunk upon some sudden diminution of their fortune, an unexpected blast of their reputation, or the loss of children or of friends. They have suffered all sensibility of pleasure to be destroyed by a single blow, have given up for ever the hopes of substituting any other object in the room of that which they lament, resigned their lives to gloom and despondency, and worn themselves out in unavailing misery.

Yet so much is this passion the natural consequence of tenderness and endearment, that, however painful and however useless, it is justly reproachful not to feel it on some occasions; and so widely and constantly has it always prevailed, that the laws of some nations, and the customs of others, have limited a time for the external appearances of grief caused by the dissolution of close alliances, and the breach of domestic union.

It seems determined by the general suffrage of mankind, that sorrow is to a certain point laudable, as the offspring of love, or at least pardonable, as the effect of weakness; but that it ought not to be suffered to increase by indulgence, but must give way, after a stated time, to social duties and the common avocations of life. It is at first unavoidable, and therefore must be allowed, whether with or without our choice; it may afterwards be admitted as a decent and affectionate testimony of kindness and esteem; something will be extorted by nature, and something may be given to the world. But all beyond the bursts of passion, or the forms of solemnity, is not only useless, but culpable; for we have no right to sacrifice, to the vain longings of affection, that time which Providence allows us for the task of our station.

Yet it too often happens that sorrow, thus lawfully entering, gains such a firm possession of the mind, that it is not afterwards to be ejected; the mournful ideas, first violently impressed and afterwards willingly received, so much engross the attention, as to predominate in every thought, to darken gaiety, and perplex ratiocination. An habitual sadness seizes upon the soul, and the faculties are chained to a single object, which can never be contemplated but with hopeless uneasiness.

From this state of dejection it is very difficult to rise to cheerfulness and alacrity; and therefore many who have laid down rules of intellectual health, think preservatives easier than remedies, and teach us not to trust ourselves with favourite enjoyments, not to indulge the luxury of fondness, but to keep our minds always suspended in such indifference, that we may change the objects about us without emotion.

An exact compliance with this rule might, perhaps, contribute to tranquillity, but surely it would never produce happiness. He that regards none so much as to be afraid of losing them, must live for ever without the gentle pleasures of sympathy and confidence; he must feel no melting fondness, no warmth of benevolence, nor any of those honest joys which nature annexes to the power of pleasing. And as no man can justly claim more tenderness than he pays, he must forfeit his share in that officious and watchful kindness which love only can dictate, and those lenient endearments by which love only can soften life. He may justly be overlooked and neglected by such as have more warmth in their heart; for who would be the friend of him, whom, with whatever assiduity he may be courted, and with whatever services obliged, his principles will not suffer to make equal returns, and who, when you have exhausted all the instances of good will can only be prevailed on not to be an enemy?

An attempt to preserve life in a state of neutrality and indifference is unreasonable and vain. If by excluding joy we could shut out grief, the scheme would deserve very serious attention; but since, however we may debar ourselves from happiness, misery will find its way at many inlets, and the assaults of pain will force our regard, though we may withhold it from the invitations of pleasure, we may surely endeavour to raise life above the middle point of apathy at one time, since it will necessarily sink below it at another.

But though it cannot be reasonable not to gain happiness for fear of losing it, yet it must be confessed that in proportion to the pleasure of possession will be for some time our sorrow for the loss; it is therefore the province of the moralist to enquire whether such pains may not quickly give way to mitigation. Some have thought that the most certain way to clear the heart from its embarrassment is to drag it by force into scenes of merriment. Others imagine that such a transition is too violent, and recommend rather to sooth it into tranquillity, by making it acquainted with miseries more dreadful and afflictive, and diverting to the calamities of others the regards which we are inclined to fix too closely upon our own misfortunes.

It may be doubted whether either of those remedies will be sufficiently powerful. The efficacy of mirth it is not always easy to try, and the indulgence of melancholy may be suspected to be one of those medicines, which will destroy, if it happens not to cure.

The safe and general antidote against sorrow is employment. It is commonly observed, that among soldiers and seamen, though there is much kindness, there is little grief; they see their friend fall without any of that lamentation which is indulged in security and idleness, because they have no leisure to spare from the care of themselves; and whoever shall keep his thoughts equally busy, will find himself equally unaffected with irretrievable losses.

Time is observed generally to wear out sorrow, and its effects might doubtless be accelerated by quickening the succession, and enlarging the variety of objects.

> *Si tempore longo*
> *Leniri poterit luctus, tu sperne morari,*
> *Qui sapiet, sibi tempus erit.*
>
> Hugo Grotius

> *'Tis long ere time can mitigate your grief;*
> *To wisdom fly, she quickly brings relief.*
>
> transl. Rev. Francis Lewis

Sorrow is a kind of rust of the soul, which every new idea contributes in its passage to scour away. It is the putrefaction of stagnant life, and is remedied by exercise and motion.

Rambler no. 52, September 15, 1750: Overcoming grief

> *Quoties flenti Theseius heros*
> *Siste modum, dixit, neque enim fortuna querenda*
> *Sola tua est, similes aliorum respice casus,*
> *Mitius ista feres.*
>
> Ovid, *Metamorphoses*, XV. 492–495

How oft in vain the son of Theseus said,
The stormy sorrows be with patience laid;
Nor are thy fortunes to be wept alone;
Weigh other's woes, and learn to bear thy own.

transl. Alexander Stopford Catcott

Among the various methods of consolation, to which the miseries inseparable from our present state have given occasion, it has been, as I have already remarked, recommended by some writers to put the sufferer in mind of heavier pressures and more excruciating calamities than those of which he has himself reason to complain.

This has, in all ages, been directed and practised; and, in conformity to this custom, Lipsius, the great modern master of the Stoic philosophy, has, in his celebrated treatise on "steadiness of mind," endeavoured to fortify the breast against too much sensibility of misfortune, by enumerating the evils which have in former ages fallen upon the world, the devastation of wide-extended regions, the sack of cities, and massacre of nations.[12] And the common voice of the multitude, uninstructed by precept and unprejudiced by authority, which, in questions that relate to the heart of man, is, in my opinion, more decisive than the learning of Lipsius, seems to justify the efficacy of this procedure; for one of the first comforts which one neighbour administers to another, is a relation of the like infelicity, combined with circumstances of greater bitterness.

But this medicine of the mind is like many remedies applied to the body, of which, though we see the effects, we are unacquainted with the manner of operation, and of which, therefore, some, who are unwilling to suppose any thing out of the reach of their own sagacity, have been inclined to doubt whether they have really those virtues for which they are celebrated, and whether their reputation is not the mere gift of fancy, prejudice, and credulity.

Consolation, or comfort, are words which, in their proper acceptation, signify some alleviation of that pain to which it is not in our power to afford the proper and adequate remedy, they imply rather an augmentation of the power of bearing, than a diminution of the burden. A prisoner is relieved by him that sets him at liberty, but receives comfort from such as suggest considerations by which he is made patient under the inconvenience of confinement. To that grief which arises from a great loss, he only brings the true remedy who makes his friend's condition the same as before; but he may be properly termed a comforter, who by persuasion extenuates the pain of poverty and shows, in the style of Hesiod, that "half is more than the whole."[13]

It is, perhaps, not immediately obvious how it can lull the memory of misfortune, or appease the throbbings of anguish, to hear that others are more miserable; others, perhaps, unknown or wholly indifferent, whose prosperity raises no envy, and whose fall can gratify no resentment. Some topics of comfort arising, like that which gave hope and spirit to the captive of Sesostris,[14] from the perpetual vicissitudes of life and mutability of human affairs, may as properly raise the dejected as depress the proud, and have an immediate tendency to exhilarate and revive. But how can it avail the man who languishes in the gloom of sorrow, without prospect of emerging into the sunshine of cheerfulness, to hear that others are sunk yet deeper in the dungeon of misery, shackled with heavier chains, and surrounded with darker desperation?

The solace arising from this consideration seems indeed the weakest of all others, and is perhaps never properly applied but in cases where there is no place for reflections of more speedy and pleasing efficacy. But even from such calamities life is by no means free; a thousand ills incurable, a thousand losses irreparable, a thousand difficulties insurmountable are known, or will be known, by all the sons of men. Native deformity cannot be rectified, a dead friend cannot return, and the hours of youth trifled away in folly, or lost in sickness, cannot be restored.

Under the oppression of such melancholy, it has been found useful to take a survey of the world, to contemplate the various scenes of distress in which mankind are struggling round us, and acquaint ourselves with the *terribiles visu formae,*[15] the various shapes of misery, which make havoc of terrestrial happiness, range all corners almost without restraint, trample down our hopes at the hour of harvest, and, when we have built our schemes to the top, ruin their foundations.

The first effect of this meditation is, that it furnishes a new employment for the mind, and engages the passions on remoter objects; as kings have sometimes freed themselves from a subject too haughty to be governed and too powerful to be crushed, by posting him in a distant province till his popularity has subsided, or his pride been repressed. The attention is dissipated by variety, and acts more weakly upon any single part as that torrent may be drawn off to different channels, which, pouring down in one collected body, cannot be resisted. This species of comfort is, therefore, unavailing in severe paroxysms of corporal pain, when the mind is every instant called back to misery, and in the first shock of any sudden evil; but will certainly be of use against encroaching melancholy, and a settled habit of gloomy thoughts.

It is further advantageous as it supplies us with opportunities of making comparisons in our own favour. We know that very little of the pain, or pleasure, which does not begin and end in our senses, is otherwise than relative; we are rich or poor, great or little, in proportion to the number that excel us, or fall beneath us, in any of these respects; and therefore, a man, whose uneasiness arises from reflection on any misfortune that throws him below those with whom he was once equal, is comforted by finding that he is not yet the lowest.

There is another kind of comparison, less tending towards the vice of envy, very well illustrated by an old poet, whose system will not afford many reasonable motives to content. "It is," says he, "pleasing to look from shore upon the tumults of a storm, and to see a ship struggling with the billows; it is pleasing, not because the pain of another can give us delight, but because we have a stronger impression of the happiness of safety."[16] Thus, when we look abroad, and behold the multitudes that are groaning under evils heavier than those which we have experienced, we shrink back to our own state, and instead of repining that so much must be felt, learn to rejoice that we have not more to feel.

By this observation of the miseries of others, fortitude is strengthened, and the mind brought to a more extensive knowledge of her own powers. As the heroes of action catch the flame from one another, so they to whom Providence has allotted the harder task of suffering with calmness and dignity, may animate themselves by the remembrance of those evils which have been laid on others, perhaps naturally as weak as themselves, and bear up with vigour and resolution against their own oppressions, when they see it possible that more severe afflictions may be born.

There is still another reason why, to many minds, the relation of other men's infelicity may give a lasting and continual relief. Some, not well instructed in the measures by which Providence distributes happiness, are perhaps misled by divines, who, as Bellarmine makes temporal prosperity one of the characters of the true church, have represented wealth and ease as the certain concomitants of virtue, and the unfailing result of the divine approbation. Such sufferers are dejected in their misfortunes, not so much for what they feel, as for what they dread; not because they cannot support the sorrows or endure the wants of their present condition, but because they consider them as only the beginnings of more sharp and more lasting pains. To these mourners it is an act of the highest charity to represent the calamities which not only virtue has suffered, but virtue has incurred; to inform them that one evidence of a future state, is the uncertainty of any present reward for goodness; and to remind them, from the highest authority, of the distresses and penury of men "of whom the world was not worthy."[17]

Rambler no. 67, November 6, 1750: The illusory promises of hope

Exiles, the proverb says, subsist on hope,
Delusive hope still points to distant good,
To good that mocks approach.
                    transl. of Euripides, *Phoenissae*, ll. 396–397

There is no temper so generally indulged as hope: other passions operate by starts on particular occasions, or in certain parts of life; but hope begins with the first power of comparing our actual with our possible state, and attends us through every stage and period, always urging us forward to new acquisitions, and holding out some distant blessing to our view, promising us either relief from pain, or increase of happiness.

Hope is necessary in every condition. The miseries of poverty, of sickness, of captivity, would, without this comfort, be insupportable; nor does it appear that the happiest lot of terrestrial existence can set us above the want of this general blessing; or that life, when the gifts of nature and of fortune are accumulated upon it, would not still be wretched were it not elevated and delighted by the expectation of some new possession, of some enjoyment yet behind, by which the wish shall be at last satisfied, and the heart filled up to its utmost extent.

Hope is indeed very fallacious, and promises what it seldom gives; but its promises are more valuable than the gifts of fortune, and it seldom frustrates us without assuring us of recompensing the delay by a greater bounty.

I was musing on this strange inclination which every man feels to deceive himself, and considering the advantages and dangers proceeding from this gay prospect of futurity, when, falling asleep, on a sudden I found myself placed in a garden, of which my sight could descry no limits. Every scene above me was gay and gladsome, light with sunshine, and fragrant with perfumes; the ground was painted with all the variety of spring, and all the choir of nature was singing in the groves. When I had recovered from the first raptures, with which the confusion of pleasure had for a time entranced me, I began to take a particular and deliberate view of this delightful region. I then perceived that I had yet higher gratifications to expect, and that, at a small distance from me, there were brighter flowers, clearer fountains, and more lofty groves, where the birds, which I yet heard but faintly, were exerting all the power of melody. The trees about me were beautiful with verdure, and fragrant with blossoms; but I was tempted to leave them by the sight of ripe fruits, which seemed to hang only to be plucked. I therefore walked hastily forwards, but found, as I proceeded, that the colours of the field faded at my approach, the fruit fell before I reached it, the birds flew still singing before me, and though I pressed onward with great celerity, I was still in sight of pleasure of which I could not yet gain the possession, and which seemed to mock my diligence, and to retire as I advanced.

Though I was confounded with so many alternations of joy and grief, I yet persisted to go forward, in hopes that these fugitive delights would in time be overtaken. At length I saw an innumerable multitude of every age and sex, who seemed all to partake of some general felicity; for every cheek was flushed with confidence, and every eye sparkled with eagerness: yet each appeared to have some particular and secret pleasure, and very few were willing to communicate their intentions, or extend their concern beyond themselves. Most of them seemed, by the rapidity of their motion, too busy to gratify the curiosity of a stranger, and therefore I was content for a while to gaze upon them, without interrupting them with troublesome inquiries. At last I observed one man worn with time, and unable to struggle in the crowd; and, therefore, supposing him more at leisure, I began to accost him: but he turned from me with anger, and told me he must not be disturbed, for the great hour of projection was now come when Mercury should lose his wings, and slavery should no longer dig the mine for gold.

I left him, and attempted another, whose softness of mien, and easy movement gave me reason to hope for a more agreeable reception; but he told me, with a low bow, that nothing would make him more happy than an opportunity of serving me, which he could not now want, for a place which he had been twenty years soliciting would be soon vacant. From him I had recourse to the next, who was departing in haste to take possession of the estate of an uncle, who by the course of nature could not live long. He that followed was preparing to dive for treasure in a new-invented bell; and another was on the point of discovering the longitude.

Being thus rejected wheresoever I applied myself for information, I began to imagine it best to desist from inquiry, and try what my own observation would discover: but seeing a young man, gay and thoughtless, I resolved upon one more experiment, and was informed that I was in the garden of Hope, the daughter of Desire, and that all those whom I saw thus tumultuously bustling round me were incited by the promises of Hope, and hastening to seize the gifts which she held in her hand.

I turned my sight upward, and saw a goddess in the bloom of youth sitting on a throne: around her lay all the gifts of fortune, and all the blessings of life were spread abroad to view; she had a perpetual gaiety of aspect, and every one imagined that her smile, which was impartial and general, was directed to himself, and triumphed in his own superiority to others, who had conceived the same confidence from the same mistake.

I then mounted an eminence, from which I had a more extensive view of the whole place, and could with less perplexity consider the different conduct of the crowds that filled it. From this station I observed, that the entrance into the garden of Hope was by two gates, one of which was kept by Reason, and the other by Fancy. Reason was surly and scrupulous, and seldom turned the key without many interrogatories and long hesitation;

but Fancy was a kind and gentle portress,[18] she held her gate wide open, and welcomed all equally to the district under her superintendency; so that the passage was crowded by all those who either feared the examination of Reason, or had been rejected by her.

From the gate of Reason there was a way to the throne of Hope, by a craggy, slippery, and winding path, called the Streight of Difficulty, which those who entered with the permission of the guard endeavoured to climb. But though they surveyed the way very carefully before they began to rise, and marked out the several stages of their progress, they commonly found unexpected obstacles, and were obliged frequently to stop on the sudden, where they imagined the way plain and even. A thousand intricacies embarrassed them, a thousand slips threw them back, and a thousand pitfalls impeded their advance. So formidable were the dangers, and so frequent the miscarriages, that many returned from the first attempt, and many fainted in the midst of the way, and only a very small number were led up to the summit of Hope, by the hand of Fortitude. Of these few the greater part, when they had obtained the gift which Hope had promised them, regretted the labour which it cost, and felt in their success the regret of disappointment; the rest retired with their prize, and were led by Wisdom to the bowers of Content.

Turning then towards the gate of Fancy, I could find no way to the seat of Hope; but though she sat full in view, and held out her gifts with an air of invitation, which filled every heart with rapture, the mountain was, on that side, inaccessibly steep, but so channelled and shaded, that none perceived the impossibility of ascending it, but each imagined himself to have discovered a way to which the rest were strangers. Many expedients were indeed tried by this industrious tribe, of whom some were making themselves wings, which others were contriving to actuate by the perpetual motion. But with all their labour and all their artifices, they never rose above the ground, or quickly fell back, nor ever approached the throne of Hope, but continued still to gaze at a distance, and laugh at the slow progress of those whom they saw toiling in the Streight of Difficulty.

Part of the favourites of Fancy, when they had entered the garden, without making, like the rest, an attempt to climb the mountain, turned immediately to the vale of Idleness, a calm and undisturbed retirement, from whence they could always have Hope in prospect, and to which they pleased themselves with believing that she intended speedily to descend. These were indeed scorned by all the rest; but they seemed very little affected by contempt, advice, or reproof, but were resolved to expect at ease the favour of the goddess.

Among this gay race I was wandering, and found them ready to answer all my questions, and willing to communicate their mirth; but turning round, I saw two dreadful monsters entering the vale, one of whom I knew to be Age, and the other Want. Sport and revelling were now at an end, and an universal shriek of affright and distress burst out and awaked me.

Rambler no. 71, November 20, 1750: Wasting life by dwelling on the future

Vivere quod propero pauper, nec inutilis annis;
  Da veniam, properat vivere nemo satis.

                    Martial, II. 90. 3–4

True, sir, to live I haste, your pardon give,
  For tell me, who makes haste enough to live?

                    transl. Rev. Francis Lewis

Many words and sentences are so frequently heard in the mouths of men, that a superficial observer is inclined to believe, that they must contain some primary principle, some great rule of action, which it is proper always to have present to the attention, and by which the use of every hour is to be adjusted. Yet, if we consider the conduct of those sententious philosophers, it will often be found, that they repeat these aphorisms, merely because they have somewhere heard them, because they have nothing else to say, or because they think veneration gained by such appearances of wisdom, but that no ideas are annexed to the words, and that, according to the old blunder of the followers of Aristotle, their souls are mere pipes or organs, which transmit sounds, but do not understand them.

Of this kind is the well-known and well-attested position "that life is short," which may be heard among mankind by an attentive auditor, many times a day, but which never yet within my reach of observation left any impression upon the mind; and perhaps, if my readers will turn their thoughts back upon their old friends, they will find it difficult to call a single man to remembrance, who appeared to know that life was short till he was about to lose it.

It is observable that Horace,[19] in his account of the characters of men, as they are diversified by the various influence of time, remarks that the old man is *dilator, spe longus,* given to procrastination, and inclined to extend his hopes to a great distance. So far are we generally from thinking what we often say of the shortness of life, that at the time when it is necessarily shortest, we form projects which we delay to execute, indulge such expectations as nothing but a long train of events can gratify, and suffer those passions to gain upon us, which are only excusable in the prime of life.

These reflections were lately excited in my mind by an evening's conversation with my friend Prospero, who, at the age of fifty-five, has bought an estate, and is now contriving to dispose and cultivate it with uncommon elegance. His great pleasure is to walk among stately trees, and lie musing in the heat of noon under their shade; he is therefore maturely considering how he shall dispose his walks and his groves, and has at last determined to send for the best plans from Italy, and forbear planting till the next season.

Thus is life trifled away in preparations to do what never can be done, if it be left unattempted till all the requisites which imagination can suggest are gathered together. Where our design terminates only in our own satisfaction, the mistake is of no great importance; for the pleasure of expecting enjoyment is often greater than that of obtaining it, and the completion of almost every wish is found a disappointment; but when many others are interested in an undertaking, when any design is formed, in which the improvement or security of mankind is involved, nothing is more unworthy either of wisdom or benevolence, than to delay it from time to time, or to forget how much every day that passes over us takes away from our power, and how soon an idle purpose to do an action sinks into a mournful wish that it had once been done.

We are frequently importuned by the bacchanalian writers to lay hold on the present hour, to catch the pleasures within our reach, and remember that futurity is not at our command.

Soon fades the rose; once past the fragrant hour,
The loiterer finds a bramble for a flow'r.
  Samuel Johnson transl. of anonymous Greek poem

But surely these exhortations may, with equal propriety, be applied to better purposes; it may be at least inculcated that pleasures are more safely postponed than virtues, and that greater loss is suffered by missing an opportunity of doing good, than an hour of giddy frolic and noisy merriment.

When [Rev. Richard Baxter] had lost a thousand pounds, which he had laid up for the erection of a school, he used frequently to mention the misfortune as an incitement to be charitable while God gives the power of bestowing, and considered himself as culpable in some degree for having left a good action in the hands of chance, and suffered his benevolence to be defeated for want of quickness and diligence.

It is lamented by [Thomas] Hearne, the learned antiquary of Oxford, that this general forgetfulness of the fragility of life, has remarkably infected the students of monuments and records; as their employment consists first in collecting, and afterwards in arranging or abstracting what libraries afford them, they ought to amass no more than they can digest; but when they have undertaken a work, they go on searching and transcribing, call for new supplies when they are already overburdened, and at last leave their work unfinished. "It is," says he, "the business of a good antiquary, as of a good man, to have mortality always before him."

Thus, not only in the slumber of sloth, but in the dissipation of ill-directed industry, is the shortness of life generally forgotten. As some men lose their hours in laziness, because they suppose that there is time enough for the reparation of neglect; others busy themselves in providing that no length of life may want employment; and it often happens that sluggishness and activity are equally surprised by the last summons, and perish not more differently from each other, than the fowl that received the shot in her flight, from her that is killed upon the bush.

Among the many improvements made by the last centuries in human knowledge, may be numbered the exact calculations of the value of life; but whatever may be their use in traffic, they seem very little to have advanced morality. They have hitherto been rather applied to the acquisition of money than of wisdom; the computer refers none of his calculations to his own tenure, but persists, in contempt of probability, to foretell old age to himself, and believes that he is marked out to reach the utmost verge of human existence, and see thousands and ten thousands fall into the grave.

So deeply is this fallacy rooted in the heart, and so strongly guarded by hope and fear against the approach of reason, that neither science nor experience can shake it, and we act as if life were without end, though we see and confess its uncertainty and shortness.

Divines have, with great strength and ardour, shown the absurdity of delaying reformation and repentance; a degree of folly, indeed, which sets eternity to hazard. It is the same weakness, in proportion to the importance of the neglect, to transfer any care, which now claims our attention, to a future time; we subject ourselves to needless dangers from accidents which early diligence would have obviated, or perplex our minds by vain precautions, and make provision for the execution of designs, of which the opportunity once missed never will return.

As he that lives longest lives but a little while, every man may be certain that he has no time to waste. The duties of life are commensurate to its duration, and every day brings its task, which if neglected is doubled on the morrow. But he that has already trifled away those months and years in which he should have laboured must remember that he has now only a part of that of which the whole is little; and that since the few moments remaining are to be considered as the last trust of heaven, not one is to be lost.

Rambler no. 108, March 30, 1751:
Making good use of time before "single minutes" pass into years

> *Sapere aude,*
> *Incipe. Vivendi recte qui prorogat horam,*
> *Rusticus expectat dum defluat amnis: at ille*
> *Labitur, & labetur in omne volubilis aevum.*
>   Horace, *Epistles,* I.2. 40–43

Begin, be bold, and venture to be wise;
He who defers this work from day to day,
Does on a river's bank expecting stay,
Till the whole stream, which stopp'd him, should be gone,
That runs, and as it runs, for ever will run on.

transl. Abraham Cowley

An ancient poet, unreasonably discontented at the present state of things, which his system of opinions obliged him to represent in its worst form, has observed of the earth, "that its greater part is covered by the uninhabitable ocean; that of the rest some is encumbered with naked mountains, and some lost under barren sands; some scorched with unintermitted[20] heat, and some petrified with perpetual frost; so that only a few regions remain for the production of fruits, the pasture of cattle, and the accommodation of man."[21]

The same observation may be transferred to the time allotted us in our present state. When we have deducted all that is absorbed in sleep, all that is inevitably appropriated to the demands of nature, or irresistibly engrossed by the tyranny of custom; all that passes in regulating the superficial decorations of life, or is given up in the reciprocations of civility to the disposal of others; all that is torn from us by the violence of disease, or stolen imperceptibly away by lassitude and languor; we shall find that part of our duration very small of which we can truly call ourselves masters, or which we can spend wholly at our own choice. Many of our hours are lost in a rotation of petty cares, in a constant recurrence of the same employments; many of our provisions for ease or happiness are always exhausted by the present day; and a great part of our existence serves no other purpose, than that of enabling us to enjoy the rest.

Of the few moments which are left in our disposal, it may reasonably be expected that we should be so frugal as to let none of them slip from us without some equivalent; and perhaps it might be found, that as the earth, however straitened by rocks and waters, is capable of producing more than all its inhabitants are able to consume, our lives, though much contracted by incidental distraction, would yet afford us a large space vacant to the exercise of reason and virtue; that we want not time, but diligence, for great performances; and that we squan-

der much of our allowance, even while we think it sparing and insufficient.

This natural and necessary comminution of our lives, perhaps, often
makes us insensible of the negligence with which we suffer them to slide
away. We never consider ourselves as possessed at once of time sufficient
for any great design, and therefore indulge ourselves in fortuitous amusements. We think it unnecessary to take an account of a few supernumer-
ary moments, which, however employed, could have produced little advantage, and which were exposed to a thousand chances of disturbance
and interruption.

It is observable that, either by nature or by habit, our faculties are fitted
to images of a certain extent, to which we adjust great things by division,
and little things by accumulation. Of extensive surfaces we can only take a
survey, as the parts succeed one another; and atoms we cannot perceive
till they are united into masses. Thus we break the vast periods of time
into centuries and years; and thus, if we would know the amount of moments, we must agglomerate them into days and weeks.

The proverbial oracles of our parsimonious ancestors have informed
us that the fatal waste of fortune is by small expenses, by the profusion of
sums too little singly to alarm our caution, and which we never suffer ourselves to consider together. Of the same kind is the prodigality of life; he
that hopes to look back hereafter with satisfaction upon past years, must
learn to know the present value of single minutes, and endeavour to let no
particle of time fall useless to the ground.

It is usual for those who are advised to the attainment of any new qualification, to look upon themselves as required to change the general course
of their conduct, to dismiss business and exclude pleasure, and to devote
their days and nights to a particular attention. But all common degrees of
excellence are attainable at a lower price; he that should steadily and resolutely assign to any science or language those interstitial vacancies which
intervene in the most crowded variety of diversion or employment, would
find every day new irradiations of knowledge, and discover how much
more is to be hoped from frequency and perseverance, than from violent
efforts and sudden desires; efforts which are soon remitted when they encounter difficulty, and desires which, if they are indulged too often, will

shake off the authority of reason, and range capriciously from one object to another.

The disposition to defer every important design to a time of leisure and a state of settled uniformity proceeds generally from a false estimate of the human powers. If we except those gigantic and stupendous intelligences who are said to grasp a system by intuition, and bound forward from one series of conclusions to another, without regular steps through intermediate propositions, the most successful students make their advances in knowledge by short flights, between each of which the mind may lie at rest. For every single act of progression a short time is sufficient; and it is only necessary that whenever that time is afforded, it be well employed.

Few minds will be long confined to severe and laborious meditation; and when a successful attack on knowledge has been made, the student recreates himself with the contemplation of his conquest, and forbears another incursion, till the new-acquired truth has become familiar, and his curiosity calls upon him for fresh gratifications. Whether the time of intermission is spent in company or in solitude, in necessary business or in voluntary levities, the understanding is equally abstracted from the object of inquiry; but, perhaps, if it be detained by occupations less pleasing, it returns again to study with greater alacrity than when it is glutted with ideal pleasures, and surfeited with intemperance of application. He that will not suffer himself to be discouraged by fancied impossibilities, may sometimes find his abilities invigorated by the necessity of exerting them in short intervals, as the force of a current is increased by the contraction of its channel.

From some cause like this, it has probably proceeded that, among those who have contributed to the advancement of learning, many have risen to eminence in opposition to all the obstacles which external circumstances could place in their way, amidst the tumult of business, the distresses of poverty, or the dissipations of a wandering and unsettled state. A great part of the life of Erasmus was one continual peregrination; ill supplied with the gifts of fortune, and led from city to city, and from kingdom to kingdom, by the hopes of patrons and preferment, hopes which always flattered and always deceived him; he yet found means, by unshaken constancy and a vigilant improvement of those hours which, in the midst of the most restless activity, will remain unengaged, to write more than another in the same condition would have hoped to read. Compelled by want to attendance and solicitation, and so much versed in common life, that he has transmitted to us the most perfect delineation of the manners of his age, he joined to his knowledge of the world such application to books that he will stand for ever in the first rank of literary heroes. How this proficiency was obtained he sufficiently discovers by informing us that the *Praise of Folly*, one of his most celebrated performances, was composed by him on the road to Italy; *ne totum illud tempus quo equo fuit insidendum, illiteratis fabulis terreretur,* lest the hours which he was obliged to spend on horseback should be tattled away without regard to literature.[22]

An Italian philosopher expressed in his motto that "time was his estate"; an estate, indeed, which will produce nothing without cultivation, but will always abundantly repay the labours of industry, and satisfy the most extensive desires, if no part of it be suffered to lie waste by negligence, to be overrun with noxious plants, or laid out for show, rather than for use.

Rambler no. 183, December 17, 1751: The monster envy

Nulla fides regni sociis, omnisque potestas
Impatiens consortis erat.

Lucan, *Pharsalia,* I. 92–93

No faith of partnership dominion owns;
Still discord hovers o'er divided thrones.

The hostility perpetually exercised between one man and another, is caused by the desire of many for that which only few can possess. Every man would be rich, powerful, and famous; yet fame, power, and riches are only the names of relative conditions, which imply the obscurity, dependence, and poverty of greater numbers.

This universal and incessant competition produces injury and malice by two motives, interest and envy; the prospect of adding to our possessions what we can take from others, and the hope of alleviating the sense of our disparity by lessening others, though we gain nothing to ourselves.

Of these two malignant and destructive powers, it seems probable at the first view, that interest has the strongest and most extensive influence. It is easy to conceive that opportunities to seize what has been long wanted, may excite desires almost irresistible; but surely the same eagerness cannot be kindled by an accidental power of destroying that which gives happiness to another. It must be more natural to rob for gain, than to ravage only for mischief.

Yet I am inclined to believe, that the great law of mutual benevolence is oftener violated by envy than by interest, and that most of the misery which the defamation of blameless actions, or the obstruction of honest endeavours, brings upon the world, is inflicted by men that propose no advantage to themselves but the satisfaction of poisoning the banquet which they cannot taste, and blasting the harvest which they have no right to reap.

Interest can diffuse itself but to a narrow compass. The number is never large of those who can hope to fill the posts of degraded power, catch the fragments of shattered fortune, or succeed to the honours of depreciated beauty. But the empire of envy has no limits, as it requires to its influence very little help from external circumstances. Envy may always be produced by idleness and pride, and in what place will they not be found?

Interest requires some qualities not universally bestowed. The ruin of another will produce no profit to him who has not discernment to mark his advantage, courage to seize, and activity to pursue it; but the cold malignity of envy may be exerted in a torpid and quiescent state, amidst the gloom of stupidity, in the coverts of cowardice. He that falls by the attacks of interest, is torn by hungry tigers; he may discover and resist his enemies. He that perishes in the ambushes of envy, is destroyed by unknown and invisible assailants, and dies like a man suffocated by a poisonous vapour, without knowledge of his danger, or possibility of contest.

Interest is seldom pursued but at some hazard. He that hopes to gain much, has commonly something to lose, and when he ventures to attack superiority, if he fails to conquer, is irrecoverably crushed. But envy may act without expense or danger. To spread suspicion, to invent calumnies, to propagate scandal, requires neither labour nor courage. It is easy for the author of a lie, however malignant, to escape detection, and infamy needs very little industry to assist its circulation.

Envy is almost the only vice which is practicable at all times, and in every place; the only passion which can never lie quiet for want of irritation: its effects therefore are every where discoverable, and its attempts always to be dreaded.

It is impossible to mention a name which any advantageous distinction has made eminent, but some latent animosity will burst out. The wealthy trader, however he may abstract himself from public affairs, will never want those who hint, with Shylock, that ships are but boards. The beauty, adorned only with the unambitious graces of innocence and modesty, provokes, whenever she appears, a thousand murmurs of detraction. The genius, even when he endeavours only to entertain or instruct, yet suffers persecution from innumerable critics, whose acrimony is excited merely by the pain of seeing others pleased, and of hearing applauses which another enjoys.

The frequency of envy makes it so familiar, that it escapes our notice; nor do we often reflect upon its turpitude or malignity, till we happen to feel its influence. When he that has given no provocation to malice, but by attempting to excel, finds himself pursued by multitudes whom he never saw, with all the implacability of personal resentment; when he perceives clamour and malice let loose upon him as a public enemy, and incited by every stratagem of defamation; when he hears the misfortunes of his family, or the follies of his youth, exposed to the world; and every failure of conduct, or defect of nature, aggravated and ridiculed; he then learns to abhor those artifices at which he only laughed before, and discovers how much the happiness of life would be advanced by the eradication of envy from the human heart.

Envy is, indeed, a stubborn weed of the mind, and seldom yields to the culture of philosophy. There are, however, considerations, which, if carefully implanted and diligently propagated, might in time overpower and repress it, since no one can nurse it for the sake of pleasure, as its effects are only shame, anguish, and perturbation. It is above all other vices inconsistent with the character of a social being, because it sacrifices truth and kindness to very weak temptations. He that plunders a wealthy neighbour gains as much as he takes away, and may improve his own condition in the same proportion as he impairs another's; but he that blasts a flourishing reputation, must be content with a small dividend of additional fame, so small as can afford very little consolation to balance the guilt by which it is obtained.

I have hitherto avoided that dangerous and empirical morality which cures one vice by means of another. But envy is so base and detestable, so vile in its original, and so pernicious in its effects, that the predominance of almost any other quality is to be preferred. It is one of those lawless enemies of society, against which poisoned arrows may honestly be used. Let it therefore be constantly remembered that whoever envies another confesses his superiority, and let those be reformed by their pride who have lost their virtue.

It is no slight aggravation of the injuries which envy incites, that they are committed against those who have given no intentional provocation; and that the sufferer is often marked out for ruin, not because he has failed in any duty, but because he has dared to do more than was required.

Almost every other crime is practised by the help of some quality which might have produced esteem or love, if it had been well employed; but envy is mere unmixed and genuine evil; it pursues a hateful end by despicable means, and desires not so much its own happiness as another's misery. To avoid depravity like this, it is not necessary that any one should aspire to heroism or sanctity, but only that he should resolve not to quit the rank which nature assigns him, and wish to maintain the dignity of a human being.

Rambler no. 193, January 21, 1752: Independent judgment

Laudis amore tumes? sunt certa piacula quae te
Ter purè lecto poterunt recreare libello.

Horace, *Epistles*, I.1. 36–37

Or art thou vain? books yield a certain spell,
To stop thy tumour; you shall cease to swell
When you have read them thrice, and studied well.

transl. Thomas Creech

Whatever is universally desired, will be sought by industry and artifice, by merit and crimes, by means good and bad, rational and absurd, according to the prevalence of virtue or vice, of wisdom or folly. Some will always mistake the degree of their own desert, and some will desire that others may mistake it. The cunning will have recourse to stratagem, and the powerful to violence, for the attainment of their wishes; some will stoop to theft, and others venture upon plunder.

Praise is so pleasing to the mind of man, that it is the original motive of almost all our actions. The desire of commendation, as of every thing else, is varied indeed by innumerable differences of temper, capacity, and knowledge; some have no higher wish than for the applause of a club; some expect the acclamations of a county; and some have hoped to fill the mouths of all ages and nations with their names. Every man pants for the highest eminence within his view; none, however mean, ever sinks below the hope of being distinguished by his fellow-beings, and very few have by magnanimity or piety been so raised above it, as to act wholly without regard to censure or opinion.

To be praised, therefore, every man resolves; but resolutions will not execute themselves. That which all think too parsimoniously distributed to their own claims, they will not gratuitously squander upon others, and some expedient must be tried, by which praise may be gained before it can be enjoyed.

Among the innumerable bidders for praise, some are willing to purchase at the highest rate, and offer ease and health, fortune and life. Yet even of these only a small part have gained what they so earnestly desired; the student wastes away in meditation, and the soldier perishes on the ramparts, but unless some accidental advantage cooperates with merit, neither perseverance nor adventure attracts attention, and learning and bravery sink into the grave, without honour or remembrance.

But ambition and vanity generally expect to be gratified on easier terms. It has been long observed, that what is procured by skill or labour to the first possessor, may be afterwards transferred for money; and that the man of wealth may partake all the acquisitions of courage without hazard, and all the products of industry without fatigue. It was easily discovered that riches would obtain praise among other conveniences, and that he whose pride was unluckily associated with laziness, ignorance, or cow-

ardice, needed only to pay the hire of a panegyrist, and he might be re-
galed with periodical eulogies; might determine, at leisure, what virtue or
science he would be pleased to appropriate, and be lulled in the evening
with soothing serenades, or waked in the morning by sprightly gratula-
tions.

The happiness which mortals receive from the celebration of beneficence which never relieved, eloquence which never persuaded, or elegance which never pleased, ought not to be envied or disturbed, when
they are known honestly to pay for their entertainment. But there are unmerciful exactors of adulation who withhold the wages of venality; retain
their encomiast from year to year by general promises and ambiguous
blandishments; and when he has run through the whole compass of flattery, dismiss him with contempt, because his vein of fiction is exhausted.

A continual feast of commendation is only to be obtained by merit or
by wealth; many are therefore obliged to content themselves with single
morsels, and recompense the infrequency of their enjoyment by excess
and riot, whenever fortune sets the banquet before them. Hunger is never
delicate; they who are seldom gorged to the full with praise, may be safely
fed with gross compliments; for the appetite must be satisfied before it is
disgusted.

It is easy to find the moment at which vanity is eager for sustenance,
and all that impudence or servility can offer will be well received. When
any one complains of the want of what he is known to possess in an uncommon degree, he certainly waits with impatience to be contradicted.
When the trader pretends anxiety about the payment of his bills, or the
beauty remarks how frightfully she looks, then is the lucky moment to talk
of riches or of charms, of the death of lovers, or the honour of a merchant.

Others there are yet more open and artless, who, instead of suborning
a flatterer, are content to supply his place, and, as some animals impregnate themselves, swell with the praises which they hear from their own
tongues. *Recte is dicitur laudare sese, cui nemo alius contigit laudator.* "It
is right," says Erasmus, "that he, whom no one else will commend, should
bestow commendations on himself." Of all the sons of vanity, these are
surely the happiest and greatest; for what is greatness or happiness but
independence on external influences, exemption from hope or fear, and

the power of supplying every want from the common stores of nature, which can neither be exhausted nor prohibited? Such is the wise man of the stoics; such is the divinity of the epicureans; and such is the flatterer of himself. Every other enjoyment malice may destroy; every other panegyric envy may withhold; but no human power can deprive the boaster of his own encomiums. Infamy may hiss, or contempt may growl, the hirelings of the great may follow fortune, and the votaries of truth may attend on virtue; but his pleasures still remain the same; he can always listen with rapture to himself, and leave those who dare not repose upon their own attestation, to be elated or depressed by chance, and toil on in the hopeless task of fixing caprice, and propitiating malice.

This art of happiness has been long practised by periodical writers, with little apparent violation of decency. When we think our excellencies overlooked by the world, or desire to recall the attention of the public to some particular performance, we sit down with great composure and write a letter to ourselves. The correspondent, whose character we assume, always addresses us with the deference due to a superior intelligence; proposes his doubts with a proper sense of his own inability; offers an objection with trembling diffidence; and at last has no other pretensions to our notice than his profundity of respect and sincerity of admiration, his submission to our dictates, and zeal for our success. To such a reader, it is impossible to refuse regard, nor can it easily be imagined with how much alacrity we snatch up the pen which indignation or despair had condemned to inactivity, when we find such candour and judgment yet remaining in the world.

A letter of this kind I had lately the honour of perusing, in which, though some of the periods were negligently closed, and some expressions of familiarity were used, which I thought might teach others to address me with too little reverence, I was so much delighted with the passages in which mention was made of universal learning—unbounded genius—soul of Homer, Pythagoras, and Plato—solidity of thought—accuracy of distinction—elegance of combination—vigour of fancy—strength of reason—and regularity of composition—that I had once determined to lay it before the public. Three times I sent it to the printer, and three times I fetched it back. My modesty was on the point of yielding, when, reflecting that I was about to waste panegyrics on myself, which might be more profitably reserved for my patron, I locked it up for a better hour, in compliance with the farmer's principle, who never eats at home what he can carry to the market.

Adventurer no. 50, April 28, 1753: Lying

Quicunque turpi fraude semel innotuit,
Etiamsi vera dicit, amittit fidem.

Plato, *Phaedrus*, I.10. 1–2

The wretch that often has deceiv'd,
Though truth he speaks, is ne'er believ'd.

When Aristotle was once asked what a man could gain by uttering falsehoods; he replied, "not to be credited when he shall tell the truth."

The character of a liar is at once so hateful and contemptible, that even of those who have lost their virtue it might be expected that from the violation of truth they should be restrained by their pride. Almost every other vice that disgraces human nature may be kept in countenance by applause and association: the corrupter of virgin innocence sees himself envied by the men, and at least not detested by the women; the drunkard may easily unite with beings devoted like himself to noisy merriments or silent insensibility, who will celebrate his victories over the novices of intemperance, boast themselves the companions of his prowess, and tell with rapture of the multitudes whom unsuccessful emulation has hurried to the grave; even the robber and the cutthroat have their followers, who admire their address and intrepidity, their stratagems of rapine, and their fidelity to the gang.

The liar, and only the liar, is invariably and universally despised, abandoned, and disowned: he has no domestic consolations which he can oppose to the censure of mankind; he can retire to no fraternity, where his crimes may stand in the place of virtues; but is given up to the hisses of the multitude, without friend and without apologist. It is the peculiar condition of falsehood to be equally detested by the good and bad: "The devils," says Sir Thomas Browne, "do not tell lies to one another; for truth is necessary to all societies: nor can the society of hell subsist without it."

It is natural to expect that a crime thus generally detested should be generally avoided; at least, that none should expose himself to unabated and unpitied infamy without an adequate temptation; and that to guilt so easily detected, and so severely punished, an adequate temptation would not readily be found.

Yet so it is, that in defiance of censure and contempt, truth is frequently violated; and scarcely the most vigilant and unremitted circumspection will secure him that mixes with mankind from being hourly deceived by men of whom it can scarcely be imagined that they mean any injury to him or profit to themselves: even where the subject of conversation could not have been expected to put the passions in motion, or to have excited either hope or fear, or zeal or malignity, sufficient to induce any man to put his reputation in hazard, however little he might value it, or to over-power the love of truth, however weak might be its influence.

The casuists have very diligently distinguished lies into their several classes, according to their various degrees of malignity: but they have, I think, generally omitted that which is most common, and perhaps, not least mischievous; which, since the moralists have not given it a name, I shall distinguish as the Lye of Vanity.

To vanity may justly be imputed most of the falsehoods which every man perceives hourly playing upon his ear, and, perhaps, most of those that are propagated with success. To the lie of commerce, and the lie of malice, the motive is so apparent, that they are seldom negligently or im-plicitly received; suspicion is always watchful over the practices of inter-est; and whatever the hope of gain, or desire of mischief, can prompt one man to assert, another is by reasons equally cogent incited to refute. But vanity pleases herself with such slight gratifications, and looks forward to pleasure so remotely consequential, that her practices raise no alarm, and her stratagems are not easily discovered.

Vanity is, indeed, often suffered to pass unpursued by suspicion, be-cause he that would watch her motions, can never be at rest: fraud and malice are bounded in their influence; some opportunity of time and place is necessary to their agency; but scarce any man is abstracted one moment from his vanity; and he to whom truth affords no gratifications is generally inclined to seek them in falsehood.

It is remarked by Sir Kenelm Digby, "that every man has a desire to appear superior to others, though it were only in having seen what they have not seen." Such an accidental advantage, since it neither implies merit nor confers dignity, one would think should not be desired so much as to be counterfeited: yet even this vanity, trifling as it is, produces innumerable narratives, all equally false; but more or less credible in proportion to the skill or confidence of the relater. How many may a man of diffusive conversation count among his acquaintances whose lives have been signalized by numberless escapes; who never cross the river but in a storm, or take a journey into the country without more adventures than befell the knights-errant of ancient times in pathless forests or enchanted castles! How many must he know to whom portents and prodigies are of daily occurrence; and for whom nature is hourly working wonders invisible to every other eye, only to supply them with subjects of conversation!

Others there are that amuse themselves with the dissemination of falsehood, at greater hazard of detection and disgrace; men marked out by some lucky planet for universal confidence and friendship, who have been consulted in every difficulty, entrusted with every secret, and summoned to every transaction: it is the supreme felicity of these men to stun all companies with noisy information; to still doubt and overbear opposition with certain knowledge or authentic intelligence. A liar of this kind, with a strong memory or brisk imagination, is often the oracle of an obscure club, and, till time discovers his impostures, dictates to his hearers with uncontrolled authority; for if a public question be started, he was present at the debate; if a new fashion be mentioned, he was at court the first day of its appearance; if a new performance of literature draws the attention of the public, he has patronized the author and seen his work in manuscript; if a criminal of eminence be condemned to die, he often predicted his fate and endeavoured his reformation: and who that lives at a distance from the scene of action will dare to contradict a man who reports from his own eyes and ears, and to whom all persons and affairs are thus intimately known?

This kind of falsehood is generally successful for a time, because it is practised at first with timidity and caution: but the prosperity of the liar is of short duration; the reception of one story is always an incitement to the forgery of another less probable; and he goes on to triumph over tacit credulity, till pride or reason rises up against him, and his companions will no longer endure to see him wiser than themselves.

It is apparent that the inventors of all these fictions intend some exaltation of themselves, and are led off by the pursuit of honour from their attendance upon truth: their narratives always imply some consequence in favour of their courage, their sagacity, or their activity, their familiarity with the learned, or their reception among the great; they are always bribed by the present pleasure of seeing themselves superior to those that surround them, and receiving the homage of silent attention and envious admiration.

But vanity is sometimes incited to fiction by less visible gratifications: the present age abounds with a race of liars who are content with the consciousness of falsehood, and whose pride is to deceive others without any gain or glory to themselves. Of this tribe it is the supreme pleasure to remark a lady in the playhouse or the park, and to publish, under the character of a man suddenly enamoured, an advertisement in the news of the next day, containing a minute description of her person and her dress. From this artifice, indeed, no other effect can be expected, than perturbations which the writer can never see, and conjectures of which he never can be informed; some mischief, however, he hopes he has done; and to have done mischief is of some importance. He sets his invention to work again, and produces a narrative of a robbery or a murder, with all the circumstances of time and place accurately adjusted. This is a jest of greater effect and longer duration: if he fixes his scene at a proper distance, he may for several days keep a wife in terror for her husband, or a mother for her son; and please himself with reflecting that by his abilities and address some addition is made to the miseries of life.

There is, I think, an ancient law of Scotland, by which leasing-making was capitally punished. I am, indeed, far from desiring to increase in this kingdom the number of executions; yet I cannot but think that they who destroy the confidence of society, weaken the credit of intelligence, and interrupt the security of life; harass the delicate with shame, and perplex the timorous with alarms; might very properly be awakened to a sense of their crimes by denunciations of a whipping-post or pillory: since many are so insensible of right and wrong, that they have no standard of action but the law; nor feel guilt, but as they dread punishment.

Adventurer no. 69, July 3, 1753: Idle hope and the waste of life

Ferè libenter homines id quod volunt credunt.

Caesar, *Gallic War,* III. 18

Men willingly believe what they wish to be true.

Tully has long ago observed that no man, however weakened by long life, is so conscious of his own decrepitude, as not to imagine that he may yet hold his station in the world for another year.

Of the truth of this remark every day furnishes new confirmation: there is no time of life in which men for the most part seem less to expect the stroke of death, than when every other eye sees it impending; or are more busy in providing for another year, than when it is plain to all but themselves that at another year they cannot arrive. Though every funeral that passes before their eyes evinces the deceitfulness of such expectations, since every man who is born to the grave thought himself equally certain of living at least to the next year; the survivor still continues to flatter himself, and is never at a loss for some reason why his life should be protracted, and the voracity of death continue to be pacified with some other prey.

But this is only one of the innumerable artifices practised in the universal conspiracy of mankind against themselves: every age and every condition indulges some darling fallacy; every man amuses himself with projects which he knows to be improbable, and which, therefore, he resolves to pursue without daring to examine them. Whatever any man ardently desires, he very readily believes that he shall some time attain: he whose intemperance has overwhelmed him with diseases, while he languishes in the spring, expects vigour and recovery from the summer sun; and while he melts away in the summer, transfers his hopes to the frosts of winter: he that gazes upon elegance or pleasure, which want of money hinders him from imitating or partaking, comforts himself that the time of distress will soon be at an end, and that every day brings him nearer to a state of happiness; though he knows it has passed not only without acquisition of advantage, but perhaps without endeavours after it, in the formation of schemes that cannot be executed, and in the contemplation of prospects which cannot be approached.

Such is the general dream in which we all slumber out our time: every man thinks the day coming in which he shall be gratified with all his wishes, in which he shall leave all those competitors behind, who are now rejoicing like himself in the expectation of victory; the day is always coming to the servile in which they shall be powerful, to the obscure in which they shall be eminent, and to the deformed in which they shall be beautiful.

If any of my readers has looked with so little attention on the world about him, as to imagine this representation exaggerated beyond probability, let him reflect a little upon his own life; let him consider what were his hopes and prospects ten years ago, and what additions he then expected to be made by ten years to his happiness; those years are now elapsed; have they made good the promise that was extorted from them? have they advanced his fortune, enlarged his knowledge, or reformed his conduct, to the degree that was once expected? I am afraid every man that recollects his hopes must confess his disappointment; and own that day has glided unprofitably after day, and that he is still at the same distance from the point of happiness.

With what consolations can those who have thus miscarried in their chief design elude the memory of their ill success? with what amusements can they pacify their discontent, after the loss of so large a portion of life? they can give themselves up again to the same delusions, they can form new schemes of airy gratifications, and fix another period of felicity; they can again resolve to trust the promise which they know will be broken, they can walk in a circle with their eyes shut, and persuade themselves to think that they go forward.

Of every great and complicated event, part depends upon causes out of our power, and part must be effected by vigour and perseverance. With regard to that which is styled in common language the work of chance, men will always find reasons for confidence or distrust, according to their different tempers or inclinations; and he that has been long accustomed to please himself with possibilities of fortuitous happiness, will not easily or willingly be reclaimed from his mistake. But the effects of human industry and skill are more easily subjected to calculation: whatever can be completed in a year is divisible into parts, of which each may be performed in the compass of a day; he, therefore, that has passed the day without attention to the task assigned him, may be certain that the lapse of life has brought him no nearer to his object; for whatever idleness may expect from time, its produce will be only in proportion to the diligence with which it has been used. He that floats lazily down the stream, in pursuit of something borne along by the same current, will find himself indeed move forward; but unless he lays his hand to the oar, and increases his speed by his own labour, must be always at the same distance from that which he is following.

There have happened in every age some contingencies of unexpected and undeserved success, by which those who are determined to believe whatever favours their inclinations, have been encouraged to delight themselves with future advantages; they support confidence by considerations of which the only proper use is to chase away despair: it is equally absurd to sit down in idleness because some have been enriched without labour, as to leap a precipice because some have fallen and escaped with life, or to put to sea in a storm because some have been driven from a wreck upon the coast to which they are bound.

We are all ready to confess, that belief ought to be proportioned to evidence or probability: let any man, therefore, compare the number of those who have been thus favoured by fortune, and of those who have failed of their expectations, and he will easily determine with what justness he has registered himself in the lucky catalogue.

But there is no need on these occasions for deep inquiries or laborious calculations; there is a far easier method of distinguishing the hopes of folly from those of reason, of finding the difference between prospects that exist before the eyes, and those that are only painted on a fond imagination. Tom Drowsy had accustomed himself to compute the profit of a darling project till he had no longer any doubt of its success; it was at last matured by close consideration, all the measures were accurately adjusted, and he wanted only five hundred pounds to become master of a fortune that might be envied by a director of a trading company. Tom was generous and grateful, and was resolved to recompense this small assistance with an ample fortune; he, therefore, deliberated for a time to whom amongst his friends he should declare his necessities; not that he suspected a refusal, but because he could not suddenly determine which of them would make the best use of riches, and was, therefore, most worthy of his favour. At last his choice was settled; and knowing that in order to borrow he must show the probability of repayment, he prepared for a minute and copious explanation of his project. But here the golden dream was at an end: he soon discovered the impossibility of imposing upon others the notions by which he had so long imposed upon himself; which way soever he turned his thoughts, impossibility and absurdity arose in opposition on every side; even credulity and prejudice were at last forced to give way, and he grew ashamed of crediting himself what shame would not suffer him to communicate to another.

To this test let every man bring his imaginations, before they have been too long predominant in his mind. Whatever is true will bear to be related, whatever is rational will endure to be explained; but when we delight to brood in secret over future happiness, and silently to employ our meditations upon schemes of which we are conscious that the bare mention would expose us to derision and contempt; we should then remember, that we are cheating ourselves by voluntary delusions; and giving up to the unreal mockeries of fancy, those hours in which solid advantages might be attained by sober thought and rational assiduity.

There is, indeed, so little certainty in human affairs, that the most cautious and severe examiner may be allowed to indulge some hopes which he cannot prove to be much favoured by probability; since, after his utmost endeavours to ascertain events, he must often leave the issue in the hands of chance. And so scanty is our present allowance of happiness, that in many situations life could scarcely be supported, if hope were not allowed to relieve the present hour by pleasures borrowed from futurity; and reanimate the languor of dejection to new efforts, by pointing to distant regions of felicity, which yet no resolution or perseverance shall ever reach.

But these, like all other cordials, though they may invigorate in a small quantity, intoxicate in a greater; these pleasures, like the rest, are lawful only in certain circumstances, and to certain degrees; they may be useful in a due subservience to nobler purposes, but become dangerous and destructive when once they gain the ascendant in the heart: to soothe the mind to tranquillity by hope, even when that hope is likely to deceive us, may be sometimes useful; but to lull our faculties in a lethargy is poor and despicable.

Vices and errors are differently modified, according to the state of the minds to which they are incident; to indulge hope beyond the warrant of reason, is the failure alike of mean and elevated understandings; but its foundation and its effects are totally different: the man of high courage and great abilities is apt to place too much confidence in himself, and to expect, from a vigorous exertion of his powers, more than spirit or diligence can attain: between him and his wish he sees obstacles indeed, but he expects to overleap or break them; his mistaken ardour hurries him forward; and though, perhaps, he misses his end, he nevertheless obtains some collateral good, and performs something useful to mankind, and honourable to himself.

The drone of timidity presumes likewise to hope, but without ground and without consequence; the bliss with which he solaces his hours he always expects from others, though very often he knows not from whom: he folds his arms about him, and sits in expectation of some revolution in the state that shall raise him to greatness, or some golden shower that shall load him with wealth; he dozes away the day in musing upon the morrow; and at the end of life is roused from his dream only to discover that the time of action is past, and that he can now show his wisdom only by repentance.

Adventurer no. 119, December 25, 1753:
The torment of fleeting pleasures and "the contagion of desire"

Latius regnes avidum domando
Spiritum, quam si Lybiam remotis
Gadibus jungas, et uterque Paenus
Serviat uni.

Horace, *Odes*, II.2. 9–12

By virtue's precepts to controul
The thirsty cravings of the soul,
Is over wider realms to reign
Unenvied monarch, than if Spain
You could to distant Lybia join,
And both the Carthages were thine.

transl. Philip Francis

When Socrates was asked, "which of mortal men was to be accounted nearest to the Gods in happiness?" he answered, "that man who is in want of the fewest things."

In this answer, Socrates left it to be guessed by his auditors, whether, by the exemption from want which was to constitute happiness, he meant amplitude of possessions or contraction of desire. And, indeed, there is so little difference between them, that Alexander the Great confessed the inhabitant of a tub the next man to the master of the world; and left a declaration to future ages, that if he was not Alexander he should wish to be Diogenes.

These two states, however, though they resemble each other in their consequence, differ widely with respect to the facility with which they may be attained. To make great acquisitions can happen to very few; and in the uncertainty of human affairs, to many it will be incident to labour without reward, and to lose what they already possess by endeavours to make it more: some will always want abilities, and others opportunities to accumulate wealth. It is therefore happy that nature has allowed us a more certain and easy road to plenty; every man may grow rich by contracting his wishes, and by quiet acquiescence in what has been given him, supply the absence of more.

Yet so far is almost every man from emulating the happiness of the gods by any other means than grasping at their power, that it seems to be the great business of life to create wants as fast as they are satisfied. It has been long observed by moralists, that every man squanders or loses a great part of that life of which every man knows and deplores the shortness: and it may be remarked with equal justness, that though every man laments his own insufficiency to his happiness, and knows himself a necessitous and precarious being, incessantly soliciting the assistance of others, and feeling wants which his own art or strength cannot supply; yet there is no man who does not, by the superaddition of unnatural cares, render himself still more dependent; who does not create an artificial poverty, and suffer himself to feel pain for the want of that of which, when it is gained, he can have no enjoyment.

It must, indeed, be allowed, that as we lose part of our time because it steals away silent and invisible, and many an hour is passed before we recollect that it is passing; so unnatural desires insinuate themselves un-observed into the mind, and we do not perceive that they are gaining upon us till the pain which they give us awakens us to notice. No man is sufficiently vigilant to take account of every minute of his life, or to watch every motion of his heart. Much of our time likewise is sacrificed to cus-tom; we trifle, because we see others trifle; in the same manner we catch from example the contagion of desire; we see all about us busied in pur-suit of imaginary good, and begin to bustle in the same chase, lest greater activity should triumph over us.

It is true that to man as a member of society many things become nec-essary which, perhaps, in a state of nature are superfluous; and that many things, not absolutely necessary, are yet so useful and convenient, that they cannot easily be spared. I will make yet a more ample and liberal concession. In opulent states and regular governments, the temptations to wealth and rank, and to the distinctions that follow them, are such as no force of understanding finds it easy to resist.

If, therefore, I saw the quiet of life disturbed only by endeavours after wealth and honour; by solicitude, which the world, whether justly or not, considered as important; I should scarcely have had courage to inculcate any precepts of moderation and forbearance. He that is engaged in a pur-suit in which all mankind profess to be his rivals is supported by the au-thority of all mankind in the prosecution of his design, and will, therefore, scarcely stop to hear the lectures of a solitary philosopher. Nor am I cer-tain that the accumulation of honest gain ought to be hindered, or the ambition of just honours always to be repressed. Whatever can enable the possessor to confer any benefit upon others, may be desired upon virtu-ous principles; and we ought not too rashly to accuse any man of intend-ing to confine the influence of his acquisitions to himself.

But if we look round upon mankind, whom shall we find among those that fortune permits to form their own manners, that is not tormenting himself with a wish for something, of which all the pleasure and all the benefit will cease at the moment of attainment? One man is beggaring his posterity to build a house, which when finished he never will inhabit; another is levelling mountains to open a prospect, which, when he has once enjoyed it, he can enjoy it no more; another is painting ceilings, carving wainscot, and filling his apartments with costly furniture, only that some neighbouring house may not be richer or finer than his own.

That splendour and elegance are not desirable, I am not so abstracted from life as to inculcate; but if we inquire closely into the reason for which they are esteemed, we shall find them valued principally as evidences of wealth. Nothing, therefore, can show greater depravity of understanding, than to delight in the show when the reality is wanting; or voluntarily to become poor, that strangers may for a time imagine us to be rich.

But there are yet minuter objects and more trifling anxieties. Men may be found who are kept from sleep by the want of a shell particularly variegated; who are wasting their lives in stratagems to obtain a book in a language which they do not understand; who pine with envy at the flowers of another man's parterre; who hover like vultures round the owner of a fossil, in hopes to plunder his cabinet at his death; and who would not much regret to see a street in flames, if a box of medals might be scattered in the tumult.

He that imagines me to speak of these sages in terms exaggerated and hyperbolical, has conversed but little with the race of virtuosos. A slight acquaintance with their studies, and a few visits to their assemblies, would inform him that nothing is so worthless, but that prejudice and caprice can give it value; nor any thing of so little use, but that by indulging an idle competition or unreasonable pride, a man may make it to himself one of the necessaries of life.

Desires like these, I may surely, without incurring the censure of moroseness, advise every man to repel when they invade his mind; or if he admits them, never to allow them any greater influence than is necessary to give petty employments the power of pleasing, and diversify the day with slight amusements.

An ardent wish, whatever be its object, will always be able to interrupt tranquillity. What we believe ourselves to want, torments us not in proportion to its real value, but according to the estimation by which we have rated it in our own minds; in some diseases, the patient has been observed to long for food, which scarce any extremity of hunger would in health have compelled him to swallow; but while his organs were thus depraved, the craving was irresistible, nor could any rest be obtained till it was appeased by compliance. Of the same nature are the irregular appetites of the mind; though they are often excited by trifles, they are equally disquieting with real wants: the Roman, who wept at the death of his lamprey, felt the same degree of sorrow that extorts tears on other occasions.

Inordinate desires, of whatever kind, ought to be repressed upon yet a higher consideration; they must be considered as enemies not only to happiness but to virtue. There are men, among those commonly reckoned the learned and the wise, who spare no stratagems to remove a competitor at an auction, who will sink the price of a rarity at the expense of truth, and whom it is not safe to trust alone in a library or cabinet. These are faults which the fraternity seem to look upon as jocular mischiefs, or to think excused by the violence of the temptation: but I shall always fear that he, who accustoms himself to fraud in little things, wants only opportunity to practise it in greater; "he that has hardened himself by killing a sheep," says Pythagoras, "will with less reluctance shed the blood of a man."

To prize every thing according to its real use ought to be the aim of a rational being. There are few things which can much conduce to happiness, and, therefore, few things to be ardently desired. He that looks upon the business and bustle of the world, with the philosophy with which Socrates surveyed the fair at Athens, will turn away at last with his exclamation, "How many things are here which I do not want!"

Idler no. 11, June 24, 1758: Not letting weather affect one's disposition

Nec te quaesiveris extra.

Persius, I. 7

It is commonly observed, that when two Englishmen meet, their first talk is of the weather; they are in haste to tell each other what each must already know, that it is hot or cold, bright or cloudy, windy or calm.

There are, among the numerous lovers of subtleties and paradoxes, some who derive the civil institutions of every country from its climate, who impute freedom and slavery to the temperature of the air, can fix the meridian of vice and virtue, and tell at what degree of latitude we are to expect courage or timidity, knowledge or ignorance.

From these dreams of idle speculation, a slight survey of life, and a little knowledge of history, are sufficient to awaken any inquirer whose ambition of distinction has not overpowered his love of truth. Forms of government are seldom the result of much deliberation; they are framed by chance in popular assemblies, or in conquered countries, by despotic authority. Laws are often occasional, often capricious, made always by a few, and sometimes by a single voice. Nations have changed their characters; slavery is now nowhere more patiently endured than in countries once inhabited by the zealots of liberty.

But national customs can arise only from general agreement; they are not imposed, but chosen, and are continued only by the continuance of their cause. An Englishman's notice of the weather is the natural consequence of changeable skies and uncertain seasons. In many parts of the world, wet weather and dry are regularly expected at certain periods; but in our island every man goes to sleep unable to guess whether he shall behold in the morning a bright or cloudy atmosphere, whether his rest shall be lulled by a shower, or broken by a tempest. We therefore rejoice mutually at good weather, as at an escape from something that we feared; and mutually complain of bad, as of the loss of something that we hoped.

Such is the reason of our practice; and who shall treat it with contempt? Surely not the attendant on a court, whose business is to watch the looks of a being weak and foolish as himself, and whose vanity is to recount the names of men, who might drop into nothing and leave no vacuity; nor the proprietor of funds, who stops his acquaintance in the street to tell him of the loss of half-a-crown; nor the inquirer after news, who fills his head with foreign events, and talks of skirmishes and sieges, of which no consequence will ever reach his hearers or himself. The weather is a nobler and more interesting subject; it is the present state of the skies, and of the earth, on which plenty and famine are suspended, on which millions depend for the necessaries of life.

The weather is frequently mentioned for another reason, less honourable to my dear countrymen. Our dispositions too frequently change with the colour of the sky; and when we find ourselves cheerful and good-natured, we naturally pay our acknowledgments to the powers of sunshine; or, if we sink into dulness and peevishness, look round the horizon for an excuse, and charge our discontent upon an easterly wind or a cloudy day.

Surely nothing is more reproachful to a being endowed with reason, than to resign its powers to the influence of the air, and live in dependence on the weather and the wind, for the only blessings which nature has put into our power, tranquillity and benevolence. To look up to the sky for the nutriment of our bodies, is the condition of nature; to call upon the sun for peace and gaiety, or deprecate the clouds lest sorrow should overwhelm us, is the cowardice of idleness, and the idolatry of folly.

Yet even in this age of inquiry and knowledge, when superstition is driven away, and omens and prodigies have lost their terrors, we find this folly countenanced by frequent examples. Those that laugh at the portentous glare of a comet, and hear a crow with equal tranquillity from the right or left, will yet talk of times and situations proper for intellectual performances, will imagine the fancy exalted by vernal breezes, and the reason invigorated by a bright calm.

If men who have given up themselves to fanciful credulity would confine their conceits in their own minds, they might regulate their lives by the barometer, with inconvenience only to themselves; but to fill the world with accounts of intellects subject to ebb and flow, of one genius that awakened in the spring, and another that ripened in the autumn, of one mind expanded in the summer, and of another concentrated in the winter, is no less dangerous than to tell children of bugbears and goblins. Fear will find every house haunted; and idleness will wait for ever for the moment of illumination.

This distinction of seasons is produced only by imagination operating on luxury. To temperance every day is bright, and every hour is propitious to diligence. He that shall resolutely excite his faculties or exert his virtues will soon make himself superior to the seasons, and may set at defiance the morning mist, and the evening damp, the blasts of the east, and the clouds of the south.

It was the boast of the Stoic philosophy to make man unshaken by calamity, and unelated by success, incorruptible by pleasure, and invulnerable by pain; these are heights of wisdom which none ever attained, and to which few can aspire; but there are lower degrees of constancy necessary to common virtue; and every man, however he may distrust himself in the extremes of good or evil, might at least struggle against the tyranny of the climate, and refuse to enslave his virtue or his reason to the most variable of all variations, the changes of the weather.

Idler no. 14, July 15, 1758: People who rob and waste others' time

When Diogenes received a visit in his tub from Alexander the Great, and was asked, according to the ancient forms of royal courtesy, what petition he had to offer; "I have nothing," said he, "to ask, but that you would remove to the other side, that you may not, by intercepting the sunshine, take from me what you cannot give me."

Such was the demand of Diogenes from the greatest monarch of the earth, which those who have less power than Alexander may, with yet more propriety, apply to themselves. He that does much good, may be allowed to do sometimes a little harm. But if the opportunities of beneficence be denied by fortune, innocence should at least be vigilantly preserved.

It is well known, that time once passed never returns; and that the moment which is lost, is lost for ever. Time therefore ought, above all other kinds of property, to be free from invasion; and yet there is no man who does not claim the power of wasting that time which is the right of others.

This usurpation is so general, that a very small part of the year is spent by choice; scarcely any thing is done when it is intended, or obtained when it is desired. Life is continually ravaged by invaders; one steals away an hour, and another a day; one conceals the robbery by hurrying us into business, another by lulling us with amusement; the depredation is continued through a thousand vicissitudes of tumult and tranquillity, till, having lost all, we can lose no more.

This waste of the lives of men has been very frequently charged upon the Great, whose followers linger from year to year in expectations, and die at last with petitions in their hands. Those who raise envy will easily incur censure. I know not whether statesmen and patrons do not suffer more reproaches than they deserve, and may not rather themselves complain that they are given up a prey to pretensions without merit, and to importunity without shame.

The truth is, that the inconveniencies of attendance are more lamented than felt. To the greater number solicitation is its own reward: to be seen in good company, to talk of familiarities with men of power, to be able to tell the freshest news, to gratify an inferior circle with predictions of increase or decline of favour, and to be regarded as a candidate for high offices are compensations more than equivalent to the delay of favours, which, perhaps, he that begs them has hardly confidence to expect.

A man conspicuous in a high station, who multiplies hopes that he may multiply dependants, may be considered as a beast of prey, justly dreaded, but easily avoided; his den is known, and they who would not be devoured need not approach it. The great danger of the waste of time is from caterpillars and moths, who are not resisted because they are not feared, and who work on with unheeded mischiefs, and invisible encroachments.

He whose rank or merit procures him the notice of mankind, must give up himself, in a great measure, to the convenience or humour of those who surround him. Every man who is sick of himself will fly to him for relief; he that wants to speak will require him to hear; and he that wants to hear will expect him to speak. Hour passes after hour, the noon succeeds to morning, and the evening to noon, while a thousand objects are forced upon his attention, which he rejects as fast as they are offered, but which the custom of the world requires to be received with appearance of regard.

If we will have the kindness of others, we must endure their follies. He who cannot persuade himself to withdraw from society, must be content to pay a tribute of his time to a multitude of tyrants; to the loiterer, who makes appointments which he never keeps; to the consulter, who asks advice which he never takes; to the boaster, who blusters only to be praised; to the complainer, who whines only to be pitied; to the projector, whose happiness is to entertain his friends with expectations which all but himself know to be vain; to the economist, who tells of bargains and settlements; to the politician, who predicts the fate of battles and breach of alliances; to the usurer, who compares the different funds; and to the talker, who talks only because he loves to be talking.

To put every man in possession of his own time, and rescue the day from this succession of usurpers, is beyond my power, and beyond my hope. Yet, perhaps, some stop might be put to this unmerciful persecution, if all would seriously reflect that whoever pays a visit that is not desired, or talks longer than the hearer is willing to attend, is guilty of an injury which he cannot repair, and takes away that which he cannot give.

Idler no. 27, October 21, 1758: Enslavement to habits

It has been the endeavour of all those whom the world has reverenced for superior wisdom, to persuade man to be acquainted with himself, to learn his own powers and his own weakness, to observe by what evils he is most dangerously beset, and by what temptations most easily overcome.

This counsel has been often given with serious dignity, and often received with appearance of conviction; but, as very few can search deep into their own minds without meeting what they wish to hide from themselves, scarcely any man persists in cultivating such disagreeable acquaintance, but draws the veil again between his eyes and his heart, leaves his passions and appetites as he found them, and advises others to look into themselves.

This is the common result of inquiry even among those that endeavour to grow wiser or better: but this endeavour is far enough from frequency; the greater part of the multitudes that swarm upon the earth have never been disturbed by such uneasy curiosity, but deliver themselves up to business or to pleasure, plunge into the current of life, whether placid or turbulent, and pass on from one point or prospect to another, attentive rather to any thing than the state of their minds; satisfied, at an easy rate, with an opinion, that they are no worse than others, that every man must mind his own interest, or that their pleasures hurt only themselves, and are therefore no proper subjects of censure.

Some, however, there are, whom the intrusion of scruples, the recollection of better notions, or the latent reprehension of good examples, will not suffer to live entirely contented with their own conduct; these are forced to pacify the mutiny of reason with fair promises, and quiet their thoughts with designs of calling all their actions to review, and planning a new scheme for the time to come.

There is nothing which we estimate so fallaciously as the force of our own resolutions, nor any fallacy which we so unwillingly and tardily detect. He that has resolved a thousand times, and a thousand times deserted his own purpose, yet suffers no abatement of his confidence, but still believes himself his own master; and able, by innate vigour of soul, to press forward to his end, through all the obstructions that inconveniencies or delights can put in his way.

That this mistake should prevail for a time is very natural. When conviction is present, and temptation out of sight, we do not easily conceive how any reasonable being can deviate from his true interest. What ought to be done, while it yet hangs only on speculation, is so plain and certain, that there is no place for doubt; the whole soul yields itself to the predominance of truth, and readily determines to do what, when the time of action comes, will be at last omitted.

I believe most men may review all the lives that have passed within their observation, without remembering one efficacious resolution, or being able to tell a single instance of a course of practice suddenly changed in consequence of a change of opinion, or an establishment of determination. Many, indeed, alter their conduct, and are not at fifty what they were at thirty; but they commonly varied imperceptibly from themselves, followed the train of external causes, and rather suffered reformation than made it.

It is not uncommon to charge the difference between promise and performance, between profession and reality, upon deep design and studied deceit; but the truth is, that there is very little hypocrisy in the world; we do not so often endeavour or wish to impose on others, as on ourselves; we resolve to do right, we hope to keep our resolutions, we declare them to confirm our own hope, and fix our own inconstancy by calling witnesses of our actions; but at last habit prevails, and those whom we invited to our triumph laugh at our defeat.

Custom is commonly too strong for the most resolute resolver, though furnished for the assault with all the weapons of philosophy. "He that endeavours to free himself from an ill habit," says Bacon, "must not change too much at a time, lest he should be discouraged by difficulty; nor too little, for then he will make but slow advances." This is a precept which may be applauded in a book, but will fail in the trial, in which every change will be found too great or too little. Those who have been able to conquer habit, are like those that are fabled to have returned from the realms of Pluto:

> *Pauci, quos aequus amavit*
> *Jupiter, atque ardens evexit ad aethera virtus.*
> *Aeneid,* VI. 129–130

They are sufficient to give hope but not security; to animate the contest, but not to promise victory.

Those who are in the power of evil habits must conquer them as they can; and conquered they must be, or neither wisdom nor happiness can be attained; but those who are not yet subject to their influence may, by timely caution, preserve their freedom; they may effectually resolve to escape the tyrant, whom they will very vainly resolve to conquer.

Idler no. 44, February 17, 1759: The pains of memory

Memory is, among the faculties of the human mind, that of which we make the most frequent use, or rather that of which the agency is incessant, or perpetual. Memory is the primary and fundamental power, without which there could be no other intellectual operation. Judgment and ratiocination suppose something already known, and draw their decisions only from experience. Imagination selects ideas from the treasures of remembrance, and produces novelty only by varied combinations. We do not even form conjectures of distant, or anticipations of future events, but by concluding what is possible from what is past.

The two offices of memory are collection and distribution; by one images are accumulated, and by the other produced for use. Collection is always the employment of our first years; and distribution commonly that of our advanced age.

To collect and reposite[23] the various forms of things, is far the most pleasing part of mental occupation. We are naturally delighted with novelty, and there is a time when all that we see is new. When first we enter into the world, whithersoever we turn our eyes, they meet knowledge with pleasure at her side; every diversity of nature pours ideas in upon the soul; neither search nor labour are necessary; we have nothing more to do than to open our eyes, and curiosity is gratified.

Much of the pleasure which the first survey of the world affords is exhausted before we are conscious of our own felicity, or able to compare our condition with some other possible state. We have, therefore, few traces of the joy of our earliest discoveries; yet we all remember a time when nature had so many untasted gratifications, that every excursion gave delight which can now be found no longer, when the noise of a torrent, the rustle of a wood, the song of birds, or the play of lambs, had power to fill the attention, and suspend all perception of the course of time.

But these easy pleasures are soon at an end; we have seen in a very little time so much, that we call out for new objects of observation, and endeavour to find variety in books and life. But study is laborious, and not always satisfactory; and conversation has its pains as well pleasures; we are willing to learn, but not willing to be taught; we are pained by ignorance, but pained yet more by another's knowledge.

From the vexation of pupilage men commonly set themselves free about the middle of life, by shutting up the avenues of intelligence, and resolving to rest in their present state; and they whose ardour of inquiry continues longer find themselves insensibly forsaken by their instructors. As every man advances in life, the proportion between those that are younger and that are older than himself is continually changing; and he that has lived half a century finds few that do not require from him that information which he once expected from those that went before him.

Then it is that the magazines of memory are opened, and the stores of accumulated knowledge are displayed by vanity or benevolence, or in honest commerce of mutual interest. Every man wants others, and is, therefore, glad when he is wanted by them. And as few men will endure the labour of intense meditation without necessity, he that has learned enough for his profit or his honour, seldom endeavours after further acquisitions.

The pleasure of recollecting speculative notions would not be much less than that of gaining them, if they could be kept pure and unmingled with the passages of life; but such is the necessary concatenation of our thoughts, that good and evil are linked together, and no pleasure recurs but associated with pain. Every revived idea reminds us of a time when something was enjoyed that is now lost, when some hope was not yet blasted, when some purpose had yet not languished into sluggishness or indifference.

Whether it be that life has more vexations than comforts, or, what is in the event just the same, that evil makes deeper impression than good, it is certain that few can review the time past without heaviness of heart. He remembers many calamities incurred by folly, many opportunities lost by negligence. The shades of the dead rise up before him; and he laments the companions of his youth, the partners of his amusements, the assistants of his labours, whom the hand of death has snatched away.

When an offer was made to Themistocles of teaching him the art of memory, he answered, that he would rather wish for the art of forgetfulness. He felt his imagination haunted by phantoms of misery which he was unable to suppress, and would gladly have calmed his thoughts with some "oblivious antidote."[24] In this we all resemble one another; the hero and the sage are, like vulgar mortals, overburdened by the weight of life; all shrink from recollection, and all wish for an art of forgetfulness.

Idler no. 72, September 1, 1759: The art and power of forgetting the past

Men complain of nothing more frequently than of deficient memory; and, indeed, every one finds that many of the ideas which he desired to retain have slipped irretrievably away; that the acquisitions of the mind are sometimes equally fugitive with the gifts of fortune; and that a short intermission of attention more certainly lessens knowledge than impairs an estate.

To assist this weakness of our nature, many methods have been proposed, all of which may be justly suspected of being ineffectual; for no art of memory, however its effects have been boasted or admired, has been ever adopted into general use, nor have those who possessed it appeared to excel others in readiness of recollection or multiplicity of attainments.

There is another art of which all have felt the want, though Themistocles only confessed it. We suffer equal pain from the pertinacious adhesion of unwelcome images, as from the evanescence of those which are pleasing and useful; and it may be doubted whether we should be more benefited by the art of memory or the art of forgetfulness.

Forgetfulness is necessary to remembrance. Ideas are retained by renovation of that impression which time is always wearing away, and which new images are striving to obliterate. If useless thoughts could be expelled from the mind, all the valuable parts of our knowledge would more frequently recur, and every recurrence would reinstate them in their former place.

It is impossible to consider, without some regret, how much might have been learned, or how much might have been invented, by a rational and vigorous application of time, uselessly or painfully passed in the revocation of events, which have left neither good nor evil behind them, in grief for misfortunes either repaired or irreparable, in resentment of injuries known only to ourselves, of which death has put the authors beyond our power.

Philosophy has accumulated precept upon precept to warn us against the anticipation of future calamities. All useless misery is certainly folly, and he that feels evils before they come may be deservedly censured; yet surely to dread the future is more reasonable than to lament the past. The business of life is to go forwards: he who sees evil in prospect meets it in his way; but he who catches it by retrospection turns back to find it. That which is feared may sometimes be avoided, but that which is regretted today may be regretted again tomorrow.

Regret is indeed useful and virtuous, and not only allowable but necessary, when it tends to the amendment of life, or to admonition of error which we may be again in danger of committing. But a very small part of the moments spent in meditation on the past, produce any reasonable caution or salutary sorrow. Most of the mortifications that we have suffered arose from the concurrence of local and temporary circumstances, which can never meet again; and most of our disappointments have succeeded those expectations, which life allows not to be formed a second time.

It would add much to human happiness, if an art could be taught of forgetting all of which the remembrance is at once useless and afflictive; if that pain which never can end in pleasure could be driven totally away, that the mind might perform its functions without encumbrance, and the past might no longer encroach upon the present.

Little can be done well to which the whole mind is not applied; the business of every day calls for the day to which it is assigned; and he will have no leisure to regret yesterday's vexations who resolves not to have a new subject of regret tomorrow.

But to forget or to remember at pleasure, are equally beyond the power of man. Yet as memory may be assisted by method, and the decays of knowledge repaired by stated times of recollection, so the power of forgetting is capable of improvement. Reason will, by a resolute contest, prevail over imagination, and the power may be obtained of transferring the attention as judgment shall direct.

The incursions of troublesome thoughts are often violent and importunate; and it is not easy to a mind accustomed to their inroads to expel them immediately by putting better images into motion; but this enemy of quiet is above all others weakened by every defeat; the reflection which has been once overpowered and ejected, seldom returns with any formidable vehemence.

Employment is the great instrument of intellectual dominion. The mind cannot retire from its enemy into total vacancy, or turn aside from one object but by passing to another. The gloomy and the resentful are always found among those who have nothing to do, or who do nothing. We must be busy about good or evil, and he to whom the present offers nothing will often be looking backward on the past.

Idler no. 74, September 15, 1759: The common failure of memory

In the mythological pedigree of learning, memory is made the mother of the muses, by which the masters of ancient wisdom, perhaps, meant to show the necessity of storing the mind copiously with true notions, before the imagination should be suffered to form fictions or collect embellishments; for the works of an ignorant poet can afford nothing higher than pleasing sound, and fiction is of no other use than to display the treasures of memory.

The necessity of memory to the acquisition of knowledge is inevitably felt and universally allowed, so that scarcely any other of the mental faculties are commonly considered as necessary to a student: he that admires the proficiency of another, always attributes it to the happiness of his memory; and he that laments his own defects, concludes with a wish that his memory was better.

It is evident that when the power of retention is weak, all the attempts at eminence of knowledge must be vain; and as few are willing to be doomed to perpetual ignorance, I may, perhaps, afford consolation to some that have fallen too easily into despondence, by observing that such weakness is, in my opinion, very rare, and that few have reason to complain of nature as unkindly sparing of the gifts of memory.

In the common business of life, we find the memory of one like that of another, and honestly impute omissions not to involuntary forgetfulness, but culpable inattention; but in literary inquiries, failure is imputed rather to want of memory than of diligence.

We consider ourselves as defective in memory, either because we remember less than we desire, or less than we suppose others to remember.

Memory is like all other human powers, with which no man can be satisfied who measures them by what he can conceive, or by what he can desire. He whose mind is most capacious, finds it much too narrow for his wishes; he that remembers most, remembers little compared with what he forgets. He, therefore, that, after the perusal of a book, finds few ideas remaining in his mind, is not to consider the disappointment as peculiar to himself, or to resign all hopes of improvement, because he does not retain what even the author has, perhaps, forgotten.

He who compares his memory with that of others, is often too hasty to lament the inequality. Nature has sometimes, indeed, afforded examples of enormous, wonderful, and gigantic memory. Scaliger reports of himself that, in his youth, he could repeat above a hundred verses, having once read them; and Barthicus declares that he wrote his *Comment upon Claudian* without consulting the text. But not to have such degrees of memory is no more to be lamented, than not to have the strength of Hercules, or the swiftness of Achilles. He that, in the distribution of good, has an equal share with common men, may justly be contented. Where there is no striking disparity, it is difficult to know of two which remembers most, and still more difficult to discover which reads with greater attention, which has renewed the first impression by more frequent repetitions, or by what accidental combination of ideas either mind might have united any particular narrative or argument to its former stock.

But memory, however impartially distributed, so often deceives our trust, that almost every man attempts, by some artifice or other, to secure its fidelity.

It is the practice of many readers to note in the margin of their books the most important passages, the strongest arguments, or the brightest sentiments. Thus they load their minds with superfluous attention, repress the vehemence of curiosity by useless deliberation, and by frequent interruption break the current of narration or the chain of reason, and at last close the volume, and forget the passages and marks together.

Others I have found unalterably persuaded, that nothing is certainly remembered but what is transcribed; and they have, therefore, passed weeks and months in transferring large quotations to a commonplace-book. Yet, why any part of a book which can be consulted at pleasure should be copied, I was never able to discover. The hand has no closer correspondence with the memory than the eye. The act of writing itself distracts the thoughts, and what is read twice is commonly better remembered than what is transcribed. This method, therefore, consumes time without assisting memory.

The true art of memory is the art of attention. No man will read with much advantage who is not able, at pleasure, to evacuate his mind, or who brings not to his author an intellect defecated and pure, neither turbid with care, nor agitated by pleasure. If the repositories of thought are already full, what can they receive? If the mind is employed on the past or future, the book will be held before the eyes in vain. What is read with delight is commonly retained, because pleasure always secures attention; but the books which are consulted by occasional necessity, and perused with impatience, seldom leave any traces on the mind.

Society and Manners

Rambler no. 39, July 31, 1750:
Marriage and the unhappy state of women in society[1]

Infelix—nulli bene nupta marito.
　Ausonius, *Epitaphia Heroum,* "To Dido," No. 8 *Loeb*

Unblest, still doom'd to wed with misery.

The condition of the female sex has been frequently the subject of compassion to medical writers, because their constitution of body is such that every state of life brings its peculiar diseases: they are placed, according to the proverb, between Scylla and Charybdis, with no other choice than of dangers equally formidable; and whether they embrace marriage, or determine upon a single life, are exposed, in consequence of their choice, to sickness, misery, and death.

　It were to be wished that so great a degree of natural infelicity might not be increased by adventitious and artificial miseries, and that beings whose beauty we cannot behold without admiration, and whose delicacy we cannot contemplate without tenderness, might be suffered to enjoy every alleviation of their sorrows. But, however it has happened, the custom of the world seems to have been formed in a kind of conspiracy against them, though it does not appear but they had themselves an equal share in its establishment; and prescriptions which, by whomsoever they were begun, are now of long continuance, and by consequence of great authority, seem to have almost excluded them from content, in whatsoever condition they shall pass their lives.

If they refuse the society of men, and continue in that state which is reasonably supposed to place happiness most in their own power, they seldom give those that frequent their conversation any exalted notions of the blessing of liberty; for whether it be that they are angry to see with what inconsiderate eagerness other heedless females rush into slavery, or with what absurd vanity the married ladies boast the change of their condition, and condemn the heroines who endeavour to assert the natural dignity of their sex; whether they are conscious that like barren countries they are free, only because they were never thought to deserve the trouble of a conquest, or imagine that their sincerity is not always unsuspected, when they declare their contempt of men; it is certain, that they generally appear to have some great and incessant cause of uneasiness, and that many of them have at last been persuaded, by powerful rhetoricians, to try the life which they had so long contemned, and put on the bridal ornaments at a time when they least became them.

What are the real causes of the impatience which the ladies discover in a virgin state, I shall perhaps take some other occasion to examine. That it is not to be envied for its happiness, appears from the solicitude with which it is avoided; from the opinion universally prevalent among the sex, that no woman continues long in it but because she is not invited to forsake it; from the disposition always shown to treat old maids as the refuse of the world; and from the willingness with which it is often quitted at last, by those whose experience has enabled them to judge at leisure, and decide with authority.

Yet such is life, that whatever is proposed, it is much easier to find reasons for rejecting than embracing. Marriage, though a certain security from the reproach and solicitude of antiquated virginity, has yet, as it is usually conducted, many disadvantages that take away much from the pleasure which society promises, and might afford, if pleasures and pains were honestly shared and mutual confidence inviolably preserved.

The miseries, indeed, which many ladies suffer under conjugal vexations, are to be considered with great pity, because their husbands are often not taken by them as objects of affection, but forced upon them by
authority and violence, or by persuasion and importunity, equally resistless when urged by those whom they have been always accustomed to
reverence and obey; and it very seldom appears that those who are thus
despotic in the disposal of their children, pay any regard to their domestic and personal felicity, or think it so much to be enquired whether they
will be happy, as whether they will be rich.

It may be urged, in extenuation of this crime, which parents, not in
any other respect to be numbered with robbers and assassins, frequently
commit, that, in their estimation, riches and happiness are equivalent
terms. They have passed their lives with no other wish than of adding
acre to acre, and filling one bag after another, and imagine the advantage
of a daughter sufficiently considered when they have secured her a large
jointure, and given her reasonable expectations of living in the midst of
those pleasures with which she had seen her father and mother solacing
their age.

There is an economical oracle received among the prudential part
of the world which advises fathers "to marry their daughters, lest they
should marry themselves"; by which I suppose it is implied, that women
left to their own conduct generally unite themselves with such partners
as can contribute very little to their felicity. Who was the author of this
maxim, or with what intention it was originally uttered, I have not yet discovered; but imagine that however solemnly it may be transmitted, or
however implicitly received, it can confer no authority which nature has
denied; it cannot license Titus to be unjust, lest Caia should be imprudent; nor give right to imprison for life, lest liberty should be ill employed.

That the ladies have sometimes incurred imputations which might
naturally produce edicts not much in their favour, must be confessed by
their warmest advocates; and I have indeed seldom observed that when
the tenderness or virtue of their parents has preserved them from forced
marriage, and left them at large to choose their own path in the labyrinth
of life, they have made any great advantage of their liberty: they commonly
take the opportunity of independence to trifle away youth and lose their

bloom in a hurry of diversions, recurring in a succession too quick to leave room for any settled reflection; they see the world without gaining experience, and at last regulate their choice by motives trifling as those of a girl, or mercenary as those of a miser.

Malanthea came to town upon the death of her father, with a very large fortune, and with the reputation of a much larger; she was therefore followed and caressed by many men of rank, and by some of understanding; but having an insatiable desire of pleasure, she was not at leisure, from the park, the gardens, the theatres, visits, assemblies, and masquerades, to attend seriously to any proposal, but was still impatient for a new flatterer, and neglected marriage as always in her power; till in time her admirers fell away, wearied with expense, disgusted at her folly, or offended by her inconstancy; she heard of concerts to which she was not invited, and was more than once forced to sit still at an assembly for want of a partner. In this distress, chance threw her way Philotryphus, a man vain, glittering, and thoughtless as herself, who had spent a small fortune in equipage and dress, and was shining in the last suit for which his tailor would give him credit. He had been long endeavouring to retrieve his extravagance by marriage, and therefore soon paid his court to Melanthea, who after some weeks of insensibility saw him at a ball, and was wholly overcome by his performance in a minuet. They married; but a man cannot always dance, and Philotryphus had no other method of pleasing; however, as neither was in any great degree vicious, they lived together with no other unhappiness than vacuity of mind, and that tastelessness of life which proceeds from a satiety of juvenile pleasures, and an utter inability to fill their place by nobler employments. As they have known the fashionable world at the same time, they agree in their notions of all those subjects on which they ever speak, and being able to add nothing to the ideas of each other, are not much inclined to conversation, but very often join in one wish, "That they could sleep more, and think less."

Argyris, after having refused a thousand offers, at last consented to marry Cotylus, the younger brother of a duke, a man without elegance of mien, beauty of person, or force of understanding; who, while he courted her, could not always forbear allusions to her birth, and hints how cheaply she would purchase an alliance to so illustrious a family. His conduct from the hour of his marriage has been insufferably tyrannical, nor has he any other regard to her than what arises from his desire that her appearance may not disgrace him. Upon this principle, however, he always orders that she should be gaily dressed, and splendidly attended; and she has, among all her mortifications, the happiness to take place of her eldest sister.

Rambler no. 45, August 21, 1750: Sober assessment of marriage

This is the chief felicity of life,
That concord smile on the connubial bed;
But now 'tis hatred all.
transl. of Euripides, *Medea,* ll. 14–16

To the Rambler.

Sir,

Though, in the dissertations which you have given us on marriage, very just cautions are laid down against the common causes of infelicity, and the necessity of having, in that important choice, the first regard to virtue, is carefully inculcated; yet I cannot think the subject so much exhausted, but that a little reflection would present to the mind many questions, in the discussion of which great numbers are interested, and many precepts which deserve to be more particularly and forcibly impressed.

You seem, like most of the writers that have gone before you, to have allowed as an uncontested principle, that "marriage is generally unhappy": but I know not whether a man who professes to think for himself, and concludes from his own observations, does not depart from his character when he follows the crowd thus implicitly, and receives maxims without recalling them to a new examination, especially when they comprise so wide a circuit of life, and include such a variety of circumstances. As I have an equal right with others to give my opinion of the objects about me, and a better title to determine concerning that state which I have tried, than many who talk of it without experience, I am unwilling to be restrained by mere authority from advancing what, I believe, an accurate view of the world will confirm, that marriage is not commonly unhappy, otherwise than as life is unhappy; and that most of those who complain of connubial miseries, have as much satisfaction as their nature would have admitted, or their conduct procured, in any other condition.

It is, indeed, common to hear both sexes repine at their change, relate the happiness of their earlier years, blame the folly and rashness of their own choice, and warn those whom they see coming into the world against the same precipitance and infatuation. But it is to be remembered, that the days which they so much wish to call back, are the days not only of celibacy but of youth, the days of novelty and improvement, of ardour and of hope, of health and vigour of body, of gaiety and lightness of heart. It is not easy to surround life with any circumstances in which youth will not be delightful; and I am afraid that whether married or unmarried, we shall find the vesture of terrestrial existence more heavy and cumbrous, the longer it is worn.

That they censure themselves for the indiscretion of their choice, is not a sufficient proof that they have chosen ill, since we see the same discontent at every other part of life which we cannot change. Converse with almost any man, grown old in a profession, and you will find him regretting that he did not enter into some different course, to which he too late finds his genius better adapted, or in which he discovers that wealth and honour are more easily attained. "The merchant," says Horace, "envies the soldier, and the soldier recounts the felicity of the merchant; the lawyer, when his clients harass him, calls out for the quiet of the countryman; and the countryman, when business calls him to town, proclaims that there is no happiness but amidst opulence and crowds."[2] Every man recounts the inconveniences of his own station, and thinks those of any other less, because he has not felt them. Thus the married praise the ease and freedom of a single state, and the single fly to marriage from the weariness of solitude. From all our observations we may collect with certainty, that misery is the lot of man, but cannot discover in what particular condition it will find most alleviations; or whether all external appendages are not, as we use them, the causes either of good or ill.

Whoever feels great pain, naturally hopes for ease from change of posture; he changes it, and finds himself equally tormented: and of the same kind are the expedients by which we endeavour to obviate or elude those uneasinesses, to which mortality will always be subject. It is not likely that the married state is eminently miserable, since we see such numbers, whom the death of their partners has set free from it, entering it again.

Wives and husbands are, indeed, incessantly complaining of each other; and there would be reason for imagining that almost every house was infested with perverseness or oppression beyond human sufferance, did we not know upon how small occasions some minds burst out into lamentations and reproaches, and how naturally every animal revenges his pain upon those who happen to be near, without any nice examination of its cause. We are always willing to fancy ourselves within a little happiness, and when, with repeated efforts, we cannot reach it, persuade ourselves that it is intercepted by an ill-paired mate, since, if we could find any other obstacle, it would be our own fault that it was not removed.

Anatomists have often remarked, that though our diseases are sufficiently numerous and severe, yet when we enquire into the structure of the body, the tenderness of some parts, the minuteness of others, and the immense multiplicity of animal functions that must concur to the healthful and vigorous exercise of all our powers, there appears reason to wonder rather that we are preserved so long, than that we perish so soon, and that our frame subsists for a single day, or hour, without disorder, rather than that it should be broken or obstructed by violence of accidents, or length of time.

The same reflection arises in my mind, upon observation of the manner in which marriage is frequently contracted. When I see the avaricious and crafty taking companions to their tables and their beds without any inquiry, but after farms and money; or the giddy and thoughtless uniting themselves for life to those whom they have only seen by the light of tapers at a ball; when parents make articles for their children, without inquiring after their consent; when some marry for heirs to disappoint their brothers, and others throw themselves into the arms of those whom they do not love, because they have found themselves rejected where they were most solicitous to please; when some marry because their servants cheat them, some because they squander their own money, some because their houses are pestered with company, some because they will live like other people, and some only because they are sick in themselves, I am not so much inclined to wonder that marriage is sometimes unhappy, as that it appears so little loaded with calamity; and cannot but conclude that society has something in itself eminently agreeable to human nature, when I find its pleasures so great, that even the ill choice of a companion can hardly overbalance them.

By the ancient customs of the Muscovites, the men and women never saw each other till they were joined beyond the power of parting. It may be suspected that by this method many unsuitable matches were produced, and many tempers associated that were not qualified to give pleasure to each other. Yet, perhaps, among a people so little delicate, where the paucity of gratifications and the uniformity of life gave no opportunity for imagination to interpose its objections, there was not much danger of capricious dislike; and while they felt neither cold nor hunger they might live quietly together, without any thought of the defects of one another.

Among us, whom knowledge has made nice and affluence wanton, there are, indeed, more cautions requisite to secure tranquillity; and yet if we observe the manner in which those converse, who have singled out each other for marriage, we shall, perhaps, not think that the Russians lost much by their restraint. For the whole endeavour of both parties during the time of courtship is to hinder themselves from being known, and to disguise their natural temper, and real desires, in hypocritical imitation, studied compliance, and continual affectation. From the time that their love is avowed, neither sees the other but in a mask, and the cheat is managed often on both sides with so much art, and discovered afterwards with so much abruptness, that each has reason to suspect that some transformation has happened on the wedding night, and that, by a strange imposture, one has been courted, and another married.

I desire you, therefore, Mr. *Rambler*, to question all who shall hereafter come to you with matrimonial complaints, concerning their behaviour in the time of courtship, and inform them that they are neither to wonder nor repine, when a contract begun with fraud has ended in disappointment.

I am, &c.

Rambler no. 50, September 8, 1750: Youth and age

Credebant hoc grande nefas, et morte piandum,
Si juvenis vetulo non assurrexerat, atque
Barbato cuicunque puer, licet ipse videret
Plura domi fraga, et majores glandis acervos.

Juvenal, *Satires*, XIII. 54–57

And had not men the hoary head rever'd,
And boys paid rev'rence when a man appear'd,
Both must have died, though richer skins they wore,
And saw more heaps of acorns in their store.

transl. Thomas Creech

I have always thought it the business of those who turn their speculations upon the living world, to commend the virtues as well as to expose the faults of their contemporaries, and to confute a false as well as to support a just accusation; not only because it is peculiarly the business of a monitor to keep his own reputation untainted, lest those who can once charge him with partiality should indulge themselves afterwards in disbelieving him at pleasure; but because he may find real crimes sufficient to give full employment to caution or repentance, without distracting the mind by needless scruples and vain solicitudes.

There are certain fixed and stated reproaches that one part of mankind has in all ages thrown upon another, which are regularly transmitted through continued successions, and which he that has once suffered them is certain to use with the same undistinguishing vehemence when he has changed his station, and gained the prescriptive right of inflicting on others what he had formerly endured himself.

To these hereditary imputations, of which no man sees the justice till it becomes his interest to see it, very little regard is to be shown; since it does not appear that they are produced by ratiocination or inquiry, but received implicitly, or caught by a kind of instantaneous contagion, and supported rather by willingness to credit, than ability to prove them.

It has been always the practice of those who are desirous to believe themselves made venerable by length of time, to censure the new comers into life, for want of respect to grey hairs and sage experience, for heady confidence in their own understandings, for hasty conclusions upon partial views, for disregard of counsels, which their fathers and grandsires are ready to afford them, and a rebellious impatience of that subordination to which youth is condemned by nature, as necessary to its security from evils into which it would be otherwise precipitated, by the rashness of passion, and the blindness of ignorance.

Every old man complains of the growing depravity of the world, of the petulance and insolence of the rising generation. He recounts the decency and regularity of former times, and celebrates the discipline and sobriety of the age in which his youth was passed; a happy age, which is now no more to be expected, since confusion has broken in upon the world, and thrown down all the boundaries of civility and reverence.

It is not sufficiently considered how much he assumes who dares to claim the privilege of complaining; for as every man has, in his own opinion, a full share of the miseries of life, he is inclined to consider all clamorous uneasiness as a proof of impatience rather than of affliction, and to ask, what merit has this man to show, by which he has acquired a right to repine at the distributions of nature? Or, why does he imagine that exemptions should be granted him from the general condition of man? We find ourselves excited rather to captiousness than pity, and instead of being in haste to soothe his complaints by sympathy and tenderness, we enquire whether the pain be proportionate to the lamentation; and whether, supposing the affliction real, it is not the effect of vice and folly rather than calamity.

The querulousness and indignation which is observed so often to disfigure the last scene of life, naturally leads us to enquiries like these. For surely it will be thought at the first view of things, that if age be thus contemned and ridiculed, insulted and neglected, the crime must at least be equal on either part. They who have had opportunities of establishing their authority over minds ductile and unresisting, they who have been the protectors of helplessness, and the instructors of ignorance, and who yet retain in their own hands the power of wealth, and the dignity of command, must defeat their influence by their own misconduct, and make use of all these advantages with very little skill, if they cannot secure to themselves an appearance of respect, and ward off open mockery and declared contempt.

The general story of mankind will evince, that lawful and settled authority is very seldom resisted when it is well employed. Gross corruption, or evident imbecility, is necessary to the suppression of that reverence with which the majority of mankind look upon their governors, and on those whom they see surrounded by splendour and fortified by power. For though men are drawn by their passions into forgetfulness of invisible rewards and punishments, yet they are easily kept obedient to those who have temporal dominion in their hands, till their veneration is dissipated by such wickedness and folly as can neither be defended nor concealed.

It may, therefore, very reasonably be suspected that the old draw upon themselves the greatest part of those insults which they so much lament, and that age is rarely despised but when it is contemptible. If men imagine that excess of debauchery can be made reverend by time, that knowledge is the consequence of long life, however idly or thoughtlessly employed, that priority of birth will supply the want of steadiness or honesty, can it raise much wonder that their hopes are disappointed, and that they see their posterity rather willing to trust their own eyes in their progress into life, than enlist themselves under guides who have lost their way?

There are, indeed, many truths which time necessarily and certainly teaches, and which might, by those who have learned them from experience, be communicated to their successors at a cheaper rate: but dictates, though liberally enough bestowed, are generally without effect, the teacher gains few proselytes by instruction which his own behaviour contradicts; and young men miss the benefit of counsel, because they are not very ready to believe that those who fell below them in practice, can much excel them in theory. Thus the progress of knowledge is retarded, the world is kept long in the same state, and every new race is to gain the prudence of their predecessors by committing and redressing the same miscarriages.

To secure to the old that influence which they are willing to claim, and which might so much contribute to the improvement of the arts of life, it is absolutely necessary that they give themselves up to the duties of declining years; and contentedly resign to youth its levity, its pleasures, its frolics, and its fopperies. It is a hopeless endeavour to unite the contrarieties of spring and winter; it is unjust to claim the privileges of age and retain the playthings of childhood. The young always form magnificent ideas of the wisdom and gravity of men whom they consider as placed at a distance from them in the ranks of existence, and naturally look on those whom they find trifling with long beards, with contempt and indignation, like that which women feel at the effeminacy of men. If dotards will contend with boys in those performances in which boys must always excel them; if they will dress crippled limbs in embroidery, endeavour at gaiety with faltering voices, and darken assemblies of pleasure with the ghastliness of disease, they may well expect those who find their diversions obstructed will hoot them away; and that if they descend to competition with youth, they must bear the insolence of successful rivals.

> *Lusisti satis, edisti satis atque bibisti:*
> *Tempus abire tibi est.*
>> Horace, *Epistles*, II.2. 214–215

> *You've had your share of mirth, of meat and drink:*
> *'Tis time to quit the scene—'tis time to think.*
>> transl. James Elphinston

Another vice of age, by which the rising generation may be alienated from it, is severity and censoriousness, that gives no allowance to the failings of early life, that expects artfulness from childhood, and constancy from youth, that is peremptory in every command, and inexorable to every failure. There are many who live merely to hinder happiness, and whose descendants can only tell of long life, that it produces suspicion, malignity, peevishness, and persecution: and yet even these tyrants can talk of the ingratitude of the age, curse their heirs for impatience, and wonder that young men cannot take pleasure in their father's company.

He that would pass the latter part of life with honour and decency, must, when he is young, consider that he shall one day be old; and remember, when he is old, that he has once been young. In youth, he must lay up knowledge for his support when his powers of acting shall forsake him; and in age forbear to animadvert with rigour on faults which experience only can correct.

Rambler no. 72, November 24, 1750: The necessity of good humour

Omnis Aristippum decuit status, et color, et res,
Sectantem majora fere; presentibus aequum.

Horace, Epistles, I.17. 23–24

Yet Aristippus ev'ry dress became,
In ev'ry various change of life the same;
And though he aim'd at things of higher kind,
Yet to the present held an equal mind.

transl. Philip Francis

To the Rambler.
Sir,

Those who exalt themselves into the chair of instruction, without enquiring whether any will submit to their authority, have not sufficiently considered how much of human life passes in little incidents, cursory conversation, slight business, and casual amusements; and therefore they have endeavoured only to inculcate the more awful virtues, without condescending to regard those petty qualities which grow important only by their frequency, and which, though they produce no single acts of heroism, nor astonish us by great events, yet are every moment exerting their influence upon us, and make the draught of life sweet or bitter by imperceptible instillations. They operate unseen and unregarded, as change of air makes us sick or healthy, though we breathe it without attention, and only know the particles that impregnate it by their salutary or malignant effects.

You have shown yourself not ignorant of the value of those subaltern endowments, yet have hitherto neglected to recommend good humour to the world, though a little reflection will show you that it is the "balm of being,"[3] the quality to which all that adorns or elevates mankind must owe its power of pleasing. Without good humour, learning and bravery can only confer that superiority which swells the heart of the lion in the desert, where he roars without reply, and ravages without resistance. Without good-humour, virtue may awe by its dignity, and amaze by its brightness; but must always be viewed at a distance, and will scarcely gain a friend or attract an imitator.

Good humour may be defined a habit of being pleased; a constant and perennial softness of manner, easiness of approach, and suavity of disposition; like that which every man perceives in himself when the first transports of new felicity have subsided, and his thoughts are only kept in motion by a slow succession of soft impulses. Good humour is a state between gaiety and unconcern; the act or emanation of a mind at leisure to regard the gratification of another.

It is imagined by many, that whenever they aspire to please, they are required to be merry, and to show the gladness of their souls by flights of pleasantry, and bursts of laughter. But though these men may be for a time heard with applause and admiration, they seldom delight us long. We enjoy them a little, and then retire to easiness and good humour, as the eye gazes awhile on eminences glittering with the sun, but soon turns aching away to verdure and to flowers.

Gaiety is to good humour as animal perfumes to vegetable fragrance; the one overpowers weak spirits, and the other recreates and revives them. Gaiety seldom fails to give some pain; the hearers either strain their faculties to accompany its towerings, or are left behind in envy and despair. Good humour boasts no faculties which every one does not believe in his own power, and pleases principally by not offending.

It is well known that the most certain way to give any man pleasure, is to persuade him that you receive pleasure from him, to encourage him to freedom and confidence, and to avoid any such appearance of superiority as may overbear and depress him. We see many that by this art only spend their days in the midst of caresses, invitations, and civilities; and without any extraordinary qualities or attainments, are the universal favourites of both sexes, and certainly find a friend in every place. The darlings of the world will, indeed, be generally found such as excite neither jealousy nor fear, and are not considered as candidates for any eminent degree of reputation, but content themselves with common accomplishments, and endeavour rather to solicit kindness than to raise esteem; therefore in assemblies and places of resort it seldom fails to happen, that though at the entrance of some particular person every face brightens with gladness, and every hand is extended in salutation, yet if you pursue him beyond the first exchange of civilities, you will find him of very small importance, and only welcome to the company as one by whom all conceive themselves admired, and with whom any one is at liberty to amuse himself when he can find no other auditor or companion; as one with whom all are at ease, who will hear a jest without criticism, and a narrative without contradiction, who laughs with every wit, and yields to every disputer.

There are many whose vanity always inclines them to associate with those from whom they have no reason to fear mortification; and there are times in which the wise and the knowing are willing to receive praise without the labour of deserving it, in which the most elevated mind is willing to descend, and the most active to be at rest. All therefore are at some hour or another fond of companions whom they can entertain upon easy terms, and who will relieve them from solitude, without condemning them to vigilance and caution. We are most inclined to love when we have nothing to fear, and he that encourages us to please ourselves, will not be long without preference in our affection to those whose learning holds us at the distance of pupils, or whose wit calls all attention from us, and leaves us without importance, and without regard.

It is remarked by prince Henry, when he sees Falstaff lying on the ground, that "he could have better spared a better man."[4] He was well acquainted with the vices and follies of him whom he lamented, but while his conviction compelled him to do justice to superior qualities, his tenderness still broke out at the remembrance of Falstaff, of the cheerful companion, the loud buffoon, with whom he had passed his time in all the luxury of idleness, who had gladded him with unenvied merriment, and whom he could at once enjoy and despise.

You may perhaps think this account of those who are distinguished for their good humour not very consistent with the praises which I have bestowed upon it. But surely nothing can more evidently show the value of this quality, than that it recommends those who are destitute of all other excellencies, and procures regard to the trifling, friendship to the worthless, and affection to the dull.

Good humour is indeed generally degraded by the characters in which it is found; for, being considered as a cheap and vulgar quality, we find it often neglected by those that, having excellencies of higher reputation and brighter splendour, perhaps imagine that they have some right to gratify themselves at the expense of others, and are to demand compliance, rather than to practise it. It is by some unfortunate mistake that almost all those who have any claim to esteem or love, press their pretensions with too little consideration of others. This mistake, my own interest, as well as my zeal for general happiness, makes me desirous to rectify; for I have a friend who, because he knows his own fidelity and usefulness, is never willing to sink into a companion: I have a wife whose beauty first subdued me, and whose wit confirmed her conquest, but whose beauty now serves no other purpose than to entitle her to tyranny, and whose wit is only used to justify perverseness.

Surely nothing can be more unreasonable than to lose the will to please, when we are conscious of the power, or show more cruelty than to choose any kind of influence before that of kindness. He that regards the welfare of others, should make his virtue approachable, that it may be loved and copied; and he that considers the wants which every man feels, or will feel, of external assistance, must rather wish to be surrounded by those that love him, than by those that admire his excellencies, or solicit his favours; for admiration ceases with novelty, and interest gains its end and retires. A man whose great qualities want the ornament of superficial attractions, is like a naked mountain with mines of gold, which will be frequented only till the treasure is exhausted.

I am, &c.

PHILOMIDES

Rambler no. 80, December 22, 1750: Variety and happiness

Vides, ut altâ stet nive candidum
Soracte, nece jam sustineant onus
Silvae laborantes

Horace, *Odes*, I.9. 1–3

Behold yon mountain's hoary height
  Made higher with new mounts of snow;
Again behold the winter's weight
  Oppress the lab'ring woods below.

transl. Dryden

As Providence has made the human soul an active being, always impatient for novelty, and struggling for something yet unenjoyed with unwearied progression, the world seems to have been eminently adapted to this disposition of the mind; it is formed to raise expectations by constant vicissitudes, and to obviate satiety by perpetual change.

Wherever we turn our eyes, we find something to revive our curiosity and engage our attention. In the dusk of the morning we watch the rising of the sun, and see the day diversify the clouds, and open new prospects in its gradual advance. After a few hours, we see the shades lengthen, and the light decline, till the sky is resigned to a multitude of shining orbs different from each other in magnitude and splendour. The earth varies its appearance as we move upon it; the woods offer their shades, and the fields their harvests; the hill flatters with an extensive view, and the valley invites with shelter, fragrance, and flowers.

The poets have numbered among the felicities of the golden age, an exemption from the change of seasons, and a perpetuity of spring; but I am not certain that in this state of imaginary happiness they have made sufficient provision for that insatiable demand of new gratifications, which seem particularly to characterize the nature of man. Our sense of delight is in a great measure comparative, and arises at once from the sensations which we feel, and those which we remember. Thus ease after torment is pleasure for a time, and we are very agreeably recreated, when the body, chilled with the weather, is gradually recovering its natural tepidity; but the joy ceases when we have forgot the cold: we must fall below ease again, if we desire to rise above it, and purchase new felicity by voluntary pain. It is therefore not unlikely, that however the fancy may be amused with the description of regions in which no wind is heard but the gentle zephyr, and no scenes are displayed but valleys enamelled with unfading flowers, and woods waving their perennial verdure, we should soon grow weary of uniformity, find our thoughts languish for want of other subjects, call on heaven for our wonted round of seasons, and think ourselves liberally recompensed for the inconveniences of summer and winter, by new perceptions of the calmness and mildness of the intermediate variations.

Every season has its particular power of striking the mind. The nakedness and asperity of the wintry world always fill the beholder with pensive and profound astonishment; as the variety of the scene is lessened, its grandeur is increased; and the mind is swelled at once by the mingled ideas of the present and the past, of the beauties which have vanished from the eyes, and the waste and desolation that are now before them.

It is observed by Milton, that he who neglects to visit the country in spring, and rejects the pleasures that are then in their first bloom and fragrance, is guilty of "sullenness against nature."[5] If we allot different duties to different seasons, he may be charged with equal disobedience to the voice of nature, who looks on the bleak hills and leafless woods without seriousness and awe. Spring is the season of gaiety, and winter of terror; in spring the heart of tranquillity dances to the melody of the groves, and the eye of benevolence sparkles at the sight of happiness and plenty. In the winter, compassion melts at universal calamity, and the tear of softness starts at the wailings of hunger, and the cries of the creation in distress.

Few minds have much inclination to indulge heaviness and sorrow, nor do I recommend them beyond the degree necessary to maintain in its full vigour that habitual sympathy and tenderness which, in a world of so much misery, is necessary to the ready discharge of our most important duties. The winter, therefore, is generally celebrated as the proper season for domestic merriment and gaiety. We are seldom invited by the votaries of pleasure to look abroad for any other purpose, than that we may shrink back with more satisfaction to our coverts, and when we have heard the howl of the tempest, and felt the gripe of the frost, congratulate each other with more gladness upon a close room, an easy chair, a large fire, and a smoking dinner.

Winter brings natural inducements to jollity and conversation. Differences, we know, are never so effectually laid asleep as by some common calamity. An enemy unites all to whom he threatens danger. The rigour of winter brings generally to the same fireside those who, by the opposition of inclinations, or difference of employment, move in various directions through the other parts of the year; and when they have met, and find it their mutual interest to remain together, they endear each other by mutual compliances, and often wish for the continuance of the social season, with all its bleakness, and all its severities.

To the men of study and imagination the winter is generally the chief time of labour. Gloom and silence produce composure of mind, and concentration of ideas; and the privation of external pleasure naturally causes an effort to find entertainment within. This is the time in which those whom literature enables to find amusements for themselves, have more than common convictions of their own happiness. When they are condemned by the elements to retirement, and debarred from most of the diversions which are called in to assist the flight of time, they can find new subjects of inquiry, and preserve themselves from that weariness which hangs always flagging upon the vacant mind.

It cannot indeed be expected of all to be poets and philosophers; it is necessary that the greater part of mankind should be employed in the minute business of common life; minute, indeed, not if we consider its influence upon our happiness, but if we respect the abilities requisite to conduct it. These must necessarily be more dependent on accident for the means of spending agreeably those hours which their occupations leave unengaged, or nature obliges them to allow to relaxation. Yet even on these I would willingly impress such a sense of the value of time, as may incline them to find out for their careless hours amusements of more use and dignity than the common games, which not only weary the mind without improving it, but strengthen the passions of envy and avarice, and often lead to fraud and to profusion, to corruption and to ruin. It is unworthy of a reasonable being to spend any of the little time allotted us, without some tendency, either direct or oblique, to the end of our existence. And though every moment cannot be laid out on the formal and regular improvement of our knowledge, or in the stated practice of a moral or religious duty, yet none should be so spent as to exclude wisdom or virtue, or pass without possibility of qualifying us more or less for the better employment of those which are to come.

It is scarcely possible to pass an hour in honest conversation, without being able, when we rise from it, to please ourselves with having given or received some advantages; but a man may shuffle cards, or rattle dice, from noon to midnight, without tracing any new idea in his mind, or being able to recollect the day by any other token than his gain or loss, and a confused remembrance of agitated passions, and clamorous altercations.

However, as experience is of more weight than precept, any of my readers who are contriving how to spend the dreary months before them may consider which of their past amusements fills them now with the greatest satisfaction, and resolve to repeat those gratifications of which the pleasure is most durable.

Rambler no. 148, August 17, 1751: Parental tyranny and cruelty

Me pater saevis oneret catenis
Quod viro clemens misero peperci,
Me vel extremis Numidarum in oris
    Classe releget.

Horace, Odes, III. ll. 45–48

   Me let my father load with chains,
Or banish to Numidia's farthest plains;
   My crime, that I a loyal wife,
In kind compassion spar'd my husband's life.

transl. Philip Francis

Politicians remark, that no oppression is so heavy or lasting as that which is inflicted by the perversion and exorbitance of legal authority. The robber may be seized, and the invader repelled, whenever they are found; they who pretend no right but that of force, may by force be punished or suppressed. But when plunder bears the name of impost, and murder is perpetrated by a judicial sentence, fortitude is intimidated, and wisdom confounded: resistance shrinks from an alliance with rebellion, and the villain remains secure in the robes of the magistrate.

Equally dangerous and equally detestable are the cruelties often exercised in private families, under the venerable sanction of parental authority; the power which we are taught to honour from the first moments of reason; which is guarded from insult and violation by all that can impress awe upon the mind of man; and which therefore may wanton in cruelty without control, and trample the bounds of right with innumerable transgressions, before duty and piety will dare to seek redress, or think themselves at liberty to recur to any other means of deliverance than supplications by which insolence is elated, and tears by which cruelty is gratified.

It was for a long time imagined by the Romans, that no son could be the murderer of his father; and they had therefore no punishment appropriated to parricide. They seem likewise to have believed with equal confidence, that no father could be cruel to his child; and therefore they allowed every man the supreme judicature in his own house, and put the lives of his offspring into his hands. But experience informed them by degrees, that they determined too hastily in favour of human nature; they found that instinct and habit were not able to contend with avarice or malice; that the nearest relation might be violated; and that power, to whomsoever entrusted, might be ill employed. They were therefore obliged to supply and to change their institutions; to deter the parricide by a new law, and to transfer capital punishments from the parent to the magistrate.

There are indeed many houses which it is impossible to enter familiarly, without discovering that parents are by no means exempt from the intoxications of dominion; and that he who is in no danger of hearing remonstrances but from his own conscience, will seldom be long without the art of controlling his convictions, and modifying justice by his own will.

If in any situation the heart were inaccessible to malignity, it might be supposed to be sufficiently secured by parental relation. To have voluntarily become to any being the occasion of its existence, produces an obligation to make that existence happy. To see helpless infancy stretching out her hands, and pouring out her cries in testimony of dependence, without any powers to alarm jealousy, or any guilt to alienate affection, must surely awaken tenderness in every human mind; and tenderness once excited will be hourly increased by the natural contagion of felicity, by the repercussion of communicated pleasure, by the consciousness of the dignity of benefaction. I believe no generous or benevolent man can see the vilest animal courting his regard, and shrinking at his anger, playing his gambols of delight before him, calling on him in distress, and flying to him in danger, without more kindness than he can persuade himself to feel for the wild and unsocial inhabitants of the air and water. We naturally endear to ourselves those to whom we impart any kind of pleasure, because we imagine their affection and esteem secured to us by the benefits which they receive.

There is, indeed, another method by which the pride of superiority may be likewise gratified. He that has extinguished all the sensations of humanity, and has no longer any satisfaction in the reflection that he is loved as the distributor of happiness, may please himself with exciting terror as the inflictor of pain: he may delight his solitude with contemplating the extent of his power and the force of his commands; in imagining the desires that flutter on the tongue which is forbidden to utter them, or the discontent which preys on the heart in which fear confines it; he may amuse himself with new contrivances of detection, multiplications of prohibition, and varieties of punishment; and swell with exultation when he considers how little of the homage that he receives he owes to choice.

That princes of this character have been known, the history of all absolute kingdoms will inform us; and since, as Aristotle observes . . . "the government of a family is naturally monarchical,"[6] it is, like other monarchies, too often arbitrarily administered. The regal and parental tyrant differ only in the extent of their dominions, and the number of their slaves. The same passions cause the same miseries; except that seldom any prince, however despotic, has so far shaken off all awe of the public eye, as to venture upon those freaks of injustice which are sometimes indulged under the secrecy of a private dwelling. Capricious injunctions, partial decisions, unequal allotments, distributions of reward, not by merit but by fancy, and punishments, regulated not by the degree of the offence, but by the humour of the judge, are too frequent where no power is known but that of a father.

That he delights in the misery of others, no man will confess, and yet what other motive can make a father cruel? The king may be instigated by one man to the destruction of another; he may sometimes think himself endangered by the virtues of a subject; he may dread the successful general or the popular orator; his avarice may point out golden confiscations; and his guilt may whisper that he can only be secure by cutting off all power of revenge.

But what can a parent hope from the oppression of those who were born to his protection, of those who can disturb him with no competition, who can enrich him with no spoils? Why cowards are cruel may be easily discovered; but for what reason, not more infamous than cowardice, can that man delight in oppression who has nothing to fear?

The unjustifiable severity of a parent is loaded with this aggravation, that those whom he injures are always in his sight. The injustice of a prince is often exercised upon those of whom he never had any personal or particular knowledge; and the sentence which he pronounces, whether of banishment, imprisonment, or death, removes from his view the man whom he condemns. But the domestic oppressor dooms himself to gaze upon those faces which he clouds with terror and with sorrow; and beholds every moment the effects of his own barbarities. He that can bear to give continual pain to those who surround him, and can walk with satisfaction in the gloom of his own presence; he that can see submissive misery without relenting, and meet without emotion the eye that implores mercy, or demands justice, will scarcely be amended by remonstrance or admonition; he has found means of stopping the avenues of tenderness, and arming his heart against the force of reason.

Even though no consideration should be paid to the great law of social beings, by which every individual is commanded to consult the happiness of others, yet the harsh parent is less to be vindicated than any other criminal, because he less provides for the happiness of himself. Every man, however little he loves others, would willingly be loved; every man hopes to live long, and therefore hopes for that time at which he shall sink back to imbecility, and must depend for ease and cheerfulness upon the officiousness of others. But how has he obviated the inconveniences of old age, who alienates from him the assistance of his children, and whose bed must be surrounded in the last hours, in the hours of languor and dejection, of impatience and of pain, by strangers to whom his life is indifferent, or by enemies to whom his death is desirable?

Piety will, indeed, in good minds overcome provocation, and those who have been harassed by brutality will forget the injuries which they have suffered, so far as to perform the last duties with alacrity and zeal. But surely no resentment can be equally painful with kindness thus undeserved, nor can severer punishment be imprecated upon a man not wholly lost in meanness and stupidity, than, through the tediousness of decrepitude, to be reproached by the kindness of his own children, to receive not the tribute but the alms of attendance, and to owe every relief of his miseries, not to gratitude but to mercy.

Rambler no. 170, November 2, 1751: Misella's history

Confiteor; si quid prodest delicta fateri.

Ovid, *Amores*, II. 4.3

I grant the charge; forgive the fault confess'd.

To the Rambler.

Sir,

I am one of those beings from whom many, that melt at the sight of all other misery, think it meritorious to withhold relief; one whom the rigour of virtuous indignation dooms to suffer without complaint, and perish without regard; and whom I myself have formerly insulted in the pride of reputation and security of innocence.

I am of a good family, but my father was burdened with more children than he could decently support. A wealthy relation, as he travelled from London to his country seat, condescending to make him a visit, was touched with compassion of his narrow fortune, and resolved to ease him of part of his charge, by taking the care of a child upon himself. Distress on one side, and ambition on the other, were too powerful for parental fondness, and the little family passed in review before him, that he might make his choice. I was then ten years old, and, without knowing for what purpose, I was called to my great cousin, endeavoured to recommend myself by my best courtesy, sung him my prettiest song, told the last story that I had read, and so much endeared myself by my innocence, that he declared his resolution to adopt me, and to educate me with his own daughters.

My parents felt the common struggles at the thought of parting, and "some natural tears they dropp'd, but wip'd them soon."[7] They considered, not without that false estimation of the value of wealth, which poverty long continued always produces, that I was raised to higher rank than they could give me, and to hopes of more ample fortune than they could bequeath. My mother sold some of her ornaments to dress me in such a manner as might secure me from contempt at my first arrival; and when she dismissed me, pressed me to her bosom with an embrace that I still feel, gave me some precepts of piety, which, however neglected, I have not forgotten, and uttered prayers for my final happiness, of which I have not yet ceased to hope that they will at last be granted.

My sisters envied my new finery, and seemed not much to regret our separation; my father conducted me to the stagecoach with a kind of cheerful tenderness; and in a very short time I was transported to splendid apartments, and a luxurious table, and grew familiar to show, noise, and gaiety.

In three years my mother died, having implored a blessing on her family with her last breath. I had little opportunity to indulge a sorrow which there was none to partake with me, and therefore soon ceased to reflect much upon my loss. My father turned all his care upon his other children, whom some fortunate adventures and unexpected legacies enabled him, when he died, four years after my mother, to leave in a condition above their expectations.

I should have shared the increase of his fortune, and had once a portion assigned me in his will; but my cousin assuring him that all care for me was needless, since he had resolved to place me happily in the world, directed him to divide my part amongst my sisters.

Thus I was thrown upon dependence without resource. Being now at an age in which young women are initiated into company, I was no longer to be supported in my former character, but at a considerable expense; so that partly lest I should waste money, and partly lest my appearance might draw too many compliments and assiduities, I was insensibly degraded from my equality, and enjoyed few privileges above the head servant, but that of receiving no wages.

I felt every indignity, but knew that resentment would precipitate my fall. I therefore endeavoured to continue my importance by little services and active officiousness, and, for a time, preserved myself from neglect by withdrawing all pretences to competition, and studying to please rather than to shine. But my interest, notwithstanding this expedient, hourly declined, and my cousin's favourite maid began to exchange repartees with me, and consult me about the alterations of a cast gown.

I was now completely depressed, and though I had seen mankind enough to know the necessity of outward cheerfulness, I often withdrew to my chamber to vent my grief, or turn my condition in my mind, and examine by what means I might escape from perpetual mortification. At last my schemes and sorrows were interrupted by a sudden change of my relation's behaviour, who one day took an occasion when we were left together in a room, to bid me suffer myself no longer to be insulted, but assume the place which he always intended me to hold in the family. He assured me that his wife's preference of her own daughters should never hurt me; and, accompanying his professions with a purse of gold, ordered me to bespeak a rich suit at the mercer's, and to apply privately to him for money when I wanted it, and insinuate that my other friends supplied me, which he would take care to confirm.

By this stratagem, which I did not then understand, he filled me with tenderness and gratitude, compelled me to repose on him as my only support, and produced a necessity of private conversation. He often appointed interviews at the house of an acquaintance, and sometimes called on me with a coach, and carried me abroad. My sense of his favour, and the desire of retaining it, disposed me to unlimited complaisance, and, though I saw his kindness grow every day more fond, I did not suffer any suspicion to enter my thoughts. At last the wretch took advantage of the familiarity which he enjoyed as my relation, and the submission which he exacted as my benefactor, to complete the ruin of an orphan, whom his own promises had made indigent, whom his indulgence had melted, and his authority subdued.

I know not why it should afford subject of exultation to overpower on any terms the resolution, or surprise the caution of a girl; but of all the boasters that deck themselves in the spoils of innocence and beauty, they surely have the least pretensions to triumph who submit to owe their success to some casual influence. They neither employ the graces of fancy, nor the force of understanding, in their attempts; they cannot please their vanity with the art of their approaches, the delicacy of their adulations, the elegance of their address, or the efficacy of their eloquence; nor applaud themselves as possessed of any qualities by which affection is attracted. They surmount no obstacles, they defeat no rivals, but attack only those who cannot resist, and are often content to possess the body, without any solicitude to gain the heart.

Many of those despicable wretches does my present acquaintance with infamy and wickedness enable me to number among the heroes of debauchery. Reptiles whom their own servants would have despised, had they not been their servants, and with whom beggary would have disdained intercourse, had she not been allured by hopes of relief. Many of the beings which are now rioting in taverns, or shivering in the streets, have been corrupted, not by arts of gallantry which stole gradually upon the affections and laid prudence asleep, but by the fear of losing benefits which were never intended, or of incurring resentment which they could not escape; some have been frighted by masters, and some awed by guardians into ruin.

Our crime had its usual consequence, and he soon perceived that I could not long continue in his family. I was distracted at the thought of the reproach which I now believed inevitable. He comforted me with hopes of eluding all discovery, and often upbraided me with the anxiety, which perhaps none but himself saw in my countenance; but at last mingled his assurances of protection and maintenance with menaces of total desertion, if, in the moments of perturbation I should suffer his secret to escape, or endeavour to throw on him any part of my infamy.

Thus passed the dismal hours, till my retreat could no longer be delayed. It was pretended that my relations had sent for me to a distant county, and I entered upon a state which shall be described in my next letter.

I am, Sir, &c.
MISELLA

***Rambler* no. 171, November 5, 1751: Misella and the miseries of prostitution**

Taedet coeli convexa tueri.

Aeneid, IV. 451

Dark is the sun, and loathsome is the day.

To the Rambler.

Sir,

Misella now sits down to continue her narrative. I am convinced that nothing would more powerfully preserve youth from irregularity, or guard inexperience from seduction, than a just description of the condition into which the wanton plunges herself; and therefore hope that my letter may be a sufficient antidote to my example.

After the distraction, hesitation, and delays which the timidity of guilt naturally produces, I was removed to lodgings in a distant part of the town, under one of the characters commonly assumed upon such occasions. Here being by my circumstances condemned to solitude, I passed most of my hours in bitterness and anguish. The conversation of the people with whom I was placed was not at all capable of engaging my attention, or dispossessing the reigning ideas. The books which I carried to my retreat were such as heightened my abhorrence of myself; for I was not so far abandoned as to sink voluntarily into corruption, or endeavour to conceal from my own mind the enormity of my crime.

My relation remitted none of his fondness, but visited me so often, that I was sometimes afraid lest his assiduity should expose him to suspicion. Whenever he came he found me weeping, and was therefore less delightfully entertained than he expected. After frequent expostulations upon the unreasonableness of my sorrow, and innumerable protestations of everlasting regard, he at last found that I was more affected with the loss of my innocence, than the danger of my fame, and that he might not be disturbed by my remorse, began to lull my conscience with the opiates of irreligion. His arguments were such as my course of life has since exposed me often to the necessity of hearing, vulgar, empty, and fallacious; yet they at first confounded me by their novelty, filled me with doubt and perplexity, and interrupted that peace which I began to feel from the sincerity of my repentance, without substituting any other support. I listened a while to his impious gabble, but its influence was soon overpowered by natural reason and early education, and the convictions which this new attempt gave me of his baseness completed my abhorrence. I have heard of barbarians who, when tempests drive ships upon their coast, decoy them to the rocks that they may plunder their lading, and have always thought that wretches, thus merciless in their depredations, ought to be destroyed by a general insurrection of all social beings; yet how light is this guilt to the crime of him who, in the agitations of remorse, cuts away the anchor of piety, and, when he has drawn aside credulity from the paths of virtue, hides the light of heaven which would direct her to return. I had hitherto considered him as a man equally betrayed with myself by the concurrence of appetite and opportunity; but I now saw with horror that he was contriving to perpetuate his gratification, and was desirous to fit me to his purpose, by complete and radical corruption.

To escape, however, was not yet in my power. I could support the expenses of my condition only by the continuance of his favour. He provided all that was necessary, and in a few weeks congratulated me upon my escape from the danger which we had both expected with so much anxicty. I then began to remind him of his promise to restore me with my fame uninjured to the world. He promised me in general terms, that nothing should be wanting which his power could add to my happiness, but forbore to release me from my confinement. I knew how much my reception in the world depended upon my speedy return, and was therefore outrageously impatient of his delays, which I now perceived to be only artifices of lewdness. He told me at last, with an appearance of sorrow, that all hopes of restoration to my former state were forever precluded; that chance had discovered my secret, and malice divulged it; and that nothing now remained, but to seek a retreat more private, where curiosity or hatred could never find us.

The rage, anguish, and resentment which I felt at this account are not to be expressed. I was in so much dread of reproach and infamy, which he represented as pursuing me with full cry, that I yielded myself implicitly to his disposal and was removed, with a thousand studied precautions, through byways and dark passages to another house, where I harassed him with perpetual solicitations for a small annuity that might enable me to live in the country in obscurity and innocence.

This demand he at first evaded with ardent professions, but in time appeared offended at my importunity and distrust; and having one day endeavoured to sooth me with uncommon expressions of tenderness, when he found my discontent immoveable, left me with some inarticulate murmurs of anger. I was pleased that he was at last roused to sensibility, and expecting that at his next visit he would comply with my request, lived with great tranquillity upon the money in my hands, and was so much pleased with this pause of persecution that I did not reflect how much his absence had exceeded the usual intervals, till I was alarmed with the danger of wanting subsistence. I then suddenly contracted my expenses, but was unwilling to supplicate for assistance. Necessity, however, soon overcame my modesty or my pride, and I applied to him by a letter, but had no answer. I writ in terms more pressing, but without effect. I then sent an agent to inquire after him, who informed me that he had quitted his house, and was gone with his family to reside for some time on his estate in Ireland.

However shocked at this abrupt departure, I was yet unwilling to believe that he could wholly abandon me, and therefore, by the sale of my clothes, I supported myself, expecting that every post would bring me relief. Thus I passed seven months between hope and dejection, in a gradual approach to poverty and distress, emaciated with discontent, and bewildered with uncertainty. At last my landlady, after many hints of the necessity of a new lover, took the opportunity of my absence to search my boxes, and missing some of my apparel, seized the remainder for rent, and led me to the door.

To remonstrate against legal cruelty was vain; to supplicate obdurate brutality was hopeless. I went away I knew not whither, and wandered about without any settled purpose, unacquainted with the usual expedients of misery, unqualified for laborious offices, afraid to meet an eye that had seen me before, and hopeless of relief from those who were strangers to my former condition. Night came on in the midst of my distraction, and I still continued to wander till the menaces of the watch obliged me to shelter myself in a covered passage.

Next day, I procured a lodging in the backward garret of a mean house, and employed my landlady to inquire for a service. My applications were generally rejected for want of a character. At length I was received at a draper's, but when it was known to my mistress that I had only one gown, and that of silk, she was of opinion that I looked like a thief, and without warning hurried me away. I then tried to support myself by my needle; and by my landlady's recommendation obtained a little work from a shop, and for three weeks lived without repining; but when my punctuality had gained me so much reputation, that I was trusted to make up a head of some value, one of my fellow lodgers stole the lace, and I was obliged to fly from a prosecution.

Thus driven again into the streets, I lived upon the least that could support me, and at night accommodated myself under penthouses as well as I could. At length I became absolutely penniless, and having strolled all day without sustenance, was, at the close of evening, accosted by an elderly man, with an invitation to a tavern. I refused him with hesitation; he seized me by the hand, and drew me into a neighbouring house, where, when he saw my face pale with hunger, and my eyes swelling with tears, he spurned me from him, and bade me cant and whine in some other place; he for his part would take care of his pockets.

I still continued to stand in the way, having scarcely strength to walk further, when another soon addressed me in the same manner. When he saw the same tokens of calamity, he considered that I might be obtained at a cheap rate, and therefore quickly made overtures, which I no longer had firmness to reject. By this man I was maintained four months in penurious wickedness, and then abandoned to my former condition, from which I was delivered by another keeper.

In this abject state I have now passed four years, the drudge of extortion and the sport of drunkenness; sometimes the property of one man, and sometimes the common prey of accidental lewdness; at one time tricked up for sale by the mistress of a brothel, at another begging in the streets to be relieved from hunger by wickedness; without any hope in the day but of finding some whom folly or excess may expose to my allurements, and without any reflections at night, but such as guilt and terror impress upon me.

If those who pass their days in plenty and security, could visit for an hour the dismal receptacles to which the prostitute retires from her nocturnal excursions, and see the wretches that lie crowded together, mad with intemperance, ghastly with famine, nauseous with filth, and noisome with disease; it would not be easy for any degree of abhorrence to harden them against compassion, or to repress the desire which they must immediately feel to rescue such numbers of human beings from a state so dreadful.

It is said, that in France they annually evacuate their streets, and ship their prostitutes and vagabonds to their colonies. If the women that infest this city had the same opportunity of escaping from their miseries, I believe very little force would be necessary; for who among them can dread any change? Many of us indeed are wholly unqualified for any but the most servile employments, and those perhaps would require the care of a magistrate to hinder them from following the same practices in another country; but others are only precluded by infamy from reformation, and would gladly be delivered on any terms from the necessity of guilt, and the tyranny of chance. No place but a populous city can afford opportunities for open prostitution; and where the eye of justice can attend to individuals, those who cannot be made good may be restrained from mischief. For my part, I should exult at the privilege of banishment, and think myself happy in any region that should restore me once again to honesty and peace.

I am, Sir, &c.

MISELLA

Rambler no. 188, January 4, 1752: Conversation

Si te colo, Sexte, non amabo.

Martial, *Epigrammata,* II.55.3

The more I honour thee, the less I love.

None of the desires dictated by vanity is more general, or less blameable, than that of being distinguished for the arts of conversation. Other accomplishments may be possessed without opportunity of exerting them, or wanted without danger that the defect can often be remarked; but as no man can live, otherwise than in an hermitage, without hourly pleasure or vexation, from the fondness or neglect of those about him, the faculty of giving pleasure is of continual use. Few are more frequently envied than those who have the power of forcing attention wherever they come, whose entrance is considered as a promise of felicity, and whose departure is lamented, like the recess of the sun from northern climates, as a privation of all that enlivens fancy, or inspirits gaiety.

It is apparent, that to excellence in this valuable art, some peculiar qualifications are necessary; for every one's experience will inform him, that the pleasure which men are able to give in conversation, holds no stated proportion to their knowledge or their virtue. Many find their way to the tables and the parties of those who never consider them as of the least importance in any other place; we have all, at one time or other, been content to love those whom we could not esteem, and been persuaded to try the dangerous experiment of admitting him for a companion, whom we knew to be too ignorant for a counsellor, and too treacherous for a friend.

I question whether some abatement of character is not necessary to general acceptance. Few spend their time with much satisfaction under the eye of uncontestable superiority; and therefore, among those whose presence is courted at assemblies of jollity, there are seldom found men eminently distinguished for powers or acquisitions. The wit whose vivacity condemns slower tongues to silence, the scholar whose knowledge allows no man to fancy that he instructs him, the critic who suffers no fallacy to pass undetected, and the reasoner who condemns the idle to thought and the negligent to attention, are generally praised and feared, reverenced and avoided.

He that would please must rarely aim at such excellence as depresses his hearers in their own opinion, or debars them from the hope of contributing reciprocally to the entertainment of the company. Merriment, extorted by sallies of imagination, sprightliness of remark, or quickness of reply, is too often what the Latins call, the "Sardinian laughter,"[8] a distortion of the face without gladness of heart.

For this reason, no style of conversation is more extensively acceptable than the narrative. He who has stored his memory with slight anecdotes, private incidents, and personal peculiarities, seldom fails to find his audience favourable. Almost every man listens with eagerness to contemporary history; for almost every man has some real or imaginary connection with a celebrated character, some desire to advance or oppose a rising name. Vanity often cooperates with curiosity. He that is a hearer in one place, qualifies himself to become a speaker in another; for though he cannot comprehend a series of argument, or transport the volatile spirit of wit without evaporation, he yet thinks himself able to treasure up the various incidents of a story, and please his hopes with the information which he shall give to some inferior society.

Narratives are for the most part heard without envy, because they are not supposed to imply any intellectual qualities above the common rate. To be acquainted with facts not yet echoed by plebeian mouths, may happen to one man as well as to another; and to relate them when they are known, has in appearance so little difficulty, that every one concludes himself equal to the task.

But it is not easy, and in some situations of life not possible, to accumulate such a stock of materials as may support the expense of continual narration; and it frequently happens, that they who attempt this method of ingratiating themselves, please only at the first interview; and, for want of new supplies of intelligence, wear out their stories by continual repetition.

There would be, therefore, little hope of obtaining the praise of a good companion, were it not to be gained by more compendious methods; but such is the kindness of mankind to all, except those who aspire to real merit and rational dignity, that every understanding may find some way to excite benevolence; and whoever is not envied may learn the art of procuring love. We are willing to be pleased, but are not willing to admire, we favour the mirth or officiousness that solicits our regard, but oppose the worth or spirit that enforces it.

The first place among those that please, because they desire only to please, is due to the "merry fellow," whose laugh is loud, and whose voice is strong; who is ready to echo every jest with obstreperous approbation, and countenance every frolic with vociferations of applause. It is not necessary to a merry fellow to have in himself any fund of jocularity, or force of conception; it is sufficient that he always appears in the highest exaltation of gladness, for the greater part of mankind are gay or serious by infection, and follow without resistance the attraction of example.

Next to the merry fellow is the "good-natured man," a being generally without benevolence, or any other virtue, than such as indolence and insensibility confer. The characteristic of a good-natured man is to bear a joke; to sit unmoved and unaffected amidst noise and turbulence, profaneness and obscenity; to hear every tale without contradiction; to endure insult without reply; and to follow the stream of folly, whatever course it shall happen to take. The good-natured man is commonly the darling of the petty wits, with whom they exercise themselves in the rudiments of raillery; for he never takes advantage of failings, nor disconcerts a puny satirist with unexpected sarcasms; but while the glass continues to circulate, contentedly bears the expense of an uninterrupted laughter, and retires rejoicing at his own importance.

The "modest man" is a companion of a yet lower rank, whose only power of giving pleasure is not to interrupt it. The modest man satisfies himself with peaceful silence, which all his companions are candid enough to consider as proceeding not from inability to speak, but willingness to hear.

Many, without being able to attain any general character of excellence, have some single art of entertainment which serves them as a passport through the world. One I have known for fifteen years the darling of a weekly club, because every night, precisely at eleven, he begins his favourite song, and during the vocal performance, by corresponding motions of his hand, chalks out a giant upon the wall. Another has endeared himself to a long succession of acquaintances by sitting among them with his wig reversed; another by contriving to smut the nose of any stranger who was to be initiated in the club; another by purring like a cat, and then pretending to be frightened; and another by yelping like a hound, and calling to the drawers to drive out the dog.

Such are the arts by which cheerfulness is promoted, and sometimes friendship established; arts, which those who despise them should not rigorously blame, except when they are practised at the expense of innocence; for it is always necessary to be loved, but not always necessary to be reverenced.

Adventurer no. 67, June 26, 1753: London, productive society, and the role of the individual

Inventas—vitam excoluere per artes.

Aeneid, VI. 663

They polish life by useful arts.

That familiarity produces neglect has been long observed. The effect of all external objects, however great or splendid, ceases with their novelty; the courtier stands without emotion in the royal presence; the rustic tramples under his foot the beauties of the spring with little attention to their colours or their fragrance; and the inhabitant of the coast darts his eye upon the immense diffusion of waters, without awe, wonder, or terror.

Those who have past much of their lives in this great city, look upon its opulence and its multitudes, its extent and variety, with cold indifference; but an inhabitant of the remoter parts of the kingdom is immediately distinguished by a kind of dissipated curiosity, a busy endeavour to divide his attention amongst a thousand objects, and a wild confusion of astonishment and alarm.

The attention of a newcomer is generally first struck by the multiplicity of cries that stun him in the streets, and the variety of merchandise and manufactures which the shopkeepers expose on every hand; and he is apt, by unwary bursts of admiration, to excite the merriment and contempt of those who mistake the use of their eyes for effects of their understanding, and confound accidental knowledge with just reasoning.

But, surely, these are subjects on which any man may without reproach employ his meditations: the innumerable occupations among which the thousands that swarm in the streets of London are distributed, may furnish employment to minds of every cast, and capacities of every degree. He that contemplates the extent of this wonderful city, finds it difficult to conceive by what method plenty is maintained in our markets, and how the inhabitants are regularly supplied with the necessaries of life; but when he examines the shops and warehouses, sees the immense stores of every kind of merchandise piled up for sale, and runs over all the manufactures of art and products of nature, which are everywhere attracting his eye and soliciting his purse, he will be inclined to conclude, that such quantities cannot easily be exhausted, and that part of mankind must soon stand still for want of employment, till the wares already provided shall be worn out and destroyed.

As Socrates was passing through the fair at Athens, and casting his eyes over the shops and customers, "how many things are here," says he, "that I do not want!"[9] The same sentiment is every moment rising in the mind of him that walks the streets of London, however inferior in philosophy to Socrates: he beholds a thousand shops crowded with goods of which he can scarcely tell the use, and which, therefore, he is apt to consider as of no value: and indeed, many of the arts by which families are supported and wealth is heaped together, are of that minute and superfluous kind, which nothing but experience could evince possible to be prosecuted with advantage, and which, as the world might easily want, it could scarcely be expected to encourage.

But so it is, that custom, curiosity, or wantonness, supplies every art with patrons, and finds purchasers for every manufacture; the world is so adjusted, that not only bread but riches may be obtained without great abilities or arduous performances: the most unskilful hand and unenlightened mind have sufficient incitements to industry; for he that is resolutely busy, can scarcely be in want. There is, indeed, no employment, however despicable, from which a man may not promise himself more than competence, when he sees thousands and myriads raised to dignity, by no other merit than that of contributing to supply their neighbours with the means of sucking smoke through a tube of clay; and others raising contributions upon those, whose elegance disdains the grossness of smoky luxury, by grinding the same materials into a powder that may at once gratify and impair the smell.

Not only by these popular and modish trifles, but by a thousand un-heeded and evanescent kinds of business, are the multitudes of this city preserved from idleness, and consequently from want. In the endless va-riety of tastes and circumstances that diversify mankind, nothing is so su-perfluous, but that some one desires it: or so common, but that some one is compelled to buy it. As nothing is useless but because it is in improper hands, what is thrown away by one is gathered up by another; and the re-fuse of part of mankind furnishes a subordinate class with the materials necessary to their support.

When I look round upon those who are thus variously exerting their qualifications, I cannot but admire the secret concatenation of society that links together the great and the mean, the illustrious and the obscure; and consider with benevolent satisfaction, that no man, unless his body or mind be totally disabled, has need to suffer the mortification of seeing himself useless or burdensome to the community: he that will diligently labour, in whatever occupation, will deserve the sustenance which he ob-tains, and the protection which he enjoys; and may lie down every night with the pleasing consciousness of having contributed something to the happiness of life.

Contempt and admiration are equally incident to narrow minds: he whose comprehension can take in the whole subordination of mankind, and whose perspicacity can pierce to the real state of things through the thin veils of fortune or of fashion, will discover meanness in the highest stations, and dignity in the meanest; and find that no man can become venerable but by virtue, or contemptible but by wickedness.

In the midst of this universal hurry, no man ought to be so little influ-enced by example, or so void of honest emulation, as to stand a lazy spec-tator of incessant labour; or please himself with the mean happiness of a drone, while the active swarms are buzzing about him: no man is without some quality, by the due application of which he might deserve well of the world; and whoever he be that has but little in his power, should be in haste to do that little, lest he be confounded with him that can do noth-ing.

By this general concurrence of endeavours, arts of every kind have been so long cultivated, that all the wants of man may be immediately supplied; idleness can scarcely form a wish which she may not gratify by the toil of others, or curiosity dream of a toy, which the shops are not ready to afford her.

Happiness is enjoyed only in proportion as it is known; and such is the state or folly of man, that it is known only by experience of its contrary: we who have long lived amidst the conveniences of a town immensely populous, have scarce an idea of a place where desire cannot be gratified by money. In order to have a just sense of this artificial plenty, it is necessary to have passed some time in a distant colony, or those parts of our island which are thinly inhabited: he that has once known how many trades every man in such situations is compelled to exercise, with how much labour the products of nature must be accommodated to human use, how long the loss or defect of any common utensil must be endured, or by what awkward expedients it must be supplied, how far men may wander with money in their hands before any can sell them what they wish to buy, will know how to rate at its proper value the plenty and ease of a great city.

But that the happiness of man may still remain imperfect, as wants in this place are easily supplied, new wants likewise are easily created; every man, in surveying the shops of London, sees numberless instruments and conveniences of which, while he did not know them, he never felt the need; and yet, when use has made them familiar, wonders how life could be supported without them. Thus it comes to pass, that our desires always increase with our possessions; the knowledge that something remains yet unenjoyed, impairs our enjoyment of the good before us.

They who have been accustomed to the refinements of science, and multiplications of contrivance, soon lose their confidence in the unassisted powers of nature, forget the paucity of our real necessities, and overlook the easy methods by which they may be supplied. It were a speculation worthy of a philosophical mind, to examine how much is taken away from our native abilities, as well as added to them, by artificial expedients. We are so accustomed to give and receive assistance, that each of us singly can do little for himself; and there is scarce anyone among us, however contracted may be his form of life, who does not enjoy the labour of a thousand artists.

But a survey of the various nations that inhabit the earth will inform us that life may be supported with less assistance; and that the dexterity which practice enforced by necessity produces is able to effect much by very scanty means. The nations of Mexico and Peru erected cities and temples without the use of iron; and at this day the rude Indian supplies himself with all the necessaries of life: sent like the rest of mankind naked into the world, as soon as his parents have nursed him up to strength, he is to provide by his own labour for his own support. His first care is to find a sharp flint among the rocks; with this he undertakes to fell the trees of the forest; he shapes his bow, heads his arrows, builds his cottage, and hollows his canoe, and from that time lives in a state of plenty and prosperity; he is sheltered from the storms, he is fortified against beasts of prey, he is enabled to pursue the fish of the sea, and the deer of the mountains; and as he does not know, does not envy the happiness of polished nations, where gold can supply the want of fortitude and skill, and he whose laborious ancestors have made him rich, may lie stretched upon a couch, and see all the treasures of all the elements poured down before him.

This picture of a savage life if it shows how much individuals may perform, shows likewise how much society is to be desired. Though the perseverance and address of the Indian excite our admiration, they nevertheless cannot procure him the conveniences which are enjoyed by the vagrant beggar of a civilized country: he hunts like a wild beast to satisfy his hunger; and when he lies down to rest after a successful chase, cannot pronounce himself secure against the danger of perishing in a few days: he is, perhaps, content with his condition, because he knows not that a better is attainable by man; as he that is born blind does not long for the perception of light, because he cannot conceive the advantages which light would afford him; but hunger, wounds, and weariness are real evils, though he believes them equally incident to all his fellow creatures; and when a tempest compels him to lie starving in his hut, he cannot justly be concluded equally happy with those whom art has exempted from the power of chance, and who make the foregoing year provide for the following.

To receive and to communicate assistance, constitutes the happiness of human life: man may, indeed, preserve his existence in solitude, but can enjoy it only in society; the greatest understanding of an individual doomed to procure food and clothing for himself, will barely supply him with expedients to keep off death from day to day; but as one of a large community performing only his share of the common business, he gains leisure for intellectual pleasures, and enjoys the happiness of reason and reflection.

Biography and Autobiography

Biography

Rambler no. 60, October 13, 1750: The value of biography

—Quid sit pulchrum, quid turpe, quid utile, quid non,
Plenius et melius Chrysippo et Crantore dicit.

Horace, Epistles, I.2. 3–4

Whose works the beautiful and base contain;
Of vice and virtue more instructive rules,
Than all the sober sages of the schools.

transl. Philip Francis

All joy or sorrow for the happiness or calamities of others is produced by an act of the imagination, that realizes the event however fictitious, or approximates it however remote, by placing us, for a time, in the condition of him whose fortune we contemplate; so that we feel, while the deception lasts, whatever motions would be excited by the same good or evil happening to ourselves.

Our passions are therefore more strongly moved, in proportion as we can more readily adopt the pains or pleasure proposed to our minds, by recognizing them as once our own, or considering them as naturally incident to our state of life. It is not easy for the most artful writer to give us an interest in happiness or misery, which we think ourselves never likely to feel, and with which we have never yet been made acquainted. Histories of the downfall of kingdoms and revolutions of empires are read with great tranquillity; the imperial tragedy pleases common auditors only by its pomp of ornament, and grandeur of ideas; and the man whose faculties have been engrossed by business, and whose heart never fluttered but at the rise or fall of the stocks, wonders how the attention can be seized, or the affection agitated, by a tale of love.

Those parallel circumstances and kindred images, to which we readily conform our minds, are, above all other writings, to be found in narratives of the lives of particular persons; and therefore no species of writing seems more worthy of cultivation than biography, since none can be more delightful or more useful, none can more certainly enchain the heart by irresistible interest, or more widely diffuse instruction to every diversity of condition.

The general and rapid narratives of history, which involve a thousand fortunes in the business of a day, and complicate innumerable incidents in one great transaction, afford few lessons applicable to private life, which derives its comforts and its wretchedness from the right or wrong management of things, which nothing but their frequency makes considerable, "Parva, si non fiant quotidie," says Pliny,[1] and which can have no place in those relations which never descend below the consultation of senates, the motions of armies, and the schemes of conspirators.

I have often thought that there has rarely passed a life of which a judicious and faithful narrative would not be useful. For, not only every man has, in the mighty mass of the world, great numbers in the same condition with himself, to whom his mistakes and miscarriages, escapes and expedients, would be of immediate and apparent use; but there is such an uniformity in the state of man, considered apart from adventitious and separable decorations and disguises, that there is scarce any possibility of good or ill, but is common to human kind. A great part of the time of those who are placed at the greatest distance by fortune, or by temper, must unavoidably pass in the same manner; and though, when the claims of nature are satisfied, caprice, and vanity, and accident begin to produce discriminations and peculiarities, yet the eye is not very heedful or quick which cannot discover the same causes still terminating their influence in the same effects, though sometimes accelerated, sometimes retarded, or perplexed by multiplied combinations. We are all prompted by the same motives, all deceived by the same fallacies, all animated by hope, obstructed by danger, entangled by desire, and seduced by pleasure.

It is frequently objected to relations of particular lives, that they are not distinguished by any striking or wonderful vicissitudes. The scholar who passed his life among his books, the merchant who conducted only his own affairs, the priest whose sphere of action was not extended beyond that of his duty, are considered as no proper objects of public regard, however they might have excelled in their several stations, whatever might have been their learning, integrity, and piety. But this notion arises from false measures of excellence and dignity, and must be eradicated by considering that in the esteem of uncorrupted reason, what is of most use is of most value.

It is, indeed, not improper to take honest advantages of prejudice, and to gain attention by a celebrated name; but the business of a biographer is often to pass slightly over those performances and incidents which produce vulgar greatness, to lead the thoughts into domestic privacies, and display the minute details of daily life, where exterior appendages are cast aside, and men excel each other only by prudence and by virtue. The account of Thuanus is, with great propriety, said by its author to have been written that it might lay open to posterity the private and familiar character of that man, "cujus ingenium et candorem ex ipsius scriptis sunt olim semper miraturi," whose candour and genius will to the end of time be by his writings preserved in admiration.[2]

There are many invisible circumstances which, whether we read as inquirers after natural and moral knowledge, whether we intend to enlarge our science or increase our virtue, are more important than public occurrences. Thus Sallust, the great master of nature, has not forgot, in his account of Cataline, to remark that "his walk was now quick, and again slow," as an indication of a mind revolving something with violent commotion.[3] Thus the story of Melancthon affords a striking lecture on the value of time, by informing us that when he made an appointment, he expected not only the hour, but the minute to be fixed, that the day might not run out in the idleness of suspense[4]: and all the plans and enterprises of [John] De Witt are now of less importance to the world, than that part of his personal character, which represents him as "careful of his health, and negligent of his life."[5]

But biography has often been allotted to writers who seem very little acquainted with the nature of their task, or very negligent about the performance. They rarely afford any other account than might be collected from public papers, but imagine themselves writing a life when they exhibit a chronological series of actions or preferments; and so little regard the manners or behaviour of their heroes, that more knowledge may be gained of a man's real character by a short conversation with one of his servants than from a formal and studied narrative, begun with his pedigree, and ended with his funeral.

If now and then they condescend to inform the world of particular facts, they are not always so happy as to select the most important. I know not well what advantage posterity can receive from the only circumstance by which [Thomas] Tickell has distinguished Addison from the rest of mankind, "the irregularity of his pulse"[6]: nor can I think myself overpaid for the time spent in reading the life of Malherb by being enabled to relate after the learned biographer, that Malherb had two predominant opinions; one, that the looseness of a single woman might destroy all her boast of ancient descent; the other, that the French beggars made use very improperly and barbarously of the phrase "noble Gentleman," because either word included the sense of both.

There are, indeed, some natural reasons why these narratives are often written by such as were not likely to give much instruction or delight, and why most accounts of particular persons are barren and useless. If a life be delayed till interest and envy are at an end, we may hope for impartiality, but must expect little intelligence; for the incidents which give excellence to biography are of a volatile and evanescent kind, such as soon escape the memory, and are rarely transmitted by tradition. We know how few can portray a living acquaintance, except by his most prominent and observable particularities and the grosser features of his mind; and it may be easily imagined how much of this little knowledge may be lost in im-parting it, and how soon a succession of copies will lose all resemblance of the original.

If the biographer writes from personal knowledge, and makes haste to gratify the public curiosity, there is danger lest his interest, his fear, his gratitude, or his tenderness, overpower his fidelity, and tempt him to con-ceal, if not to invent. There are many who think it an act of piety to hide the faults or failings of their friends, even when they can no longer suffer by their detection; we therefore see whole ranks of characters adorned with uniform panegyric, and not to be known from one another, but by extrinsic and casual circumstances. "Let me remember," says Hale, "when I find myself inclined to pity a criminal, that there is likewise a pity due to the country."[7] If we owe regard to the memory of the dead, there is yet more respect to be paid to knowledge, to virtue, and to truth.

Idler no. 84, November 24, 1759: The uses of biography

Biography is, of the various kinds of narrative writing, that which is most eagerly read, and most easily applied to the purposes of life.

In romances, when the wide field of possibility lies open to invention, the incidents may easily be made more numerous, the vicissitudes more sudden, and the events more wonderful; but from the time of life when fancy begins to be overruled by reason and corrected by experience, the most artful tale raises little curiosity when it is known to be false; though it may, perhaps, be sometimes read as a model of a neat or elegant style, not for the sake of knowing what it contains, but how it is written; or those that are weary of themselves may have recourse to it as a pleasing dream, of which, when they awake, they voluntarily dismiss the images from their minds.

The examples and events of history press, indeed, upon the mind with the weight of truth; but when they are reposited in the memory, they are oftener employed for show than use, and rather diversify conversation than regulate life. Few are engaged in such scenes as give them opportuni-ties of growing wiser by the downfall of statesmen or the defeat of gener-als. The stratagems of war and the intrigues of courts are read by far the greater part of mankind with the same indifference as the adventures of fabled heroes, or the revolutions of a fairy region. Between falsehood and useless truth there is little difference. As gold which he cannot spend will make no man rich, so knowledge which he cannot apply will make no man wise.

The mischievous consequences of vice and folly, of irregular desires and predominant passions, are best discovered by those relations which are levelled with the general surface of life, which tell not how any man became great, but how he was made happy; not how he lost the favour of his prince, but how he became discontented with himself.

Those relations are, therefore, commonly of most value in which the writer tells his own story. He that recounts the life of another, commonly dwells most upon conspicuous events, lessens the familiarity of his tale to increase its dignity, shows his favourite at a distance, decorated and magnified like the ancient actors in their tragic dress, and endeavours to hide the man that he may produce a hero.

But if it be true, which was said by a French prince, "that no man was a hero to the servants of his chamber," it is equally true, that every man is yet less a hero to himself. He that is most elevated above the crowd by the importance of his employments, or the reputation of his genius, feels himself affected by fame or business but as they influence his domestic life. The high and low, as they have the same faculties and the same senses, have no less similitude in their pains and pleasures. The sensations are the same in all, though produced by very different occasions. The prince feels the same pain when an invader seizes a province, as the farmer when a thief drives away his cow. Men thus equal in themselves will appear equal in honest and impartial biography; and those whom fortune or nature place at the greatest distance may afford instruction to each other.

The writer of his own life has, at least, the first qualification of an historian, the knowledge of the truth; and though it may be plausibly objected that his temptations to disguise it are equal to his opportunities of knowing it, yet I cannot but think that impartiality may be expected with equal confidence from him that relates the passages of his own life, as from him that delivers the transactions of another.

Certainty of knowledge not only excludes mistake, but fortifies veracity. What we collect by conjecture, and by conjecture only, can one man judge of another's motives or sentiments, is easily modified by fancy or by desire; as objects imperfectly discerned take forms from the hope or fear of the beholder. But that which is fully known cannot be falsified but with reluctance of understanding, and alarm of conscience; of understanding, the lover of truth; of conscience, the sentinel of virtue.

He that writes the life of another is either his friend or his enemy, and wishes either to exalt his praise or aggravate his infamy; many temptations to falsehood will occur in the disguise of passions, too specious to fear much resistance. Love of virtue will animate panegyric, and hatred of wickedness embitter censure. The zeal of gratitude, the ardour of patriotism, fondness for an opinion, or fidelity to a party, may easily overpower the vigilance of a mind habitually well disposed, and prevail over unassisted and unfriended veracity.

But he that speaks of himself has no motive to falsehood or partiality except self-love, by which all have so often been betrayed, that all are on the watch against its artifices. He that writes an apology for a single action, to confute an accusation, or recommend himself to favour, is, indeed, always to be suspected of favouring his own cause; but he that sits down calmly and voluntarily to review his life for the admonition of posterity, or to amuse himself, and leaves this account unpublished, may be commonly presumed to tell truth, since falsehood cannot appease his own mind, and fame will not be heard beneath the tomb.

Idler no. 102, March 29, 1760: The value of an author's autobiography

It very seldom happens to man that his business is his pleasure. What is done from necessity is so often to be done when against the present inclination, and so often fills the mind with anxiety, that an habitual dislike steals upon us, and we shrink involuntarily from the remembrance of our task. This is the reason why almost every one wishes to quit his employment; he does not like another state, but is disgusted with his own.

From this unwillingness to perform more than is required of that which is commonly performed with reluctance, it proceeds that few authors write their own lives. Statesmen, courtiers, ladies, generals, and seamen have given to the world their own stories, and the events with which their different stations have made them acquainted. They retired to the closet as to a place of quiet and amusement, and pleased themselves with writing, because they could lay down the pen whenever they were weary. But the author, however conspicuous, or however important, either in the public eye or in his own, leaves his life to be related by his successors, for he cannot gratify his vanity but by sacrificing his ease.

It is commonly supposed that the uniformity of a studious life affords no matter for a narration; but the truth is that of the most studious life a great part passes without study. An author partakes of the common condition of humanity; he is born and married like another man; he has hopes and fears, expectations and disappointments, griefs and joys, and friends and enemies, like a courtier or a statesman; nor can I conceive why his affairs should not excite curiosity as much as the whisper of a drawing-room or the factions of a camp.

Nothing detains the reader's attention more powerfully than deep involutions of distress, or sudden vicissitudes of fortune; and these might be abundantly afforded by memoirs of the sons of literature. They are entangled by contracts which they know not how to fulfil, and obliged to write on subjects which they do not understand. Every publication is a new period of time from which some increase or declension of fame is to be reckoned. The gradations of a hero's life are from battle to battle, and of an author's from book to book.

Success and miscarriage have the same effects in all conditions. The prosperous are feared, hated, and flattered; and the unfortunate avoided, pitied, and despised. No sooner is a book published than the writer may judge of the opinion of the world. If his acquaintance press round him in public places, or salute him from the other side of the street; if invitations to dinner come thick upon him, and those with whom he dines keep him to supper; if the ladies turn to him when his coat is plain, and the footmen serve him with attention and alacrity; he may be sure that his work has been praised by some leader of literary fashions.

Of declining reputation the symptoms are not less easily observed. If the author enters a coffee-house, he has a box to himself; if he calls at a bookseller's, the boy turns his back and, what is the most fatal of all prognostics, authors will visit him in a morning, and talk to him hour after hour of the malevolence of critics, the neglect of merit, the bad taste of the age and the candour of posterity.

All this modified and varied by accident and custom would form very amusing scenes of biography, and might recreate many a mind which is very little delighted with conspiracies or battles, intrigues of a court, or debates of a parliament; to this might be added all the changes of the countenance of a patron, traced from the first glow which flattery raises in his cheek, through ardour of fondness, vehemence of promise, magnificence of praise, excuse of delay, and lamentation of inability, to the last chill look of final dismission, when the one grows weary of soliciting, and the other of hearing solicitation.

Thus copious are the materials which have been hitherto suffered to lie neglected, while the repositories of every family that has produced a soldier or a minister are ransacked, and libraries are crowded with useless folios of state papers which will never be read, and which contribute nothing to valuable knowledge.

I hope the learned will be taught to know their own strength and their value, and, instead of devoting their lives to the honour of those who seldom thank them for their labours, resolve at last to do justice to themselves.

Autobiography

[The following essays may be seen to have autobiographical relevance to Johnson at various points in his life.]

Rambler no. 89, January 22, 1751:
Dangers of "airy gratifications" and lonely fantasies

Dulce est desipere in loco.

Horace, Odes, IV. 12. 28

Wisdom at proper times is well forgot.

Locke, whom there is no reason to suspect of being a favourer of idleness or libertinism, has advanced, that whoever hopes to employ any part of his time with efficacy and vigour, must allow some of it to pass in trifles. It is beyond the powers of humanity to spend a whole life in profound study and intense meditation, and the most rigorous exacters of industry and seriousness have appointed hours for relaxation and amusement.

It is certain that, with or without our consent, many of the few moments allotted us will slide imperceptibly away, and that the mind will break, from confinement to its stated task, into sudden excursions. Severe and connected attention is preserved but for a short time; and when a man shuts himself up in his closet, and bends his thoughts to the discussion of any abstruse question, he will find his faculties continually stealing away to more pleasing entertainments. He often perceives himself transported, he knows not how, to distant tracts of thought, and returns to his first object as from a dream, without knowing when he forsook it, or how long he has been abstracted from it.

It has been observed that the most studious are not always the most learned. There is, indeed, no great difficulty in discovering that this difference of proficiency may arise from the difference of intellectual powers, of the choice of books, or the convenience of information. But I believe it likewise frequently happens that the most recluse are not the most vigorous prosecutors of study. Many impose upon the world, and many upon themselves, by an appearance of severe and exemplary diligence, when they, in reality, give themselves up to the luxury of fancy, please their minds with regulating the past, or planning out the future; place themselves at will in varied situations of happiness, and slumber away their days in voluntary visions. In the journey of life some are left behind, because they are naturally feeble and slow; some because they miss the way, and many because they leave it by choice, and instead of pressing onward with a steady pace, delight themselves with momentary deviations, turn aside to pluck every flower, and repose in every shade.

There is nothing more fatal to a man whose business is to think than to have learned the art of regaling his mind with those airy gratifications. Other vices or follies are restrained by fear, reformed by admonition, or rejected by the conviction which the comparison of our conduct with that of others may in time produce. But this invisible riot of the mind, this secret prodigality of being, is secure from detection, and fearless of reproach. The dreamer retires to his apartments, shuts out the cares and interruptions of mankind, and abandons himself to his own fancy; new worlds rise up before him, one image is followed by another, and a long succession of delights dances round him. He is at last called back to life by nature, or by custom, and enters peevish into society, because he cannot model it to his own will. He returns from his idle excursions with the asperity, though not with the knowledge of a student, and hastens again to the same felicity with the eagerness of a man bent upon the advancement of some favourite science. The infatuation strengthens by degrees, and like the poison of opiates, weakens his powers, without any external symptoms of malignity.

It happens, indeed, that these hypocrites of learning are in time detected, and convinced by disgrace and disappointment of the difference between the labour of thought, and the sport of musing. But this discovery is often not made till it is too late to recover the time that has been fooled away. A thousand accidents may, indeed, awaken drones to a more early sense of their danger and their shame. But they who are convinced of the necessity of breaking from this habitual drowsiness, too often relapse in spite of their resolution; for these ideal seducers are always near, and neither any particularity of time nor place is necessary to their influence; they invade the soul without warning, and have often charmed down resistance before their approach is perceived or suspected.

This captivity, however, it is necessary for every man to break, who has any desire to be wise or useful, to pass his life with the esteem of others, or to look back with satisfaction from his old age upon his earlier years. In order to regain liberty, he must find the means of flying from himself; he must, in opposition to the Stoic precept, teach his desires to fix upon external things; he must adopt the joys and the pains of others, and excite in his mind the want of social pleasures and amicable communication.

It is perhaps not impossible to promote the cure of this mental malady by close application to some new study, which may pour in fresh ideas, and keep curiosity in perpetual motion. But study requires solitude, and solitude is a state dangerous to those who are too much accustomed to sink into themselves. Active employment or public pleasure is generally a necessary part of this intellectual regimen, without which, though some remission may be obtained, a complete cure will scarcely be effected.

This is a formidable and obstinate disease of the intellect, of which, when it has once become radicated[8] by time, the remedy is one of the hardest tasks of reason and of virtue. Its slightest attacks, therefore, should be watchfully opposed; and he that finds the frigid and narcotic infection beginning to seize him, should turn his whole attention against it, and check it at the first discovery by proper counteraction.

The great resolution to be formed, when happiness and virtue are thus formidably invaded, is, that no part of life be spent in a state of neutrality or indifference; but that some pleasure be found for every moment that is not devoted to labour; and that, whenever the necessary business of life grows irksome or disgusting, an immediate transition be made to diversion and gaiety.

After the exercises which the health of the body requires, and which have themselves a natural tendency to actuate and invigorate the mind, the most eligible amusement of a rational being seems to be that interchange of thoughts which is practised in free and easy conversation; where suspicion is banished by experience, and emulation by benevolence; where every man speaks with no other restraint than unwillingness to offend, and hears with no other disposition than desire to be pleased.

There must be a time in which every man trifles; and the only choice that nature offers us is to trifle in company or alone. To join profit with pleasure has been an old precept among men who have had very different conceptions of profit. All have agreed that our amusements should not terminate wholly in the present moment, but contribute more or less to future advantage. He that amuses himself among well-chosen companions, can scarcely fail to receive, from the most careless and obstreperous merriment which virtue can allow, some useful hints; nor can converse on the most familiar topics without some casual information. The loose sparkles of thoughtless wit may give new light to the mind, and the gay contention for paradoxical positions rectify the opinions.

This is the time in which those friendships that give happiness or consolation, relief or security, are generally formed. A wise and good man is never so amiable as in his unbended and familiar intervals. Heroic generosity or philosophical discoveries may compel veneration and respect, but love always implies some kind of natural or voluntary equality, and is only to be excited by that levity and cheerfulness which disencumber all minds from awe and solicitude, invite the modest to freedom, and exalt the timorous to confidence. This easy gaiety is certain to please, whatever be the character of him that exerts it; if our superiors descend from their elevation, we love them for lessening the distance at which we are placed below them; and inferiors, from whom we can receive no lasting advantage, will always keep our affections while their sprightliness and mirth contribute to our pleasure.

Every man finds himself differently affected by the sight of fortresses of war, and palaces of pleasure; we look on the height and strength of the bulwarks with a kind of gloomy satisfaction, for we cannot think of defence without admitting images of danger, but we range delighted and jocund through the gay apartments of the palace, because nothing is impressed by them on the mind but joy and festivity. Such is the difference between great and amiable characters; with protectors we are safe, with companions we are happy.

Rambler no. 117, April 30, 1751: The advantages of living in a garret

The gods they challenge, and affect the skies:
Heav'd on Olympus tott'ring Ossa stood;
On Ossa, Pelion nods with all his wood.
transl. Pope, *Odyssey*, XI, 315–316

To the Rambler.
Sir,
Nothing has more retarded the advancement of learning than the disposition of vulgar minds to ridicule and vilify what they cannot comprehend. All industry must be excited by hope; and as the student often proposes no other reward to himself than praise, he is easily discouraged by contempt and insult. He who brings with him into a clamorous multitude the timidity of recluse speculation, and has never hardened his front in public life, or accustomed his passions to the vicissitudes and accidents,

the triumphs and defeats of mixed conversation, will blush at the stare of petulant incredulity, and suffer himself to be driven by a burst of laughter from the fortresses of demonstration. The mechanist will be afraid to assert before hardy contradiction, the possibility of tearing down bulwarks with a silkworm's thread; and the astronomer of relating the rapidity of light, the distance of the fixed stars, and the height of the lunar mountains.

If I could by any efforts have shaken off this cowardice, I had not sheltered myself under a borrowed name, nor applied to you for the means of communicating to the public the theory of a garret; a subject which, except some slight and transient strictures, has been hitherto neglected by those who were best qualified to adorn it, either for want of leisure to prosecute the various researches in which a nice discussion must engage them, or because it requires such diversity of knowledge, and such extent of curiosity, as is scarcely to be found in any single intellect: or perhaps others foresaw the tumults which would be raised against them, and confined their knowledge to their own breasts, and abandoned prejudice and folly to the direction of chance.

That the professors of literature generally reside in the highest stories, has been immemorially observed. The wisdom of the ancients was well acquainted with the intellectual advantages of an elevated situation: why else were the Muses stationed on Olympus or Parnassus, by those who could with equal right have raised them bowers in the vale of Tempe, or erected their altars among the flexures of Meander? Why was Jove himself nursed upon a mountain? or why did the goddesses, when the prize of beauty was contested, try the cause upon the top of Ida? Such were the fictions by which the great masters of the earlier ages endeavoured to inculcate to posterity the importance of a garret, which, though they had been long obscured by the negligence and ignorance of succeeding times, were well enforced by the celebrated symbol of Pythagoras . . . "when the wind blows, worship its echo." This could not but be understood by his disciples as an inviolable injunction to live in a garret, which I have found frequently visited by the echo and the wind. Nor was the tradition wholly obliterated in the age of Augustus, for Tibullus evidently congratulates himself upon his garret, not without some allusion to the Pythagorean precept:

Quàm juvat immites ventos audire cubantem—
Aut, gelidas hybernus aquas cùm fuderit auster,
   Securum somnos, imbre juvante, sequi!
                     Elegies, I.l. 45, 47–48

How sweet in sleep to pass the careless hours,
Lull'd by the beating winds and dashing show'rs!

And it is impossible not to discover the fondness of Lucretius, an earlier writer, for a garret, in his description of the lofty towers of serene learning, and of the pleasure with which a wise man looks down upon the confused and erratic state of the world moving below him:

Sed nil dulcius est, bene quàm munita tenere
Editâ doctrinâ sapientum templa serena;
Despicere unde queas alios, passimque videre
Errare, atque viam palanteis quaerere vitae.
               De Rerum Natura, II. 7–10

—'Tis sweet thy lab'ring steps to guide
To virtue's heights, with wisdom well supply'd,
And all the magazines of learning fortify'd:
From thence to look below on human kind,
Bewilder'd in the maze of life, and blind.
                    transl. Dryden

The institution has, indeed, continued to our own time; the garret is still the usual receptacle of the philosopher and poet; but this, like many ancient customs, is perpetuated only by an accidental imitation, without knowledge of the original reason for which it was established.

Causa latet; res est notissima.
        Ovid, *Metamorphoses,* IV. 287

The cause is secret, but th' effect is known.
                    transl. Addison

Conjectures have, indeed, been advanced concerning these habitations of literature, but without much satisfaction to the judicious inquirer. Some have imagined that the garret is generally chosen by the wits as most easily rented; and concluded that no man rejoices in his aerial abode, but on the days of payment. Others suspect that a garret is chiefly convenient, as it is remoter than any other part of the house from the outer door, which is often observed to be infested by visitants, who talk incessantly of beer, or linen, or a coat, and repeat the same sounds every morning, and sometimes again in the afternoon, without any variation, except that they grow daily more importunate and clamorous, and raise their voices in time from mournful murmurs to raging vociferations. This eternal monotony is always detestable to a man whose chief pleasure is to enlarge his knowledge, and vary his ideas. Others talk of freedom from noise, and abstraction from common business or amusements; and some, yet more visionary, tell us, that the faculties are enlarged by open prospects, and that the fancy is at more liberty, when the eye ranges without confinement.

These conveniences may perhaps all be found in a well-chosen garret; but surely they cannot be supposed sufficiently important to have operated invariably upon different climates, distant ages, and separate nations. Of an universal practice, there must still be presumed an universal cause, which, however recondite and abstruse, may be perhaps reserved to make me illustrious by its discovery, and you by its promulgation.

It is universally known that the faculties of the mind are invigorated or weakened by the state of the body, and that the body is in a great measure regulated by the various compressions of the ambient element. The effects of the air in the production or cure of corporeal maladies have been acknowledged from the time of Hippocrates; but no man has yet sufficiently considered how far it may influence the operations of the genius, though every day affords instances of local understanding, of wits and reasoners, whose faculties are adapted to some single spot, and who, when they are removed to any other place, sink at once into silence and stupidity. I have discovered, by a long series of observations, that invention and elocution suffer great impediments from dense and impure vapours, and that the tenuity of a defecated air at a proper distance from the surface of the earth accelerates the fancy, and sets at liberty those intellectual powers which were before shackled by too strong attraction, and unable to expand themselves under the pressure of a gross atmosphere. I have found dulness to quicken into sentiment in a thin ether, as water, though not very hot, boils in a receiver partly exhausted; and heads, in appearance empty, have teemed with notions upon rising ground, as the flaccid sides of a football would have swelled out into stiffness and extension.

For this reason I never think myself qualified to judge decisively of any man's faculties, whom I have only known in one degree of elevation; but take some opportunity of attending him from the cellar to the garret, and try upon him all the various degrees of rarefaction and condensation, tension and laxity. If he is neither vivacious aloft, nor serious below, I then consider him as hopeless; but as it seldom happens, that I do not find the temper to which the texture of his brain is fitted, I accommodate him in time with a tube of mercury, first marking the points most favourable to his intellects, according to rules which I have long studied, and which I may, perhaps, reveal to mankind in a complete treatise of barometrical pneumatology.

Another cause of the gaiety and sprightliness of the dwellers in garrets is probably the increase of that vertiginous motion, with which we are carried round by the diurnal revolution of the earth. The power of agitation upon the spirits is well known; every man has felt his heart lightened in a rapid vehicle, or on a galloping horse; and nothing is plainer, than that he who towers to the fifth story, is whirled through more space by every circumrotation, than another that grovels upon the ground floor. The nations between the topics are known to be fiery, inconstant, inventive, and fanciful; because, living at the utmost length of the earth's diameter, they are carried about with more swiftness than those whom nature has placed nearer to the poles; and therefore, as it becomes a wise man to struggle with the inconveniences of his country, whenever celerity and acuteness are requisite, we must actuate our languor by taking a few turns round the centre in a garret.

If you imagine that I ascribe to air and motion effects which they cannot produce, I desire you to consult your own memory, and consider whether you have never known a man acquire reputation in his garret, which, when fortune or a patron had placed him upon the first floor, he was unable to maintain; and who never recovered his former vigour of understanding, till he was restored to his original situation. That a garret will make every man a wit, I am very far from supposing; I know there are some who would continue blockheads even on the summit of the Andes, or on the peak of Tenerife. But let not any man be considered as unimprovable till this potent remedy has been tried; for perhaps he was formed to be great only in a garret, as the joiner of Aretaeus was rational in no other place but his own shop.

I think a frequent removal to various distances from the centre, so necessary to a just estimate of intellectual abilities, and consequently of so great use in education, that if I hoped that the public could be persuaded to so expensive an experiment, I would propose that there should be a cavern dug, and a tower erected, like those which Bacon describes in Solomon's house, for the expansion and concentration of understanding, according to the exigency of different employments, or constitutions. Perhaps some that fume away in meditations upon time and space in the tower, might compose tables of interest at a certain depth; and he that upon level ground stagnates in silence, or creeps in narrative, might at the height of half a mile, ferment into merriment, sparkle with repartee, and froth with declamation.

Addison observes that we may find the heat of Virgil's climate in some lines of his Georgic: so, when I read a composition, I immediately determine the height of the author's habitation. As an elaborate performance is commonly said to smell of the lamp, my commendation of a noble thought, a sprightly sally, or a bold figure, is to pronounce it fresh from the garret; an expression which would break from me upon the perusal of most of your papers, did I not believe, that you sometimes quit the garret, and ascend into the cock-loft.

HYPERTATUS

Rambler no. 134, June 29, 1751: Causes of idleness

Quis scit, an adjiciant hodiernae crastina summae
Tempora Dî superi!

Horace, *Odes*, IV.7. 17–18

Who knows if Heav'n, with ever-bounteous pow'r,
Shall add to-morrow to the present hour?

transl. Philip Francis

I sat yesterday morning employed in deliberating on which among the various subjects that occurred to my imagination I should bestow the paper of today. After a short effort of meditation by which nothing was determined, I grew every moment more irresolute, my ideas wandered from the first intention, and I rather wished to think, than thought upon any settled subject; till at last I was awakened from this dream of study by a summons from the press: the time was come for which I had been thus negligently purposing to provide, and, however dubious or sluggish, I was now necessitated to write.

Though to a writer whose design is so comprehensive and miscellaneous, that he may accommodate himself with a topic from every scene of life, or view of nature, it is no great aggravation of his task to be obliged to a sudden composition; yet I could not forbear to reproach myself for having so long neglected what was unavoidably to be done, and of which every moment's idleness increased the difficulty. There was however some pleasure in reflecting that I, who had only trifled till diligence was necessary, might still congratulate myself upon my superiority to multitudes, who have trifled till diligence is vain; who can by no degree of activity or resolution recover the opportunities which have slipped away; and who are condemned by their own carelessness to hopeless calamity and barren sorrow.

The folly of allowing ourselves to delay what we know cannot be finally escaped, is one of the general weaknesses which, in spite of the instruction of moralists and the remonstrances of reason, prevail to a greater or less degree in every mind: even they who most steadily withstand it, find it, if not the most violent, the most pertinacious of their passions, always renewing its attacks, and though often vanquished, never destroyed.

It is indeed natural to have particular regard to the time present, and to be most solicitous for that which is by its nearness enabled to make the strongest impressions. When therefore any sharp pain is to be suffered, or any formidable danger to be incurred, we can scarcely exempt ourselves wholly from the seducements of imagination; we readily believe that another day will bring some support or advantage which we now want; and are easily persuaded that the moment of necessity which we desire never to arrive, is at a great distance from us.

Thus life is languished away in the gloom of anxiety, and consumed in collecting resolutions which the next morning dissipates; in forming purposes which we scarcely hope to keep, and reconciling ourselves to our own cowardice by excuses which, while we admit them, we know to be absurd. Our firmness is by the continual contemplation of misery, hourly impaired; every submission to our fear enlarges its dominion; we not only waste that time in which the evil we dread might have been suffered and surmounted, but even where procrastination produces no absolute increase of our difficulties, make them less superable to ourselves by habitual terrors. When evils cannot be avoided, it is wise to contract the interval of expectation; to meet the mischiefs which will overtake us if we fly; and suffer only their real malignity, without the conflicts of doubt, and anguish of anticipation.

To act is far easier than to suffer; yet we every day see the progress of life retarded by the *vis inertiae,* the mere repugnance to motion, and find multitudes repining at the want of that which nothing but idleness hinders them from enjoying. The case of Tantalus, in the region of poetic punishment, was somewhat to be pitied, because the fruits that hung about him retired from his hand; but what tenderness can be claimed by those who, though perhaps they suffer the pains of Tantalus, will never lift their hands for their own relief?

There is nothing more common among this torpid generation than murmurs and complaints; murmurs at uneasiness which only vacancy and suspicion expose them to feel, and complaints of distresses which it is in their own power to remove. Laziness is commonly associated with timidity. Either fear originally prohibits endeavours by infusing despair of success; or the frequent failure of irresolute struggles, and the constant desire of avoiding labour, impress by degrees false terrors on the mind. But fear, whether natural or acquired, when once it has full possession of the fancy, never fails to employ it upon visions of calamity, such as, if they are not dissipated by useful employment, will soon overcast it with horrors, and embitter life not only with those miseries by which all earthly beings are really more or less tormented, but with those which do not yet exist, and which can only be discerned by the perspicacity of cowardice.

Among all who sacrifice future advantage to present inclination, scarcely any gain so little as those that suffer themselves to freeze in idleness. Others are corrupted by some enjoyment of more or less power to gratify the passions; but to neglect our duties, merely to avoid the labour of performing them, a labour which is always punctually rewarded, is surely to sink under weak temptations. Idleness never can secure tranquillity; the call of reason and of conscience will pierce the closest pavilion of the sluggard, and though it may not have force to drive him from his down, will be loud enough to hinder him from sleep. Those moments which he cannot resolve to make useful, by devoting them to the great business of his being, will still be usurped by powers that will not leave them to his disposal; remorse and vexation will seize upon them, and forbid him to enjoy what he is so desirous to appropriate.

There are other causes of inactivity incident to more active faculties and more acute discernment. He to whom many objects of pursuit arise at the same time, will frequently hesitate between different desires, till a rival has precluded him, or change his course as new attractions prevail, and harass himself without advancing. He who sees different ways to the same end, will, unless he watches carefully over his own conduct, lay out too much of his attention upon the comparison of probabilities, and the adjustment of expedients, and pause in the choice of his road till some accident intercepts his journey. He whose penetration extends to remote consequences, and who, whenever he applies his attention to any design, discovers new prospects of advantage and possibilities of improvement, will not easily be persuaded that his project is ripe for execution; but will superadd one contrivance to another, endeavour to unite various purposes in one operation, multiply complications, and refine niceties, till he is entangled in his own scheme, and bewildered in the perplexity of various intentions. He that resolves to unite all the beauties of situation in a new purchase, must waste his life in roving to no purpose from province to province. He that hopes in the same house to obtain every convenience, may draw plans and study Palladio, but will never lay a stone. He will attempt a treatise on some important subject, and amass materials, consult authors, and study all the dependant and collateral parts of learning, but never conclude himself qualified to write. He that has abilities to conceive perfection, will not easily be content without it; and since perfection cannot be reached, will lose the opportunity of doing well in the vain hope of unattainable excellence.

The certainty that life cannot be long, and the probability that it will be much shorter than nature allows, ought to awaken every man to the active prosecution of whatever he is desirous to perform. It is true, that no diligence can ascertain success; death may intercept the swiftest career; but he who is cut off in the execution of an honest undertaking, has at least the honour of falling in his rank, and has fought the battle though he missed the victory.

Rambler no. 161, October 1, 1751: The several garrets of a man of letters

Frail as the leaves that quiver on the sprays,
Like them man flourishes, like them decays.

Pope, *Iliad*, VI. 146

Mr. Rambler.
Sir,
You have formerly observed that curiosity often terminates in barren knowledge, and that the mind is prompted to study and inquiry rather by the uneasiness of ignorance, than the hope of profit. Nothing can be of less importance to any present interest, than the fortune of those who have been long lost in the grave, and from whom nothing now can be hoped or feared. Yet, to rouse the zeal of a true antiquary, little more is necessary than to mention a name which mankind have conspired to forget; he will make his way to remote scenes of action through obscurity and contradiction, as Tully sought amidst bushes and brambles the tomb of Archimedes.[9]

It is not easy to discover how it concerns him that gathers the produce, or receives the rent of an estate, to know through what families the land has passed, who is registered in the Conqueror's survey[10] as its possessor, how often it has been forfeited by treason, or how often sold by prodigality. The power or wealth of the present inhabitants of a country cannot be much increased by an inquiry after the names of those barbarians who destroyed one another twenty centuries ago, in contests for the shelter of woods, or convenience of pasturage. Yet we see that no man can be at rest in the enjoyment of a new purchase till he has learned the history of his grounds from the ancient inhabitants of the parish, and that no nation omits to record the actions of their ancestors, however bloody, savage, and rapacious.

The same disposition, as different opportunities call it forth, discovers itself in great or little things. I have always thought it unworthy of a wise man to slumber in total inactivity, only because he happens to have no employment equal to his ambition or genius; it is therefore my custom to apply my attention to the objects before me, and as I cannot think any place wholly unworthy of notice that affords a habitation to a man of letters, I have collected the history and antiquities of the several garrets in which I have resided.

> *Quantulacunque estis, vos ego magna voco.*
> Ovid, *Amores*, III.15. 14

> *How small to others, but how great to me!*

Many of these narratives my industry has been able to extend to a considerable length; but the woman with whom I now lodge has lived only eighteen months in the house, and can give no account of its ancient revolutions; the plasterer having, at her entrance, obliterated by his whitewash all the smoky memorials which former tenants had left upon the ceiling, and perhaps drawn the veil of oblivion over politicians, philosophers, and poets.

When I first cheapened my lodgings, the landlady told me that she hoped I was not an author, for the lodgers on the first floor had stipulated that the upper rooms should not be occupied by a noisy trade. I very readily promised to give no disturbance to her family, and soon dispatched a bargain on the usual terms.

I had not slept many nights in my new apartment before I began to inquire after my predecessors, and found my landlady, whose imagination is filled chiefly with her own affairs, very ready to give me information.

Curiosity, like all other desires, produces pain as well as pleasure. Before she began her narrative, I had heated my head with expectations of adventures and discoveries, of elegance in disguise, and learning in distress; and was somewhat mortified when I heard that the first tenant was a tailor, of whom nothing was remembered but that he complained of his room for want of light; and, after having lodged in it a month, and paid only a week's rent, pawned a piece of cloth which he was trusted to cut out, and was forced to make a precipitate retreat from this quarter of the town.

The next was a young woman newly arrived from the country, who lived for five weeks with great regularity, and became by frequent treats very much the favourite of the family, but at last received visits so frequently from a cousin in Cheapside, that she brought the reputation of the house into danger, and was therefore dismissed with good advice.

The room then stood empty for a fortnight; my landlady began to think that she had judged hardly, and often wished for such another lodger. At last, an elderly man of a grave aspect read the bill, and bargained for the room at the very first price that was asked. He lived in close retirement, seldom went out till evening, and then returned early, sometimes cheerful, and at other times dejected. It was remarkable, that whatever he purchased, he never had small money in his pocket; and, though cool and temperate on other occasions, was always vehement and stormy till he received his change. He paid his rent with great exactness, and seldom failed once a week to requite my landlady's civility with a supper. At last, such is the fate of human felicity, the house was alarmed at midnight by the constable, who demanded to search the garrets. My landlady assuring him that he had mistaken the door, conducted him upstairs, where he found the tools of a coiner; but the tenant had crawled along the roof to an empty house, and escaped; much to the joy of my landlady, who declares him a very honest man, and wonders why anybody should be hanged for making money when such numbers are in want of it. She however confesses that she shall, for the future, always question the character of those who take her garret without beating down the price.

The bill was then placed again in the window, and the poor woman was teased for seven weeks by innumerable passengers, who obliged her to climb with them every hour up five stories, and then disliked the prospect, hated the noise of a public street, thought the stairs narrow, objected to a low ceiling, required the walls to be hung with fresher paper, asked questions about the neighbourhood, could not think of living so far from their acquaintance, wished the windows had looked to the south rather than the west, told how the door and chimney might have been better disposed, bid her half the price that she asked, or promised to give her earnest the next day, and came no more.

At last, a short meagre man, in a tarnished waistcoat, desired to see the garret, and when he had stipulated for two long shelves, and a larger table, hired it at a low rate. When the affair was completed, he looked round him with great satisfaction, and repeated some words which the woman did not understand. In two days he brought a great box of books, took possession of his room, and lived very inoffensively, except that he frequently disturbed the inhabitants of the next floor by unseasonable noises. He was generally in bed at noon, but from evening to midnight he sometimes talked aloud with great vehemence, sometimes stamped as in rage, sometimes threw down his poker, then clattered his chairs, then sat down in deep thought, and again burst out into loud vociferations; sometimes he would sigh as oppressed with misery, and sometimes shaken with convulsive laughter. When he encountered any of the family, he gave way or bowed, but rarely spoke, except that as he went upstairs he often repeated,

> *This habitant th'aerial regions boast.*
> Hesiod, *Works and Days,* l. 8

hard words, to which his neighbours listened so often, that they learned them without understanding them. What was his employment she did not venture to ask him, but at last heard a printer's boy inquire for the author.

My landlady was very often advised to beware of this strange man, who, though he was quiet for the present, might perhaps become outrageous in the hot months; but, as she was punctually paid, she could not find any sufficient reason for dismissing him, till one night he convinced her, by setting fire to his curtains, that it was not safe to have an author for her inmate.

She had then for six weeks a succession of tenants, who left the house on Saturday, and, instead of paying their rent, stormed at their landlady. At last she took in two sisters, one of whom had spent her little fortune in procuring remedies for a lingering disease, and was now supported and attended by the other: she climbed with difficulty to the apartment, where she languished eight weeks without impatience, or lamentation, except for the expense and fatigue which her sister suffered, and then calmly and contentedly expired. The sister followed her to the grave, paid the few debts which they had contracted, wiped away the tears of useless sorrow, and, returning to the business of common life, resigned to me the vacant habitation.

Such, Mr. *Rambler*, are the changes which have happened in the narrow space where my present fortune has fixed my residence. So true it is that amusement and instruction are always at hand for those who have skill and willingness to find them; and, so just is the observation of Juvenal,[11] that a single house will show whatever is done or suffered in the world.

I am, Sir, &c.

Rambler no. 163, October 8, 1751: The perils of having a patron

Mitte superba pati fastidia, spemque caducam
  Despice; vive tibi, nam moriere tibi.

Seneca

Bow to no patron's insolence; rely
On no frail hopes, in freedom live and die.

transl. Rev. Francis Lewis

None of the cruelties exercised by wealth and power upon indigence and dependence is more mischievous in its consequences, or more frequently practised with wanton negligence, than the encouragement of expectations which are never to be gratified, and the elation and depression of the heart by needless vicissitudes of hope and disappointment.

Every man is rich or poor, according to the proportion between his desires and enjoyments; any enlargement of wishes is therefore equally destructive to happiness with the diminution of possession; and he that teaches another to long for what he never shall obtain, is no less an enemy to his quiet, than if he had robbed him of part of his patrimony.

But representations thus refined exhibit no adequate idea of the guilt of pretended friendship; of artifices by which followers are attracted only to decorate the retinue of pomp, and swell the shout of popularity, and to be dismissed with contempt and ignominy, when their leader has succeeded or miscarried, when he is sick of show, and weary of noise. While a man infatuated with the promises of greatness, wastes his hours and days in attendance and solicitation, the honest opportunities of improving his condition pass by without his notice; he neglects to cultivate his own barren soil, because he expects every moment to be placed in regions of spontaneous fertility, and is seldom roused from his delusion, but by the gripe of distress which he cannot resist, and the sense of evils which cannot be remedied.

The punishment of Tantalus in the infernal regions affords a just image of hungry servility, flattered with the approach of advantage, doomed to lose it before it comes into his reach, always within a few days of felicity, and always sinking back to his former wants: . . . "I saw," says Homer's Ulysses, "the severe punishment of Tantalus. In a lake, whose waters approached to his lips, he stood burning with thirst, without the power to drink. Whenever he inclined his head to the stream, some deity commanded it to be dry, and the dark earth appeared at his feet. Around him lofty trees spread their fruits to view; the pear, the pomegranate, and the apple, the green olive and the luscious fig quivered before him, which, whenever he extended his hand to seize them, were snatched by the winds into clouds and obscurity."[12]

This image of misery was perhaps originally suggested to some poet by the conduct of his patron, by the daily contemplation of splendour which he never must partake, by fruitless attempts to catch at interdicted happiness, and by the sudden evanescence of his reward, when he thought his labours almost at an end. To groan with poverty, when all about him was opulence, riot, and superfluity, and to find the favours which he had long been encouraged to hope, and had long endeavoured to deserve, squandered at last on nameless ignorance, was to thirst with water flowing before him, and to see the fruits, to which his hunger was hastening, scattered by the wind. Nor can my correspondent, whatever he may have suffered, express with more justness or force the vexations of dependence.

To the Rambler.

Sir,

I am one of those mortals who have been courted and envied as the favourites of the great. Having often gained the prize of composition at the university, I began to hope that I should obtain the same distinction in every other place, and determined to forsake the profession to which I was destined by my parents, and in which the interest of my family would have procured me a very advantageous settlement. The pride of wit fluttered in my heart, and when I prepared to leave the college, nothing entered my imagination but honours, caresses, and rewards, riches without labour, and luxury without expense.

I however delayed my departure for a time, to finish the performance by which I was to draw the first notice of mankind upon me. When it was completed I hurried to London, and considered every moment that passed before its publication, as lost in a kind of neutral existence, and cut off from the golden hours of happiness and fame. The piece was at last printed and disseminated by a rapid sale; I wandered from one place of concourse to another, feasted from morning to night on the repetition of my own praises, and enjoyed the various conjectures of critics, the mistaken candour of my friends, and the impotent malice of my enemies. Some had read the manuscript, and rectified its inaccuracies; others had seen it in a state so imperfect, that they could not forbear to wonder at its present excellence; some had conversed with the author at the coffee-house; and others gave hints that they had lent him money.

I knew that no performance is so favourably read as that of a writer who suppresses his name, and therefore resolved to remain concealed, till those by whom literary reputation is established had given their suffrages too publicly to retract them. At length my bookseller informed me that Aurantius, the standing patron of merit, had sent inquiries after me, and invited me to his acquaintance.

The time which I had long expected was now arrived. I went to Aurantius with a beating heart, for I looked upon our interview as the critical moment of my destiny. I was received with civilities which my academic rudeness made me unable to repay; but when I had recovered from my confusion, I prosecuted the conversation with such liveliness and propriety, that I confirmed my new friend in his esteem of my abilities, and was dismissed with the utmost ardour of profession, and raptures of fondness.

I was soon summoned to dine with Aurantius, who had assembled the most judicious of his friends to partake of the entertainment. Again I exerted my powers of sentiment and expression, and again found every eye sparkling with delight, and every tongue silent with attention. I now became familiar at the table of Aurantius, but could never, in his most private or jocund hours, obtain more from him than general declarations of esteem, or endearments of tenderness, which included no particular promise, and therefore conferred no claim. This frigid reserve somewhat disgusted me, and when he complained of three days absence, I took care to inform him with how much importunity of kindness I had been detained by his rival Pollio.

Aurantius now considered his honour as endangered by the desertion of a wit, and, lest I should have an inclination to wander, told me that I could never find a friend more constant and zealous than himself; that indeed he had made no promises, because he hoped to surprise me with advancement, but had been silently promoting my interest, and should continue his good offices, unless he found the kindness of others more desired.

If you, Mr. Rambler, have ever ventured your philosophy within the attraction of greatness, you know the force of such language introduced with a smile of gracious tenderness, and impressed at the conclusion with an air of solemn sincerity. From that instant I gave myself up wholly to Aurantius, and, as he immediately resumed his former gaiety, expected every morning a summons to some employment of dignity and profit. One month succeeded another, and, in defiance of appearances, I still fancied myself nearer to my wishes, and continued to dream of success, and wake to disappointment. At last the failure of my little fortune compelled me to abate the finery which I hitherto thought necessary to the company with whom I associated, and the rank to which I should be raised. Aurantius, from the moment in which he discovered my poverty, considered me as fully in his power, and afterwards rather permitted my attendance than invited it; thought himself at liberty to refuse my visits, whenever he had other amusements within reach, and often suffered me to wait, without pretending any necessary business. When I was admitted to his table, if any man of rank equal to his own was present, he took occasion to mention my writings and commend my ingenuity, by which he intended to apologize for the confusion of distinctions, and the improper assortment of his company; and often called upon me to entertain his friends with my productions, as a sportsman delights the squires of his neighbourhood with the curvets of his horse, or the obedience of his spaniels.

To complete my mortification, it was his practice to impose tasks upon me, by requiring me to write upon such subjects as he thought susceptible of ornament and illustration. With these extorted performances he was little satisfied, because he rarely found in them the ideas which his own imagination had suggested, and which he therefore thought more natural than mine.

When the pale of ceremony is broken, rudeness and insult soon enter the breach. He now found that he might safely harass me with vexation, that he had fixed the shackles of patronage upon me, and that I could neither resist him nor escape. At last, in the eighth year of my servitude, when the clamour of creditors was vehement, and my necessity known to be extreme, he offered me a small office, but hinted his expectation that I should marry a young woman with whom he had been acquainted.

I was not so far depressed by my calamities as to comply with this proposal; but, knowing that complaints and expostulations would but gratify his insolence, I turned away with that contempt with which I shall never want spirit to treat the wretch who can outgo the guilt of a robber without the temptation of his profit, and who lures the credulous and thoughtless to maintain the show of his levee, and the mirth of his table, at the expense of honour, happiness, and life.

I am, Sir, &c.

LIBERALIS

Rambler no. 165, October 15, 1751: No man is a prophet in his hometown[13]

> *Young was I once and poor, now rich and old;*
> *A harder case than mine was never told;*
> *Blest with the power to use them—I had none;*
> *Loaded with riches now, the power is gone.*
>   *Greek Anthology,* IX. 138, Antiphilus,
>   transl. Rev. Francis Lewis

To the Rambler.

Sir,

The writers who have undertaken the unpromising task of moderating desire exert all the power of their eloquence to show that happiness is not the lot of man, and have, by many arguments and examples, proved the instability of every condition by which envy or ambition are excited. They have set before our eyes all the calamities to which we are exposed from the frailty of nature, the influence of accident, or the stratagems of malice; they have terrified greatness with conspiracies, and riches with anxieties, wit with criticism, and beauty with disease.

All the force of reason, and all the charms of language, are indeed necessary to support positions which every man hears with a wish to confute them. Truth finds an easy entrance into the mind when she is introduced by desire, and attended by pleasure; but when she intrudes uncalled, and brings only fear and sorrow in her train, the passes of the intellect are barred against her by prejudice and passion; if she sometimes forces her way by the batteries of argument, she seldom long keeps possession of her conquests, but is ejected by some favoured enemy, or at best obtains only a nominal sovereignty, without influence and without authority.

That life is short we are all convinced, and yet suffer not that conviction to repress our projects or limit our expectations; that life is miserable we all feel, and yet we believe that the time is near when we shall feel it no longer. But to hope happiness and immortality is equally vain. Our state may indeed be more or less embittered as our duration may be more or less contracted; yet the utmost felicity which we can ever attain will be little better than alleviation of misery, and we shall always feel more pain from our wants than pleasure from our enjoyments. The incident which I am going to relate will show, that to destroy the effect of all our success, it is not necessary that any signal calamity should fall upon us, that we should be harassed by implacable persecution, or excruciated by irremediable pains: the brightest hours of prosperity have their clouds, and the stream of life, if it is not ruffled by obstructions, will grow putrid by stagnation.

My father, resolving not to imitate the folly of his ancestors, who had hitherto left the younger sons encumbrances on the eldest, destined me to a lucrative profession; and I, being careful to lose no opportunity of improvement, was, at the usual time in which young men enter the world, well qualified for the exercise of the business which I had chosen.

My eagerness to distinguish myself in public, and my impatience of the narrow scheme of life to which my indigence confined me, did not suffer me to continue long in the town where I was born. I went away as from a place of confinement, with a resolution to return no more, till I should be able to dazzle with my splendour those who now looked upon me with contempt, to reward those who had paid honours to my dawning merit, and to show all who had suffered me to glide by them unknown and neglected, how much they mistook their interest in omitting to propitiate a genius like mine.

Such were my intentions when I sallied forth into the unknown world, in quest of riches and honours, which I expected to procure in a very short time; for what could withhold them from industry and knowledge? He that indulges hope will always be disappointed. Reputation I very soon obtained; but as merit is much more cheaply acknowledged than rewarded, I did not find myself yet enriched in proportion to my celebrity.

I had, however, in time, surmounted the obstacles by which envy and competition obstruct the first attempts of a new claimant, and saw my opponents and censurers tacitly confessing their despair of success, by courting my friendship and yielding to my influence. They who once pursued me, were now satisfied to escape from me; and they who had before thought me presumptuous in hoping to overtake them, had now their utmost wish, if they were permitted, at no great distance, quietly to follow me.

My wants were not madly multiplied as my acquisitions increased, and the time came, at length when I thought myself enabled to gratify all reasonable desires, and when, therefore, I resolved to enjoy that plenty and serenity which I had been hitherto labouring to procure, to enjoy them while I was yet neither crushed by age into infirmity, nor so habituated to a particular manner of life as to be unqualified for new studies or entertainments.

I now quitted my profession, and, to set myself at once free from all importunities to resume it, changed my residence, and devoted the remaining part of my time to quiet and amusement. Amidst innumerable projects of pleasure which restless idleness incited me to form, and of which most, when they came to the moment of execution, were rejected for others of no longer continuance, some accident revived in my imagination the pleasing ideas of my native place. It was now in my power to visit those from whom I had been so long absent, in such a manner as was consistent with my former resolution, and I wondered how it could happen that I had so long delayed my own happiness.

Full of the admiration which I should excite, and the homage which I should receive, I dressed my servants in a more ostentatious livery, purchased a magnificent chariot, and resolved to dazzle the inhabitants of the little town with an unexpected blaze of greatness.

While the preparations that vanity required were made for my departure, which, as workmen will not easily be hurried beyond their ordinary rate, I thought very tedious, I solaced my impatience with imaging the various censures that my appearance would produce; the hopes which some would feel from my bounty; the terror which my power would strike on others; the awkward respect with which I should be accosted by timorous officiousness; and the distant reverence with which others, less familiar to splendour and dignity, would be contented to gaze upon me. I deliberated a long time, whether I should immediately descend to a level with my former acquaintances; or make my condescension more grateful by a gentle transition from haughtiness and reserve. At length I determined to forget some of my companions, till they discovered themselves by some indubitable token, and to receive the congratulations of others upon my good fortune with indifference, to show that I always expected what I had now obtained. The acclamations of the populace I purposed to reward with six hogsheads of ale, and a roasted ox, and then recommend to them to return to their work.

At last all the trappings of grandeur were fitted, and I began the journey of triumph, which I could have wished to have ended in the same moment; but my horses felt none of their master's ardour, and I was shaken four days upon rugged roads. I then entered the town, and, having graciously let fall the glasses, that my person might be seen, passed slowly through the street. The noise of the wheels brought the inhabitants to their doors, but I could not perceive that I was known by them. At last I alighted, and my name, I suppose, was told by my servants, for the barber stepped from the opposite house, and seized me by the hand with honest joy in his countenance, which, according to the rule that I had prescribed to myself, I repressed with a frigid graciousness. The fellow, instead of sinking into dejection, turned away with contempt, and left me to consider how the second salutation should be received. The next fellow was better treated, for I soon found that I must purchase by civility that regard which I had expected to enforce by insolence.

There was yet no smoke of bonfires, no harmony of bells, no shout of crowds, nor riot of joy; the business of the day went forward as before; and, after having ordered a splendid supper, which no man came to partake, and which my chagrin hindered me from tasting, I went to bed, where the vexation of disappointment overpowered the fatigue of my journey, and kept me from sleep.

I rose so much humbled by those mortifications as to inquire after the present state of the town, and found that I had been absent too long to obtain the triumph which had flattered my expectation. Of the friends whose compliments I expected, some had long ago moved to distant provinces, some had lost in the maladies of age all sense of another's prosperity, and some had forgotten our former intimacy amidst care and distresses. Of three whom I had resolved to punish for their former offences by a longer continuance of neglect, one was, by his own industry, raised above my scorn, and two were sheltered from it in the grave. All those whom I loved, feared, or hated, all whose envy or whose kindness I had hopes of contemplating with pleasure, were swept away, and their place was filled by a new generation with other views and other competitions;

and among many proofs of the impotence of wealth, I found that it conferred upon me very few distinctions in my native place.

I am, Sir, &c.

SEROTINUS

Rambler no. 208, March 14, 1752: Concluding the *Rambler*

Begone, ye blockheads, Heraclitus cries,
And leave my labours to the learn'd and wise:
By wit, by knowledge, studious to be read,
I scorn the multitude, alive and dead.

Greek Anthology, VII. 128

Time, which puts an end to all human pleasures and sorrows, has likewise concluded the labours of the *Rambler.* Having supported, for two years, the anxious employment of a periodical writer, and multiplied my essays to upwards of two hundred, I have now determined to desist.

The reasons of this resolution it is of little importance to declare, since justification is unnecessary when no objection is made. I am far from supposing, that the cessation of my performances will raise any inquiry, for I have never been much a favourite of the public, nor can boast that, in the progress of my undertaking, I have been animated by the rewards of the liberal, the caresses of the great, or the praises of the eminent.

But I have no design to gratify pride by submission, or malice by lamentation; nor think it reasonable to complain of neglect from those whose regard I never solicited. If I have not been distinguished by the distributors of literary honours, I have seldom descended to the arts by which favour is obtained. I have seen the meteors of fashions rise and fall, without any attempt to add a moment to their duration. I have never complied with temporary curiosity, nor enabled my readers to discuss the topic of the day; I have rarely exemplified my assertions by living characters; in my papers, no man could look for censures of his enemies, or praises of himself; and they only were expected to peruse them, whose passions left them leisure for abstracted truth, and whom virtue could please by its naked dignity.

To some, however, I am indebted for encouragement, and to others for assistance. The number of my friends was never great, but they have been such as would not suffer me to think that I was writing in vain, and I did not feel much dejection from the want of popularity.

My obligations having not been frequent, my acknowledgments may be soon dispatched. I can restore to all my correspondents their productions, with little diminution of the bulk of my volumes, though not without the loss of some pieces to which particular honours have been paid.

The parts from which I claim no other praise than that of having given them an opportunity of appearing, are the four billets in the tenth paper, the second letter in the fifteenth, the thirtieth, the forty-fourth, the ninety-seventh, and the hundredth papers, and the second letter in the hundred and seventh.

Having thus deprived myself of many excuses which candour might have admitted for the inequality of my compositions, being no longer able to allege the necessity of gratifying correspondents, the importunity with which publication was solicited, or obstinacy with which correction was rejected, I must remain accountable for all my faults, and submit, without subterfuge, to the censures of criticism, which, however, I shall not endeavour to soften by a formal deprecation, or to overbear by the influence of a patron. The supplications of an author never yet reprieved him a moment from oblivion; and, though greatness has sometimes sheltered guilt, it can afford no protection to ignorance or dulness. Having hitherto attempted only the propagation of truth, I will not at last violate it by the confession of terrors which I do not feel; having laboured to maintain the dignity of virtue, I will not now degrade it by the meanness of dedication.

The seeming vanity with which I have sometimes spoken of myself, would perhaps require an apology, were it not extenuated by the example of those who have published essays before me, and by the privilege which every nameless writer has been hitherto allowed. "A mask," says Castiglione,[14] "confers a right of acting and speaking with less restraint, even when the wearer happens to be known." He that is discovered without his own consent, may claim some indulgence, and cannot be rigorously called to justify those sallies or frolics which his disguise must prove him desirous to conceal.

But I have been cautious lest this offence should be frequently or grossly committed; for, as one of the philosophers directs us to live with a friend, as with one that is some time to become an enemy, I have always thought it the duty of an anonymous author to write as if he expected to be hereafter known.

I am willing to flatter myself with hopes that, by collecting these papers, I am not preparing, for my future life, either shame or repentance. That all are happily imagined, or accurately polished, that the same sentiments have not sometimes recurred, or the same expressions been too frequently repeated, I have not confidence in my abilities sufficient to warrant. He that condemns himself to compose on a stated day will often bring to his task an attention dissipated, a memory embarrassed, an imagination overwhelmed, a mind distracted with anxieties, a body languishing with disease: he will labour on a barren topic, till it is too late to change it; or, in the ardour of invention, diffuse his thoughts into wild exuberance, which the pressing hour of publication cannot suffer judgment to examine or reduce.

Whatever shall be the final sentence of mankind, I have at least endeavoured to deserve their kindness. I have laboured to refine our language to grammatical purity, and to clear it from colloquial barbarisms, licentious idioms, and irregular combinations. Something, perhaps, I have added to the elegance of its construction, and something to the harmony of its cadence. When common words were less pleasing to the ear, or less distinct in their signification, I have familiarized the terms of philosophy, by applying them to popular ideas, but have rarely admitted any words not authorized by former writers; for I believe that whoever knows the English tongue in its present extent, will be able to express his thoughts without further help from other nations.

As it has been my principal design to inculcate wisdom or piety, I have allotted few papers to the idle sports of imagination. Some, perhaps, may be found, of which the highest excellence is harmless merriment; but scarcely any man is so steadily serious as not to complain, that the severity of dictatorial instruction has been too seldom relieved, and that he is driven by the sternness of the *Rambler*'s philosophy to more cheerful and airy companions.

Next to the excursions of fancy are the disquisitions of criticism, which, in my opinion, is only to be ranked among the subordinate and instrumental arts. Arbitrary decision and general exclamation I have carefully avoided, by asserting nothing without a reason, and establishing all my principles of judgment on unalterable and evident truth.

In the pictures of life I have never been so studious of novelty or surprise, as to depart wholly from all resemblance; a fault which writers deservedly celebrated frequently commit, that they may raise, as the occasion requires, either mirth or abhorrence. Some enlargement may be allowed to declamation, and some exaggeration to burlesque; but as they deviate farther from reality, they become less useful, because their lessons will fail of application. The mind of the reader is carried away from the contemplation of his own manners; he finds in himself no likeness to the phantom before him; and though he laughs or rages, is not reformed.

The essays professedly serious, if I have been able to execute my own intentions, will be found exactly conformable to the precepts of Christianity, without any accommodation to the licentiousness and levity of the present age. I therefore look back on this part of my work with pleasure, which no blame or praise of man shall diminish or augment. I shall never envy the honours which wit and learning obtain in any other cause, if I can be numbered among the writers who have given ardour to virtue, and confidence to truth.

> *Celestial pow'rs! that piety regard,*
> *From you my labours wait their last reward.*
> Dionysius Periegetes, l. 1186, transl. Samuel Johnson

Adventurer no. 39, March 20, 1753: Sleep

> *—Pallas pour'd sweet slumbers on his soul;*
> *And balmy dreams, the gift of soft repose,*
> *Calm'd all his pains, and banish'd all his woes.*
> *Odyssey,* V. 491–493, transl. Pope (incorrectly cited)

If every day did not produce fresh instances of the ingratitude of mankind, we might, perhaps, be at a loss, why so liberal and impartial a benefactor as sleep, should meet with so few historians or panegyrists. Writers are so totally absorbed by the business of the day, as never to turn their attention to that power, whose officious hand so seasonably suspends the burden of life; and without whose interposition man would not be able to endure the fatigue of labour, however rewarded, or the struggle with opposition, however successful.

Night, though she divides to many the longest part of life, and to almost all the most innocent and happy, is yet unthankfully neglected, except by those who pervert her gifts.

The astronomers, indeed, expect her with impatience, and felicitate themselves upon her arrival: Fontenelle has not failed to celebrate her praises; and to chide the sun for hiding from his view the worlds, which he imagines to appear in every constellation. Nor have the poets been always deficient in her praises: Milton has observed of the night, that it is "the pleasant time, the cool, the silent."[15]

These men may, indeed, well be expected to pay particular homage to night; since they are indebted to her, not only for cessation of pain, but increase of pleasure; not only for slumber, but for knowledge. But the greater part of her avowed votaries are the sons of luxury; who appropriate to festivity the hours designed for rest; who consider the reign of pleasure as commencing when day begins to withdraw her busy multitudes, and ceases to dissipate attention by intrusive and unwelcome variety; who begin to awake to joy when the rest of the world sinks into insensibility; and revel in the soft effluence of flattering and artificial lights, which "more shadowy set off the face of things."[16]

Without touching upon the fatal consequences of a custom which, as Ramazzini observes, will be for ever condemned, and for ever retained; it may be observed, that however sleep may be put off from time to time, yet the demand is of so importunate a nature, as not to remain long unsatisfied: and if, as some have done, we consider it as the tax of life, we cannot but observe it as a tax that must be paid, unless we could cease to be men; for Alexander declared, that nothing convinced him that he was not a divinity, but his not being able to live without sleep.

To live without sleep in our present fluctuating state, however desirable it might seem to the lady in Clelia,[17] can surely be the wish only of the young or the ignorant; to everyone else, a perpetual vigil will appear to be a state of wretchedness, second only to that of the miserable beings whom Swift has in his travels so elegantly described as "supremely cursed with immortality."

Sleep is necessary to the happy to prevent satiety, and to endear life by a short absence; and to the miserable, to relieve them by intervals of quiet. Life is to most, such as could not be endured without frequent intermissions of existence: Homer, therefore, has thought it an office worthy of the goddess of wisdom, to lay Ulysses asleep when landed on Phaeacia.

It is related of [Jean Philippe] Barretier, whose early advances in literature scarce any human mind has equalled, that he spent twelve hours of the four-and-twenty in sleep: yet this appears from the bad state of his health, and the shortness of his life, to have been too small a respite for a mind so vigorously and intensely employed: it is to be regretted, therefore, that he did not exercise his mind less, and his body more: since by this means, it is highly probable, that though he would not then have astonished with the blaze of a comet, he would yet have shone with the permanent radiance of a fixed star.

Nor should it be objected that there have been many men who daily spend fifteen or sixteen hours in study: for by some of whom this is reported it has never been done; others have done it for a short time only; and of the rest it appears, that they employed their minds in such operations as required neither celerity nor strength, in the low drudgery of collating copies, comparing authorities, digesting dictionaries, or accumulating compilations.

Men of study and imagination are frequently upbraided by the industrious and plodding sons of care, with passing too great a part of their life in a state of inaction. But these defiers of sleep seem not to remember that though it must be granted them that they are crawling about before the break of day, it can seldom be said that they are perfectly awake; they exhaust no spirits, and require no repairs; but lie torpid as a toad in marble, or at least are known to live only by an inert and sluggish locomotive faculty, and may be said, like a wounded snake, to "drag their slow length along."[18]

Man has been long known among philosophers by the appellation of the microcosm, or epitome of the world: the resemblance between the great and little world might, by a rational observer, be detailed to many particulars; and to many more by a fanciful speculatist. I know not in which of these two classes I shall be ranged for observing, that as the total quantity of light and darkness allotted in the course of the year to every region of the earth is the same, though distributed at various times and in different portions; so, perhaps, to each individual of the human species, nature has ordained the same quantity of wakefulness and sleep; though divided by some into a total quiescence and vigorous exertion of their faculties, and, blended by others in a kind of twilight of existence, in a state between dreaming and reasoning, in which they either think without action, or act without thought.

The poets are generally well affected to sleep: as men who think with vigour, they require respite from thought; and gladly resign themselves to that gentle power, who not only bestows rest, but frequently leads them to happier regions, where patrons are always kind, and audiences are always candid; where they are feasted in the bowers of imagination, and crowned with flowers divested of their prickles, and laurels of unfading verdure.

The more refined and penetrating part of mankind, who take wide surveys of the wilds of life, who see the innumerable terrors and distresses that are perpetually preying on the heart of man, and discern with unhappy perspicuity, calamities yet latent in their causes, are glad to close their eyes upon the gloomy prospect, and lose in a short insensibility the remembrance of others' miseries and their own. The hero has no higher hope than that, after having routed legions after legions, and added kingdom to kingdom, he shall retire to milder happiness, and close his days in social festivity. The wit or the sage can expect no greater happiness than that, after having harassed his reason in deep researches, and fatigued his fancy in boundless excursions, he shall sink at night in the tranquillity of sleep.

The poets, among all those that enjoy the blessings of sleep, have been least ashamed to acknowledge their benefactor. How much Statius[19] considered the evils of life as assuaged and softened by the balm of slumber, we may discover by that pathetic invocation, which he poured out in his waking nights: and that Cowley, among the other felicities of his darling solitude, did not forget to number the privilege of sleeping without disturbance, we may learn from the rank that he assigns among the gifts of nature to the poppy, "which is scattered," says he, "over the fields of corn, that all the needs of man may be easily satisfied, and that bread and sleep may be found together."[20]

Si quis invisum Cereri benignae
Me putat germen, vehementer errat;
Illa me in partem recipit libenter Fertilis agri.

Meque frumentumque simul per omnes
Consulens mundo Dea spargit oras;
Crescite, O! dixit, duo magna sustentacula vitae.

Carpe, mortalis, mea dona laetus,
Carpe, nec plantas alias require,
Sed satur panis, satur et soporis, Caetera sperne.

He widely errs who thinks I yield
Precedence in the well-cloth'd field,
 Tho' mix'd with wheat I grow:
Indulgent Ceres knew my worth,
And to adorn the teeming earth,
She bade the Poppy blow.

Nor vainly gay the sight to please,
But blest with power mankind to ease,
 The Goddess saw me rise:
"Thrive with the life-supporting grain,"
She cry'd, "the solace of the swain,
The cordial of his eyes."

"Seize, happy mortal, seize the good;
My hand supplies thy sleep and food,
 And makes thee truly blest:
With plenteous meals enjoy the day,
In slumbers pass the night away,
And leave to fate the rest."

Sleep, therefore, as the chief of all earthly blessings, is justly appropriated to industry and temperance; the refreshing rest, and the peaceful
night, are the portion only of him who lies down weary with honest labour, and free from the fumes of indigested luxury; it is the just doom of
laziness and gluttony, to be inactive without ease, and drowsy without
tranquillity.

Sleep has been often mentioned as the image of death; "so like it," says Sir Thomas Browne, "that I dare not trust it without my prayers";[21] their resemblance is, indeed, apparent and striking; they both, when they seize the body, leave the soul at liberty: and wise is he that remembers of both, that they can be safe and happy only by virtue.

Idler no. 31, November 18, 1758: Sober and the disguises of idleness

[*The character of Sober is commonly thought to be Johnson's portrait of himself.*]

Many moralists have remarked that pride has of all human vices the widest dominion, appears in the greatest multiplicity of forms, and lies hid under the greatest variety of disguises; of disguises which, like the moon's "veil of brightness," are both its "lustre and its shade"[22] and betray it to others, though they hide it from ourselves.

It is not my intention to degrade pride from this pre-eminence of mischief; yet I know not whether idleness may not maintain a very doubtful and obstinate competition.

There are some that profess idleness in its full dignity, who call themselves the "Idle," as Busiris in the play calls himself the "Proud";[23] who boast that they do nothing, and thank their stars that they have nothing to do; who sleep every night till they can sleep no longer, and rise only that exercise may enable them to sleep again; who prolong the reign of darkness by double curtains, and never see the sun but to "tell him how they hate his beams";[24] whose whole labour is to vary the posture of indolence, and whose day differs from their night, but as a couch or chair differs from a bed.

These are the true and open votaries of idleness, for whom she weaves the garlands of poppies, and into whose cup she pours the waters of oblivion; who exist in a state of unruffled stupidity, forgetting and forgotten; who have long ceased to live, and at whose death the survivors can only say, that they have ceased to breathe.

But idleness predominates in many lives where it is not suspected; for, being a vice which terminates in itself, it may be enjoyed without injury to others; and it is therefore not watched like fraud, which endangers property; or like pride, which naturally seeks its gratifications in another's inferiority. Idleness is a silent and peaceful quality that neither raises envy by ostentation, nor hatred by opposition; and therefore nobody is busy to censure or detect it.

As pride sometimes is hid under humility, idleness is often covered by turbulence and hurry. He that neglects his known duty and real employment, naturally endeavours to crowd his mind with something that may bar out the remembrance of his own folly, and does any thing but what he ought to do with eager diligence, that he may keep himself in his own favour.

Some are always in a state of preparation, occupied in previous measures, forming plans, accumulating materials, and providing for the main affair. These are certainly under the secret power of idleness. Nothing is to be expected from the workman whose tools are for ever to be sought. I was once told by a great master, that no man ever excelled in painting, who was eminently curious about pencils and colours.

There are others to whom idleness dictates another expedient, by which life may be passed unprofitably away without the tediousness of many vacant hours. The art is, to fill the day with petty business, to have always something in hand which may raise curiosity, but not solicitude, and keep the mind in a state of action, but not of labour.

This art has for many years been practised by my old friend Sober with wonderful success. Sober is a man of strong desires and quick imagination, so exactly balanced by the love of ease, that they can seldom stimulate him to any difficult undertaking; they have, however, so much power, that they will not suffer him to lie quite at rest; and though they do not make him sufficiently useful to others, they make him at least weary of himself.

Mr. Sober's chief pleasure is conversation; there is no end of his talk or his attention; to speak or to hear is equally pleasing; for he still fancies that he is teaching or learning something, and is free for the time from his own reproaches.

But there is one time at night when he must go home, that his friends may sleep; and another time in the morning, when all the world agrees to shut out interruption. These are the moments of which poor Sober trembles at the thought. But the misery of these tiresome intervals he has many means of alleviating. He has persuaded himself that the manual arts are undeservedly overlooked; he has observed in many trades the effects of close thought, and just ratiocination. From speculation he proceeded to practice, and supplied himself with the tools of a carpenter, with which he mended his coal-box very successfully, and which he still continues to employ, as he finds occasion.

He has attempted at other times the crafts of the shoemaker, tinman, plumber, and potter; in all these arts he has failed, and resolves to qualify himself for them by better information. But his daily amusement is chemistry. He has a small furnace, which he employs in distillation, and which has long been the solace of his life. He draws oils and waters, and essences and spirits, which he knows to be of no use; sits and counts the drops, as they come from his retort, and forgets that, whilst a drop is falling, a moment flies away.

Poor Sober! I have often teased him with reproof, and he has often promised reformation; for no man is so much open to conviction as the idler, but there is none on whom it operates so little. What will be the effect of this paper I know not; perhaps, he will read it and laugh, and light the fire in his furnace; but my hope is, that he will quit his trifles, and betake himself to rational and useful diligence.

Idler no. 103, April 5, 1760: Concluding the *Idler:* the last of anything

Respicere ad longae jussit spatia ultima vitae.

Juvenal, *Satires,* X. 275

Much of the pain and pleasure of mankind arises from the conjectures which every one makes of the thoughts of others; we all enjoy praise which we do not hear, and resent contempt which we do not see. The Idler may, therefore, be forgiven, if he suffers his imagination to represent to him what his readers will say or think when they are informed that they have now his last paper in their hands.

Value is more frequently raised by scarcity than by use. That which lay neglected when it was common, rises in estimation as its quantity becomes less. We seldom learn the true want of what we have till it is discovered that we can have no more.

This essay will, perhaps, be read with care even by those who have not yet attended to any other; and he that finds this late attention recompensed, will not forbear to wish that he had bestowed it sooner.

Though the Idler and his readers have contracted no close friendship, they are, perhaps, both unwilling to part. There are few things not purely evil of which we can say, without some emotion of uneasiness, "this is the last." Those who never could agree together, shed tears when mutual discontent has determined them to final separation; of a place which has been frequently visited, though without pleasure, the last look is taken with heaviness of heart; and the Idler, with all his chillness of tranquillity, is not wholly unaffected by the thought that his last essay is now before him.

The secret horror of the last is inseparable from a thinking being, whose life is limited, and to whom death is dreadful. We always make a secret comparison between a part and the whole; the termination of any period of life reminds us that life itself has likewise its termination; when we have done any thing for the last time, we involuntarily reflect that a part of the days allotted us is past, and that as more is past there is less remaining.

It is very happily and kindly provided, that in every life there are certain pauses and interruptions, which force consideration upon the careless, and seriousness upon the light; points of time where one course of action ends, and another begins; and by vicissitudes of fortune or alteration of employment, by change of place or loss of friendship, we are forced to say of something, "this is the last."

An even and unvaried tenor of life always hides from our apprehension the approach of its end. Succession is not perceived but by variation; he that lives today as he lived yesterday, and expects that, as the present day is, such will be the morrow, easily conceives time as running in a circle and returning to itself. The uncertainty of our duration is impressed commonly by dissimilitude of condition; it is only by finding life changeable that we are reminded of its shortness.

This conviction, however forcible at every new impression, is every moment fading from the mind; and partly by the inevitable incursion of new images, and partly by voluntary exclusion of unwelcome thoughts, we are again exposed to the universal fallacy; and we must do another thing for the last time, before we consider that the time is nigh when we shall do no more.

As the last *Idler* is published in that solemn week which the Christian world has always set apart for the examination of the conscience, the review of life, the extinction of earthly desires, and the renovation of holy purposes; I hope that my readers are already disposed to view every incident with seriousness, and improve it by meditation; and that, when they see this series of trifles brought to a conclusion, they will consider that, by outliving the *Idler*, they have passed weeks, months, and years which are now no longer in their power; that an end must in time be put to every thing great as to every thing little; that to life must come its last hour, and to this system of being its last day, the hour at which probation ceases, and repentance will be vain; the day in which every work of the hand, and imagination of the heart shall be brought to judgment, and an everlasting futurity shall be determined by the past.

Literature and Authorship

Rambler no. 4, March 31, 1750: Vice and virtue in fiction

Simul et jucunda et idonea dicere vitæ.
$\qquad\qquad$ Horace, *Ars Poetica*, l. 334

And join both profit and delight in one.
$\qquad\qquad$ transl. Thomas Creech

The works of fiction, with which the present generation seems more particularly delighted, are such as exhibit life in its true state, diversified only by accidents that daily happen in the world, and influenced by passions and qualities which are really to be found in conversing with mankind.

This kind of writing may be termed not improperly the comedy of romance, and is to be conducted nearly by the rules of comic poetry. Its province is to bring about natural events by easy means, and to keep up curiosity without the help of wonder: it is therefore precluded from the machines and expedients of the heroic romance, and can neither employ giants to snatch away a lady from the nuptial rites, nor knights to bring her back from captivity; it can neither bewilder its personages in deserts, nor lodge them in imaginary castles.

I remember a remark made by Scaliger upon Pontanus, that all his writings are filled with the same images; and that if you take from him his lilies and his roses, his satyrs and his dryads, he will have nothing left that can be called poetry. In like manner almost all the fictions of the last age will vanish, if you deprive them of a hermit and a wood, a battle and a shipwreck.

Why this wild strain of imagination found reception so long in polite and learned ages, it is not easy to conceive; but we cannot wonder that while readers could be procured, the authors were willing to continue it; for when a man had by practice gained some fluency of language, he had no further care than to retire to his closet, let loose his invention, and heat his mind with incredibilities; a book was thus produced without fear of criticism, without the toil of study, without knowledge of nature, or acquaintance with life.

The task of our present writers is very different; it requires, together with that learning which is to be gained from books, that experience which can never be attained by solitary diligence, but must arise from general converse and accurate observation of the living world. Their performances have, as Horace expresses it, *plus oneris quantum veniae minus,*[1] little indulgence, and therefore more difficulty. They are engaged in portraits of which every one knows the original, and can detect any deviation from exactness of resemblance. Other writings are safe, except from the malice of learning, but these are in danger from every common reader; as the slipper ill executed was censured by a shoemaker who happened to stop in his way at the Venus of Apelles.[2]

But the fear of not being approved as just copiers of human manners, is not the most important concern that an author of this sort ought to have before him. These books are written chiefly to the young, the ignorant, and the idle, to whom they serve as lectures of conduct, and introductions into life. They are the entertainment of minds unfurnished with ideas, and therefore easily susceptible of impressions; not fixed by principles, and therefore easily following the current of fancy; not informed by experience, and consequently open to every false suggestion and partial account.

That the highest degree of reverence should be paid to youth, and that nothing indecent should be suffered to approach their eyes or ears, are precepts extorted by sense and virtue from an ancient writer, by no means eminent for chastity of thought. The same kind, though not the same degree, of caution, is required in every thing which is laid before them, to secure them from unjust prejudices, perverse opinions, and incongruous combinations of images.

In the romances formerly written, every transaction and sentiment was so remote from all that passes among men, that the reader was in very little danger of making any applications to himself; the virtues and crimes were equally beyond his sphere of activity; and he amused himself with heroes and with traitors, deliverers and persecutors, as with beings of another species, whose actions were regulated upon motives of their own, and who had neither faults nor excellencies in common with himself.

But when an *Adventurer* is leveled with the rest of the world, and acts in such scenes of the universal drama as may be the lot of any other man; young spectators fix their eyes upon him with closer attention, and hope, by observing his behaviour and success, to regulate their own practices, when they shall be engaged in the like part.

For this reason these familiar histories may perhaps be made of greater use than the solemnities of professed morality, and convey the knowledge of vice and virtue with more efficacy than axioms and definitions. But if the power of example is so great as to take possession of the memory by a kind of violence, and produce effects almost without the intervention of the will, care ought to be taken that, when the choice is unrestrained, the best examples only should be exhibited; and that which is likely to operate so strongly, should not be mischievous or uncertain in its effects.

The chief advantage which these fictions have over real life is, that their authors are at liberty, though not to invent, yet to select objects, and to cull from the mass of mankind those individuals upon which the attention ought most to be employed; as a diamond, though it cannot be made, may be polished by art, and placed in such a situation as to display that lustre which before was buried among common stones.

It is justly considered as the greatest excellency of art, to imitate nature; but it is necessary to distinguish those parts of nature which are most proper for imitation: greater care is still required in representing life, which is so often discoloured by passion, or deformed by wickedness. If the world be promiscuously described, I cannot see of what use it can be to read the account; or why it may not be as safe to turn the eye immediately upon mankind as upon a mirrour which shows all that presents itself without discrimination.

It is therefore not a sufficient vindication of a character, that it is drawn as it appears; for many characters ought never to be drawn: nor of a narrative, that the train of events is agreeable to observation and experience, for that observation which is called knowledge of the world, will be found much more frequently to make men cunning than good. The purpose of these writings is surely not only to show mankind, but to provide that they may be seen hereafter with less hazard; to teach the means of avoiding the snares which are laid by treachery for innocence, without infusing any wish for that superiority with which the betrayer flatters his vanity; to give the power of counteracting fraud, without the temptation to practise it; to initiate youth by mock encounters in the art of necessary defence, and to increase prudence without impairing virtue.

Many writers, for the sake of following nature, so mingle good and bad qualities in their principal personages, that they are both equally conspicuous; and as we accompany them through their adventures with delight, and are led by degrees to interest ourselves in their favour, we lose the abhorrence of their faults, because they do not hinder our pleasure, or, perhaps, regard them with some kindness, for being united with so much merit.

There have been men indeed splendidly wicked, whose endowments threw a brightness on their crimes, and whom scarce any villainy made perfectly detestable, because they never could be wholly divested of their excellencies; but such have been in all ages the great corrupters of the world, and their resemblance ought no more to be preserved, than the art of murdering without pain.

Some have advanced, without due attention to the consequences of this notion, that certain virtues have their correspondent faults, and therefore that to exhibit either apart is to deviate from probability. Thus men are observed by Swift to be "grateful in the same degree as they are resentful." This principle, with others of the same kind, supposes man to act from a brute impulse, and pursue a certain degree of inclination, without any choice of the object; for, otherwise, though it should be allowed that gratitude and resentment arise from the same constitution of the passions, it follows not that they will be equally indulged when reason is consulted; yet, unless that consequence be admitted, this sagacious maxim becomes an empty sound, without any relation to practice or to life.

Nor is it evident, that even the first motions to these effects are always in the same proportion. For pride, which produces quickness of resentment, will obstruct gratitude, by unwillingness to admit that inferiority which obligation implies; and it is very unlikely that he who cannot think he receives a favour, will acknowledge or repay it.

It is of the utmost importance to mankind, that positions of this tendency should be laid open and confuted; for while men consider good and evil as springing from the same root, they will spare the one for the sake of the other, and in judging, if not of others at least of themselves, will be apt to estimate their virtues by their vices. To this fatal error all those will contribute, who confound the colours of right and wrong, and, instead of helping to settle their boundaries, mix them with so much art, that no common mind is able to disunite them.

In narratives where historical veracity has no place, I cannot discover why there should not be exhibited the most perfect idea of virtue; of virtue not angelical, nor above probability, for what we cannot credit, we shall never imitate, but the highest and purest that humanity can reach, which, exercised in such trials as the various revolutions of things shall bring upon it, may, by conquering some calamities and enduring others, teach us what we may hope, and what we can perform. Vice, for vice is necessary to be shown, should always disgust; nor should the graces of gaiety, or the dignity of courage, be so united with it, as to reconcile it to the mind. Wherever it appears, it should raise hatred by the malignity of its practices, and contempt by the meanness of its stratagems: for while it is supported by either parts or spirit, it will be seldom heartily abhorred. The Roman tyrant was content to be hated, if he was but feared; and there are thousands of the readers of romances willing to be thought wicked, if they may be allowed to be wits. It is therefore to be steadily inculcated, that virtue is the highest proof of understanding, and the only solid basis of greatness; and that vice is the natural consequence of narrow thoughts; that it begins in mistake, and ends in ignominy.

Rambler no. 21, May 29, 1750: Uncertainty of literary fame

Terra salutiferas herbas, eademque nocentes,
Nutrit; & urtiae proxima saepe rosa est.

Ovid, *Remedia Amoris,* ll. 45–46

Our bane and physic the same earth bestows,
And near the noisome nettle blooms the rose.

Every man is prompted by the love of himself to imagine that he possesses some qualities superior, either in kind or in degree, to those which he sees allotted to the rest of the world; and, whatever apparent disadvantages he may suffer in the comparison with others, he has some invisible distinctions, some latent reserve of excellence, which he throws into the balance, and by which he generally fancies that it is turned in his favour.

The studious and speculative part of mankind always seem to consider their fraternity as placed in a state of opposition to those who are engaged in the tumult of public business; and have pleased themselves, from age to age, with celebrating the felicity of their own condition, and with recounting the perplexity of politics, the dangers of greatness, the anxieties of ambition, and the miseries of riches.

Among the numerous topics of declamation, that their industry has discovered on this subject, there is none which they press with greater efforts, or on which they have more copiously laid out their reason and their imagination, than the instability of high stations, and the uncertainty with which the profits and honours are possessed, that must be acquired with so much hazard, vigilance, and labour.

This they appear to consider as an irrefragable argument against the choice of the statesman and the warrior; and swell with confidence of victory, thus furnished by the muses with the arms which never can be blunted, and which no art or strength of their adversaries can elude or resist.

It was well known by experience to the nations which employed elephants in war, that though by the terror of their bulk, and the violence of their impression, they often threw the enemy into disorder, yet there was always danger in the use of them, very nearly equivalent to the advantage;

for if their first charge could be supported, they were easily driven back upon their confederates; they then broke through the troops behind them, and made no less havoc in the precipitation of their retreat, than in the fury of their onset.

I know not whether those who have so vehemently urged the inconveniences and dangers of an active life, have not made use of arguments that may be retorted with equal force upon themselves; and whether the happiness of a candidate for literary fame be not subject to the same uncertainty with that of him who governs provinces, commands armies, presides in the senate, or dictates in the cabinet.

That eminence of learning is not to be gained without labour, at least equal to that which any other kind of greatness can require, will be allowed by those who wish to elevate the character of a scholar; since they cannot but know, that every human acquisition is valuable in proportion to the difficulty employed in its attainment. And that those who have gained the esteem and veneration of the world, by their knowledge or their genius, are by no means exempt from the solicitude which any other kind of dignity produces, may be conjectured from the innumerable artifices which they make use of to degrade a superior, to repress a rival, or obstruct a follower; artifices so gross and mean, as to prove evidently how much a man may excel in learning, without being either more wise or more virtuous than those whose ignorance he pities or despises.

Nothing therefore remains, by which the student can gratify his desire of appearing to have built his happiness on a more firm basis than his antagonist, except the certainty with which his honours are enjoyed. The garlands gained by the heroes of literature must be gathered from summits equally difficult to climb with those that bear the civic or triumphal wreaths, they must be worn with equal envy, and guarded with equal care from those hands that are always employed in efforts to tear them away; the only remaining hope is, that their verdure is more lasting, and that they are less likely to fade by time, or less obnoxious to the blasts of accident.

Even this hope will receive very little encouragement from the examination of the history of learning, or observation of the fate of scholars in the present age. If we look back into past times, we find innumerable names of authors once in high reputation, read perhaps by the beautiful, quoted by the witty, and commented by the grave; but of whom we now know only that they once existed. If we consider the distribution of literary fame in our own time, we shall find it a possession of very uncertain tenure; sometimes bestowed by a sudden caprice of the public, and again transferred to a new favourite, for no other reason than that he is new; sometimes refused to long labour and eminent desert, and sometimes granted to very slight pretentions; lost sometimes by security and negligence, and sometimes by too diligent endeavours to retain it.

A successful author is equally in danger of the diminution of his fame, whether he continues or ceases to write. The regard of the public is not to be kept but by tribute, and the remembrance of past service will quickly languish, unless successive performances frequently revive it. Yet in every new attempt there is new hazard, and there are few who do not at some unlucky time, injure their own characters by attempting to enlarge them.

There are many possible causes of that inequality which we may so frequently observe in the performances of the sane man, from the influence of which no ability or industry is sufficiently secured, and which have so often sullied the splendour of genius, that the wit, as well as the conqueror, may be properly cautioned not to indulge his pride with too early triumphs, but to defer to the end of life his estimate of happiness.

> —*Ultima semper*
> *Expectanda dies homini, dicique beatus*
> *Ante obitum nemo, supremaque funera debet.*
> > Ovid, *Metamorphoses*, III. 135–137

> *But no frail man, however great or high,*
> *Can be concluded blest before he die.*
> > transl. Addison

Among the motives that urge an author to undertakings by which his reputation is impaired, one of the most frequent must be mentioned with tenderness, because it is not to be counted among his follies, but his miseries. It very often happens that the works of learning or of wit are performed at the direction of those by whom they are to be rewarded; the writer has not always the choice of his subject, but is compelled to accept any task which is thrown before him without much consideration of his own convenience, and without time to prepare himself by previous studies.

Miscarriages of this kind are likewise frequently the consequence of that acquaintance with the great, which is generally considered as one of the chief privileges of literature and genius. A man who has once learned to think himself exalted by familiarity with those whom nothing but their birth, or their fortunes, or such stations as are seldom gained by moral excellence, set above him, will not be long without submitting his understanding to their conduct; he will suffer them to prescribe the course of his studies, and employ him for their own purposes either of diversion or interest. His desire of pleasing those whose favour he has weakly made necessary to himself, will not suffer him always to consider how little he is qualified for the work imposed. Either his vanity will tempt him to conceal his deficiencies, or that cowardice, which always encroaches fast upon such as spend their lives in the company of persons higher than themselves, will not leave him resolution to assert the liberty of choice.

But, though we suppose that a man by his fortune can avoid the necessity of dependence, and by his spirit can repel the usurpations of patronage, yet he may easily, by writing long, happen to write ill. There is a general succession of events in which contraries are produced by periodical vicissitudes; labour and care are rewarded with success, success produces confidence, confidence relaxes industry, and negligence ruins that reputation which accuracy had raised.

He that happens not to be lulled by praise into supineness, may be animated by it to undertakings above his strength, or incited to fancy himself alike qualified for every kind of composition, and able to comply with the public taste through all its variations. By some opinion like this, many men have been engaged, at an advanced age, in attempts which they had not time to complete, and after a few weak efforts, sunk into the grave with vexation to see the rising generation gain ground upon them. From these failures the highest genius is not exempt; that judgment which appears so penetrating, when it is employed upon the works of others, very often fails where interest or passion can exert their power. We are blinded in examining our own labours by innumerable prejudices. Our juvenile compositions please us, because they bring to our minds the remembrance of youth; our later performances we are ready to esteem, because we are un-willing to think that we have made no improvement; what flows easily from the pen charms us, because we read with pleasure that which flatters our opinion of our own powers; what was composed with great strug-gles of the mind we do not easily reject, because we cannot bear that so much labour should be fruitless. But the reader has none of these prepos-sessions, and wonders that the author is so unlike himself, without con-sidering that the same soil will, with different culture, afford different products.

Rambler no. 23, June 5, 1750:
An author must depend on his own and not critics' judgments

Tres mihi convivae prope dissentire videntur;
Poscentur vario multum diversa palato.

Horace, *Epistles,* II.2. 61–62

Three guests I have, dissenting at my feast,
Requiring each to gratify his taste
With different food.

transl. Philip Francis

That every man should regulate his actions by his own conscience, with-out any regard to the opinions of the rest of the world, is one of the first precepts of moral prudence; justified not only by the suffrage of reason, which declares that none of the gifts of heaven are to lie useless, but by the voice likewise of experience, which will soon inform us that, if we make the praise or blame of others the rule of our conduct, we shall be dis-tracted by a boundless variety of irreconcilable judgments, be held in per-petual suspense between contrary impulses, and consult forever without determination.

I know not whether, for the same reason, it is not necessary for an au-thor to place some confidence in his own skill, and to satisfy himself in the knowledge that he has not deviated from the established laws of com-position, without submitting his works to frequent examinations before he gives them to the public, or endeavouring to secure success by a solicitous conformity to advice and criticism.

It is, indeed, quickly discoverable, that consultation and compliance can conduce little to the perfection of any literary performance; for whoever is so doubtful of his own abilities as to encourage the remarks of others, will find himself every day embarrassed with new difficulties, and will harass his mind, in vain, with the hopeless labour of uniting heterogeneous ideas, digesting independent hints, and collecting into one point the several rays of borrowed light, emitted often with contrary directions.

Of all authors, those who retail their labours in periodical sheets would be most unhappy, if they were much to regard the censures or the admonitions of their readers; for, as their works are not sent into the world at once, but by small parts in gradual succession, it is always imagined, by those who think themselves qualified to give instructions, that they may yet redeem their former failings by hearkening to better judges, and supply the deficiencies of their plan, by the help of the criticisms which are so liberally afforded.

I have had occasion to observe, sometimes with vexation, and sometimes with merriment, the different temper with which the same man reads a printed and manuscript performance. When a book is once in the hands of the public, it is considered as permanent and unalterable; and the reader, if he be free from personal prejudices, takes it up with no other intention than of pleasing or instructing himself: he accommodates his mind to the author's design; and, having no interest in refusing the amusement that is offered him, never interrupts his own tranquillity by studied cavils, or destroys his satisfaction in that which is already well, by an anxious inquiry how it might be better; but is often contented without pleasure, and pleased without perfection.

But if the same man be called to consider the merit of a production yet unpublished, he brings an imagination heated with objections to passages which he has yet never heard; he invokes all the powers of criticism, and stores his memory with taste and grace, purity and delicacy, manners and unities, sounds which, having been once uttered by those that understood them, have been since reechoed without meaning, and kept up to the disturbance of the world by a constant repercussion from one coxcomb to another. He considers himself as obliged to show, by some proof of his abilities, that he is not consulted to no purpose, and therefore watches every opening for objection, and looks round for every opportunity to propose some specious alteration. Such opportunities a very small degree of sagacity will enable him to find; for, in every work of imagination, the disposition of parts, the insertion of incidents, and use of decorations, may be varied a thousand ways with equal propriety; and as in things nearly equal, that will always seem best to every man which he himself produces; the critic, whose business is only to propose, without the care of execution, can never want the satisfaction of believing that he has suggested very important improvements, nor the power of enforcing his advice by arguments, which, as they appear convincing to himself, either his kindness or his vanity will press obstinately and importunately, without suspicion that he may possibly judge too hastily in favour of his own advice, or inquiry whether the advantage of the new scheme be proportionate to the labour.

It is observed by the younger Pliny[3] that an orator ought not so much to select the strongest arguments which his cause admits, as to employ all which his imagination can afford: for, in pleading, those reasons are of most value which will most affect the judges; and the judges, says he, will be always most touched with that which they had before conceived. Every man who is called to give his opinion of a performance, decides upon the same principle; he first suffers himself to form expectations, and then is angry at his disappointment. He lets his imagination rove at large, and wonders that another, equally unconfined in the boundless ocean of possibility, takes a different course.

But, though the rule of Pliny be judiciously laid down, it is not applicable to the writer's cause, because there always lies an appeal from domestic criticism to a higher judicature, and the public, which is never corrupted, nor often deceived, is to pass the last sentence upon literary claims.

Of the great force of preconceived opinions I had many proofs, when I first entered upon this weekly labour. My readers having, from the performances of my predecessors, established an idea of unconnected essays, to which they believed all future authors under a necessity of conforming, were impatient of the least deviation from their system, and numerous remonstrances were accordingly made by each, as he found his favourite subject omitted or delayed. Some were angry that the Rambler did not, like the Spectator, introduce himself to the acquaintance of the public, by an account of his own birth and studies, an enumeration of his adventures, and a description of his physiognomy. Others soon began to remark that he was a solemn, serious, dictatorial writer, without sprightliness or gaiety, and called out with vehemence for mirth and humour. Another admonished him to have a special eye upon the various clubs of this great city, and informed him that much of the Spectator's vivacity was laid out upon such assemblies. He has been censured for not imitating the politeness of his predecessors, having hitherto neglected to take the ladies under his protection, and give them rules for the just opposition of colours, and the proper dimensions of ruffles and pinners.[4] He has been required by one to fix a particular censure upon those matrons who play at cards with spectacles: and another is very much offended whenever he meets with a speculation in which naked precepts are comprised without the illustration of examples and characters.

I make not the least question that all these monitors intend the promotion of my design, and the instruction of my readers; but they do not know, or do not reflect, that an author has a rule of choice peculiar to himself; and selects those subjects which he is best qualified to treat, by the course of his studies, or the accidents of his life; that some topics of amusement have been already treated with too much success to invite a competition; and that he who endeavours to gain many readers must try various arts of invitation, essay every avenue of pleasure, and make frequent changes in his methods of approach.

I cannot but consider myself, amidst this tumult of criticism, as a ship in a poetical tempest, impelled at the same time by opposite winds, and dashed by the waves from every quarter, but held upright by the contrariety of the assailants, and secured in some measure by multiplicity of distress. Had the opinion of my censurers been unanimous, it might perhaps have overset my resolution; but since I find them at variance with each other, I can, without scruple, neglect them, and endeavour to gain the favour of the public by following the direction of my own reason, and indulging the sallies of my own imagination.

Rambler no. 77, December 11, 1750: Morally unworthy authors

Os dignum aeterno nitidum quod fulgeat auro,
Si mallet laudare Deum, cui sordida monstra
Praetulit, et liquidam temeravit crimine vocem.
  Prudentius, *Contra Symmachi Orationem,* I. 635–637

A golden statue such a wit might claim,
Had God and virtue rais'd the noble flame;
But ah! how lewd a subject has he sung,
What vile obscenity profanes his tongue.
                              transl. Rev. Francis Lewis

Among those whose hopes of distinction, or riches, arise from an opinion of their intellectual attainments, it has been, from age to age, an established custom to complain of the ingratitude of mankind to their instructors, and the discouragement which men of genius and study suffer from avarice and ignorance, from the prevalence of false taste, and the encroachment of barbarity.

Men are most powerfully affected by those evils which themselves feel, or which appear before their own eyes; and as there has never been a time of such general felicity, but that many have failed to obtain the rewards to which they had, in their own judgment, a just claim, some offended writer has always declaimed, in the rage of disappointment, against his age or nation; nor is there one who has not fallen upon times more unfavourable to learning than any former century, or who does not wish that he had been reserved in the insensibility of non-existence to some happier hour, when literary merit shall no longer be despised, and the gifts and caresses of mankind shall recompense the toils of study, and add lustre to the charms of wit.

Many of these clamours are undoubtedly to be considered only as the bursts of pride never to be satisfied, as the prattle of affectation, mimicking distresses unfelt, or as the common places of vanity solicitous for splendour of sentences, and acuteness of remark. Yet it cannot be denied that frequent discontent must proceed from frequent hardships, and though it is evident that not more than one age or people can deserve the censure of being more averse from learning than any other, yet at all times knowledge must have encountered impediments, and wit been mortified with contempt, or harassed with persecution.

It is not necessary, however, to join immediately in the outcry, or to condemn mankind as pleased with ignorance, or always envious of superior abilities. The miseries of the learned have been related by themselves, and since they have not been found exempt from that partiality with which men look upon their own actions and sufferings, we may conclude that they have not forgotten to deck their cause with the brightest ornaments, and strongest colours. The logician collected all his subtleties when they were to be employed in his own defence; and the master of rhetoric exerted against his adversary all the arts by which hatred is embittered, and indignation inflamed.

To believe no man in his own cause is the standing and perpetual rule of distributive justice. Since therefore, in the controversy between the learned and their enemies, we have only the pleas of one party, of the party more able to delude our understandings, and engage our passions, we must determine our opinion by facts uncontested, and evidences on each side allowed to be genuine.

By this procedure, I know not whether the students will find their cause promoted, or the compassion which they expect much increased. Let their conduct be impartially surveyed; let them be allowed no longer to direct attention at their pleasure, by expatiating on their own deserts; let neither the dignity of knowledge overawe the judgment, nor the graces of elegance seduce it. It will then, perhaps, be found, that they were not able to produce claims to kinder treatment, but provoked the calamities which they suffered, and seldom wanted friends, but when they wanted virtue.

That few men, celebrated for theoretic wisdom, live with conformity to their precepts, must be readily confessed; and we cannot wonder that the indignation of mankind rises with great vehemence against those who neglect the duties which they appear to know with so strong conviction the necessity of performing. Yet since no man has power of acting equal to that of thinking, I know not whether the speculatist[5] may not sometimes incur censures too severe, and by those who form ideas of his life from their knowledge of his books, be considered as worse than others, only because he was expected to be better.

He by whose writings the heart is rectified, the appetites counteracted, and the passions repressed, may be considered as not unprofitable to the great republic of humanity, even though his behaviour should not always exemplify his rules. His instructions may diffuse their influence to regions in which it will not be inquired whether the author be "albus an ater," good or bad; to times when all his faults and all his follies shall be lost in forgetfulness, among things of no concern or importance to the world; and he may kindle in thousands and ten thousands that flame which burnt but dimly in himself, through the fumes of passion, or the damps of cowardice. The vicious moralist may be considered as a taper, by which we are lighted through the labyrinth of complicated passions: he extends his radiance further than his heat, and guides all that are within view, but burns only those who make too near approaches.

Yet since good or harm must be received for the most part from those to whom we are familiarly known, he whose vices overpower his virtues, in the compass to which his vices can extend, has no reason to complain that he meets not with affection or veneration, when those with whom he passes his life are more corrupted by his practice than enlightened by his ideas. Admiration begins where acquaintance ceases; and his favourers are distant, but his enemies at hand.

Yet many have dared to boast of neglected merit, and to challenge their age for cruelty and folly, of whom it cannot be alleged that they have endeavoured to increase the wisdom or virtue of their readers. They have been at once profligate in their lives, and licentious in their compositions; have not only forsaken the paths of virtue, but attempted to lure others after them. They have smoothed the road of perdition, covered with flowers the thorns of guilt, and taught temptation sweeter notes, softer blandishments, and stronger allurements.

It has been apparently the settled purpose of some writers, whose powers and acquisitions place them high in the rank of literature, to set fashion on the side of wickedness; to recommend debauchery and lewdness, by associating them with qualities most likely to dazzle the discernment, and attract the affections; and to show innocence and goodness with such attendant weaknesses as necessarily expose them to contempt and derision.

Such naturally found intimates among the corrupt, the thoughtless, and the intemperate; passed their lives amidst the levities of sportive idleness, or the warm professions of drunken friendship; and fed their hopes with the promises of wretches, whom their precepts had taught to scoff at truth. But when fools had laughed away their sprightliness, and the languors of excess could no longer be relieved, they saw their protectors hourly drop away, and wondered and stormed to find themselves abandoned. Whether their companions persisted in wickedness, or returned to virtue, they were left equally without assistance; for debauchery is selfish and negligent, and from virtue the virtuous only can expect regard.

It is said by Florus of Catiline, who died in the midst of slaughtered enemies, that "his death had been illustrious, had it been suffered for his country." Of the wits who have languished away life under the pressures of poverty, or in the restlessness of suspense, caressed and rejected, flattered and despised, as they were of more or less use to those who styled themselves their patrons, it might be observed, that their miseries would enforce compassion, had they been brought upon them by honesty and religion.

The wickedness of a loose or profane author is more atrocious than that of the giddy libertine, or drunken ravisher, not only because it extends its effects wider, as a pestilence that taints the air is more destructive than poison infused in a draught, but because it is committed with cool deliberation. By the instantaneous violence of desire, a good man may sometimes be surprised before reflection can come to his rescue; when the appetites have strengthened their influence by habit, they are not easily resisted or suppressed; but for the frigid villainy of studious lewdness, for the calm malignity of laboured impiety, what apology can be invented? What punishment can be adequate to the crime of him who retires to solitudes for the refinement of debauchery; who tortures his fancy, and ransacks his memory, only that he may leave the world less virtuous than he found it; that he may intercept the hopes of the rising generation; and spread snares for the soul with more dexterity?

What were their motives, or what their excuses, is below the dignity of reason to examine. If having extinguished in themselves the distinction of right and wrong, they were insensible of the mischief which they promoted, they deserved to be hunted down by the general compact, as no longer partaking of social nature; if influenced by the corruption of patrons, or readers, they sacrificed their own convictions to vanity or interest, they were to be abhorred with more acrimony than he that murders for pay; since they committed greater crimes without greater temptations.

"Of him, to whom much is given, much shall be required."[6] Those, whom God has favoured with superior faculties, and made eminent for quickness of intuition, and accuracy of distinctions, will certainly be regarded as culpable in his eye, for defects and deviations which, in souls less enlightened, may be guiltless. But, surely, none can think without horror on that man's condition, who has been more wicked in proportion as he had more means of excelling in virtue, and used the light imparted from heaven only to embellish folly, and shed lustre upon crimes.

Rambler no. 137, July 9, 1751: Necessity of literary courage

Dum vitant stulti vitia, in contraria currunt.
Horace, *Satires,* I.2. 24

—Whilst fools one vice condemn,
They run into the opposite extreme.
transl. Thomas Creech

That wonder is the effect of ignorance, has been often observed. The awful stillness of attention, with which the mind is overspread at the first view of an unexpected effect, ceases when we have leisure to disentangle complications and investigate causes. Wonder is a pause of reason, a sudden cessation of the mental progress, which lasts only while the understanding is fixed upon some single idea, and is at an end when it recovers force enough to divide the object into its parts, or mark the intermediate gradations from the first agent to the last consequence.

It may be remarked with equal truth, that ignorance is often the effect of wonder. It is common for those who have never accustomed themselves to the labour of inquiry, nor invigorated their confidence by conquests over difficulty, to sleep in the gloomy quiescence of astonishment, without any effort to animate inquiry, or dispel obscurity. What they cannot immediately conceive, they consider as too high to be reached, or too extensive to be comprehended; they therefore content themselves with the gaze of folly, forbear to attempt what they have no hopes of performing, and resign the pleasure of rational contemplation to more pertinacious study, or more active faculties.

Among the productions of mechanic art, many are of a form so different from that of their first materials, and many consist of parts so numerous and so nicely adapted to each other, that it is not possible to view them without amazement. But when we enter the shops of artificers, observe the various tools by which every operation is facilitated, and trace the progress of a manufacture through the different hands that, in succession to each other, contribute to its perfection, we soon discover that every single man has an easy task, and that the extremes, however remote, of natural rudeness and artificial elegance, are joined by a regular concatenation of effects, of which every one is introduced by that which precedes it, and equally introduces that which is to follow.

The same is the state of intellectual and manual performances. Long calculations or complex diagrams affright the timorous and inexperienced from a second view; but if we have skill sufficient to analyze them into simple principles, it will be discovered that our fear was groundless. "Divide and conquer," is a principle equally just in science as in policy. Complication is a species of confederacy which, while it continues united, bids defiance to the most active and vigorous intellect; but of which every member is separately weak, and which may therefore be quickly subdued, if it can once be broken.

The chief art of learning, as Locke has observed, is to attempt but little at a time.[7] The widest excursions of the mind are made by short flights frequently repeated; the most lofty fabrics of science are formed by the continued accumulation of single propositions.

It often happens, whatever be the cause, that impatience of labour, or dread of miscarriage, seizes those who are most distinguished for quickness of apprehension; and that they who might with greatest reason promise themselves victory, are least willing to hazard the encounter. This diffidence, where the attention is not laid asleep by laziness or dissipated by pleasures, can arise only from confused and general views, such as negligence snatches in haste, or from the disappointment of the first hopes formed by arrogance without reflection. To expect that the intricacies of science will be pierced by a careless glance, or the eminences of fame ascended without labour, is to expect a particular privilege, a power denied to the rest of mankind; but to suppose that the maze is inscrutable to diligence, or the heights inaccessible to perseverance, is to submit tamely to the tyranny of fancy, and enchain the mind in voluntary shackles.

It is the proper ambition of the heroes in literature to enlarge the boundaries of knowledge by discovering and conquering new regions of the intellectual world. To the success of such undertakings perhaps some degree of fortuitous happiness is necessary, which no man can promise or procure to himself; and therefore doubt and irresolution may be forgiven in him that ventures into the unexplored abysses of truth, and attempts to find his way through the fluctuations of uncertainty, and the conflicts of contradiction. But when nothing more is required than to pursue a path already beaten, and to trample obstacles which others have demolished, why should any man so much distrust his own intellect as to imagine himself unequal to the attempt?

It were to be wished that they who devote their lives to study would at once believe nothing too great for their attainment, and consider nothing as too little for their regard; that they would extend their notice alike to science and to life, and unite some knowledge of the present world to their acquaintance with past ages and remote events.

Nothing has so much exposed men of learning to contempt and ridicule, as their ignorance of things which are known to all but themselves. Those who have been taught to consider the institutions of the schools as giving the last perfection to human abilities, are surprised to see men wrinkled with study, yet wanting to be instructed in the minute circumstances of propriety, or the necessary forms of daily transaction; and quickly shake off their reverence for modes of education, which they find to produce no ability above the rest of mankind.

"Books," says Bacon, "can never teach the use of books."[8] The student must learn by commerce with mankind to reduce his speculations to practice, and accommodate his knowledge to the purposes of life.

It is too common for those who have been bred to scholastic professions, and passed much of their time in academies where nothing but learning confers honours, to disregard every other qualification, and to imagine that they shall find mankind ready to pay homage to their knowledge, and to crowd about them for instruction. They therefore step out from their cells into the open world with all the confidence of authority and dignity of importance; they look round about them at once with ignorance and scorn on a race of beings to whom they are equally unknown and equally contemptible, but whose manners they must imitate, and with whose opinions they must comply, if they desire to pass their time happily among them.

To lessen that disdain with which scholars are inclined to look on the common business of the world, and the unwillingness with which they condescend to learn what is not to be found in any system of philosophy, it may be necessary to consider that though admiration is excited by abstruse researches and remote discoveries, yet pleasure is not given, nor affection conciliated, but by softer accomplishments, and qualities more easily communicable to those about us. He that can only converse upon questions about which only a small part of mankind has knowledge sufficient to make them curious, must lose his days in unsocial silence, and live in the crowd of life without a companion. He that can only be useful on great occasions, may die without exerting his abilities, and stand a helpless spectator of a thousand vexations which fret away happiness, and which nothing is required to remove but a little dexterity of conduct and readiness of expedients.

No degree of knowledge attainable by man is able to set him above the want of hourly assistance, or to extinguish the desire of fond endearments, and tender officiousness; and therefore, no one should think it unnecessary to learn those arts by which friendship may be gained. Kindness is preserved by a constant reciprocation of benefits or interchange of pleasures; but such benefits only can be bestowed, as others are capable to receive, and such pleasures only imparted, as others are qualified to enjoy.

By this descent from the pinnacles of art no honour will be lost; for the condescensions of learning are always overpaid by gratitude. An elevated genius employed in little things, appears, to use the simile of Longinus, like the sun in his evening declination: he remits his splendour but retains his magnitude, and pleases more though he dazzles less.[9]

Rambler no. 156, September 14, 1751:
Rules of writing based on human nature and usefulness

Nunquam aliud natura, aliud sapientia dicit.
Juvenal, *Satires*, XIV. 321

For wisdom ever echoes nature's voice.

Every government, say the politicians, is perpetually degenerating towards corruption, from which it must be rescued at certain periods by the
resuscitation of its first principles, and the re-establishment of its original
constitution. Every animal body, according to the methodic physicians,
is, by the predominance of some exuberant quality, continually declining
towards disease and death, which must be obviated by a seasonable re-
duction of the peccant humour to the just equipoise which health requires.

In the same manner the studies of mankind, all at least which, not being subject to rigorous demonstration, admit the influence of fancy and
caprice, are perpetually tending to error and confusion. Of the great principles of truth which the first speculatists discovered, the simplicity is
embarrassed by ambitious additions, or the evidence obscured by inaccurate argumentation; and as they descend from one succession of writers to another, like light transmitted from room to room, they lose their
strength and splendour, and fade at last in total evanescence.

The systems of learning therefore must be sometimes reviewed, complications analyzed into principles, and knowledge disentangled from
opinion. It is not always possible, without a close inspection, to separate
the genuine shoots of consequential reasoning, which grow out of some
radical postulate, from the branches which art has engrafted on it. The
accidental prescriptions of authority, when time has procured them veneration, are often confounded with the laws of nature, and those rules
are supposed coeval with reason, of which the first rise cannot be discovered.

Criticism has sometimes permitted fancy to dictate the laws by which
fancy ought to be restrained, and fallacy to perplex the principles by
which fallacy is to be detected; her superintendence of others has betrayed her to negligence of herself; and, like the ancient Scythians, by ex-

tending her conquests over distant regions, she has left her throne vacant to her slaves.

Among the laws of which the desire of extending authority, or ardour of promoting knowledge, has prompted the prescription, all which writers have received, had not the same original right to our regard. Some are to be considered as fundamental and indispensable, others only as useful and convenient; some as dictated by reason and necessity, others as enacted by despotic antiquity; some as invincibly supported by their conformity to the order of nature and operations of the intellect; others as formed by accident, or instituted by example, and therefore always liable to dispute and alteration.

That many rules have been advanced without consulting nature or reason, we cannot but suspect, when we find it peremptorily decreed by the ancient masters, that "only three speaking personages should appear at once upon the stage";[10] a law which, as the variety and intricacy of modern plays has made it impossible to be observed, we now violate without scruple, and, as experience proves, without inconvenience.

The original of this precept was merely accidental. Tragedy was a monody, or solitary song in honour of Bacchus, improved afterwards into a dialogue by the addition of another speaker; but the ancients, remembering that the tragedy was at first pronounced only by one, durst not for some time venture beyond two; at last, when custom and impunity had made them daring, they extended their liberty to the admission of three, but restrained themselves by a critical edict from further exorbitance.

By what accident the number of acts was limited to five, I know not that any author has informed us; but certainly it is not determined by any necessity arising either from the nature of action, or propriety of exhibition. An act is only the representation of such a part of the business of the play as proceeds in an unbroken tenor, or without any intermediate pause. Nothing is more evident than that of every real, and by consequence of every dramatic action, the intervals may be more or fewer than five; and indeed the rule is upon the English stage everyday broken in effect, without any other mischief than that which arises from an absurd endeavour to observe it in appearance. Whenever the scene is shifted the act ceases, since some time is necessarily supposed to elapse while the personages of the drama change their place.

With no greater right to our obedience have the critics confined the dramatic action to a certain number of hours. Probability requires that the time of action should approach somewhat nearly to that of exhibition, and those plays will always be thought most happily conducted which crowd the greatest variety into the least space. But since it will frequently happen that some delusion must be admitted, I know not where the limits of imagination can be fixed. It is rarely observed that minds, not prepossessed by mechanical criticism, feel any offence from the extension of the intervals between the acts; nor can I conceive it absurd or impossible, that he who can multiply three hours into twelve or twenty-four, might imagine with equal ease a greater number.

I know not whether he that professes to regard no other laws than those of nature, will not be inclined to receive tragicomedy to his protection, whom, however generally condemned, her own laurels have hitherto shaded from the fulminations of criticism. For what is there in the mingled drama which impartial reason can condemn? The connection of important with trivial incidents, since it is not only common but perpetual in the world, may surely be allowed upon the stage, which pretends only to be the mirror of life. The impropriety of suppressing passions before we have raised them to the intended agitation, and of diverting the expectation from an event which we keep suspended only to raise it, may be speciously urged. But will not experience show this objection to be rather subtle than just? Is it not certain that the tragic and comic affections have been moved alternately with equal force, and that no plays have oftener filled the eye with tears, and the breast with palpitation, than those which are variegated with interludes of mirth?

I do not however think it safe to judge of works of genius merely by the event. The resistless vicissitudes of the heart, this alternate prevalence of merriment and solemnity, may sometimes be more properly ascribed to the vigour of the writer than the justness of the design: and, instead of vindicating tragicomedy by the success of Shakespeare, we ought, perhaps, to pay new honours to that transcendent and unbounded genius that could preside over the passions in sport; who, to actuate the affections, needed not the slow gradation of common means, but could fill the heart with instantaneous jollity or sorrow, and vary our disposition as he changed his scenes. Perhaps the effects even of Shakespeare's poetry might have been yet greater, had he not counteracted himself; and we might have been more interested in the distresses of his heroes, had we not been so frequently diverted by the jokes of his buffoons.

There are other rules more fixed and obligatory. It is necessary that of every play the chief action should be single; for since a play represents some transaction, through its regular maturation to its final event, two actions equally important must evidently constitute two plays.

As the design of tragedy is to instruct by moving the passions, it must always have a hero, a personage apparently and incontestably superior to the rest, upon whom the attention may be fixed, and the anxiety suspended. For though, of two persons opposing each other with equal abilities and equal virtue, the auditor will inevitably, in time, choose his favourite, yet as that choice must be without any cogency of conviction, the hopes or fears which it raises will be faint and languid. Of two heroes acting in confederacy against a common enemy, the virtues or dangers will give little emotion, because each claims our concern with the same right, and the heart lies at rest between equal motives.

It ought to be the first endeavour of a writer to distinguish nature from custom; or that which is established because it is right, from that which is right only because it is established; that he may neither violate essential principles by a desire of novelty, nor debar himself from the attainment of beauties within his view, by a needless fear of breaking rules which no literary dictator had authority to enact.

Rambler no. 184, December 21, 1751:
Writing as an analogy for the vagaries of life

Permittes ipsis expendere numinibus, quid
Conveniat nobis, rebusque sit utile nostris.

Juvenal, Satires, X. 347–348

Intrust thy fortune to the pow'rs above:
Leave them to manage for thee, and to grant
What their unerring wisdom sees thee want.

transl. Dryden

As every scheme of life, so every form of writing, has its advantages and inconveniences, though not mingled in the same proportions. The writer of essays escapes many embarrassments to which a large work would have exposed him; he seldom harasses his reason with long trains of consequences, dims his eyes with the perusal of antiquated volumes, or burdens his memory with great accumulations of preparatory knowledge. A careless glance upon a favourite author, or transient survey of the varieties of life, is sufficient to supply the first hint or seminal idea, which, enlarged by the gradual accretion of matter stored in the mind, is by the warmth of fancy easily expanded into flowers, and sometimes ripened into fruit.

The most frequent difficulty by which the authors of these petty compositions are distressed, arises from the perpetual demand of novelty and change. The compiler of a system of science lays his invention at rest, and employs only his judgment, the faculty exerted with least fatigue. Even the relater of feigned adventures, when once the principal characters are established, and the great events regularly connected, finds incidents and episodes crowding upon his mind; every change opens new views, and the latter part of the story grows without labour out of the former. But he that attempts to entertain his reader with unconnected pieces, finds the irksomeness of his task rather increased than lessened by every production. The day calls afresh upon him for a new topic, and he is again obliged to choose, without any principle to regulate his choice.

It is indeed true that there is seldom any necessity of looking far or inquiring long for a proper subject. Every diversity of art or nature, every public blessing or calamity, every domestic pain or gratification, every sally of caprice, blunder of absurdity, or stratagem of affectation, may supply matter to him whose only rule is to avoid uniformity. But it often happens that the judgment is distracted with boundless multiplicity, the imagination ranges from one design to another, and the hours pass imperceptibly away, till the composition can be no longer delayed, and necessity enforces the use of those thoughts which then happen to be at hand. The mind, rejoicing at deliverance on any terms from perplexity and suspense, applies herself vigorously to the work before her, collects embellishments and illustrations, and sometimes finishes, with great elegance and happiness, what in a state of ease and leisure she never had begun.

It is not commonly observed how much, even of actions considered as particularly subject to choice, is to be attributed to accident, or some cause out of our own power, by whatever name it be distinguished. To close tedious deliberations with hasty resolves, and after long consultations with reason to refer the question to caprice, is by no means peculiar to the essayist. Let him that peruses this paper review the series of his life, and inquire how he was placed in his present condition. He will find, that of the good or ill which he has experienced, a great part came unexpected, without any visible gradations of approach; that every event has been influenced by causes acting without his intervention; and that whenever he pretended to the prerogative of foresight, he was mortified with new conviction of the shortness of his views.

The busy, the ambitious, the inconstant, and the adventurous, may be said to throw themselves by design into the arms of fortune, and voluntarily to quit the power of governing themselves; they engage in a course of life in which little can be ascertained by previous measures; nor is it any wonder that their time is passed between elation and despondency, hope and disappointment.

Some there are who appear to walk the road of life with more circumspection, and make no step till they think themselves secure from the hazard of a precipice, when neither pleasure nor profit can tempt them from the beaten path; who refuse to climb lest they should fall, or to run lest they should stumble, and move slowly forward without any compliance with those passions by which the heady and vehement are seduced and betrayed.

Yet even the timorous prudence of this judicious class is far from exempting them from the dominion of chance, a subtle and insidious power, who will intrude upon privacy and embarrass caution. No course of life is so prescribed and limited, but that many actions must result from arbitrary election. Every one must form the general plan of his conduct by his own reflections; he must resolve whether he will endeavour at riches or at content; whether he will exercise private or public virtues; whether he will labour for the general benefit of mankind, or contract his beneficence to his family and dependents.

This question has long exercised the schools of philosophy, but remains yet undecided; and what hope is there that a young man, unacquainted with the arguments on either side, should determine his own destiny otherwise than by chance?

When chance has given him a partner of his bed, whom he prefers to all other women, without any proof of superior desert, chance must again direct him in the education of his children; for, who was ever able to convince himself by arguments, that he had chosen for his son that mode of instruction to which his understanding was best adapted, or by which he would most easily be made wise or virtuous?

Whoever shall inquire by what motives he was determined on these important occasions, will find them such as his pride will scarcely suffer him to confess; some sudden ardour of desire, some uncertain glimpse of advantage, some petty competition, some inaccurate conclusion, or some example implicitly reverenced. Such are often the first causes of our resolves; for it is necessary to act, but impossible to know the consequences of action, or to discuss all the reasons which offer themselves on every part to inquisitiveness and solicitude.

Since life itself is uncertain, nothing which has life for its basis can boast much stability. Yet this is but a small part of our perplexity. We set out on a tempestuous sea in quest of some port, where we expect to find rest, but where we are not sure of admission, we are not only in danger of sinking in the way, but of being misled by meteors mistaken for stars, of being driven from our course by the changes of the wind, and of losing it by unskillful steerage; yet it sometimes happens, that crosswinds blow us to a safer coast, that meteors draw us aside from whirlpools, and that negligence or error contributes to our escape from mischiefs to which a direct course would have exposed us. Of those that, by precipitate conclusions, involve themselves in calamities without guilt, very few, however they may reproach themselves, can be certain that other measures would have been more successful.

In this state of universal uncertainty, where a thousand dangers hover about us, and none can tell whether the good that he pursues is not evil in disguise, or whether the next step will lead him to safety or destruction, nothing can afford any rational tranquillity, but the conviction that, however we amuse ourselves with unideal sounds, nothing in reality is governed by chance, but that the universe is under the perpetual superintendence of Him who created it; that our being is in the hands of omnipotent goodness, by whom what appears casual to us, is directed for ends ultimately kind and merciful; and that nothing can finally hurt him who debars not himself from the divine favour.

Adventurer no. 137, February 26, 1754: The usefulness of an author

What have I been doing?

Pythagoras, *Aurea Carmina*, 42

As man is a being very sparingly furnished with the power of prescience, he can provide for the future only by considering the past; and as futurity is all in which he has any real interest, he ought very diligently to use the only means by which he can be enabled to enjoy it, and frequently to revolve the experiments which he has hitherto made upon life, that he may gain wisdom from his mistakes, and caution from his miscarriages.

Though I do not so exactly conform to the precepts of Pythagoras as to practise every night this solemn recollection, yet I am not so lost in dissipation as wholly to omit it; nor can I forbear sometimes to inquire of myself in what employment my life has passed away. Much of my time has sunk into nothing, and left no trace by which it can be distinguished; and of this I now only know, that it was once in my power, and might once have been improved.

Of other parts of life, memory can give some account: at some hours I have been gay, and at others serious; I have sometimes mingled in conversation, and sometimes meditated in solitude; one day has been spent in consulting the ancient sages, and another in writing *Adventurers*.

At the conclusion of any undertaking, it is usual to compute the loss and profit. As I shall soon cease to write *Adventurers*, I could not forbear lately to consider what has been the consequence of my labours; and whether I am to reckon the hours laid out in these compositions as applied to a good and laudable purpose, or suffered to fume away in useless evaporations.

That I have intended well, I have the attestation of my own heart: but good intentions may be frustrated when they are executed without suitable skill, or directed to an end unattainable in itself.

Some there are, who leave writers very little room for self-congratulation; some who affirm that books have no influence upon the public, that no age was ever made better by its authors, and that to call upon mankind to correct their manners, is, like Xerxes, to scourge the wind, or shackle the torrent.

This opinion they pretend to support by unfailing experience. The world is full of fraud and corruption, rapine and malignity; interest is the ruling motive of mankind, and every one is endeavouring to increase his own stores of happiness by perpetual accumulation, without reflecting upon the numbers whom his superfluity condemns to want: in this state of things a book of morality is published, in which charity and benevolence are strongly enforced; and it is proved beyond opposition, that men are happy in proportion as they are virtuous, and rich as they are liberal. The book is applauded, and the author is preferred; he imagines his applause deserved, and receives less pleasure from the acquisition of reward than the consciousness of merit. Let us look again upon mankind: interest is still the ruling motive, and the world is yet full of fraud and corruption, malevolence and rapine.

The difficulty of confuting this assertion, arises merely from its generality and comprehension; to overthrow it by a detail of distinct facts, requires a wider survey of the world than human eyes can take; the progress of reformation is gradual and silent, as the extension of evening shadows; we know that they were short at noon, and are long at sunset, but our senses were not able to discern their increase: we know of every civil nation, that it was once savage, and how was it reclaimed but by precept and admonition?

Mankind are universally corrupt, but corrupt in different degrees; as they are universally ignorant, yet with greater or less irradiations of knowledge. How has knowledge or virtue been increased and preserved in one place beyond another, but by diligent inculcation and rational enforcement?

Books of morality are daily written, yet its influence is still little in the world; so the ground is annually ploughed, and yet multitudes are in want of bread. But, surely, neither the labours of the moralist nor of the husbandman are vain: let them for a while neglect their tasks, and their usefulness will be known; the wickedness that is now frequent will become universal, the bread that is now scarce would wholly fail.

The power, indeed, of every individual is small, and the consequence of his endeavours imperceptible, in a general prospect of the world. Providence has given no man ability to do much, that something might be left for every man to do. The business of life is carried on by a general cooperation; in which the part of any single man can be no more distinguished than the effect of a particular drop when the meadows are floated by a summer shower: yet every drop increases the inundation, and every hand adds to the happiness or misery of mankind.

That a writer, however zealous or eloquent, seldom works a visible effect upon cities or nations, will readily be granted. The book which is read most, is read by few, compared with those that read it not; and of those few, the greater part peruse it with dispositions that very little favour their own improvement.

It is difficult to enumerate the several motives which procure to books the honour of perusal: spite, vanity, and curiosity, hope and fear, love and hatred, every passion which incites to any other action, serves at one time or other to stimulate a reader.

Some are fond to take a celebrated volume into their hands, because they hope to distinguish their penetration by finding faults which have escaped the public; others eagerly buy it in the first bloom of reputation, that they may join the chorus of praise, and not lag, as Falstaff terms it, in "the rearward of the fashion."[11]

Some read for style, and some for argument: one has little care about the sentiment, he observes only how it is expressed; another regards not the conclusion, but is diligent to mark how it is inferred: they read for other purposes than the attainment of practical knowledge; and are no more likely to grow wise by an examination of a treatise of moral prudence, than an architect to inflame his devotion by considering attentively the proportions of a temple.

Some read that they may embellish their conversation, or shine in dispute; some that they may not be detected in ignorance, or want the reputation of literary accomplishments: but the most general and prevalent reason of study is the impossibility of finding another amusement equally cheap or constant, equally independent on the hour or the weather. He that wants money to follow the chase of pleasure through her yearly circuit, and is left at home when the gay world rolls to Bath or Tunbridge; he whose gout compels him to hear from his chamber the rattle of chariots transporting happier beings to plays and assemblies, will be forced to seek in books a refuge from himself.

The author is not wholly useless, who provides innocent amusements for minds like these. There are, in the present state of things, so many more instigations to evil than incitements to good, that he who keeps men in a neutral state, may be justly considered as a benefactor to life.

But, perhaps, it seldom happens, that study terminates in mere pastime. Books have always a secret influence on the understanding; we cannot, at pleasure, obliterate ideas; he that reads books of science, though without any fixed desire of improvement, will grow more knowing; he that entertains himself with moral or religious treatises, will imperceptibly advance in goodness; the ideas which are often offered to the mind, will at last find a lucky moment when it is disposed to receive them.

It is, therefore, urged without reason, as a discouragement to writers, that there are already books sufficient in the world; that all the topics of persuasion have been discussed, and every important question clearly stated and justly decided; and that, therefore, there is no room to hope, that pigmies should conquer where heroes have been defeated, or that the petty copiers of the present time should advance the great work of reformation, which their predecessors were forced to leave unfinished.

Whatever be the present extent of human knowledge, it is not only finite, and therefore in its own nature capable of increase, but so narrow, that almost every understanding may, by a diligent application of its powers, hope to enlarge it. It is, however, not necessary that a man should forbear to write, till he has discovered some truth unknown before; he may be sufficiently useful, by only diversifying the surface of knowledge, and luring the mind by a new appearance to a second view of those beauties which it had passed over inattentively before. Every writer may find intellects correspondent to his own, to whom his expressions are familiar, and his thoughts congenial; and, perhaps, truth is often more successfully propagated by men of moderate abilities, who, adopting the opinions of others, have no care but to explain them clearly, than by subtle speculatists and curious searchers, who exact from their readers powers equal to their own, and if their fabrics of science be strong, take no care to render them accessible.

For my part, I do not regret the hours which I have laid out in these little compositions. That the world has grown apparently better, since the publication of the *Adventurer,* I have not observed; but am willing to think that many have been affected by single sentiments, of which it is their business to renew the impression; that many have caught hints of truth, which it is now their duty to pursue; and that those who have received no improvement, have wanted not opportunity but intention to improve.

Idler no. 59, June 2, 1759: The transitory fame of books

In the common enjoyments of life, we cannot very liberally indulge the present hour, but by anticipating part of the pleasure which might have relieved the tediousness of another day; and any uncommon exertion of strength, or perseverance in labour, is succeeded by a long interval of languor and weariness. Whatever advantage we snatch beyond the certain portion allotted us by nature, is like money spent before it is due, which, at the time of regular payment, will be missed and regretted.

Fame, like all other things which are supposed to give or to increase happiness, is dispensed with the same equality of distribution. He that is loudly praised will be clamorously censured; he that rises hastily into fame will be in danger of sinking suddenly into oblivion.

Of many writers who filled their age with wonder, and whose names we find celebrated in the books of their contemporaries, the works are now no longer to be seen, or are seen only amidst the lumber of libraries which are seldom visited, where they lie only to show the deceitfulness of hope, and the uncertainty of honour.

Of the decline of reputation many causes may be assigned. It is commonly lost because it never was deserved; and was conferred at first, not by the suffrage of criticism, but by the fondness of friendship, or servility of flattery. The great and popular are very freely applauded; but all soon grow weary of echoing to each other a name which has no other claim to notice, but that many mouths are pronouncing it at once.

But many have lost the final reward of their labours, because they were too hasty to enjoy it. They have laid hold on recent occurrences, and eminent names, and delighted their readers with allusions and remarks, in which all were interested, and to which all, therefore, were attentive. But the effect ceased with its cause; the time quickly came when new events drove the former from memory, when the vicissitudes of the world brought new hopes and fears, transferred the love and hatred of the public to other agents; and the writer, whose works were no longer assisted by gratitude or resentment, was left to the cold regard of idle curiosity.

He that writes upon general principles, or delivers universal truths, may hope to be often read, because his work will be equally useful at all times and in every country; but he cannot expect it to be received with eagerness, or to spread with rapidity, because desire can have no particular stimulation: that which is to be loved long, must be loved with reason rather than with passion. He that lays out his labours upon temporary subjects, easily finds readers, and quickly loses them; for what should make the book valued when the subject is no more.

These observations will show the reason why the poem of *Hudibras* is almost forgotten, however embellished with sentiments and diversified with allusions, however bright with wit, and however solid with truth. The hypocrisy which it detected, and the folly which it ridiculed, have long vanished from public notice. Those who had felt the mischief of discord, and the tyranny of usurpation, read it with rapture; for every line brought back to memory something known, and gratified resentment by the just censure of something hated. But the book, which was once quoted by princes, and which supplied conversation to all the assemblies of the gay and witty, is now seldom mentioned, and even by those that affect to mention it, is seldom read. So vainly is wit lavished upon fugitive topics; so little can architecture secure duration when the ground is false.

Idler no. 60, June 9, 1759: Dick Minim the critic

Criticism is a study by which men grow important and formidable at a very small expense. The power of invention has been conferred by nature upon few, and the labour of learning those sciences, which may by mere labour be obtained, is too great to be willingly endured; but every man can exert such judgment as he has upon the works of others; and he whom nature has made weak, and idleness keeps ignorant, may yet support his vanity by the name of a critic.

I hope it will give comfort to great numbers who are passing through the world in obscurity, when I inform them how easily distinction may be obtained. All the other powers of literature are coy and haughty, they must be long courted, and at last are not always gained; but Criticism is a goddess easy of access and forward of advance, who will meet the slow, and encourage the timorous; the want of meaning she supplies with words, and the want of spirit she recompenses with malignity.

This profession has one recommendation peculiar to itself, that it gives vent to malignity without real mischief. No genius was ever blasted by the breath of critics. The poison which, if confined, would have burst the heart, fumes away in empty hisses, and malice is set at ease with very little danger to merit. The critic is the only man whose triumph is without another's pain, and whose greatness does not rise upon another's ruin.

To a study at once so easy and so reputable, so malicious and so harmless, it cannot be necessary to invite my readers by a long or laboured exhortation; it is sufficient, since all would be critics if they could, to show, by one eminent example, that all can be critics if they will.

Dick Minim, after the common course of puerile studies, in which he was no great proficient, was put an apprentice to a brewer, with whom he had lived two years when his uncle died in the city, and left him a large fortune in the stocks. Dick had for six months before used the company of the lower players, of whom he had learned to scorn a trade, and, being now at liberty to follow his genius, he resolved to be a man of wit and humour. That he might be properly initiated in his new character, he frequented the coffee-houses near the theatres, where he listened very diligently, day after day, to those who talked of language and sentiments, and unities and catastrophes, till, by slow degrees, he began to think that he understood something of the stage, and hoped in time to talk himself.

But he did not trust so much to natural sagacity as wholly to neglect the help of books. When the theatres were shut, he retired to Richmond with a few select writers, whose opinions he impressed upon his memory by unwearied diligence; and, when he returned with other wits to the town, was able to tell, in very proper phrases, that the chief business of art is to copy nature; that a perfect writer is not to be expected, because genius decays as judgment increases; that the great art is the art of blotting; and that, according to the rule of Horace, every piece should be kept nine years.

Of the great authors he now began to display the characters, laying

---

y bubble,
rs such trouble
d, the whole does fly,
o find out why.

Hudibras, II. 385–388

nim, we have two striking accommodations o
is impossible to utter the two lines emphatically
nat which they describe; "bubble", and "trouble"
inflation of the cheeks by the retention of the breath,
rcibly emitted, as in the practice of "blowing bub-
st excellence is in the third line, which is "crack'd", in
orcibly emitted, and then shivers into monosyllables. Yet
in neglected with common stones, and among the in-
ss a crack, and then the observation of this superlative pas-
s of *Hudibras* the observation of this superlative pas-
ved for the sagacity of Minim.

er no. 6i. June 16, 1759: Dick Minim the critic

now advanced himself to the zenith of critical reputation;
the pit, every eye in the boxes was fixed upon him; when
coffee-house, he was surrounded by circles of candidates,
ir noviciate of literature under his tuition; his opinion was
o composition was supposed to pass in safety to posterity,
no had no opinion of their own, and yet loved to debate and
n secured by Minim's approbation.
ofesses great admiration of the wisdom and munificence by
academies of the continent were raised, and often wishes for
rd of taste, for some tribunal, to which merit may appeal from
judice, and malignity. He has formed a plan for an academy
, where every work of imagination may be read before it is

down as an universal position, that all had beauties a
ion was that Shakespeare, committing himself wh
nature, wanted that correctness which learning wo
and that [Ben] Jonson, trusting to learning, did not sufficiently
eyes on nature. He blamed the stanzas of Spenser, and could not bear
hexameters of Sidney. Denham and Waller he held the first reformers o
English numbers; and thought that if Waller could have obtained the
strength of Denham, or Denham the sweetness of Waller, there had been
nothing wanting to complete a poet. He often expressed his commisera-
tion of Dryden's poverty, and his indignation at the age which suffered
him to write for bread; he repeated with rapture the first lines of *All for
Love,* but wondered at the corruption of taste which could bear anything
so unnatural as rhyming tragedies.

In Otway he found uncommon powers of moving the passions, but
was disgusted by his general negligence, and blamed him for making a
conspirator his hero; and never concluded his disquisition, without remarking how happily the sound of the clock is made to alarm the audience. Southern would have been his favourite, but that he mixes comic
with tragic scenes, intercepts the natural course of the passions, and fills
the mind with a wild confusion of mirth and melancholy. The versification of Rowe he thought too melodious for the stage, and too little varied
in different passions. He made it the great fault of Congreve, that all his
persons were wits, and that he always wrote with more art than nature. He
considered *Cato* rather as a poem than a play, and allowed Addison to be
the complete master of allegory and grave humour, but paid no great deference to him as a critic. He thought the chief merit of Prior was in his
easy tales and lighter poems, though he allowed that his *Solomon* had
many noble sentiments elegantly expressed. In Swift he discovered an inimitable vein of irony, and an easiness which all would hope and few
would attain. Pope he was inclined to degrade from a poet to a versifier,
and thought his numbers rather luscious than sweet. He often lamented
the neglect of *Phaedra and Hippolytus,* and wished to see the stage under
better regulations.

These assertions passed commonly uncontradicted; and if now and
then an opponent started up, he was quickly repressed by the suffrages of

printed, and which shall authoritatively direct the theatres what pieces to receive or reject, to exclude or to revive.

Such an institution would, in Dick's opinion, spread the fame of English literature over Europe, and make London the metropolis of elegance and politeness, the place to which the learned and ingenious of all countries would repair for instruction and improvement, and where nothing would any longer be applauded or endured that was not conformed to the nicest rules, and finished with the highest elegance.

Till some happy conjunction of the planets shall dispose our princes or ministers to make themselves immortal by such an academy, Minim contents himself to preside four nights in a week in a critical society selected by himself, where he is heard without contradiction, and whence his judgment is disseminated through the great vulgar and the small.

When he is placed in the chair of criticism, he declares loudly for the noble simplicity of our ancestors, in opposition to the petty refinements, and ornamental luxuriance. Sometimes he is sunk in despair, and perceives false delicacy daily gaining ground, and sometimes brightens his countenance with a gleam of hope, and predicts the revival of the true sublime. He then fulminates his loudest censures against the monkish barbarity of rhyme; wonders how beings that pretend to reason can be pleased with one line always ending like another; tells how unjustly and unnaturally sense is sacrificed to sound; how often the best thoughts are mangled by the necessity of confining or extending them to the dimensions of a couplet; and rejoices that genius has, in our days, shaken off the shackles which had encumbered it so long. Yet he allows that rhyme may sometimes be borne, if the lines be often broken, and the pauses judiciously diversified.

From blank verse he makes an easy transition to Milton, whom he produces as an example of the slow advance of lasting reputation. Milton is the only writer in whose books Minim can read forever without weariness. What cause it is that exempts this pleasure from satiety he has long and diligently inquired, and believes it to consist in the perpetual variation of the numbers, by which the ear is gratified and the attention awakened. The lines that are commonly thought rugged and unmusical, he conceives to have been written to temper the melodious luxury of the rest, or to express things by a proper cadence: for he scarcely finds a verse that has not this favourite beauty; he declares that he could shiver in a hothouse when he reads that

> *the ground*
> *Burns frore, and cold performs th' effect of fire;*

and that when Milton bewails his blindness the verse,

> *So thick a drop serene has quench'd these orbs,*

has, he knows not how, something that strikes him with an obscure sensation like that which he fancies would be felt from the sound of darkness.

Minim is not so confident of his rules of judgment as not very eagerly to catch new light from the name of the author. He is commonly so prudent as to spare those whom he cannot resist, unless, as will sometimes happen, he finds the public combined against them. But a fresh pretender to fame he is strongly inclined to censure, till his own honour requires that he commend him. Till he knows the success of a composition, he entrenches himself in general terms; there are some new thoughts and beautiful passages, but there is likewise much which he would have advised the author to expunge. He has several favourite epithets, of which he has never settled the meaning, but which are very commodiously applied to books which he has not read, or cannot understand. One is "manly," another is "dry," another "stiff," and another "flimsy"; sometimes he discovers delicacy of style, and sometimes meets with "strange expressions."

He is never so great, or so happy, as when a youth of promising parts is brought to receive his directions for the prosecution of his studies. He then puts on a very serious air; he advises the pupil to read none but the best authors; and when he finds one congenial to his own mind, to study his beauties, but avoid his faults; and, when he sits down to write, to consider how his favourite author would think at the present time on the present occasion. He exhorts him to catch those moments when he finds his thoughts expanded and his genius exalted, but to take care lest imagination hurry him beyond the bounds of nature. He holds diligence the mother of success; yet enjoins him, with great earnestness, not to read more than he can digest, and not to confuse his mind by pursuing studies of contrary tendencies. He tells him that every man has his genius, and that Cicero could never be a poet. The boy retires illuminated, resolves to follow his genius, and to think how Milton would have thought: and Minim feasts upon his own beneficence till another day brings another pupil.

Death

Rambler no. 78, December 15, 1750: Remembering death in our behaviour

—Mors sola fatetur
Quantula sint hominum corpuscula.

Juvenal, *Satires*, X. 172–173

Death only this mysterious truth unfolds,
The mighty soul how small a body holds.

transl. Dryden

Corporal sensation is known to depend so much upon novelty, that custom takes away from many things their power of giving pleasure or pain. Thus a new dress becomes easy by wearing it, and the palate is reconciled by degrees to dishes which at first disgusted it. That by long habit of carrying a burden, we lose, in great part, our sensibility of its weight, any man may be convinced by putting on for an hour the armour of our ancestors; for he will scarcely believe that men would have had much inclination to marches and battles, encumbered and oppressed, as he will find himself, with the ancient panoply. Yet the heroes that overran regions, and stormed towns in iron accoutrements, he knows not to have been bigger, and has no reason to imagine them stronger, than the present race of men; he therefore must conclude, that their peculiar powers were conferred only by peculiar habits, and that their familiarity with the dress of war enabled them to move in it with ease, vigour, and agility.

Yet it seems to be the condition of our present state, that pain should be more fixed and permanent than pleasure. Uneasiness gives way by slow degrees, and is long before it quits its possession of the sensory; but all our gratifications are volatile, vagrant, and easily dissipated. The fragrance of the jessamine bower is lost after the enjoyment of a few moments, and the Indian wanders among his native spices without any sense of their exhalations. It is, indeed, not necessary to show by many instances what all mankind confess, by an incessant call for variety, and restless pursuit of enjoyments, which they value only because unpossessed.

Something similar, or analogous, may be observed in effects produced immediately upon the mind; nothing can strongly strike or affect us, but what is rare or sudden. The most important events, when they become familiar, are no longer considered with wonder or solicitude, and that which at first filled up our whole attention, and left no place for any other thought, is soon thrust aside into some remote repository of the mind, and lies among other lumber of the memory, overlooked and neglected. Thus far the mind resembles the body, but here the similitude is at an end.

The manner in which external force acts upon the body is very little subject to the regulation of the will; no man can at pleasure obtund or invigorate his senses, prolong the agency of any impulse, or continue the presence of any image traced upon the eye, or any sound infused into the ear. But our ideas are more subjected to choice; we can call them before us, and command their stay, we can facilitate and promote their recurrence, we can either repress their intrusion, or hasten their retreat. It is therefore the business of wisdom and virtue, to select among numberless objects striving for our notice, such as may enable us to exalt our reason, extend our views, and secure our happiness. But this choice is to be made with very little regard to rareness or frequency; for nothing is valuable merely because it is either rare or common, but because it is adapted to some useful purpose, and enables us to supply some deficiency of our nature.

Milton has judiciously represented the father of mankind, as seized with horror and astonishment at the sight of death, exhibited to him on the mount of vision.[1] For surely, nothing can so much disturb the passions, or perplex the intellects of man, as the disruption of his union with visible nature; a separation from all that has hitherto delighted or engaged him; a change not only of the place, but the manner of his being; an entrance into a state not simply which he knows not, but which perhaps he has not faculties to know; an immediate and perceptible communication with the Supreme Being, and, what is above all distressful and alarming, the final sentence, and unalterable allotment.

Yet we to whom the shortness of life has given frequent occasions of contemplating mortality, can, without emotion, see generations of men pass away, and are at leisure to establish modes of sorrow, and adjust the ceremonial of death. We can look upon funeral pomp as a common spectacle in which we have no concern, and turn away from it to trifles and amusements, without dejection of look, or inquietude of heart.

It is, indeed, apparent, from the constitution of the world, that there must be a time for other thoughts; and a perpetual meditation upon the last hour, however it may become the solitude of a monastery, is inconsistent with many duties of common life. But surely the remembrance of death ought to predominate in our minds, as an habitual and settled principle, always operating, though not always perceived; and our attention should seldom wander so far from our own condition, as not to be recalled and fixed by sight of an event, which must soon, we know not how soon, happen likewise to ourselves, and of which, though we cannot appoint the time, we may secure the consequence.

Every instance of death may justly awaken our fears and quicken our vigilance; but its frequency so much weakens its effect, that we are seldom alarmed unless some close connection is broken, some scheme frustrated, or some hope defeated. Many therefore seem to pass on from youth to decrepitude without any reflection on the end of life, because they are wholly involved within themselves, and look on others only as inhabitants of the common earth, without any expectation of receiving good, or intention of bestowing it.

Events of which we confess the importance, excite little sensibility, unless they affect us more nearly than as sharers in the common interest of mankind; that desire which every man feels of being remembered and lamented, is often mortified when we remark how little concern is caused by the eternal departure even of those who have passed their lives with public honours, and been distinguished by extraordinary performances. It is not possible to be regarded with tenderness except by a few. That merit which gives greatness and renown, diffuses its influence to a wide compass, but acts weakly on every single breast; it is placed at a distance from common spectators, and shines like one of the remote stars, of which the light reaches us, but not the heat. The wit, the hero, the philosopher, whom their tempers or their fortunes have hindered from intimate relations, die, without any other effect than that of adding a new topic to the conversation of the day. They impress none with any fresh conviction of the fragility of our nature, because none had any particular interest in their lives, or was united to them by a reciprocation of benefits and endearments.

Thus it often happens that those who in their lives were applauded and admired are laid at last in the ground without the common honour of a stone; because by those excellencies with which many were delighted, none had been obliged, and though they had many to celebrate, they had none to love them.

Custom so far regulates the sentiments, at least of common minds, that I believe men may be generally observed to grow less tender as they advance in age. He who, when life was new, melted at the loss of every companion, can look in time, without concern, upon the grave into which his last friend was thrown, and into which himself is ready to fall; not that he is more willing to die than formerly, but that he is more familiar to the death of others, and therefore is not alarmed so far as to consider how much nearer he approaches to his end. But this is to submit tamely to the tyranny of accident, and to suffer our reason to lie useless. Every funeral may justly be considered as a summons to prepare for that state, into which it shows us that we must some time enter; and the summons is more loud and piercing, as the event of which it warns us is at less distance. To neglect at any time preparation for death, is to sleep on our post at a siege; but to omit it in old age, is to sleep at an attack.

It has always appeared to me one of the most striking passages in the visions of [Francisco de] Quevedo, which stigmatises those as fools who complain that they failed of happiness by sudden death. "How," says he, "can death be sudden to a being who always knew that he must die, and that the time of his death was uncertain?"[2]

Since business and gaiety are always drawing our attention away from a future state, some admonition is frequently necessary to recall it to our minds; and what can more properly renew the impression than the examples of mortality which every day supplies? The great incentive to virtue is the reflection that we must die; it will therefore be useful to accustom ourselves, whenever we see a funeral, to consider how soon we may be added to the number of those whose probation is past, and whose happiness or misery shall endure for ever.

Idler no. 41, January 27, 1759: On the death of a friend

[A few days earlier Johnson's mother had died.]

The following letter relates to an affliction perhaps not necessary to be imparted to the public; but I could not persuade myself to suppress it, because I think, I know the sentiments to be sincere, and I feel no disposition to provide for this day any other entertainment.

> *At tu quisquis eris, miseri qui cruda poetae*
> *Credideris fletu funera digna tuo,*
> *Haec postrema tibi sit flendi causa, fluatque*
> *Lenis inoffenso vitaque morsque gradu.*
>
> Unknown source

Mr. Idler,

Notwithstanding the warnings of philosophers, and the daily examples of losses and misfortunes which life forces upon our observation, such is the absorption of our thoughts in the business of the present day, such the resignation of our reason to empty hopes of future felicity, or such our unwillingness to foresee what we dread, that every calamity comes suddenly upon us, and not only presses us as a burden, but crushes as a blow.

There are evils which happen out of the common course of nature, against which it is no reproach not to be provided. A flash of lightning intercepts the traveller in his way. The concussion of an earthquake heaps the ruins of cities upon their inhabitants. But other miseries time brings, though silently yet visibly, forward by its even lapse, which yet approach us unseen, because we turn our eyes away, and seize us unresisted, because we could not arm ourselves against them but by setting them before us.

That it is vain to shrink from what cannot be avoided, and to hide that from ourselves which must some time be found, is a truth which we all know, but which all neglect, and, perhaps, none more than the speculative reasoner, whose thoughts are always from home, whose eye wanders over life, whose fancy dances after meteors of happiness kindled by itself, and who examines everything rather than his own state.

Nothing is more evident than that the decays of age must terminate in death; yet there is no man, says Tully,[3] who does not believe that he may yet live another year; and there is none who does not, upon the same principle, hope another year for his parent or his friend: but the fallacy will be in time detected; the last year, the last day, must come. It has come, and is past. The life which made my own life pleasant is at an end, and the gates of death are shut upon my prospects.

The loss of a friend upon whom the heart was fixed, to whom every wish and endeavour tended, is a state of dreary desolation, in which the mind looks abroad impatient of itself, and finds nothing but emptiness and horror. The blameless life, the artless tenderness, the pious simplicity, the modest resignation, the patient sickness, and the quiet death, are remembered only to add value to the loss, to aggravate regret for what cannot be amended, to deepen sorrow for what cannot be recalled.

These are the calamities by which Providence gradually disengages us from the love of life. Other evils fortitude may repel, or hope may mitigate; but irreparable privation leaves nothing to exercise resolution or flatter expectation. The dead cannot return, and nothing is left us here but languishment and grief.

Yet such is the course of nature, that whoever lives long must outlive those whom he loves and honours. Such is the condition of our present existence, that life must one time lose its associations, and every inhabitant of the earth must walk downward to the grave alone and unregarded, without any partner of his joy or grief, without any interested witness of his misfortunes or success.

Misfortune, indeed, he may yet feel; for where is the bottom of the misery of man? But what is success to him that has none to enjoy it? Happiness is not found in self-contemplation; it is perceived only when it is reflected from another.

We know little of the state of departed souls because such knowledge is not necessary to a good life. Reason deserts us at the brink of the grave, and can give no further intelligence. Revelation is not wholly silent. "There is joy in the angels of heaven over one sinner that repenteth";[4] and, surely, this joy is not incommunicable to souls disentangled from the body, and made like angels.

Let hope therefore dictate what revelation does not confute, that the union of souls may still remain; and that we who are struggling with sin, sorrow, and infirmities, may have our part in the attention and kindness of those who have finished their course, and are now receiving their reward.

These are the great occasions which force the mind to take refuge in religion: when we have no help in ourselves, what can remain but that we look up to a higher and a greater power; and to what hope may we not raise our eyes and hearts, when we consider that the greatest power is the best.

Surely there is no man who, thus afflicted, does not seek succour in the Gospel, which has brought "life and immortality to light."[5] The precepts of Epicurus, who teaches us to endure what the laws of the universe make necessary, may silence, but not content us. The dictates of Zeno, who commands us to look with indifference on external things, may dispose us to conceal our sorrow, but cannot assuage it. Real alleviation of the loss of friends, and rational tranquillity, in the prospect of our own dissolution, can be received only from the promises of Him in whose hands are life and death, and from the assurance of another and better state, in which all tears will be wiped from the eyes, and the whole soul shall be filled with joy. Philosophy may infuse stubbornness, but religion only can give patience.

I am, & c.

Politics

Idler no. 10, June 17, 1758: **Political zealots**

Credulity, or confidence of opinion too great for the evidence from which opinion is derived, we find to be a general weakness imputed by every sect and party to all others, and indeed by every man to every other man.

Of all kinds of credulity, the most obstinate and wonderful is that of political zealots; of men who being numbered, they know not how or why, in any of the parties that divide a state, resign the use of their own eyes and ears, and resolve to believe nothing that does not favour those whom they profess to follow.

The bigot of philosophy is seduced by authorities which he has not always opportunities to examine, is entangled in systems by which truth and falsehood are inextricably complicated, or undertakes to talk on subjects which nature did not form him able to comprehend.

The Cartesian who denies that his horse feels the spur, or that the hare is afraid when the hounds approach her; the disciple of Malbranche, who maintains that the man was not hurt by the bullet, which, according to vulgar apprehension, swept away his legs; the follower of Berkeley, who while he sits writing at his table, declares that he has neither table, paper, nor fingers; have all the honour at least of being deceived by fallacies not easily detected, and may plead that they did not forsake truth, but for appearances which they were not able to distinguish from it.

But the man who engages in a party has seldom to do with any thing remote or abstruse. The present state of things is before his eyes; and, if he cannot be satisfied without retrospection, yet he seldom extends his views beyond the historical events of the last century. All the knowledge that he can want is within his attainment, and most of the arguments which he can hear are within his capacity.

Yet so it is, that an Idler meets every hour of his life with men who have different opinions upon everything past, present, and future; who deny the most notorious facts, contradict the most cogent truths, and persist in asserting today what they asserted yesterday, in defiance of evidence, and contempt of confutation.

Two of my companions, who are grown old in idleness, are Tom Tempest and Jack Sneaker. Both of them consider themselves as neglected by their parties, and therefore entitled to credit; for why should they favour ingratitude? They are both men of integrity, where no factious interest is to be promoted; and both lovers of truth, when they are not heated with political debate.

Tom Tempest is a steady friend to the house of Stuart. He can recount the prodigies that have appeared in the sky, and the calamities that have afflicted the nation every year from the Revolution; and is of opinion, that, if the exiled family had continued to reign, there would have neither been worms in our ships nor caterpillars in our trees. He wonders that the nation was not awakened by the hard frost to a revocation of the true king, and is hourly afraid that the whole island will be lost in the sea. He believes that king William burned Whitehall that he might steal the furniture; and that Tillotson died an atheist. Of Queen Anne he speaks with more tenderness, owns that she meant well, and can tell by whom and why she was poisoned. In the succeeding reigns all has been corruption, malice, and design. He believes that nothing ill has ever happened for these forty years by chance or error; he holds that the battle of Dettingen was won by mistake, and that of Fontenoy lost by contract; that the *Victory* was sunk by a private order; that Cornhill was fired by emissaries from the council; and the arch of Westminster Bridge was so contrived as to sink on purpose that the nation might be put to charge. He considers the new road to Islington as an encroachment on liberty, and often asserts that "broad wheels" will be the ruin of England.[1]

Tom is generally vehement and noisy, but nevertheless has some secrets which he always communicates in a whisper. Many and many a time has Tom told me, in a corner, that our miseries were almost at an end, and that we should see, in a month, another monarch on the throne; the time elapses without a revolution; Tom meets me again with new intelligence, the whole scheme is now settled, and we shall see great events in another month.

Jack Sneaker is a hearty adherent to the present establishment; he has known those who saw the bed into which the Pretender was conveyed in a warming pan. He often rejoices that the nation was not enslaved by the Irish. He believes that King William never lost a battle, and that if he had lived one year longer he would have conquered France. He holds that Charles the First was a Papist. He allows there were some good men in the reign of Queen Anne, but the Peace of Utrecht brought a blast upon the nation, and has been the cause of all the evil that we have suffered to the present hour. He believes that the scheme of the South Sea was well intended, but that it miscarried by the influence of France. He considers a standing army as the bulwark of liberty, thinks us secured from corruption by septennial parliaments, relates how we are enriched and strengthened by the electoral dominions, and declares that the public debt is a blessing to the nation.

Yet, amidst all this prosperity, poor Jack is hourly disturbed by the dread of Popery. He wonders that some stricter laws are not made against Papists, and is sometimes afraid that they are busy with French gold among the bishops and judges.

He cannot believe that the Nonjurors are so quiet for nothing, they must certainly be forming some plot for the establishment of Popery; he does not think the present oaths sufficiently binding, and wishes that some better security could be found for the succession of Hanover. He is zealous for the naturalization of foreign Protestants, and rejoiced at the admission of the Jews to the English privileges, because he thought a Jew would never be a Papist.

Idler no. 20, August 26, 1758: Current events and writing history truthfully

There is no crime more infamous than the violation of truth. It is apparent that men can be social beings no longer than they believe each other. When speech is employed only as the vehicle of falsehood, every man must disunite himself from others, inhabit his own cave, and seek prey only for himself.

Yet the law of truth, thus sacred and necessary, is broken without punishment, without censure, in compliance with inveterate prejudice and prevailing passions. Men are willing to credit what they wish, and encourage rather those who gratify them with pleasure, than those that instruct them with fidelity.

For this reason every historian discovers his country; and it is impossible to read the different accounts of any great event, without a wish that truth had more power over partiality.

Amidst the joy of my countrymen for the acquisition of Louisbourg, I could not forbear to consider how differently this revolution of American power is not only now mentioned by the contending nations, but will be represented by the writers of another century.

The English historian will imagine himself barely doing justice to English virtue, when he relates the capture of Louisbourg in the following manner:

"The English had hitherto seen, with great indignation, their attempts baffled and their force defied by an enemy whom they considered themselves as entitled to conquer by the right of prescription, and whom many ages of hereditary superiority had taught them to despise. Their fleets were more numerous, and their seamen braver, than those of France; yet they only floated useless on the ocean, and the French derided them from their ports. Misfortunes, as is usual, produced discontent, the people murmured at the ministers, and the ministers censured the commanders.

"In the summer of this year, the English began to find their success answerable to their cause. A fleet and an army were sent to America to dislodge the enemies from the settlements which they had so perfidiously made, and so insolently maintained, and to repress that power which was growing more every day by the association of the Indians, with whom these degenerate Europeans intermarried, and whom they secured to their party by presents and promises.

"In the beginning of June the ships of war and vessels containing the land forces appeared before Louisbourg, a place so secured by nature that art was almost superfluous, and yet fortified by art as if nature had left it open. The French boasted that it was impregnable, and spoke with scorn of all attempts that could be made against it. The garrison was numerous, the stores equal to the longest siege, and their engineers and commanders high in reputation. The mouth of the harbour was so narrow, that three ships within might easily defend it against all attacks from the sea. The French had, with that caution which cowards borrow from fear and attribute to policy, eluded our fleets, and sent into that port five great ships and six smaller, of which they sunk four in the mouth of the passage, having raised batteries and posted troops at all the places where they thought it possible to make a descent. The English, however, had more to dread from the roughness of the sea, than from the skill or bravery of the defendants. Some days passed before the surges, which rise very high round that island, would suffer them to land. At last their impatience could be restrained no longer; they got possession of the shore with little loss by the sea, and with less by the enemy. In a few days the artillery was landed, the batteries were raised, and the French had no other hope than to escape from one post to another. A shot from the batteries fired the powder in one of their largest ships, the flame spread to the two next, and all three were destroyed; the English admiral sent his boats against the two large ships yet remaining, took them without resistance, and terrified the garrison to an immediate capitulation."

Let us now oppose to this English narrative the relation which will be produced, about the same time, by the writer of the age of Louis XV.

"About this time the English admitted to the conduct of affairs a man [William Pitt] who undertook to save from destruction that ferocious and turbulent people, who, from the mean insolence of wealthy traders, and the lawless confidence of successful robbers, were now sunk in despair and stupefied with horror. He called in the ships which had been dispersed over the ocean to guard their merchants, and sent a fleet and an army, in which almost the whole strength of England was comprised, to secure their possessions in America, which were endangered alike by the French arms and the French virtue. We had taken the English fortresses by force, and gained the Indian nations by humanity. The English, wherever they come, are sure to have the natives for their enemies; for the only motive of their settlements is avarice, and the only consequence of their success is oppression. In this war they acted like other barbarians; and, with a degree of outrageous cruelty, which the gentleness of our manners scarcely suffers us to conceive, offered rewards by open proclamation to those who should bring in the scalps of Indian women and children. A trader always makes war with the cruelty of a pirate.

"They had long looked with envy and with terror upon the influence which the French exerted over all the northern regions of America by the possession of Louisbourg, a place naturally strong, and new-fortified with some slight outworks. They hoped to surprise the garrison unprovided; but that sluggishness, which always defeats their malice, gave us time to send supplies, and to station ships for the defence of the harbour. They came before Louisbourg in June, and were for some time in doubt whether they should land. But the commanders, who had lately seen an admiral beheaded for not having done what he had not power to do,[2] durst not leave the place unassaulted. An Englishman has no ardour for honour, nor zeal for duty; he neither values glory nor loves his king, but balances one danger with another, and will fight rather than be hanged. They therefore landed, but with great loss their engineers had, in the last war with the French, learned something of the military science, and made their approaches with sufficient skill; but all their efforts had been without effect, had not a ball unfortunately fallen into the powder of one of our ships, which communicated the fire to the rest, and, by opening the passage of the harbour, obliged the garrison to capitulate. Thus was Louisbourg lost, and our troops marched out with the admiration of their enemies, who durst hardly think themselves masters of the place."

Idler no. 22, September 16, 1758: Imprisonment for debt

O nomen dulce libertatis! O jus eximium nostrae civitatis!
Cicero, *Actionis Secundae in C. Verrem*, V. 163

To the Idler.

Sir,

As I was passing lately under one of the gates of this city, I was struck with horror by a rueful cry, which summoned me "to remember the poor debtors."

The wisdom and justice of the English laws are, by Englishmen at least, loudly celebrated: but scarcely the most zealous admirers of our institutions can think that law wise, which, when men are capable of work, obliges them to beg; or just, which exposes the liberty of one to the passions of another.

The prosperity of a people is proportionate to the number of hands and minds usefully employed. To the community, sedition is a fever, corruption is a gangrene, and idleness an atrophy. Whatever body, and whatever society, wastes more than it acquires, must gradually decay; and every being that continues to be fed, and ceases to labour, takes away something from the public stock.

The confinement, therefore, of any man in the sloth and darkness of a prison, is a loss to the nation, and no gain to the creditor. For of the multitudes who are pining in those cells of misery, a very small part is suspected of any fraudulent act by which they retain what belongs to others. The rest are imprisoned by the wantonness of pride, the malignity of revenge, or the acrimony of disappointed expectation.

If those who thus rigorously exercise the power which the law has put into their hands, be asked, why they continue to imprison those whom they know to be unable to pay them; one will answer, that his debtor once lived better than himself; another, that his wife looked above her neighbours, and his children went in silk clothes to the dancing school; and another, that he pretended to be a joker and a wit. Some will reply, that if they were in debt, they should meet with the same treatment; some, that they owe no more than they can pay, and need therefore give no account of their actions. Some will confess their resolution that their debtors shall rot in jail; and some will discover that they hope, by cruelty, to wring the payment from their friends.

The end of all civil regulations is to secure private happiness from private malignity; to keep individuals from the power of one another; but this end is apparently neglected, when a man, irritated with loss, is allowed to be the judge of his own cause, and to assign the punishment of his own pain; when the distinction between guilt and happiness, between casualty and design, is entrusted to eyes blind with interest, to understandings depraved by resentment.

Since poverty is punished among us as a crime, it ought at least to be treated with the same lenity as other crimes; the offender ought not to languish at the will of him whom he has offended, but to be allowed some appeal to the justice of his country. There can be no reason why any debtor should be imprisoned, but that he may be compelled to payment; and a term should therefore be fixed, in which the creditor should exhibit his accusation of concealed property. If such property can be discovered, let it be given to the creditor; if the charge is not offered, or cannot be proved, let the prisoner be dismissed.

Those who made the laws have apparently supposed, that every deficiency of payment is the crime of the debtor. But the truth is, that the creditor always shares the act, and often more than shares the guilt, of improper trust. It seldom happens that any man imprisons another but for debts which he suffered to be contracted in hope of advantage to himself, and for bargains in which he proportioned his profit to his own opinion of the hazard; and there is no reason why one should punish the other for a contract in which both concurred.

Many of the inhabitants of prisons may justly complain of harder treatment. He that once owes more than he can pay, is often obliged to bribe his creditor to patience, by increasing his debt. Worse and worse commodities, at a higher and higher price, are forced upon him; he is impoverished by compulsive traffic, and at last overwhelmed, in the common receptacles of misery, by debts, which, without his own consent, were accumulated on his head. To the relief of this distress, no other objection can be made, but that by an easy dissolution of debts fraud will be left without punishment, and imprudence without awe; and that when insolvency should be no longer punishable, credit will cease.

The motive to credit is the hope of advantage. Commerce can never be at a stop, while one man wants what another can supply; and credit will never be denied, while it is likely to be repaid with profit. He that trusts one whom he designs to sue, is criminal by the act of trust: the cessation of such insidious traffic is to be desired, and no reason can be given why a change of the law should impair any other.

We see nation trade with nation, where no payment can be compelled. Mutual convenience produces mutual confidence; and the merchants continue to satisfy the demands of each other, though they have nothing to dread but the loss of trade.

It is vain to continue an institution which experience shows to be ineffectual. We have now imprisoned one generation of debtors after another, but we do not find that their numbers lessen. We have now learned that rashness and imprudence will not be deterred from taking credit; let us try whether fraud and avarice may be more easily restrained from giving it.

I am, Sir, &c.

Idler no. 38, January 6, 1759: Imprisonment for debt

Since the publication of the letter concerning the condition of those who are confined in gaols by their creditors, an inquiry is said to have been made, by which it appears that more than twenty thousand are at this time prisoners for debt.

We often look with indifference on the successive parts of that which, if the whole were seen together, would shake us with emotion. A debtor is dragged to prison, pitied for a moment, and then forgotten; another follows him, and is lost alike in the caverns of oblivion; but when the whole mass of calamity rises up at once, when twenty thousand reasonable beings are heard all groaning in unnecessary misery, not by the infirmity of nature, but the mistake or negligence of policy, who can forbear to pity and lament, to wonder and abhor.

There is here no need of declamatory vehemence: we live in an age of commerce and computation; let us, therefore, coolly inquire what is the sum of evil which the imprisonment of debtors brings upon our country.

It seems to be the opinion of the later computists, that the inhabitants of England do not exceed six millions, of which twenty thousand is the three-hundredth part. What shall we say of the humanity or the wisdom of a nation, that voluntarily sacrifices one in every three hundred to lingering destruction?

The misfortunes of an individual do not extend their influence to many; yet, if we consider the effects of consanguinity and friendship, and the general reciprocation of wants and benefits, which make one man dear or necessary to another, it may reasonably be supposed that every man languishing in prison gives trouble of some kind to two others who love or need him. By this multiplication of misery we see distress extended to the hundredth part of the whole society.

If we estimate at a shilling a day what is lost by the inaction, and consumed in the support of each man thus chained down to involuntary idleness, the public loss will rise in one year to three hundred thousand pounds; in ten years to more than a sixth part of our circulating coin.

I am afraid that those who are best acquainted with the state of our prisons will confess that my conjecture is too near the truth, when I suppose that the corrosion of resentment, the heaviness of sorrow, the corruption of confined air, the want of exercise, and sometimes of food, the contagion of diseases, from which there is no retreat, and the severity of tyrants, against whom there can be no resistance, and all the complicated horrors of a prison, put an end every year to the life of one in four of those that are shut up from the common comforts of human life.

Thus perish yearly five thousand men overborne with sorrow, consumed by famine, or putrefied by filth; many of them in the most vigorous and useful part of life; for the thoughtless and imprudent are commonly young, and the active and busy are seldom old.

According to the rule generally received, which supposes that one in thirty dies yearly, the race of man may be said to be renewed at the end of thirty years. Who would have believed till now, that of every English generation, a hundred and fifty thousand perish in our gaols! That in every century, a nation eminent for science, studious of commerce, ambitious of empire, should willingly lose, in noisome dungeons, five hundred thousand of its inhabitants; a number greater than has ever been destroyed in the same time by pestilence and the sword!

A very late occurrence may show us the value of the number which we thus condemn to be useless; in the reestablishment of the trained bands, thirty thousand are considered as a force sufficient against all exigencies. While, therefore, we detain twenty thousand in prison, we shut up in darkness and uselessness two-thirds of an army which ourselves judge equal to the defence of our country.

The monastic institutions have been often blamed, as tending to retard the increase of mankind. And, perhaps, retirement ought rarely to be permitted, except to those whose employment is consistent with abstraction, and who, though solitary, will not be idle; to those whom infirmity makes useless to the commonwealth, or to those who have paid their due proportion to society, and who, having lived for others, may be honourably dismissed to live for themselves. But whatever be the evil or the folly of these retreats, those have no right to censure them whose prisons contain greater numbers than the monasteries of other countries. It is, surely, less foolish and less criminal to permit inaction than compel it; to comply with doubtful opinions of happiness, than condemn to certain and apparent misery; to indulge the extravagancies of erroneous piety, than to multiply and enforce temptations to wickedness.

The misery of gaols is not half their evil: they are filled with every corruption which poverty and wickedness can generate between them; with all the shameless and profligate enormities that can be produced by the impudence of ignominy, the rage of want, and the malignity of despair. In a prison the awe of the public eye is lost, and the power of the law is spent; there are few fears, there are no blushes. The lewd inflame the lewd, the audacious harden the audacious. Every one fortifies himself as he can against his own sensibility, endeavours to practise on others the arts which are practised on himself, and gains the kindness of his associates by similitude of manners.

Thus some sink amidst their misery, and others survive only to propagate villainy. It may be hoped, that our lawgivers will at length take away from us this power of starving and depraving one another; but, if there be any reason why this inveterate evil should not be removed in our age, which true policy has enlightened beyond any former time, let those whose writings form the opinions and the practices of their contemporaries, endeavour to transfer the reproach of such imprisonment from the debtor to the creditor, till universal infamy shall pursue the wretch whose wantonness of power, or revenge of disappointment, condemns another to torture and to ruin; till he shall be hunted through the world as an enemy to man, and find in riches no shelter from contempt.

Surely, he whose debtor has perished in prison, although he may acquit himself of deliberate murder, must at least have his mind clouded with discontent when he considers how much another has suffered from him; when he thinks on the wife bewailing her husband, or the children begging the bread which their father would have earned. If there are any made so obdurate by avarice or cruelty, as to revolve these consequences without dread or pity, I must leave them to be awakened by some other power, for I write only to human beings.[3]

Idler no. 81, November 3, 1759:
Rape and oppression of North American Indians

As the English army was passing towards Quebec[4] along a soft savanna between a mountain and a lake, one of the petty chiefs of the inland regions stood upon a rock surrounded by his clan, and from behind the shelter of the bushes contemplated the art and regularity of European war. It was evening, the tents were pitched: he observed the security with which the troops rested in the night, and the order with which the march was renewed in the morning. He continued to pursue them with his eye till they could be seen no longer, and then stood for some time silent and pensive.

Then turning to his followers, "My children," said he, "I have often heard from men hoary with long life, that there was a time when our ancestors were absolute lords of the woods, the meadows, and the lakes, wherever the eye can reach or the foot can pass. They fished and hunted, feasted and danced, and when they were weary lay down under the first thicket, without danger and without fear. They changed their habitations, as the seasons required, convenience prompted, or curiosity allured them; and sometimes gathered the fruits of the mountain, and sometimes sported in canoes along the coast.

"Many years and ages are supposed to have been thus passed in plenty and security; when, at last, a new race of men entered our country from the great ocean. They enclosed themselves in habitations of stone, which our ancestors could neither enter by violence, nor destroy by fire. They issued from those fastnesses, sometimes covered, like the armadillo, with shells, from which the lance rebounded on the striker, and sometimes carried by mighty beasts which had never been seen in our vales or forests, of such strength and swiftness, that flight and opposition were vain alike. Those invaders ranged over the continent slaughtering, in their rage, those that resisted, and those that submitted, in their mirth. Of those that remained, some were buried in caverns, and condemned to dig metals for their masters; some were employed in tilling the ground, of which foreign tyrants devour the produce; and, when the sword and the mines have destroyed the natives, they supply their place by human beings of another colour, brought from some distant country to perish here under toil and torture.

"Some there are who boast their humanity, and content themselves to seize our chases and fisheries, who drive us from every tract of ground where fertility and pleasantness invite them to settle, and make no war upon us except when we intrude upon our own lands.

"Others pretend to have purchased a right of residence and tyranny; but surely the insolence of such bargains is more offensive than the avowed and open dominion of force. What reward can induce the possessor of a country to admit a stranger more powerful than himself? Fraud or terror must operate in such contracts; either they promised protection which they never have afforded, or instruction which they never imparted. We hoped to be secured by their favour from some other evil, or to learn the arts of Europe, by which we might be able to secure ourselves. Their power they never have exerted in our defence, and their arts they have studiously concealed from us. Their treaties are only to deceive, and their traffic only to defraud us. They have a written law among them, of which they boast, as derived from Him who made the earth and sea, and by which they profess to believe that man will be made happy when life shall forsake him. Why is not this law communicated to us? It is concealed because it is violated. For how can they preach it to an Indian nation, when I am told that one of its first precepts forbids them to do to others what they would not that others should do to them.

"But the time perhaps is now approaching when the pride of usurpation shall be crushed and the cruelties of invasion shall be revenged. The sons of rapacity have now drawn their swords upon each other, and referred their claims to the decision of war; let us look unconcerned upon the slaughter, and remember that the death of every European delivers the country from a tyrant and a robber; for what is the claim of either nation, but the claim of the vulture to the leveret, of the tiger to the fawn? Let them then continue to dispute their title to regions which they cannot people, to purchase by danger and blood the empty dignity of dominion over mountains which they will never climb, and rivers which they will never pass. Let us endeavour, in the mean time, to learn their discipline, and to forge their weapons; and, when they shall be weakened with mutual slaughter, let us rush down upon them, force their remains to take shelter in their ships, and reign once more in our native country."[5]

PART II

Excerpts from the Preface to
A Dictionary of
the English Language (1755)

I t is the fate of those who toil at the lower employments of life, to be rather driven by the fear of evil, than attracted by the prospect of good; to be exposed to censure, without hope of praise; to be disgraced by miscarriage, or punished for neglect, where success would have been without applause, and diligence without reward.

Among these unhappy mortals is the writer of dictionaries; whom mankind have considered, not as the pupil, but the slave of science, the pioneer of literature, doomed only to remove rubbish and clear obstructions from the paths through which learning and genius press forward to conquest and glory, without bestowing a smile on the humble drudge that facilitates their progress. Every other author may aspire to praise; the lexicographer can only hope to escape reproach, and even this negative recompense has been yet granted to very few.

I have, notwithstanding this discouragement, attempted a dictionary of the English language, which, while it was employed in the cultivation of every species of literature, has itself been hitherto neglected; suffered to spread, under the direction of chance, into wild exuberance; resigned to the tyranny of time and fashion; and exposed to the corruptions of ignorance, and caprices of innovation.

When I took the first survey of my undertaking, I found our speech copious without order, and energetic without rules: wherever I turned my view, there was perplexity to be disentangled, and confusion to be regulated; choice was to be made out of boundless variety, without any established principle of selection; adulterations were to be detected, without a settled test of purity; and modes of expression to be rejected or received, without the suffrages of any writers of classical reputation or acknowledged authority.

Having therefore no assistance but from general grammar, I applied myself to the perusal of our writers; and noting whatever might be of use to ascertain or illustrate any word or phrase, accumulated in time the materials of a dictionary, which, by degrees, I reduced to method, establishing to myself, in the progress of the work, such rules as experience and analogy suggested to me; experience, which practice and observation were continually increasing; and analogy, which, though in some words obscure, was evident in others.

In adjusting the ORTHOGRAPHY, which has been to this time unsettled and fortuitous, I found it necessary to distinguish those irregularities that are inherent in our tongue, and perhaps coeval with it, from others which the ignorance or negligence of later writers has produced. Every language has its anomalies, which, though inconvenient, and in themselves once unnecessary, must be tolerated among the imperfections of human things, and which require only to be registered, that they may not be increased, and ascertained, that they may not be confounded: but every language has likewise its improprieties and absurdities, which it is the duty of the lexicographer to correct or proscribe.

As language was at its beginning merely oral, all words of necessary or common use were spoken before they were written; and while they were unfixed by any visible signs, must have been spoken with great diversity, as we now observe those who cannot read catch sounds imperfectly, and utter them negligently. When this wild and barbarous jargon was first reduced to an alphabet, every penman endeavoured to express, as he could, the sounds which he was accustomed to pronounce or to receive, and vitiated in writing such words as were already vitiated in speech. The powers of the letters, when they were applied to a new language, must have been vague and unsettled, and therefore different hands would exhibit the same sound by different combinations.

From this uncertain pronunciation arise in a great part the various dialects of the same country, which will always be observed to grow fewer, and less different, as books are multiplied; and from this arbitrary representation of sounds by letters, proceeds that diversity of spelling observable in the Saxon remains, and I suppose in the first books of every nation, which perplexes or destroys analogy, and produces anomalous formations that, being once incorporated, can never be afterward dismissed or reformed.

Of this kind are the derivatives *length* from *long, strength* from *strong, darling* from *dear, breadth* from *broad,* from *dry, drought,* and from *high, height,* which Milton, in zeal for analogy, writes *highth;* "Quid te exempta juvat spinis de pluribus una";[1] to change all would be too much, and to change one is nothing.

This uncertainty is most frequent in the vowels, which are so capriciously pronounced, and so differently modified, by accident or affectation, not only in every province, but in every mouth, that to them, as is well known to etymologists, little regard is to be shown in the deduction of one language from another.

Such defects are not errors in orthography, but spots of barbarity impressed so deep in the English language, that criticism can never wash them away: these, therefore, must be permitted to remain untouched; but many words have likewise been altered by accident, or depraved by ignorance, as the pronunciation of the vulgar has been weakly followed; and some still continue to be variously written, as authors differ in their care or skill: of these it was proper to enquire the true orthography, which I have always considered as depending on their derivation, and have therefore referred them to their original languages: thus I write *enchant, enchantment, enchanter,* after the French and *incantation* after the Latin; thus *entire* is chosen rather than *intire,* because it passed to us not from the Latin *integer,* but from the French *entier.*

Of many words it is difficult to say whether they were immediately received from the Latin or the French, since at the time when we had dominions in France, we had Latin service in our churches. It is, however, my opinion, that the French generally supplied us; for we have few Latin words, among the terms of domestic use, which are not French; but many French, which are very remote from Latin.

Even in words of which the derivation is apparent, I have been often obliged to sacrifice uniformity to custom; thus I write, in compliance with a numberless majority, *convey* and *inveigh, deceit* and *receipt, fancy* and *phantom;* sometimes the derivative varies from the primitive, as *explain* and *explanation, repeat* and *repetition.*

Some combinations of letters having the same power are used indifferently without any discoverable reason of choice, as in *choak, choke; soap, sope; fewel, fuel,* and many others; which I have sometimes inserted twice, that those who search for them under either form, may not search in vain.

In examining the orthography of any doubtful word, the mode of spelling by which it is inserted in the series of the dictionary, is to be considered as that to which I give, perhaps not often rashly, the preference. I have left, in the examples, to every author his own practice unmolested, that the reader may balance suffrages, and judge between us: but this question is not always to be determined by reputed or by real learning; some men, intent upon greater things, have thought little on sounds and derivations; some, knowing in the ancient tongues, have neglected those in which our words are commonly to be sought. Thus Hammond[2] writes *fecibleness* for *feasibleness,* because I suppose he imagined it derived immediately from the Latin; and some words, such as *dependant, dependent, dependance, dependence,* vary their final syllable, as one or another language is present to the writer.

In this part of the work, where caprice has long wantoned without control, and vanity sought praise by petty reformation, I have endeavoured to proceed with a scholar's reverence for antiquity, and a grammarian's regard to the genius of our tongue. I have attempted few alterations, and among those few, perhaps the greater part is from the modern to the ancient practice; and I hope I may be allowed to recommend to those whose thoughts have been perhaps employed too anxiously on verbal singularities, not to disturb, upon narrow views or for minute propriety, the orthography of their fathers. It has been asserted, that for the law to be *known,* is of more importance than to be *right.* Change, says Hooker,[3] is not made without inconvenience, even from worse to better. There is in constancy and stability a general and lasting advantage, which will always overbalance the slow improvements of gradual correction. Much less ought our written language to comply with the corruptions of oral utterance, or copy that which every variation of time or place makes different from itself, and imitate those changes, which will again be changed, while imitation is employed in observing them.

This recommendation of steadiness and uniformity does not proceed from an opinion that particular combinations of letters have much influence on human happiness; or that truth may not be successfully taught by modes of spelling fanciful and erroneous: I am not yet so lost in lexicography as to forget that words are the daughters of earth, and that things are the sons of heaven. Language is only the instrument of science, and words are but the signs of ideas: I wish, however, that the instrument might be less apt to decay, and that signs might be permanent, like the things which they denote.

In settling the orthography, I have not wholly neglected the pronunciation, which I have directed by printing an accent upon the acute or elevated syllable. It will sometimes be found, that the accent is placed by the author quoted, on a different syllable from that marked in the alphabetical series; it is then to be understood that custom has varied, or that the author has, in my opinion, pronounced wrong. Short directions are sometimes given where the sound of letters is irregular; and if they are sometimes omitted, defect in such minute observations will be more easily excused, than superfluity.

In the investigation both of the orthography and signification of words, their ETYMOLOGY was necessarily to be considered. . . .

The etymology, so far as it is yet known, was easily found in the volumes where it is particularly and professedly delivered; and, by proper attention to the rules of derivation, the orthography was soon adjusted. But to COLLECT the WORDS of our language was a task of greater difficulty: the deficiency of dictionaries was immediately apparent; and when they were exhausted, what was yet wanting must be sought by fortuitous and unguided excursions into books, and gleaned as industry should find, or chance should offer it, in the boundless chaos of a living speech. My search, however, has been either skilful or lucky; for I have much augmented the vocabulary. . . .

Many words yet stand supported only by the name of Bailey, Ainsworth, Philips,[4] or the contracted *Dict.* for *Dictionaries* subjoined; of these I am not always certain that they are read in any book but the works of lexicographers. Of such I have omitted many, because I had never read them; and many I have inserted, because they may perhaps exist, though they have escaped my notice: they are, however, to be yet considered as resting only upon the credit of former dictionaries. Others which I considered as useful or know to be proper, though I could not at present support them by authorities, I have suffered to stand upon my own attestation, claiming the same privilege with my predecessors of being sometimes credited without proof. . . .

That part of my work on which I expect malignity most frequently to fasten, is the *explanation* [definition]; in which I cannot hope to satisfy those who are perhaps not inclined to be pleased, since I have not always been able to satisfy myself. To interpret a language by itself is very difficult; many words cannot be explained by synonyms, because the idea signified by them has not more than one appellation; nor by paraphrase, because simple ideas cannot be described. When the nature of things is unknown, or the notion unsettled and indefinite, and various in various minds, the words by which such notions are conveyed, or such things denoted, will be ambiguous and perplexed. And such is the fate of hapless lexicography, that not only darkness, but light, impedes and distresses it; things may be not only too little, but too much known, to be happily illustrated. To explain, requires the use of terms less abstruse than that which is to be explained, and such terms cannot always be found; for as nothing can be proved but by supposing something intuitively known, and evident without proof, so nothing can be defined but by the use of words too plain to admit a definition.

Other words there are, of which the sense is too subtle and evanescent to be fixed in a paraphrase; such are all those which are by the grammarians termed *expletives,* and, in dead languages, are suffered to pass for empty sounds, of no other use than to fill a verse, or to modulate a period, but which are easily perceived in living tongues to have power and emphasis, though it be sometimes such as no other form of expression can convey.

My labour has likewise been much increased by a class of verbs too frequent in the English language, of which the signification is so loose and general, the use so vague and indeterminate, and the senses detorted[5] so widely from the first idea, that it is hard to trace them through the maze of variation, to catch them on the brink of utter inanity, to circumscribe them by any limitations, or interpret them by any words of distinct and settled meaning; such are *bear, break, come, cast, fall, get, give, do, put, set, go, run, make, take, turn, throw.* If of these the whole power is not accurately delivered, it must be remembered that while our language is yet living, and variable by the caprice of every one that speaks it, these words are hourly shifting their relations, and can no more be ascertained in a dictionary, than a grove, in the agitation of a storm, can be accurately delineated from its picture in the water.

The particles are among all nations applied with so great latitude, that they are not easily reducible under any regular scheme of explication: this difficulty is not less, nor perhaps greater, in English, than in other languages. I have laboured them with diligence, I hope with success; such at least as can be expected in a task which no man, however learned or sagacious, has yet been able to perform.

Some words there are which I cannot explain, because I do not understand them; these might have been omitted very often with little inconvenience, but I would not so far indulge my vanity as to decline this confession . . . I may surely, without shame, leave some obscurities to happier industry, or future information. . . .

In every word of extensive use, it was requisite to mark the progress of its meaning, and show by what gradations of intermediate sense it has passed from its primitive to its remote and accidental signification; so that every foregoing explanation should tend to that which follows, and the series be regularly concatenated from the first notion to the last.

This is specious, but not always practicable; kindred senses may be so interwoven, that the perplexity cannot be disentangled, nor any reason be assigned why one should be ranged before the other. When the radical idea branches out into parallel ramifications, how can a consecutive series be formed of senses in their nature collateral? The shades of meaning sometimes pass imperceptibly into each other; so that though on one side they apparently differ, yet it is impossible to mark the point of contact. Ideas of the same race, though not exactly alike, are sometimes so little different, that no words can express the dissimilitude, though the mind easily perceives it when they are exhibited together; and sometimes there is such a confusion of acceptations, that discernment is wearied and distinction puzzled, and perseverance herself hurries to an end, by crowding together what she cannot separate.

These complaints of difficulty will, by those that have never considered words beyond their popular use, be thought only the jargon of a man willing to magnify his labours, and procure veneration to his studies by involution and obscurity. But every art is obscure to those that have not learned it: this uncertainty of terms, and commixture of ideas, is well known to those who have joined philosophy with grammar; and if I have not expressed them very clearly, it must be remembered that I am speaking of that which words are insufficient to explain.

The original sense of words is often driven out of use by their metaphorical acceptations, yet must be inserted for the sake of a regular origination. Thus I know not whether *ardour* is used for *material heat,* or whether *flagrant,* in English, ever signifies the same with *burning;* yet such are the primitive ideas of these words, which are therefore set first, though without examples, that the figurative senses may be commodiously deduced.

Such is the exuberance of signification which many words have obtained, that it was scarcely possible to collect all their senses; sometimes the meaning of derivatives must be sought in the mother term, and sometimes deficient explanations of the primitive may be supplied in the train of derivation. In any case of doubt or difficulty, it will be always proper to examine all the words of the same race; for some words are slightly passed over to avoid repetition, some admitted easier and clearer explanation than others, and all will be better understood, as they are considered in greater variety of structures and relations.

All the interpretations of words are not written with the same skill, or the same happiness: things equally easy in themselves, are not all equally easy to any single mind. Every writer of a long work commits errors, where there appears neither ambiguity to mislead, nor obscurity to confound him; and in a search like this, many felicities of expression will be casually overlooked, many convenient parallels will be forgotten, and many particulars will admit improvement from a mind utterly unequal to the whole performance.

But many seeming faults are to be imputed rather to the nature of the undertaking, than the negligence of the performer. Thus some explanations are unavoidably reciprocal or circular, as *hind, the female of the stag; stag, the male of the hind:* sometimes easier words are changed into harder, as *burial* into *sepulture* or *interment, drier* into *desiccative, dryness* into *siccity*[6] or *aridity, fit* into *paroxysm;* for the easiest word, whatever it be, can never be translated into one more easy. But easiness and difficulty are merely relative, and if the present prevalence of our language should invite foreigners to this dictionary, many will be assisted by those words which now seem only to increase or produce obscurity. . . .

The solution of all difficulties, and the supply of all defects, must be sought in the examples, subjoined to the various senses of each word, and ranged according to the time of their authors.

When first I collected these authorities, I was desirous that every quotation should be useful to some other end than the illustration of a word; I therefore extracted from philosophers principles of science; from historians remarkable facts; from chemists complete processes; from divines striking exhortations; and from poets beautiful descriptions. Such is design, while it is yet at a distance from execution. When the time called upon me to range this accumulation of elegance and wisdom into an alphabetical series, I soon discovered that the bulk of my volumes would fright away the student, and was forced to depart from my scheme of including all that was pleasing or useful in English literature, and reduce my transcripts very often to clusters of words, in which scarcely any meaning is retained; thus to the weariness of copying, I was condemned to add the vexation of expunging. Some passages I have yet spared, which may relieve the labour of verbal searches, and intersperse with verdure and flowers the dusty deserts of barren philology.

The examples, thus mutilated, are no longer to be considered as conveying the sentiments or doctrine of their authors; the word for the sake of which they are inserted, with all its appendant clauses, has been carefully preserved; but it may sometimes happen, by hasty detruncation,[7] that the general tendency of the sentence may be changed: the divine may desert his tenets, or the philosopher his system.

Some of the examples have been taken from writers who were never mentioned as masters of elegance or models of style; but words must be sought where they are used; and in what pages, eminent for purity, can terms of manufacture or agriculture be found? Many quotations serve no other purpose than that of proving the bare existence of words, and are therefore selected with less scrupulousness than those which are to teach their structures and relations.

My purpose was to admit no testimony of living authors, that I might not be misled by partiality, and that none of my contemporaries might have reason to complain; nor have I departed from this resolution, but when some performance of uncommon excellence excited my veneration, when my memory supplied me, from late books, with an example that was wanting, or when my heart, in the tenderness of friendship, solicited admission for a favourite name.

So far have I been from any care to grace my pages with modern decorations, that I have studiously endeavoured to collect examples and authorities from the writers before the restoration, whose works I regard as *the wells of English undefiled,* as the pure sources of genuine diction. Our language, for almost a century, has, by the concurrence of many causes, been gradually departing from its original Teutonic character, and deviating towards a Gallic structure and phraseology, from which it ought to be our endeavour to recall it, by making our ancient volumes the groundwork of style, admitting among the additions of later times, only such as may supply real deficiencies, such as are readily adopted by the genius of our tongue, and incorporate easily with our native idioms.

But as every language has a time of rudeness antecedent to perfection, as well as of false refinement and declension, I have been cautious lest my zeal for antiquity might drive me into times too remote, and crowd my book with words now no longer understood. I have fixed Sidney's work for the boundary, beyond which I make few excursions. From the authors which rose in the time of Elizabeth, a speech might be formed adequate to all the purposes of use and elegance. If the language of theology were extracted from Hooker and the translation of the Bible; the terms of natural knowledge from Bacon; the phrases of policy, war, and navigation from Raleigh; the dialect of poetry and fiction from Spenser and Sidney; and the diction of common life from Shakespeare, few ideas would be lost to mankind, for want of English words in which they might be expressed.

It is not sufficient that a word is found, unless it be so combined as that its meaning is apparently determined by the tract and tenor of the sentence; such passages I have therefore chosen, and when it happened that any author gave a definition of a term, or such an explanation as is equivalent to a definition, I have placed his authority as a supplement to my own, without regard to the chronological order that is otherwise observed.

Some words, indeed, stand unsupported by any authority, but they are commonly derivative nouns or adverbs, formed from their primitives by regular and constant analogy, or names of things seldom occurring in books, or words of which I have reason to doubt the existence.

There is more danger of censure from the multiplicity than paucity of examples; authorities will sometimes seem to have been accumulated without necessity or use, and perhaps some will be found which might, without loss, have been omitted. But a work of this kind is not hastily to be charged with superfluities: those quotations, which to careless or unskilful perusers appear only to repeat the same sense, will often exhibit, to a more accurate examiner, diversities of signification, or, at least, afford different shades of the same meaning: one will show the word applied to persons, another to things; one will express an ill, another a good, and a third a neutral sense; one will prove the expression genuine from an ancient author; another will show it elegant from a modern: a doubtful authority is corroborated by another of more credit; an ambiguous sentence is ascertained by a passage clear and determinate; the word, how often soever repeated, appears with new associates and in different combinations, and every quotation contributes something to the stability or enlargement of the language.

When words are used equivocally, I receive them in either sense; when they are metaphorical, I adopt them in their primitive acceptation.

I have sometimes, though rarely, yielded to the temptation of exhibiting a genealogy of sentiments, by showing how one author copied the thoughts and diction of another: such quotations are indeed little more than repetitions, which might justly be censured, did they not gratify the mind, by affording a kind of intellectual history.

The various syntactical structures occurring in the examples have been carefully noted; the licence or negligence with which many words have been hitherto used, has made our style capricious and indeterminate; when the different combinations of the same word are exhibited together, the preference is readily given to propriety, and I have often endeavoured to direct the choice.

Thus have I laboured by settling the orthography, displaying the analogy, regulating the structures, and ascertaining the signification of English words, to perform all the parts of a faithful lexicographer: but I have not always executed my own scheme, or satisfied my own expectations. The work, whatever proofs of diligence and attention it may exhibit, is yet capable of many improvements: the orthography which I recommend is still controvertible, the etymology which I adopt is uncertain, and perhaps frequently erroneous; the explanations are sometimes too much contracted, and sometimes too much diffused, the significations are distinguished rather with subtlety than skill, and the attention is harassed with unnecessary minuteness.

The examples are too often injudiciously truncated, and perhaps sometimes, I hope very rarely, alleged in a mistaken sense; for in making this collection I trusted more to memory, than, in a state of disquiet and embarrassment, memory can contain, and purposed to supply at the review what was left incomplete in the first transcription.

Many terms appropriated to particular occupations, though necessary and significant, are undoubtedly omitted; and of the words most studiously considered and exemplified, many senses have escaped observation.

Yet these failures, however frequent, may admit extenuation and apology. To have attempted much is always laudable, even when the enterprise is above the strength that undertakes it. To rest below his own aim is incident to every one whose fancy is active, and whose views are comprehensive; nor is any man satisfied with himself because he has done much, but because he can conceive little. When first I engaged in this work, I resolved to leave neither words nor things unexamined, and pleased myself with a prospect of the hours which I should revel away in feasts of literature, with the obscure recesses of northern learning, which I should enter and ransack; the treasures with which I expected every search into those neglected mines to reward my labour, and the triumph with which I should display my acquisitions to mankind. When I had thus enquired into the original of words, I resolved to show likewise my attention to things; to pierce deep into every science, to enquire the nature of every substance of which I inserted the name, to limit every idea by a definition strictly logical, and exhibit every production of art or nature in an accurate description, that my book might be in place of all other dictionaries whether appellative or technical. But these were the dreams of a poet doomed at last to wake a lexicographer. I soon found that it is too late to look for instruments, when the work calls for execution, and that whatever abilities I had brought to my task, with those I must finally perform it. To deliberate whenever I doubted, to enquire whenever I was ignorant, would have protracted the undertaking without end, and, perhaps, without much improvement; for I did not find by my first experiments, that what I had not of my own was easily to be obtained: I saw that one enquiry only gave occasion to another, that book referred to book, that to search was not always to find, and to find was not always to be informed; and that thus to pursue perfection, was, like the first inhabitants of Arcadia, to chase the sun, which, when they had reached the hill where he seemed to rest, was still beheld at the same distance from them.

I then contracted my design, determining to confide in myself, and no longer to solicit auxiliaries which produced more encumbrance than assistance: by this I obtained at least one advantage, that I set limits to my work, which would in time be ended, though not completed.

Despondency has never so far prevailed as to depress me to negligence; some faults will at last appear to be the effects of anxious diligence and persevering activity. The nice and subtle ramifications of meaning were not easily avoided by a mind intent upon accuracy, and convinced of the necessity of disentangling combinations, and separating similitudes. Many of the distinctions which to common readers appear useless and idle, will be found real and important by men versed in the school philosophy, without which no dictionary shall ever be accurately compiled, or skilfully examined.

Some senses however there are which, though not the same, are yet so nearly allied, that they are often confounded. Most men think indistinctly, and therefore cannot speak with exactness; and consequently some examples might be indifferently put to either signification: this uncertainty is not to be imputed to me, who do not form, but register the language; who do not teach men how they should think, but relate how they have hitherto expressed their thoughts.

The imperfect sense of some examples I lamented, but could not remedy, and hope they will be compensated by innumerable passages selected with propriety, and preserved with exactness; some shining with sparks of imagination, and some replete with treasures of wisdom.

The orthography and etymology, though imperfect, are not imperfect for want of care, but because care will not always be successful, and recollection or information come too late for use.

That many terms of art and manufacture are omitted, must be frankly acknowledged; but for this defect I may boldly allege that it was unavoidable: I could not visit caverns to learn the miner's language, nor take a voyage to perfect my skill in the dialect of navigation, nor visit the warehouses of merchants and shops of artificers, to gain the names of wares, tools, and operations, of which no mention is found in books; what favourable accident, or easy enquiry brought within my reach, has not been neglected; but it had been a hopeless labour to glean up words, by courting living information, and contesting with the sullenness of one, and the roughness of another. . . .

Nor are all words which are not found in the vocabulary, to be lamented as omissions. Of the laborious and mercantile part of the people, the diction is in a great measure casual and mutable; many of their terms are formed for some temporary or local convenience, and though current at certain times and places, are in others utterly unknown. This fugitive cant, which is always in a state of increase or decay, cannot be regarded as any part of the durable materials of a language, and therefore must be suffered to perish with other things unworthy of preservation.

Care will sometimes betray to the appearance of negligence. He that is catching opportunities which seldom occur, will suffer those to pass by unregarded, which he expects hourly to return; he that is searching for rare and remote things, will neglect those that are obvious and familiar: thus many of the most common and cursory words have been inserted with little illustration, because in gathering the authorities, I forbore to copy those which I thought likely to occur whenever they were wanted. It is remarkable that, in reviewing my collection, I found the word SEA unexemplified.

Thus it happens, that in things difficult there is danger from ignorance, and in things easy from confidence; the mind, afraid of greatness, and disdainful of littleness, hastily withdraws herself from painful searches, and passes with scornful rapidity over tasks not adequate to her powers, sometimes too secure for caution, and again too anxious for vigorous effort; sometimes idle in a plain path, and sometimes distracted in labyrinths, and dissipated by different intentions.

A large work is difficult because it is large, even though all its parts might singly be performed with facility; where there are many things to be done, each must be allowed its share of time and labour, in the proportion only which it bears to the whole; nor can it be expected, that the stones which form the dome of a temple, should be squared and polished like the diamond of a ring.

Of the event of this work, for which, having laboured it with so much application, I cannot but have some degree of parental fondness, it is natural to form conjectures. Those who have been persuaded to think well of my design, will require that it should fix our language, and put a stop to those alterations which time and chance have hitherto been suffered to make in it without opposition. With this consequence I will confess that I flattered myself for awhile; but now begin to fear that I have indulged expectation which neither reason nor experience can justify. When we see men grow old and die at a certain time one after another, from century to century, we laugh at the elixir that promises to prolong life to a thousand years; and with equal justice may the lexicographer be derided, who being able to produce no example of a nation that has preserved their words and phrases from mutability, shall imagine that his dictionary can embalm his language, and secure it from corruption and decay, that it is in his power to change sublunary nature, and clear the world at once from folly, vanity, and affectation.

With this hope, however, academies have been instituted, to guard the avenues of their languages, to retain fugitives, and repulse intruders; but their vigilance and activity have hitherto been vain; sounds are too volatile and subtle for legal restraints; to enchain syllables, and to lash the wind, are equally the undertakings of pride, unwilling to measure its desires by its strength....

Total and sudden transformations of a language seldom happen; conquests and migrations are now very rare: but there are other causes of change which, though slow in their operation, and invisible in their progress, are perhaps as much superior to human resistance as the revolutions of the sky, or intumescence of the tide. Commerce, however necessary, however lucrative, as it depraves the manners, corrupts the language; they that have frequent intercourse with strangers, to whom they endeavour to accommodate themselves, must in time learn a mingled dialect, like the jargon which serves the traffickers on the Mediterranean and Indian coasts. This will not always be confined to the exchange, the warehouse, or the port, but will be communicated by degrees to other ranks of the people, and be at last incorporated with the current speech.

There are likewise internal causes equally forcible. The language most likely to continue long without alteration, would be that of a nation raised a little, and but a little above barbarity, secluded from strangers, and totally employed in procuring the conveniences of life; either without books, or, like some of the Mahometan countries, with very few: men thus busied and unlearned, having only such words as common use requires, would perhaps long continue to express the same notions by the same signs. But no such constancy can be expected in a people polished by arts, and classed by subordination, where one part of the community is sustained and accommodated by the labour of the other. Those who have much leisure to think, will always be enlarging the stock of ideas, and every increase of knowledge, whether real or fancied, will produce new words, or combinations of words. When the mind is unchained from necessity, it will range after convenience; when it is left at large in the fields of speculation, it will shift opinions; as any custom is disused, the words that expressed it must perish with it; as any opinion grows popular, it will innovate speech in the same proportion as it alters practice.

As by the cultivation of various sciences, a language is amplified, it will be more furnished with words deflected from original sense; the geometrician will talk of a courtier's zenith, or the eccentric virtue of a wild hero, and the physician of sanguine expectations and phlegmatic delays. Copiousness of speech will give opportunities to capricious choice, by which some words will be preferred, and others degraded; vicissitudes of fashion will enforce the use of new, or extend the signification of known terms. The tropes of poetry will make hourly encroachments, and the metaphorical will become the current sense: pronunciation will be varied by levity or ignorance, and the pen must at length comply with the tongue; illiter-

ate writers will at one time or other, by public infatuation, rise into renown who, not knowing the original import of words, will use them with
colloquial licentiousness, confound distinction, and forget propriety. As
politeness increases, some expressions will be considered as too gross
and vulgar for the delicate, others as too formal and ceremonious for the
gay and airy; new phrases are therefore adopted which must, for the same
reasons, be in time dismissed. Swift, in his petty treatise on the English
language, allows that new words must sometimes be introduced, but proposes that none should be suffered to become obsolete. But what makes a
word obsolete, more than general agreement to forbear it? And how shall
it be continued, when it conveys an offensive idea, or recalled again into
the mouths of mankind, when it has once become unfamiliar by disuse,
and unpleasing by unfamiliarity?

There is another cause of alteration more prevalent than any other,
which yet in the present state of the world cannot be obviated. A mixture
of two languages will produce a third distinct from both, and they will always be mixed, where the chief part of education, and the most conspicuous accomplishment, is skill in ancient or in foreign tongues. He that has
long cultivated another language, will find its words and combinations
crowd upon his memory; and haste and negligence, refinement and affectation, will obtrude borrowed terms and exotic expressions.

The great pest of speech is frequency of translation. No book was ever
turned from one language into another, without imparting something of
its native idiom; this is the most mischievous and comprehensive innovation; single words may enter by thousands, and the fabric of the tongue
continue the same, but new phraseology changes much at once; it alters
not the single stones of the building, but the order of the columns. If an
academy should be established for the cultivation of our style, which I,
who can never wish to see dependence multiplied, hope the spirit of English liberty will hinder or destroy, let them, instead of compiling gram-
mars and dictionaries, endeavour, with all their influence, to stop the license of translators, whose idleness and ignorance, if it be suffered to
proceed, will reduce us to babble a dialect of France.

If the changes that we fear be thus irresistible, what remains but to acquiesce with silence, as in the other insurmountable distresses of humanity? It remains that we retard what we cannot repel, that we palliate what

we cannot cure. Life may be lengthened by care, though death cannot be ultimately defeated: tongues, like governments, have a natural tendency to degeneration; we have long preserved our constitution, let us make some struggles for our language.

In hope of giving longevity to that which its own nature forbids to be immortal, I have devoted this book, the labour of years, to the honour of my country, that we may no longer yield the palm of philology, without a contest, to the nations of the continent. The chief glory of every people arises from its authors: whether I shall add any thing by my own writings to the reputation of English literature, must be left to time: much of my life has been lost under the pressures of disease; much has been trifled away; and much has always been spent in provision for the day that was passing over me; but I shall not think my employment useless or ignoble, if by my assistance foreign nations, and distant ages, gain access to the propagators of knowledge, and understand the teachers of truth; if my labours afford light to the repositories of science, and add celebrity to Bacon, to Hooker, to Milton, and to Boyle.[8]

When I am animated by this wish, I look with pleasure on my book, however defective, and deliver it to the world with the spirit of a man that has endeavoured well. That it will immediately become popular I have not promised to myself: a few wild blunders, and risible absurdities, from which no work of such multiplicity was ever free, may for a time furnish folly with laughter, and harden ignorance in contempt; but useful diligence will at last prevail, and there never can be wanting some who distinguish desert; who will consider that no dictionary of a living tongue ever can be perfect, since while it is hastening to publication, some words are budding, and some falling away; that a whole life cannot be spent upon syntax and etymology, and that even a whole life would not be sufficient; that he, whose design includes whatever language can express, must often speak of what he does not understand; that a writer will sometimes be hurried by eagerness to the end, and sometimes faint with weariness under a task, which Scaliger compares to the labours of the anvil and the mine; that what is obvious is not always known, and what is known is not always present; that sudden fits of inadvertency will surprise vigilance, slight avocations will seduce attention, and casual eclipses of the mind will darken learning; and that the writer shall often in vain trace his memory at the moment of need, for that which yesterday he knew with intuitive readiness, and which will come uncalled into his thoughts tomorrow.

In this work, when it shall be found that much is omitted, let it not be forgotten that much likewise is performed; and though no book was ever spared out of tenderness to the author, and the world is little solicitous to know whence proceeded the faults of that which it condemns; yet it may gratify curiosity to inform it, that the *English Dictionary* was written with little assistance of the learned, and without any patronage of the great; not in the soft obscurities of retirement, or under the shelter of academic bowers, but amidst inconvenience and distraction, in sickness and in sorrow. It may repress the triumph of malignant criticism to observe, that if our language is not here fully displayed, I have only failed in an attempt which no human powers have hitherto completed. If the lexicons of ancient tongues, now immutably fixed, and comprised in a few volumes, be yet, after the toil of successive ages, inadequate and delusive; if the aggregated knowledge, and cooperating diligence of the Italian academicians, did not secure them from the censure of Beni; if the embodied critics of France, when fifty years had been spent upon their work, were obliged to change its economy, and give their second edition another form, I may surely be contented without the praise of perfection, which, if I could obtain, in this gloom of solitude, what would it avail me? I have protracted my work till most of those whom I wished to please have sunk into the grave, and success and miscarriage are empty sounds: I therefore dismiss it with frigid tranquillity, having little to fear or hope from censure or from praise.

PART III

Rasselas, Prince of Abyssinia
(1759)

Chapter I—Description of a Palace in a Valley

Ye who listen with credulity to the whispers of fancy, and pursue with eagerness the phantoms of hope; who expect that age will perform the promises of youth, and that the deficiencies of the present day will be supplied by the morrow; attend to the history of Rasselas, prince of Abyssinia.

Rasselas was the fourth son of the mighty emperor in whose dominions the Father of waters begins his course; whose bounty pours down the streams of plenty, and scatters over the world the harvests of Egypt.

According to the custom which has descended from age to age among the monarchs of the torrid zone, Rasselas was confined in a private palace, with the other sons and daughters of Abyssinian royalty, till the order of succession should call him to the throne.

The place which the wisdom or policy of antiquity had destined for the residence of the Abyssinian princes was a spacious valley in the kingdom of Amhara, surrounded on every side by mountains, of which the summits overhang the middle part. The only passage by which it could be entered was a cavern that passed under a rock, of which it had long been disputed whether it was the work of nature or of human industry.

The outlet of the cavern was concealed by a thick wood, and the mouth which opened into the valley was closed with gates of iron, forged by the artificers of ancient days, so massy that no man, without the help of engines, could open or shut them.

From the mountains on every side rivulets descended that filled all the valley with verdure and fertility, and formed a lake in the middle, inhabited by fish of every species, and frequented by every fowl whom nature has taught to dip the wing in water. This lake discharged its superfluities by a stream, which entered a dark cleft of the mountain on the northern side, and fell with dreadful noise from precipice to precipice till it was heard no more.

The sides of the mountains were covered with trees, the banks of the brooks were diversified with flowers; every blast shook spices from the rocks, and every month dropped fruits upon the ground. All animals that bite the grass or browse the shrubs, whether wild or tame, wandered in this extensive circuit, secured from beasts of prey by the mountains which confined them. On one part were flocks and herds feeding in the pastures, on another all the beasts of chase frisking in the lawns, the sprightly kid was bounding on the rocks, the subtle monkey frolicking in the trees, and the solemn elephant reposing in the shade. All the diversities of the world were brought together, the blessings of nature were collected, and its evils extracted and excluded.

The valley, wide and fruitful, supplied its inhabitants with all the necessaries of life, and all delights and superfluities were added at the annual visit which the emperor paid his children, when the iron gate was opened to the sound of music, and during eight days every one that resided in the valley was required to propose whatever might contribute to make seclusion pleasant, to fill up the vacancies of attention, and lessen the tediousness of time. Every desire was immediately granted. All the artificers of pleasure were called to gladden the festivity; the musicians exerted the power of harmony, and the dancers showed their activity before the princes, in hope that they should pass their lives in this blissful captivity, to which those only were admitted whose performance was thought able to add novelty to luxury. Such was the appearance of security and delight which this retirement afforded, that they to whom it was new always desired that it might be perpetual; and as those on whom the iron gate had once closed were never suffered to return, the effect of longer experience could not be known. Thus every year produced new schemes of delight, and new competitors for imprisonment.

The palace stood on an eminence, raised about thirty paces above the surface of the lake. It was divided into many squares or courts, built with greater or less magnificence according to the rank of those for whom they were designed. The roofs were turned into arches of massive stone, joined by a cement that grew harder by time, and the building stood from century to century, deriding the solstitial rains and equinoctial hurricanes, without need of reparation.

This house, which was so large as to be fully known to none but some ancient officers who successively inherited the secrets of the place, was built as if suspicion herself had dictated the plan. To every room there was an open and secret passage; every square had a communication with the rest, either from the upper stories by private galleries, or by subterranean passages from the lower apartments. Many of the columns had unsuspected cavities, in which a long race of monarchs had reposited their treasures. They then closed up the opening with marble, which was never to be removed but in the utmost exigencies of the kingdom, and recorded their accumulations in a book, which was itself concealed in a tower, not entered but by the emperor, attended by the prince who stood next in succession.

Chapter II—The Discontent of Rassclas in the Happy Valley

Here the sons and daughters of Abyssinia lived only to know the soft vicissitudes of pleasure and repose, attended by all that were skilful to delight, and gratified with whatever the senses can enjoy. They wandered in gardens of fragrance, and slept in the fortresses of security. Every art was practised to make them pleased with their own condition. The sages who instructed them told them of nothing but the miseries of public life, and described all beyond the mountains as regions of calamity, where discord was always raging, and where man preyed upon man.

To heighten their opinion of their own felicity, they were daily entertained with songs, the subject of which was the Happy Valley. Their appetites were excited by frequent enumerations of different enjoyments, and revelry and merriment were the business of every hour, from the dawn of morning to the close of even.

These methods were generally successful; few of the princes had ever wished to enlarge their bounds, but passed their lives in full conviction that they had all within their reach that art or nature could bestow, and pitied those whom fate had excluded from this seat of tranquillity as the sport of chance and the slaves of misery.

Thus they rose in the morning and lay down at night, pleased with each other and with themselves, all but Rasselas, who, in the twenty-sixth year of his age, began to withdraw himself from their pastimes and assemblies, and to delight in solitary walks and silent meditation. He often sat before tables covered with luxury, and forgot to taste the dainties that were placed before him; he rose abruptly in the midst of the song, and hastily retired beyond the sound of music. His attendants observed the change, and endeavoured to renew his love of pleasure. He neglected their officiousness, repulsed their invitations, and spent day after day on the banks of rivulets sheltered with trees, where he sometimes listened to the birds in the branches, sometimes observed the fish playing in the stream, and anon cast his eyes upon the pastures and mountains filled with animals, of which some were biting the herbage, and some sleeping among the bushes.

This singularity of his humour made him much observed. One of the sages, in whose conversation he had formerly delighted, followed him secretly, in hope of discovering the cause of his disquiet. Rasselas, who knew not that anyone was near him, having for some time fixed his eyes upon the goats that were browsing among the rocks, began to compare their condition with his own.

"What," said he, "makes the difference between man and all the rest of the animal creation? Every beast that strays beside me has the same corporal necessities with myself: he is hungry, and crops the grass; he is thirsty, and drinks the stream; his thirst and hunger are appeased; he is satisfied, and sleeps; he rises again, and is hungry; he is again fed, and is at rest. I am hungry and thirsty, like him, but when thirst and hunger cease, I am not at rest. I am, like him, pained with want, but am not, like him, satisfied with fullness. The intermediate hours are tedious and gloomy; I long again to be hungry that I may again quicken my attention. The birds peck the berries or the corn, and fly away to the groves, where they sit in seeming happiness on the branches, and waste their lives in tuning one unvaried series of sounds. I likewise can call the lutanist and the singer; but the sounds that pleased me yesterday weary me today, and will grow yet more wearisome tomorrow. I can discover within me no power of perception which is not glutted with its proper pleasure, yet I do not feel myself delighted. Man has surely some latent sense for which this place affords no gratification; or he has some desire distinct from sense which must be satisfied before he can be happy."

After this he lifted up his head, and seeing the moon rising, walked towards the palace. As he passed through the fields, and saw the animals around him, "Ye," said he, "are happy, and need not envy me that walk thus among you, burdened with myself; nor do I, ye gentle beings, envy your felicity; for it is not the felicity of man. I have many distresses from which ye are free; I fear pain when I do not feel it; I sometimes shrink at evils recollected, and sometimes start at evils anticipated: surely the equity of Providence has balanced peculiar sufferings with peculiar enjoyments."

With observations like these the prince amused himself as he returned, uttering them with a plaintive voice, yet with a look that discovered him to feel some complacence in his own perspicacity, and to receive some solace of the miseries of life from consciousness of the delicacy with which he felt and the eloquence with which he bewailed them. He mingled cheerfully in the diversions of the evening, and all rejoiced to find that his heart was lightened.

Chapter III—The Wants of Him That Wants Nothing

On the next day, his old instructor, imagining that he had now made himself acquainted with his disease of mind, was in hope of curing it by counsel, and officiously sought an opportunity of conference, which the prince, having long considered him as one whose intellects were exhausted, was not very willing to afford. "Why," said he, "does this man thus intrude upon me; shall I never be suffered to forget those lectures which pleased only while they were new, and to become new again must be forgotten?" He then walked into the wood, and composed himself to his usual meditations; when, before his thoughts had taken any settled form, he perceived his pursuer at his side, and was at first prompted by his impatience to go hastily away; but being unwilling to offend a man whom he had once reverenced and still loved, he invited him to sit down with him on the bank.

The old man, thus encouraged, began to lament the change which had been lately observed in the prince, and to inquire why he so often retired from the pleasures of the palace to loneliness and silence. "I fly from pleasure," said the prince, "because pleasure has ceased to please: I am lonely because I am miserable, and am unwilling to cloud with my presence the happiness of others." "You, sir," said the sage, "are the first who has complained of misery in the Happy Valley. I hope to convince you that your complaints have no real cause. You are here in full possession of all the emperor of Abyssinia can bestow; here is neither labour to be endured nor danger to be dreaded, yet here is all that labour or danger can procure or purchase. Look round and tell me which of your wants is without supply: if you want nothing, how are you unhappy?"

"That I want nothing," said the prince, "or that I know not what I want, is the cause of my complaint: if I had any known want, I should have a certain wish; that wish would excite endeavour, and I should not then repine to see the sun move so slowly towards the western mountain, or lament when the day breaks, and sleep will no longer hide me from myself. When I see the kids and the lambs chasing one another, I fancy that I should be happy if I had something to pursue. But, possessing all that I can want, I find one day and one hour exactly like another, except that the latter is still more tedious than the former. Let your experience inform me how the day may now seem as short as in my childhood, while nature was yet fresh, and every moment showed me what I never had observed before. I have already enjoyed too much; give me something to desire."

The old man was surprised at this new species of affliction, and knew not what to reply, yet was unwilling to be silent. "Sir," said he, "if you had seen the miseries of the world, you would know how to value your present state." "Now," said the prince, "you have given me something to desire; I shall long to see the miseries of the world, since the sight of them is necessary to happiness."

Chapter IV—The Prince Continues to Grieve and Muse

At this time the sound of music proclaimed the hour of repast, and the conversation was concluded. The old man went away sufficiently discontented to find that his reasonings had produced the only conclusion which they were intended to prevent. But in the decline of life, shame and grief are of short duration; whether it be that we bear easily what we have borne long; or that, finding ourselves in age less regarded, we less regard others; or that we look with slight regard upon afflictions to which we know that the hand of death is about to put an end.

The prince, whose views were extended to a wider space, could not speedily quiet his emotions. He had been before terrified at the length of life which nature promised him, because he considered that in a long time much must be endured; he now rejoiced in his youth, because in many years much might be done.

The first beam of hope that had been ever darted into his mind rekindled youth in his cheeks, and doubled the lustre of his eyes. He was fired with the desire of doing something, though he knew not yet, with distinctness, either end or means.

He was now no longer gloomy and unsocial; but considering himself as master of a secret stock of happiness, which he could enjoy only by concealing it, he affected to be busy in all schemes of diversion, and endeavoured to make others pleased with the state of which he himself was weary. But pleasures can never be so multiplied or continued as not to leave much of life unemployed; there were many hours, both of the night and day, which he could spend without suspicion in solitary thought. The load of life was much lightened; he went eagerly into the assemblies, because he supposed the frequency of his presence necessary to the success of his purposes; he retired gladly to privacy, because he had now a subject of thought.

His chief amusement was to picture to himself that world which he had never seen, to place himself in various conditions, to be entangled in imaginary difficulties, and to be engaged in wild adventures; but, his benevolence always terminated his projects in the relief of distress, the detection of fraud, the defeat of oppression, and the diffusion of happiness.

Thus passed twenty months of the life of Rasselas. He busied himself so intensely in visionary bustle that he forgot his real solitude; and amidst hourly preparations for the various incidents of human affairs, neglected to consider by what means he should mingle with mankind.

One day, as he was sitting on a bank, he feigned to himself an orphan virgin robbed of her little portion by a treacherous lover, and crying after him for restitution and redress. So strongly was the image impressed upon his mind that he started up in the maid's defence, and ran forward to seize the plunderer with all the eagerness of real pursuit. Fear naturally quickens the flight of guilt. Rasselas could not catch the fugitive with his utmost efforts; but, resolving to weary by perseverance him whom he could not surpass in speed, he pressed on till the foot of the mountain stopped his course.

Here he recollected himself, and smiled at his own useless impetuosity. Then raising his eyes to the mountain, "This," said he, "is the fatal obstacle that hinders at once the enjoyment of pleasure and the exercise of virtue. How long is it that my hopes and wishes have flown beyond this boundary of my life, which yet I never have attempted to surmount!"

Struck with this reflection, he sat down to muse, and remembered that since he first resolved to escape from his confinement, the sun had passed twice over him in his annual course. He now felt a degree of regret with which he had never been before acquainted. He considered how much might have been done in the time which had passed, and left nothing real behind it. He compared twenty months with the life of man. "In life," said he, "is not to be counted the ignorance of infancy or imbecility of age. We are long before we are able to think, and we soon cease from the power of acting. The true period of human existence may be reasonably estimated at forty years, of which I have mused away the four-and-twentieth part. What I have lost was certain, for I have certainly possessed it; but of twenty months to come, who can assure me?"

The consciousness of his own folly pierced him deeply, and he was long before he could be reconciled to himself. "The rest of my time," said he, "has been lost by the crime or folly of my ancestors, and the absurd

institutions of my country; I remember it with disgust, yet without remorse: but the months that have passed since new light darted into my
soul, since I formed a scheme of reasonable felicity, have been squandered
by my own fault. I have lost that which can never be restored; I have seen
the sun rise and set for twenty months, an idle gazer on the light of heaven.
In this time the birds have left the nest of their mother, and committed
themselves to the woods and to the skies; the kid has forsaken the teat,
and learned by degrees to climb the rocks in quest of independent sustenance. I only have made no advances, but am still helpless and ignorant.
The moon, by more than twenty changes, admonished me of the flux
of life; the stream that rolled before my feet upbraided my inactivity. I
sat feasting on intellectual luxury, regardless alike of the examples of the
earth and the instructions of the planets. Twenty months are passed: who
shall restore them!"

These sorrowful meditations fastened upon his mind; he passed four
months in resolving to lose no more time in idle resolves, and was awakened to more vigorous exertion by hearing a maid, who had broken a por-
celain cup, remark that what cannot be repaired is not to be regretted.

This was obvious; and Rasselas reproached himself that he had not
discovered it, having not known, or not considered, how many useful
hints are obtained by chance, and how often the mind, hurried by her
own ardour to distant views, neglects the truths that lie open before her.
He for a few hours regretted his regret, and from that time bent his whole
mind upon the means of escaping from the valley of happiness.

Chapter V—The Prince Meditates His Escape

He now found that it would be very difficult to effect that which it was
very easy to suppose effected. When he looked round about him, he saw
himself confined by the bars of nature, which had never yet been broken,
and by the gate through which none that had once passed it were ever
able to return. He was now impatient as an eagle in a grate. He passed
week after week in clambering the mountains to see if there was any aper-
ture which the bushes might conceal, but found all the summits inaccessible by their prominence. The iron gate he despaired to open for it was
not only secured with all the power of art, but was always watched by suc-

cessive sentinels, and was, by its position, exposed to the perpetual observation of all the inhabitants.

He then examined the cavern through which the waters of the lake were discharged; and, looking down at a time when the sun shone strongly upon its mouth, he discovered it to be full of broken rocks, which, though they permitted the stream to flow through many narrow passages, would stop any body of solid bulk. He returned discouraged and dejected; but having now known the blessing of hope, resolved never to despair.

In these fruitless searches he spent ten months. The time, however, passed cheerfully away: in the morning he rose with new hope; in the evening applauded his own diligence; and in the night slept sound after his fatigue. He met a thousand amusements, which beguiled his labour and diversified his thoughts. He discerned the various instincts of animals and properties of plants, and found the place replete with wonders, of which he proposed to solace himself with the contemplation if he should never be able to accomplish his flight; rejoicing that his endeavours, though yet unsuccessful, had supplied him with a source of inexhaustible enquiry.

But his original curiosity was not yet abated; he resolved to obtain some knowledge of the ways of men. His wish still continued, but his hope grew less. He ceased to survey any longer the walls of his prison, and spared to search by new toils for interstices which he knew could not be found, yet determined to keep his design always in view, and lay hold on any expedient that time should offer.

Chapter VI—A Dissertation on the Art of Flying

Among the artists that had been allured into the Happy Valley, to labour for the accommodation and pleasure of its inhabitants, was a man eminent for his knowledge of the mechanic powers, who had contrived many engines both of use and recreation. By a wheel which the stream turned he forced the water into a tower, whence it was distributed to all the apartments of the palace. He erected a pavilion in the garden, around which he kept the air always cool by artificial showers. One of the groves, appropriated to the ladies, was ventilated by fans, to which the rivulets that ran through it gave a constant motion; and instruments of soft music were placed at proper distances, of which some played by the impulse of the wind, and some by the power of the stream.

This artist was sometimes visited by Rasselas who was pleased with every kind of knowledge, imagining that the time would come when all his acquisitions should be of use to him in the open world. He came one day to amuse himself in his usual manner, and found the master busy in building a sailing chariot: he saw that the design was practicable upon a level surface, and with expressions of great esteem solicited its completion. The workman was pleased to find himself so much regarded by the prince, and resolved to gain yet higher honours. "Sir," said he, "you have seen but a small part of what the mechanic sciences can perform. I have been long of opinion that, instead of the tardy conveyance of ships and chariots, man might use the swifter migration of wings, that the fields of air are open to knowledge, and that only ignorance and idleness need crawl upon the ground."

This hint rekindled the prince's desire of passing the mountains; having seen what the mechanist had already performed, he was willing to fancy that he could do more, yet resolved to inquire further before he suffered hope to afflict him by disappointment. "I am afraid," said he to the artist, "that your imagination prevails over your skill, and that you now tell me rather what you wish than what you know. Every animal has his element assigned him; the birds have the air, and man and beasts the earth." "So," replied the mechanist, "fishes have the water, in which yet beasts can swim by nature and man by art. He that can swim needs not despair to fly; to swim is to fly in a grosser fluid, and to fly is to swim in a subtler. We are only to proportion our power of resistance to the different density of matter through which we are to pass. You will be necessarily upbourne by the air if you can renew any impulse upon it faster than the air can recede from the pressure."

"But the exercise of swimming," said the prince, "is very laborious; the strongest limbs are soon wearied; I am afraid the act of flying will be yet more violent; and wings will be of no great use unless we can fly further than we can swim."

"The labour of rising from the ground," said the artist, "will be great, as we see it in the heavier domestic fowls; but as we mount higher the earth's attraction and the body's gravity will be gradually diminished, till we shall arrive at a region where the man will float in the air without any tendency to fall; no care will then be necessary but to move forward, which the gentlest impulse will effect. You, sir, whose curiosity is so extensive, will easily conceive with what pleasure a philosopher, furnished with wings and hovering in the sky, would see the earth and all its inhabitants rolling beneath him, and presenting to him successively, by its diurnal motion, all the countries within the same parallel. How must it amuse the pendent spectator to see the moving scene of land and ocean, cities and deserts! To survey with equal security the marts of trade and the fields of battle; mountains infested by barbarians, and fruitful regions gladdened by plenty and lulled by peace! How easily shall we then trace the Nile through all his passages, pass over to distant regions, and examine the face of nature from one extremity of the earth to the other!"

"All this," said the prince, "is much to be desired, but I am afraid that no man will be able to breathe in these regions of speculation and tranquillity. I have been told that respiration is difficult upon lofty mountains, yet from these precipices, though so high as to produce great tenuity[1] of the air, it is very easy to fall; therefore I suspect that from any height where life can be supported, there may be danger of too quick descent."

"Nothing," replied the artist, "will ever be attempted if all possible objections must be first overcome. If you will favour my project, I will try the first flight at my own hazard. I have considered the structure of all volant[2] animals, and find the folding continuity of the bat's wings most easily accommodated to the human form. Upon this model I shall begin my task tomorrow, and in a year expect to tower into the air beyond the malice and pursuit of man. But I will work only on this condition, that the art shall not be divulged, and that you shall not require me to make wings for any but ourselves."

"Why," said Rasselas, "should you envy others so great an advantage? All skill ought to be exerted for universal good; every man has owed much to others, and ought to repay the kindness that he has received."

"If men were all virtuous," returned the artist, "I should with great alacrity teach them all to fly. But what would be the security of the good if the bad could at pleasure invade them from the sky? Against an army sailing through the clouds neither walls, nor mountains, nor seas could afford any security. A flight of northern savages might hover in the wind and light at once with irresistible violence upon the capital of a fruitful region that was rolling under them. Even this valley, the retreat of princes, the abode of happiness, might be violated by the sudden descent of some of the naked nations that swarm on the coast of the southern sea."

The prince promised secrecy, and waited for the performance, not wholly hopeless of success. He visited the work from time to time, observed its progress, and remarked many ingenious contrivances to facilitate motion and unite levity with strength. The artist was every day more certain that he should leave vultures and eagles behind him, and the contagion of his confidence seized upon the prince.

In a year the wings were finished; and on a morning appointed the maker appeared, furnished for flight, on a little promontory; he waved his pinions awhile to gather air, then leaped from his stand, and in an instant dropped into the lake. His wings, which were of no use in the air, sustained him in the water; and the prince drew him to land half dead with terror and vexation.

Chapter VII—The Prince Finds a Man of Learning

The prince was not much afflicted by this disaster, having suffered himself to hope for a happier event only because he had no other means of escape in view. He still persisted in his design to leave the Happy Valley by the first opportunity.

His imagination was now at a stand; he had no prospect of entering into the world, and, notwithstanding all his endeavours to support himself, discontent by degrees preyed upon him, and he began again to lose his thoughts in sadness when the rainy season, which in these countries is periodical, made it inconvenient to wander in the woods.

The rain continued longer and with more violence than had ever been known; the clouds broke on the surrounding mountains, and the torrents streamed into the plain on every side, till the cavern was too narrow to discharge the water. The lake overflowed its banks, and all the level of the valley was covered with the inundation. The eminence on which the palace was built, and some other spots of rising ground, were all that the eye could now discover. The herds and flocks left the pastures, and both the wild beasts and the tame retreated to the mountains.

This inundation confined all the princes to domestic amusements, and the attention of Rasselas was particularly seized by a poem which Imlac rehearsed upon the various conditions of humanity. He commanded the poet to attend him in his apartment, and recite his verses a second time; then entering into familiar talk, he thought himself happy in having found a man who knew the world so well, and could so skilfully paint the scenes of life. He asked a thousand questions about things to which, though common to all other mortals, his confinement from childhood had kept him a stranger. The poet pitied his ignorance, and loved his curiosity, and entertained him from day to day with novelty and instruction so that the prince regretted the necessity of sleep, and longed till the morning should renew his pleasure.

As they were sitting together, the prince commanded Imlac to relate his history, and to tell by what accident he was forced, or by what motive induced, to close his life in the Happy Valley. As he was going to begin his narrative, Rasselas was called to a concert, and obliged to restrain his curiosity till the evening.

Chapter VIII—The History of Imlac

The close of the day is, in the regions of the torrid zone, the only season of diversion and entertainment, and it was therefore midnight before the music ceased and the princesses retired. Rasselas then called for his companion, and required him to begin the story of his life.

"Sir," said Imlac, "my history will not be long: the life that is devoted to knowledge passes silently away, and is very little diversified by events. To talk in public, to think in solitude, to read and to hear, to inquire and answer inquiries, is the business of a scholar. He wanders about the world without pomp or terror, and is neither known nor valued but by men like himself.

"I was born in the kingdom of Goiama, at no great distance from the fountain of the Nile. My father was a wealthy merchant, who traded between the inland countries of Africa and the ports of the Red Sea. He was honest, frugal, and diligent, but of mean sentiments and narrow comprehension; he desired only to be rich, and to conceal his riches, lest he should be spoiled by the governors of the province."

"Surely," said the prince, "my father must be negligent of his charge if any man in his dominions dares take that which belongs to another. Does he not know that kings are accountable for injustice permitted as well as done? If I were emperor, not the meanest of my subjects should be oppressed with impunity. My blood boils when I am told that a merchant durst not enjoy his honest gains for fear of losing them by the rapacity of power. Name the governor who robbed the people that I may declare his crimes to the emperor."

"Sir," said Imlac, "your ardour is the natural effect of virtue animated by youth: the time will come when you will acquit your father, and perhaps hear with less impatience of the governor. Oppression is, in the Abyssinian dominions, neither frequent nor tolerated; but no form of government has been yet discovered by which cruelty can be wholly prevented. Subordination supposes power on one part and subjection on the other; and if power be in the hands of men it will sometimes be abused. The vigilance of the supreme magistrate may do much, but much will still remain undone. He can never know all the crimes that are committed, and can seldom punish all that he knows."

"This," said the prince, "I do not understand; but I had rather hear thee than dispute. Continue thy narration."

"My father," proceeded Imlac, "originally intended that I should have no other education than such as might qualify me for commerce; and discovering in me great strength of memory and quickness of apprehension, often declared his hope that I should be some time the richest man in Abyssinia."

"Why," said the prince, "did thy father desire the increase of his wealth when it was already greater than he durst discover or enjoy? I am unwilling to doubt thy veracity, yet inconsistencies cannot both be true."

"Inconsistencies," answered Imlac, "cannot both be right; but, imputed to man, they may both be true. Yet diversity is not inconsistency. My father might expect a time of greater security. However, some desire is necessary to keep life in motion; and he whose real wants are supplied must admit those of fancy."

"This," said the prince, "I can in some measure conceive. I repent that I interrupted thee."

"With this hope," proceeded Imlac, "he sent me to school. But when I had once found the delight of knowledge, and felt the pleasure of intelligence and the pride of invention, I began silently to despise riches, and determined to disappoint the purpose of my father, whose grossness of conception raised my pity. I was twenty years old before his tenderness would expose me to the fatigue of travel; in which time I had been instructed, by successive masters, in all the literature of my native country. As every hour taught me something new, I lived in a continual course of gratification; but as I advanced towards manhood, I lost much of the reverence with which I had been used to look on my instructors; because when the lessons were ended I did not find them wiser or better than common men.

"At length my father resolved to initiate me in commerce; and, opening one of his subterranean treasuries, counted out ten thousand pieces of gold. 'This, young man,' said he, 'is the stock with which you must negotiate. I began with less than a fifth part, and you see how diligence and parsimony have increased it. This is your own, to waste or improve. If you squander it by negligence or caprice, you must wait for my death before you will be rich; if in four years you double your stock, we will thenceforward let subordination cease, and live together as friends and partners, for he shall be always equal with me who is equally skilled in the art of growing rich.'

"We laid out our money upon camels, concealed in bales of cheap goods, and travelled to the shore of the Red Sea. When I cast my eye on the expanse of waters, my heart bounded like that of a prisoner escaped. I felt an unextinguishable curiosity kindle in my mind, and resolved to snatch this opportunity of seeing the manners of other nations, and of learning sciences unknown in Abyssinia.

"I remembered that my father had obliged me to the improvement of my stock, not by a promise, which I ought not to violate, but by a penalty, which I was at liberty to incur; and therefore determined to gratify my predominant desire, and, by drinking at the fountain of knowledge, to quench the thirst of curiosity.

"As I was supposed to trade without connection with my father, it was easy for me to become acquainted with the master of a ship, and procure a passage to some other country. I had no motives of choice to regulate my voyage. It was sufficient for me that, wherever I wandered, I should see a country which I had not seen before. I therefore entered a ship bound for Surat, having left a letter for my father declaring my intention."

Chapter IX—The History of Imlac *(continued)*

"When I first entered upon the world of waters, and lost sight of land, I looked round about me with pleasing terror, and thinking my soul enlarged by the boundless prospect, imagined that I could gaze around me forever without satiety; but in a short time I grew weary of looking on barren uniformity, where I could only see again what I had already seen. I then descended into the ship, and doubted for a while whether all my future pleasures would not end, like this, in disgust and disappointment. 'Yet surely,' said I, 'the ocean and the land are very different. The only variety of water is rest and motion. But the earth has mountains and valleys, deserts and cities; it is inhabited by men of different customs and contrary opinions; and I may hope to find variety in life, though I should miss it in nature.'

"With this thought I quieted my mind, and amused myself during the voyage, sometimes by learning from the sailors the art of navigation, which I have never practised, and sometimes by forming schemes for my conduct in different situations, in not one of which I have been ever placed.

"I was almost weary of my naval amusements when we landed safely at Surat. I secured my money and, purchasing some commodities for show, joined myself to a caravan that was passing into the inland country. My companions, for some reason or other, conjecturing that I was rich, and, by my inquiries and admiration, finding that I was ignorant, considered me as a novice whom they had a right to cheat, and who was to learn, at the usual expense, the art of fraud. They exposed me to the theft of servants and the exaction of officers, and saw me plundered upon false pretences, without any advantage to themselves but that of rejoicing in the superiority of their own knowledge."

"Stop a moment," said the prince. "Is there such depravity in man as that he should injure another without benefit to himself? I can easily conceive that all are pleased with superiority; but your ignorance was merely accidental, which, being neither your crime nor your folly, could afford them no reason to applaud themselves; and the knowledge which they had, and which you wanted, they might as effectually have shown by warning as betraying you."

"Pride," said Imlac, "is seldom delicate; it will please itself with very mean advantages, and envy feels not its own happiness but when it may be compared with the misery of others. They were my enemies because they grieved to think me rich, and my oppressors because they delighted to find me weak."

"Proceed," said the prince; "I doubt not of the facts which you relate, but imagine that you impute them to mistaken motives."

"In this company," said Imlac, "I arrived at Agra, the capital of Indostan, the city in which the great Mogul commonly resides. I applied myself to the language of the country, and in a few months was able to converse with the learned men; some of whom I found morose and reserved, and others easy and communicative; some were unwilling to teach another what they had with difficulty learned themselves; and some showed that the end of their studies was to gain the dignity of instructing.

"To the tutor of the young princes I recommended myself so much that I was presented to the emperor as a man of uncommon knowledge. The emperor asked me many questions concerning my country and my travels, and though I cannot now recollect anything that he uttered above the power of a common man, he dismissed me astonished at his wisdom and enamoured of his goodness.

"My credit was now so high that the merchants with whom I had travelled applied to me for recommendations to the ladies of the court. I was surprised at their confidence of solicitation and gently reproached them with their practices on the road. They heard me with cold indifference, and showed no tokens of shame or sorrow.

"They then urged their request with the offer of a bribe, but what I would not do for kindness I would not do for money, and refused them, not because they had injured me, but because I would not enable them to injure others; for I knew they would have made use of my credit to cheat those who should buy their wares.

"Having resided at Agra till there was no more to be learned, I travelled into Persia, where I saw many remains of ancient magnificence and observed many new accommodations of life. The Persians are a nation eminently social, and their assemblies afforded me daily opportunities of remarking characters and manners, and of tracing human nature through all its variations.

"From Persia I passed into Arabia, where I saw a nation at once pastoral and warlike, who live without any settled habitation, whose only wealth is their flocks and herds, yet carried on through all ages an hereditary war with all mankind, though they neither covet nor envy their possessions."

Chapter X—Imlac's History *(continued)*
A Dissertation upon Poetry[3]

"Wherever I went I found that poetry was considered as the highest learning, and regarded with a veneration somewhat approaching to that which man would pay to the angelic nature. And yet it fills me with wonder that in almost all countries the most ancient poets are considered as the best; whether it be that every other kind of knowledge is an acquisition gradually attained, and poetry is a gift conferred at once; or that the first poetry of every nation surprised them as a novelty, and retained the credit by consent which it received by accident at first; or whether, as the province of poetry is to describe nature and passion, which are always the same, the first writers took possession of the most striking objects for description and the most probable occurrences for fiction, and left nothing to those that followed them but transcription of the same events and new combinations of the same images. Whatever be the reason, it is commonly observed that the early writers are in possession of nature, and their followers of art; that the first excel in strength and invention, and the latter in elegance and refinement.

"I was desirous to add my name to this illustrious fraternity. I read all the poets of Persia and Arabia, and was able to repeat by memory the volumes that are suspended in the mosque of Mecca. But I soon found that no man was ever great by imitations. My desire of excellence impelled me to transfer my attention to nature and to life. Nature was to be my subject, and men to be my auditors. I could never describe what I had not seen. I could not hope to move those with delight or terror whose interests and opinions I did not understand.

"Being now resolved to be a poet, I saw everything with a new purpose; my sphere of attention was suddenly magnified; no kind of knowledge was to be overlooked. I ranged mountains and deserts for images and resemblances, and pictured upon my mind every tree of the forest and flower of the valley. I observed with equal care the crags of the rock and the pinnacles of the palace. Sometimes I wandered along the mazes of the rivulet, and sometimes watched the changes of the summer clouds. To a poet nothing can be useless. Whatever is beautiful and whatever is dreadful must be familiar to his imagination; he must be conversant with all that is awfully vast or elegantly little. The plants of the garden, the animals of the wood, the minerals of the earth, and meteors of the sky, must all concur to store his mind with inexhaustible variety; for every idea is useful for the enforcement or decoration of moral or religious truth, and he who knows most will have most power of diversifying his scenes and of gratifying his reader with remote allusions and unexpected instruction.

"All the appearances of nature I was therefore careful to study, and every country which I have surveyed has contributed something to my poetical powers."

"In so wide a survey," said the prince, "you must surely have left much unobserved. I have lived till now within the circuit of these mountains, and yet cannot walk abroad without the sight of something which I had never beheld before, or never heeded."

"This business of a poet," said Imlac, "is to examine, not the individual, but the species; to remark general properties and large appearances. He does not number the streaks of the tulip, or describe the different shades of the verdure of the forest. He is to exhibit in his portraits of nature such prominent and striking features as recall the original to every mind, and must neglect the minuter discriminations, which one may have remarked and another have neglected, for those characteristics which are alike obvious to vigilance and carelessness.

"But the knowledge of nature is only half the task of a poet; he must be acquainted likewise with all the modes of life. His character requires that he estimate the happiness and misery of every condition, observe the power of all the passions in all their combinations, and trace the changes of the human mind, as they are modified by various institutions and accidental influences of climate or custom, from the sprightliness of infancy to the despondence of decrepitude. He must divest himself of the prejudices of his age or country; he must consider right and wrong in their abstracted and invariable state; he must disregard present laws and opinions, and rise to general and transcendental truths, which will always be the same. He must, therefore, content himself with the slow progress of his name, contemn the applause of his own time, and commit his claims to the justice of posterity. He must write as the interpreter of nature and the legislator of mankind, and consider himself as presiding over the thoughts and manners of future generations, as a being superior to time and place.

"His labour is not yet at an end. He must know many languages and many sciences, and, that his style may be worthy of his thoughts, must by incessant practice familiarise to himself every delicacy of speech and grace of harmony."

Chapter XI—Imlac's Narrative *(continued)*—A Hint of Pilgrimage

Imlac now felt the enthusiastic fit, and was proceeding to aggrandize his own profession, when the prince cried out: "Enough! thou hast convinced me that no human being can ever be a poet. Proceed with thy narration."

"To be a poet," said Imlac, "is indeed very difficult." "So difficult," returned the prince, "that I will at present hear no more of his labours. Tell me whither you went when you had seen Persia."

"From Persia," said the poet, "I travelled through Syria, and for three years resided in Palestine, where I conversed with great numbers of the northern and western nations of Europe, the nations which are now in possession of all power and all knowledge, whose armies are irresistible, and whose fleets command the remotest parts of the globe. When I compared these men with the natives of our own kingdom and those that surround us, they appeared almost another order of beings. In their countries it is difficult to wish for anything that may not be obtained; a thousand arts, of which we never heard, are continually labouring for their convenience and pleasure, and whatever their own climate has denied them is supplied by their commerce."

"By what means," said the prince, "are the Europeans thus powerful? or why, since they can so easily visit Asia and Africa for trade or conquest, cannot the Asiatics and Africans invade their coasts, plant colonies in their ports, and give laws to their natural princes? The same wind that carries them back would bring us thither."

"They are more powerful, sir, than we," answered Imlac, "because they are wiser; knowledge will always predominate over ignorance, as man governs the other animals. But why their knowledge is more than ours I know not what reason can be given but the unsearchable will of the Supreme Being."

"When," said the prince with a sigh, "shall I be able to visit Palestine, and mingle with this mighty confluence of nations? Till that happy moment shall arrive, let me fill up the time with such representations as thou canst give me. I am not ignorant of the motive that assembles such numbers in that place, and cannot but consider it as the centre of wisdom and piety, to which the best and wisest men of every land must be continually resorting."

"There are some nations," said Imlac, "that send few visitants to Palestine; for many numerous and learned sects in Europe concur to censure pilgrimage as superstitious, or deride it as ridiculous."

"You know," said the prince, "how little my life has made me acquainted with diversity of opinions; it will be too long to hear the arguments on both sides; you, that have considered them, tell me the result."

"Pilgrimage," said Imlac, "like many other acts of piety, may be reasonable or superstitious, according to the principles upon which it is performed. Long journeys in search of truth are not commanded. Truth, such as is necessary to the regulation of life, is always found where it is honestly sought. Change of place is no natural cause of the increase of piety, for it inevitably produces dissipation of mind. Yet, since men go every day to view the fields where great actions have been performed, and return with stronger impressions of the event, curiosity of the same kind may naturally dispose us to view that country whence our religion had its beginning, and I believe no man surveys those awful scenes without some confirmation of holy resolutions. That the Supreme Being may be more easily propitiated in one place than in another is the dream of idle superstition, but that some places may operate upon our own minds in an uncommon manner is an opinion which hourly experience will justify. He who supposes that his vices may be more successfully combated in Palestine, will perhaps find himself mistaken; yet he may go thither without folly; he who thinks they will be more freely pardoned, dishonours at once his reason and religion."

"These," said the prince, "are European distinctions. I will consider them another time. What have you found to be the effect of knowledge? Are those nations happier than we?"

"There is so much infelicity," said the poet, "in the world, that scarce any man has leisure from his own distresses to estimate the comparative happiness of others. Knowledge is certainly one of the means of pleasure, as is confessed by the natural desire which every mind feels of increasing its ideas. Ignorance is mere privation, by which nothing can be produced; it is a vacuity in which the soul sits motionless and torpid for want of attraction, and, without knowing why, we always rejoice when we learn, and grieve when we forget. I am therefore inclined to conclude that if nothing counteracts the natural consequence of learning, we grow more happy as our minds take a wider range.

"In enumerating the particular comforts of life, we shall find many advantages on the side of the Europeans. They cure wounds and diseases with which we languish and perish. We suffer inclemencies of weather which they can obviate. They have engines for the dispatch of many laborious works, which we must perform by manual industry. There is such communication between distant places that one friend can hardly be said to be absent from another. Their policy removes all public inconveniences; they have roads cut through the mountains, and bridges laid over their rivers. And, if we descend to the privacies of life, their habitations are more commodious and their possessions are more secure."

"They are surely happy," said the prince, "who have all these conveniences, of which I envy none so much as the facility with which separated friends interchange their thoughts."

"The Europeans," answered Imlac, "are less unhappy than we, but they are not happy. Human life is everywhere a state in which much is to be endured and little to be enjoyed."[4]

Chapter XII—The Story of Imlac *(continued)*

"I am not yet willing," said the prince, "to suppose that happiness is so parsimoniously distributed to mortals, nor can I believe but that, if I had the choice of life,[5] I should be able to fill every day with pleasure. I would injure no man, and should provoke no resentments; I would relieve every distress, and should enjoy the benedictions of gratitude. I would choose my friends among the wise and my wife among the virtuous, and therefore should be in no danger from treachery or unkindness. My children should by my care be learned and pious, and would repay to my age what their childhood had received. What would dare to molest him who might call on every side to thousands enriched by his bounty or assisted by his power? And why should not life glide quietly away in the soft reciprocation of protection and reverence? All this may be done without the help of European refinements, which appear by their effects to be rather specious than useful. Let us leave them and pursue our journey."

"From Palestine," said Imlac, "I passed through many regions of Asia; in the more civilised kingdoms as a trader, and among the barbarians of the mountains as a pilgrim. At last I began to long for my native country, that I might repose after my travels and fatigues in the places where I had spent my earliest years, and gladden my old companions with the recital of my adventures. Often did I figure to myself those with whom I had sported away the gay hours of dawning life, sitting round me in its evening, wondering at my tales and listening to my counsels.

"When this thought had taken possession of my mind, I considered every moment as wasted which did not bring me nearer to Abyssinia. I hastened into Egypt, and, notwithstanding my impatience, was detained ten months in the contemplation of its ancient magnificence and in inquiries after the remains of its ancient learning. I found in Cairo a mixture of all nations: some brought thither by the love of knowledge, some by the hope of gain; many by the desire of living after their own manner without observation, and of lying hid in the obscurity of multitudes; for in a city populous as Cairo it is possible to obtain at the same time the gratifications of society and the secrecy of solitude.

"From Cairo I travelled to Suez, and embarked on the Red Sea, passing along the coast till I arrived at the port from which I had departed twenty years before. Here I joined myself to a caravan, and re-entered my native country.

"I now expected the caresses of my kinsmen and the congratulations of my friends, and was not without hope that my father, whatever value he had set upon riches, would own with gladness and pride a son who was able to add to the felicity and honour of the nation. But I was soon convinced that my thoughts were vain. My father had been dead fourteen years, having divided his wealth among my brothers, who were removed to some other provinces. Of my companions, the greater part was in the grave; of the rest, some could with difficulty remember me, and some considered me as one corrupted by foreign manners.

"A man used to vicissitudes is not easily dejected. I forgot, after a time, my disappointment, and endeavoured to recommend myself to the nobles of the kingdom; they admitted me to their tables, heard my story, and dismissed me. I opened a school, and was prohibited to teach. I then resolved to sit down in the quiet of domestic life, and addressed a lady that was fond of my conversation, but rejected my suit because my father was a merchant.

"Wearied at last with solicitation and repulses, I resolved to hide myself forever from the world, and depend no longer on the opinion or caprice of others. I waited for the time when the gate of the Happy Valley should open, that I might bid farewell to hope and fear; the day came, my performance was distinguished with favour, and I resigned myself with joy to perpetual confinement."

"Hast thou here found happiness at last?" said Rasselas. "Tell me, without reserve, art thou content with thy condition, or dost thou wish to be again wandering and inquiring? All the inhabitants of this valley celebrate their lot, and at the annual visit of the emperor invite others to partake of their felicity."

"Great prince," said Imlac, "I shall speak the truth. I know not one of all your attendants who does not lament the hour when he entered this retreat. I am less unhappy than the rest, because I have a mind replete with images, which I can vary and combine at pleasure. I can amuse my solitude by the renovation of the knowledge which begins to fade from my memory, and by recollection of the accidents of my past life. Yet all this ends in the sorrowful consideration that my acquirements are now useless, and that none of my pleasures can be again enjoyed. The rest, whose minds have no impression but of the present moment, are either corroded by malignant passions or sit stupid in the gloom of perpetual vacancy."

"What passions can infest those," said the prince, "who have no rivals?

We are in a place where impotence precludes malice, and where all envy is repressed by community of enjoyments."

"There may be community," said Imlac, "of material possessions, but there can never be community of love or of esteem. It must happen that one will please more than another; he that knows himself despised will always be envious, and still more envious and malevolent if he is condemned to live in the presence of those who despise him. The invitations by which they allure others to a state which they feel to be wretched, proceed from the natural malignity of hopeless misery. They are weary of themselves and of each other, and expect to find relief in new companions. They envy the liberty which their folly has forfeited, and would gladly see all mankind imprisoned like themselves.

"From this crime, however, I am wholly free. No man can say that he is wretched by my persuasion. I look with pity on the crowds who are annually soliciting admission to captivity, and wish that it were lawful for me to warn them of their danger."

"My dear Imlac," said the prince, "I will open to thee my whole heart. I have long meditated an escape from the Happy Valley. I have examined the mountain on every side, but find myself insuperably barred: teach me the way to break my prison; thou shalt be the companion of my flight, the guide of my rambles, the partner of my fortune, and my sole director in the *choice of life*."

"Sir," answered the poet, "your escape will be difficult, and perhaps you may soon repent your curiosity. The world, which you figure to yourself smooth and quiet as the lake in the valley, you will find a sea foaming with tempests and boiling with whirlpools; you will be sometimes overwhelmed by the waves of violence, and sometimes dashed against the rocks of treachery. Amidst wrongs and frauds, competitions and anxieties, you will wish a thousand times for these seats of quiet, and willingly quit hope to be free from fear." "Do not seek to deter me from my purpose," said the prince. "I am impatient to see what thou hast seen; and since thou art thyself weary of the valley, it is evident that thy former state was better than this. Whatever be the consequence of my experiment, I am resolved to judge with my own eyes of the various conditions of men, and then to make deliberately my *choice of life*."

"I am afraid," said Imlac, "you are hindered by stronger restraints than my persuasions; yet, if your determination is fixed, I do not counsel you to despair. Few things are impossible to diligence and skill."

Chapter XIII—Rasselas Discovers the Means of Escape

The prince now dismissed his favourite to rest, but the narrative of wonders and novelties filled his mind with perturbation. He revolved all that he had heard, and prepared innumerable questions for the morning.

Much of his uneasiness was now removed. He had a friend to whom he could impart his thoughts, and whose experience could assist him in his designs. His heart was no longer condemned to swell with silent vexation. He thought that even the Happy Valley might be endured with such a companion, and that if they could range the world together he should have nothing further to desire.

In a few days the water was discharged, and the ground dried. The prince and Imlac then walked out together, to converse without the notice of the rest. The prince, whose thoughts were always on the wing, as he passed by the gate said, with a countenance of sorrow, "Why art thou so strong, and why is man so weak?"

"Man is not weak," answered his companion; "knowledge is more than equivalent to force. The master of mechanics laughs at strength. I can burst the gate, but cannot do it secretly. Some other expedient must be tried."

As they were walking on the side of the mountain they observed that the coneys, which the rain had driven from their burrows, had taken shelter among the bushes, and formed holes behind them tending upwards in an oblique line. "It has been the opinion of antiquity," said Imlac, "that human reason borrowed many arts from the instinct of animals; let us, therefore, not think ourselves degraded by learning from the cony. We may escape by piercing the mountain in the same direction. We will begin where the summit hangs over the middle part, and labour upward till we shall issue out beyond the prominence."

The eyes of the prince, when he heard this proposal, sparkled with joy. The execution was easy and the success certain.

No time was now lost. They hastened early in the morning to choose a place proper for their mine. They clambered with great fatigue among crags and brambles, and returned without having discovered any part that favoured their design. The second and the third day were spent in the same manner, and with the same frustration; but on the fourth day they found a small cavern concealed by a thicket, where they resolved to make their experiment.

Imlac procured instruments proper to hew stone and remove earth, and they fell to their work on the next day with more eagerness than vigour. They were presently exhausted by their efforts, and sat down to pant upon the grass. The prince for a moment appeared to be discouraged. "Sir," said his companion, "practice will enable us to continue our labour for a longer time. Mark, however, how far we have advanced, and you will find that our toil will some time have an end. Great works are performed not by strength, but perseverance; yonder palace was raised by single stones, yet you see its height and spaciousness. He that shall walk with vigour three hours a day, will pass in seven years a space equal to the circumference of the globe."

They returned to their work day after day, and in a short time found a fissure in the rock, which enabled them to pass far with very little obstruction. This Rasselas considered as a good omen. "Do not disturb your mind," said Imlac, "with other hopes or fears than reason may suggest; if you are pleased with the prognostics of good, you will be terrified likewise with tokens of evil, and your whole life will be a prey to superstition. Whatever facilitates our work is more than an omen; it is a cause of success. This is one of those pleasing surprises which often happen to active resolution. Many things difficult to design prove easy to performance."

Chapter XIV—Rasselas and Imlac Receive an Unexpected Visit

They had now wrought their way to the middle, and solaced their toil with the approach of liberty, when the prince, coming down to refresh himself with air, found his sister Nekayah standing before the mouth of the cavity. He started, and stood confused, afraid to tell his design, and yet hopeless to conceal it. A few moments determined him to repose on her fidelity, and secure her secrecy by a declaration without reserve.

"Do not imagine," said the princess, "that I came hither as a spy. I had long observed from my window that you and Imlac directed your walk every day towards the same point, but I did not suppose you had any better reason for the preference than a cooler shade or more fragrant bank, nor followed you with any other design than to partake of your conversation. Since, then, not suspicion, but fondness, has detected you, let me not lose the advantage of my discovery. I am equally weary of confinement with yourself, and not less desirous of knowing what is done or suffered in the world. Permit me to fly with you from this tasteless tranquillity, which will yet grow more loathsome when you have left me. You may deny me to accompany you, but cannot hinder me from following."

The prince, who loved Nekayah above his other sisters, had no inclination to refuse her request, and grieved that he had lost an opportunity of showing his confidence by a voluntary communication. It was, therefore, agreed that she should leave the valley with them; and that in the meantime she should watch, lest any other straggler should, by chance or curiosity, follow them to the mountain.

At length their labour was at an end. They saw light beyond the prominence, and, issuing to the top of the mountain, beheld the Nile, yet a narrow current, wandering beneath them.

The prince looked round with rapture, anticipated all the pleasures of travel, and in thought was already transported beyond his father's dominions. Imlac, though very joyful at his escape, had less expectation of pleasure in the world, which he had before tried and of which he had been weary.

Rasselas was so much delighted with a wider horizon, that he could not soon be persuaded to return into the valley. He informed his sister that the way was open, and that nothing now remained but to prepare for their departure.

Chapter XV—The Prince and Princess Leave the Valley and See Many Wonders

The prince and princess had jewels sufficient to make them rich whenever they came into a place of commerce, which, by Imlac's direction, they hid in their clothes, and on the night of the next full moon all left the valley. The princess was followed only by a single favourite, who did not know whither she was going.

They clambered through the cavity, and began to go down on the other side. The princess and her maid turned their eyes toward every part, and seeing nothing to bound their prospect, considered themselves in danger of being lost in a dreary vacuity. They stopped and trembled. "I am almost afraid," said the princess, "to begin a journey of which I cannot perceive an end, and to venture into this immense plain where I may be approached on every side by men whom I never saw." The prince felt nearly the same emotions, though he thought it more manly to conceal them.

Imlac smiled at their terrors, and encouraged them to proceed. But the princess continued irresolute till she had been imperceptibly drawn forward too far to return.

In the morning they found some shepherds in the field, who set milk and fruits before them. The princess wondered that she did not see a palace ready for her reception and a table spread with delicacies; but being faint and hungry, she drank the milk and ate the fruits, and thought them of a higher flavour than the products of the valley.

They travelled forward by easy journeys, being all unaccustomed to toil or difficulty, and knowing that, though they might be missed, they could not be pursued. In a few days they came into a more populous region, where Imlac was diverted with the admiration which his companions expressed at the diversity of manners, stations, and employments.

Their dress was such as might not bring upon them the suspicion of having anything to conceal; yet the prince, wherever he came, expected to be obeyed, and the princess was frightened because those who came into her presence did not prostrate themselves before her. Imlac was forced to observe them with great vigilance, lest they should betray their rank by their unusual behaviour, and detained them several weeks in the first village to accustom them to the sight of common mortals.

By degrees the royal wanderers were taught to understand that they had for a time laid aside their dignity, and were to expect only such regard as liberality and courtesy could procure. And Imlac having by many admonitions prepared them to endure the tumults of a port and the ruggedness of the commercial race, brought them down to the sea-coast.

The prince and his sister, to whom everything was new, were gratified equally at all places, and therefore remained for some months at the port without any inclination to pass further. Imlac was content with their stay, because he did not think it safe to expose them, unpractised in the world, to the hazards of a foreign country.

At last he began to fear lest they should be discovered, and proposed to fix a day for their departure. They had no pretensions to judge for themselves, and referred the whole scheme to his direction. He therefore took passage in a ship to Suez, and, when the time came, with great difficulty prevailed on the princess to enter the vessel. They had a quick and prosperous voyage, and from Suez travelled by land to Cairo.

Chapter XVI—They Enter Cairo, and Find Every Man Happy

As they approached the city, which filled the strangers with astonishment, "This," said Imlac to the prince, "is the place where travellers and merchants assemble from all corners of the earth. You will here find men of every character and every occupation. Commerce is here honourable. I will act as a merchant, and you shall live as strangers who have no other end of travel than curiosity; it will soon be observed that we are rich. Our reputation will procure us access to all whom we shall desire to know; you shall see all the concerns of humanity, and enable yourselves at leisure to make your *choice of life*."

They now entered the town, stunned by the noise and offended by the crowds. Instruction had not yet so prevailed over habit but that they wondered to see themselves pass undistinguished along the streets, and met by the lowest of the people without reverence or notice. The princess could not at first bear the thought of being levelled with the vulgar, and for some time continued in her chamber, where she was served by her favourite Pekuah, as in the palace of the valley.

Imlac, who understood traffic, sold part of the jewels the next day, and hired a house, which he adorned with such magnificence that he was immediately considered as a merchant of great wealth. His politeness attracted many acquaintances, and his generosity made him courted by many dependants. His table was crowded by men of every nation, who all admired his knowledge, and solicited his favour. His companions, not being able to mix in the conversation, could make no discovery of their ignorance or surprise, and were gradually initiated in the world as they gained knowledge of the language.

The prince had by frequent lectures been taught the use and nature of money; but the ladies could not for a long time comprehend what the merchants did with small pieces of gold and silver, or why things of so little use should be received as an equivalent to the necessaries of life.

They studied the language two years, while Imlac was preparing to set before them the various ranks and conditions of mankind. He grew acquainted with all who had anything uncommon in their fortune or conduct. He frequented the voluptuous and the frugal, the idle and the busy, the merchants and the men of learning.

The prince, being now able to converse with fluency, and having learned the caution necessary to be observed in his intercourse with strangers, began to accompany Imlac to places of resort, and to enter into all assemblies, that he might make his *choice of life*.

For some time he thought choice needless, because all appeared to him really happy. Wherever he went he met gaiety and kindness, and heard the song of joy or the laugh of carelessness. He began to believe that the world overflowed with universal plenty, and that nothing was withheld either from want or merit; that every hand showered liberality and every heart melted with benevolence: "And who then," says he, "will be suffered to be wretched?"

Imlac permitted the pleasing delusion, and was unwilling to crush the hope of inexperience: till one day, having sat awhile silent, "I know not," said the prince, "what can be the reason that I am more unhappy than any of our friends. I see them perpetually and unalterably cheerful, but feel my own mind restless and uneasy. I am unsatisfied with those pleasures which I seem most to court. I live in the crowds of jollity, not so much to enjoy company as to shun myself, and am only loud and merry to conceal my sadness."

"Every man," said Imlac, "may by examining his own mind guess what passes in the minds of others; when you feel that your own gaiety is counterfeit, it may justly lead you to suspect that of your companions not to be sincere. Envy is commonly reciprocal. We are long before we are convinced that happiness is never to be found, and each believes it possessed by others, to keep alive the hope of obtaining it for himself. In the assembly where you passed the last night there appeared such sprightliness of air and volatility of fancy as might have suited beings of an higher order, formed to inhabit serener regions, inaccessible to care or sorrow; yet, believe me, prince, was there not one who did not dread the moment when solitude should deliver him to the tyranny of reflection."

"This," said the prince, "may be true of others since it is true of me; yet, whatever be the general infelicity of man, one condition is more happy than another, and wisdom surely directs us to take the least evil in the *choice of life.*"

"The causes of good and evil," answered Imlac, "are so various and uncertain, so often entangled with each other, so diversified by various relations, and so much subject to accidents which cannot be foreseen, that he who would fix his condition upon incontestable reasons of preference must live and die inquiring and deliberating."

"But, surely," said Rasselas, "the wise men, to whom we listen with reverence and wonder, chose that mode of life for themselves which they thought most likely to make them happy."

"Very few," said the poet, "live by choice. Every man is placed in the present condition by causes which acted without his foresight, and with which he did not always willingly cooperate, and therefore you will rarely meet one who does not think the lot of his neighbour better than his own."

"I am pleased to think," said the prince, "that my birth has given me at least one advantage over others by enabling me to determine for myself. I have here the world before me. I will review it at leisure: surely happiness is somewhere to be found."

Chapter XVII—The Prince Associates with Young Men of Spirit and Gaiety

Rasselas rose next day, and resolved to begin his experiments upon life. "Youth," cried he, "is the time of gladness: I will join myself to the young men whose only business is to gratify their desires, and whose time is all spent in a succession of enjoyments."

To such societies he was readily admitted, but a few days brought him back weary and disgusted. Their mirth was without images, their laughter without motive; their pleasures were gross and sensual, in which the mind had no part; their conduct was at once wild and mean; they laughed at order and at law, but the frown of power dejected and the eye of wisdom abashed them.

The prince soon concluded that he should never be happy in a course of life of which he was ashamed. He thought it unsuitable to a reasonable being to act without a plan, and to be sad or cheerful only by chance. "Happiness," said he, "must be something solid and permanent, without fear and without uncertainty."

But his young companions had gained so much of his regard by their frankness and courtesy that he could not leave them without warning and remonstrance. "My friends," said he, "I have seriously considered our manners and our prospects, and find that we have mistaken our own interest. The first years of man must make provision for the last. He that never thinks, never can be wise. Perpetual levity must end in ignorance; and intemperance, though it may fire the spirits for an hour, will make life short or miserable. Let us consider that youth is of no long duration, and that in mature age, when the enchantments of fancy shall cease, and phantoms of delight dance no more about us, we shall have no comforts but the esteem of wise men and the means of doing good. Let us therefore stop while to stop is in our power: let us live as men who are some time to grow old, and to whom it will be the most dreadful of all evils not to count their past years but by follies, and to be reminded of their former luxuriance of health only by the maladies which riot has produced."

They stared awhile in silence one upon another, and at last drove him away by a general chorus of continued laughter.

The consciousness that his sentiments were just and his intention kind was scarcely sufficient to support him against the horror of derision. But he recovered his tranquillity and pursued his search.

Chapter XVIII—The Prince Finds a Wise and Happy Man

As he was one day walking in the street he saw a spacious building which all were by the open doors invited to enter: he followed the stream of people, and found it a hall or school of declamation, in which professors read lectures to their auditory. He fixed his eye upon a sage raised above the rest, who discoursed with great energy on the government of the passions. His look was venerable, his action graceful, his pronunciation clear, and his diction elegant. He showed with great strength of sentiment and variety of illustration that human nature is degraded and debased when the lower faculties predominate over the higher; that when fancy, the parent of passion, usurps the dominion of the mind, nothing ensues but the natural effect of unlawful government, perturbation, and confusion; that she betrays the fortresses of the intellect to rebels, and excites her children to sedition against reason their lawful sovereign. He compared reason to the sun, of which the light is constant, uniform, and lasting; and fancy to a meteor, of bright but transitory lustre, irregular in its motion and delusive in its direction.

He then communicated the various precepts given from time to time for the conquest of passion, and displayed the happiness of those who had obtained the important victory, after which man is no longer the slave of fear nor the fool of hope; is no more emaciated by envy, inflamed by anger, emasculated by tenderness, or depressed by grief; but walks on calmly through the tumults or the privacies of life, as the sun pursues alike his course through the calm or the stormy sky.

He enumerated many examples of heroes immovable by pain or pleasure, who looked with indifference on those modes or accidents to which the vulgar give the names of good and evil. He exhorted his hearers to lay aside their prejudices, and arm themselves against the shafts of malice or misfortune, by invulnerable patience: concluding that this state only was happiness, and that this happiness was in everyone's power.

Rasselas listened to him with the veneration due to the instructions of a superior being, and waiting for him at the door, humbly implored the liberty of visiting so great a master of true wisdom. The lecturer hesitated a moment, when Rasselas put a purse of gold into his hand, which he received with a mixture of joy and wonder.

"I have found," said the prince at his return to Imlac, "a man who can teach all that is necessary to be known; who, from the unshaken throne of rational fortitude, looks down on the scenes of life changing beneath him. He speaks, and attention watches his lips. He reasons, and conviction closes his periods. This man shall be my future guide: I will learn his doctrines and imitate his life."

"Be not too hasty," said Imlac, "to trust or to admire the teachers of morality: they discourse like angels, but they live like men."

Rasselas, who could not conceive how any man could reason so forcibly without feeling the cogency of his own arguments, paid his visit in a few days, and was denied admission. He had now learned the power of money, and made his way by a piece of gold to the inner apartment, where he found the philosopher in a room half darkened, with his eyes misty and his face pale. "Sir," said he, "you are come at a time when all human friendship is useless; what I suffer cannot be remedied: what I have lost cannot be supplied. My daughter, my only daughter, from whose tenderness I expected all the comforts of my age, died last night of a fever. My views, my purposes, my hopes, are at an end: I am now a lonely being, disunited from society."

"Sir," said the prince, "mortality is an event by which a wise man can never be surprised: we know that death is always near, and it should therefore always be expected." "Young man," answered the philosopher, "you speak like one that has never felt the pangs of separation." "Have you then forgot the precepts," said Rasselas, "which you so powerfully enforced? Has wisdom no strength to arm the heart against calamity? Consider that external things are naturally variable, but truth and reason are always the same." "What comfort," said the mourner, "can truth and reason afford me? Of what effect are they now, but to tell me that my daughter will not be restored?"

The prince, whose humanity would not suffer him to insult misery with reproof, went away, convinced of the emptiness of rhetorical sounds, and the inefficacy of polished periods and studied sentences.

Chapter XIX—A Glimpse of Pastoral Life

He was still eager upon the same inquiry; and having heard of a hermit that lived near the lowest cataract of the Nile, and filled the whole country with the fame of his sanctity, resolved to visit his retreat, and inquire whether that felicity which public life could not afford was to be found in solitude, and whether a man whose age and virtue made him venerable could teach any peculiar art of shunning evils or enduring them.

Imlac and the princess agreed to accompany him, and after the necessary preparations, they began their journey. Their way lay through fields, where shepherds tended their flocks and the lambs were playing upon the pasture. "This," said the poet, "is the life which has been often celebrated for its innocence and quiet; let us pass the heat of the day among the shepherds' tents, and know whether all our searches are not to terminate in pastoral simplicity."

The proposal pleased them; and they induced the shepherds, by small presents and familiar questions, to tell the opinion of their own state. They were so rude and ignorant, so little able to compare the good with the evil of the occupation, and so indistinct in their narratives and descriptions, that very little could be learned from them. But it was evident that their hearts were cankered with discontent; that they considered themselves as condemned to labour for the luxury of the rich, and looked up with stupid malevolence towards those that were placed above them.

The princess pronounced with vehemence that she would never suffer these envious savages to be her companions, and that she should not soon be desirous of seeing any more specimens of rustic happiness; but could not believe that all the accounts of primeval pleasures were fabulous, and was yet in doubt whether life had anything that could be justly preferred to the placid gratification of fields and woods. She hoped that the time would come when, with a few virtuous and elegant companions, she should gather flowers planted by her own hands, fondle the lambs of her own ewe, and listen without care, among brooks and breezes, to one of her maidens reading in the shade.

Chapter XX—The Danger of Prosperity

On the next day they continued their journey till the heat compelled them to look round for shelter. At a small distance they saw a thick wood, which they no sooner entered than they perceived that they were approaching the habitations of men. The shrubs were diligently cut away to open walks where the shades ware darkest; the boughs of opposite trees were artificially interwoven; seats of flowery turf were raised in vacant spaces; and a rivulet that wantoned along the side of a winding path had its banks sometimes opened into small basins, and its stream sometimes obstructed by little mounds of stone heaped together to increase its murmurs.

They passed slowly through the wood, delighted with such unexpected accommodations, and entertained each other with conjecturing what or who he could be that in those rude and unfrequented regions had leisure and art for such harmless luxury.

As they advanced they heard the sound of music, and saw youths and virgins dancing in the grove; and going still further beheld a stately palace built upon a hill surrounded by woods. The laws of eastern hospitality allowed them to enter, and the master welcomed them like a man liberal and wealthy.

He was skilful enough in appearances soon to discern that they were no common guests, and spread his table with magnificence. The eloquence of Imlac caught his attention, and the lofty courtesy of the princess excited his respect. When they offered to depart, he entreated their stay, and was the next day more unwilling to dismiss them than before. They were easily persuaded to stop, and civility grew up in time to freedom and confidence.

The prince now saw all the domestics cheerful and all the face of nature smiling round the place, and could not forbear to hope that he should find here what he was seeking; but when he was congratulating the master upon his possessions he answered with a sigh, "My condition has indeed the appearance of happiness, but appearances are delusive. My prosperity puts my life in danger; the Bassa of Egypt is my enemy, incensed only by my wealth and popularity. I have been hitherto protected against him by the princes of the country; but as the favour of the great is uncertain I know not how soon my defenders may be persuaded to share the plunder with the Bassa. I have sent my treasures into a distant country, and upon the first alarm am prepared to follow them. Then will my enemies riot in my mansion, and enjoy the gardens which I have planted."

They all joined in lamenting his danger and deprecating his exile; and the princess was so much disturbed with the tumult of grief and indignation that she retired to her apartment. They continued with their kind inviter a few days longer, and then went further to find the hermit.

Chapter XXI—The Happiness of Solitude. The Hermit's History

They came on the third day, by the direction of the peasants, to the hermit's cell. It was a cavern in the side of a mountain, overshadowed with palm trees, at such a distance from the cataract that nothing more was heard than a gentle uniform murmur, such as composed the mind to pensive meditation, especially when it was assisted by the wind whistling among the branches. The first rude essay of nature had been so much improved by human labour that the cave contained several apartments appropriated to different uses, and often afforded lodging to travellers whom darkness or tempests happened to overtake.

The hermit sat on a bench at the door, to enjoy the coolness of the evening. On one side lay a book with pens and paper; on the other mechanical instruments of various kinds. As they approached him unregarded, the princess observed that he had not the countenance of a man that had found or could teach the way to happiness.

They saluted him with great respect, which he repaid like a man not unaccustomed to the forms of courts. "My children," said he, "if you have lost your way, you shall be willingly supplied with such conveniences for the night as this cavern will afford. I have all that nature requires, and you will not expect delicacies in a hermit's cell."

They thanked him; and, entering, were pleased with the neatness and regularity of the place. The hermit set flesh and wine before them, though he fed only upon fruits and water. His discourse was cheerful without levity, and pious without enthusiasm. He soon gained the esteem of his guests, and the princess repented her hasty censure.

At last Imlac began thus: "I do not now wonder that your reputation is so far extended: we have heard at Cairo of your wisdom, and came hither to implore your direction for this young man and maiden in the *choice of life*."

"To him that lives well," answered the hermit, "every form of life is good; nor can I give any other rule for choice than to remove all apparent evil."

"He will remove most certainly from evil," said the prince, "who shall devote himself to that solitude which you have recommended by your example."

"I have indeed lived fifteen years in solitude," said the hermit, "but have no desire that my example should gain any imitators. In my youth I professed arms, and was raised by degrees to the highest military rank. I have traversed wide countries at the head of my troops, and seen many

battles and sieges. At last, being disgusted by the preferments of a younger officer, and feeling that my vigour was beginning to decay, I resolved
to close my life in peace, having found the world full of snares, discord,
and misery. I had once escaped from the pursuit of the enemy by the shelter of this cavern, and therefore chose it for my final residence. I employed artificers to form it into chambers, and stored it with all that I was
likely to want.

"For some time after my retreat I rejoiced like a tempest-beaten sailor
at his entrance into the harbour, being delighted with the sudden change
of the noise and hurry of war to stillness and repose. When the pleasure
of novelty went away, I employed my hours in examining the plants which
grow in the valley, and the minerals which I collected from the rocks. But
that inquiry is now grown tasteless and irksome. I have been for some
time unsettled and distracted: my mind is disturbed with a thousand per-
plexities of doubt and vanities of imagination, which hourly prevail upon
me, because I have no opportunities of relaxation or diversion. I am sometimes ashamed to think that I could not secure myself from vice but by
retiring from the exercise of virtue, and begin to suspect that I was rather
impelled by resentment than led by devotion into solitude. My fancy riots
in scenes of folly, and I lament that I have lost so much, and have gained
so little. In solitude, if I escape the example of bad men, I want likewise
the counsel and conversation of the good. I have been long comparing the
evils with the advantages of society, and resolve to return into the world
tomorrow. The life of a solitary man will be certainly miserable, but not
certainly devout."

They heard his resolution with surprise, but after a short pause offered
to conduct him to Cairo. He dug up a considerable treasure which he had
hid among the rocks, and accompanied them to the city, on which, as he
approached it, he gazed with rapture.

Chapter XXII—The Happiness of a Life Led
According to Nature

Rasselas went often to an assembly of learned men, who met at stated
times to unbend their minds and compare their opinions. Their manners
were somewhat coarse, but their conversation was instructive, and their
disputations acute, though sometimes too violent, and often continued

till neither controvertist[6] remembered upon what question they began. Some faults were almost general among them: everyone was desirous to dictate to the rest, and everyone was pleased to hear the genius or knowledge of another depreciated.

In this assembly Rasselas was relating his interview with the hermit, and the wonder with which he heard him censure a course of life which he had so deliberately chosen and so laudably followed. The sentiments of the hearers were various. Some were of opinion that the folly of his choice had been justly punished by condemnation to perpetual perseverance. One of the youngest among them, with great vehemence, pronounced him a hypocrite. Some talked of the right of society to the labour of individuals, and considered retirement as a desertion of duty. Others readily allowed that there was a time when the claims of the public were satisfied, and when a man might properly sequester himself, to review his life and purify his heart.

One who appeared more affected with the narrative than the rest thought it likely that the hermit would in a few years go back to his retreat, and perhaps, if shame did not restrain or death intercept him, return once more from his retreat into the world. "For the hope of happiness," said he, "is so strongly impressed that the longest experience is not able to efface it. Of the present state, whatever it be, we feel and are forced to confess the misery; yet when the same state is again at a distance, imagination paints it as desirable. But the time will surely come when desire will no longer be our torment and no man shall be wretched but by his own fault."

"This," said a philosopher who had heard him with tokens of great impatience, "is the present condition of a wise man. The time is already come when none are wretched but by their own fault. Nothing is more idle than to inquire after happiness which nature has kindly placed within our reach. The way to be happy is to live according to nature, in obedience to that universal and unalterable law with which every heart is originally impressed; which is not written on it by precept, but engraved by destiny; not instilled by education, but infused at our nativity. He that lives according to nature will suffer nothing from the delusions of hope or importunities of desire; he will receive and reject with equability of temper; and act or suffer as the reason of things shall alternately prescribe. Other men may amuse themselves with subtle definitions or intricate ratiocination. Let them learn to be wise by easier means: let them observe the hind of the forest and the linnet of the grove: let them consider the life of animals, whose motions are regulated by instinct; they obey their guide, and are happy. Let us therefore at length cease to dispute, and learn to live: throw away the encumbrance of precepts, which they who utter them with so much pride and pomp do not understand, and carry with us this simple and intelligible maxim: that deviation from nature is deviation from happiness."

When he had spoken he looked round him with a placid air, and enjoyed the consciousness of his own beneficence. "Sir," said the prince with great modesty, "as I, like all the rest of mankind, am desirous of felicity, my closest attention has been fixed upon your discourse: I doubt not the truth of a position which a man so learned has so confidently advanced. Let me only know what it is to live according to nature."

"When I find young men so humble and so docile," said the philosopher, "I can deny them no information which my studies have enabled me to afford. To live according to nature is to act always with due regard to the fitness arising from the relations and qualities of causes and effects; to concur with the great and unchangeable scheme of universal felicity; to cooperate with the general disposition and tendency of the present system of things."

The prince soon found that this was one of the sages whom he should understand less as he heard him longer. He therefore bowed and was silent; and the philosopher, supposing him satisfied and the rest vanquished, rose up and departed with the air of a man that had cooperated with the present system.

Chapter XXIII—The Prince and His Sister Divide between Them the Work of Observation

Rasselas returned home full of reflections, doubtful how to direct his future steps. Of the way to happiness he found the learned and simple equally ignorant; but as he was yet young, he flattered himself that he had time remaining for more experiments and further inquiries. He communicated to Imlac his observations and his doubts, but was answered by him with new doubts and remarks that gave him no comfort. He therefore discoursed more frequently and freely with his sister, who had yet the same hope with himself, and always assisted him to give some reason why, though he had been hitherto frustrated, he might succeed at last.

"We have hitherto," said she, "known but little of the world; we have never yet been either great or mean. In our own country, though we had royalty, we had no power; and in this we have not yet seen the private recesses of domestic peace. Imlac favours not our search, lest we should in time find him mistaken. We will divide the task between us; you shall try what is to be found in the splendour of courts, and I will range the shades of humbler life. Perhaps command and authority may be the supreme blessings, as they afford the most opportunities of doing good; or perhaps what this world can give may be found in the modest habitations of middle fortune—too low for great designs, and too high for penury and distress."

Chapter XXIV—The Prince Examines the Happiness of High Stations

Rasselas applauded the design, and appeared next day with a splendid retinue at the court of the Bassa. He was soon distinguished for his magnificence, and admitted, as a prince whose curiosity had brought him from distant countries, to an intimacy with the great officers and frequent conversation with the Bassa himself.

He was at first inclined to believe that the man must be pleased with his own condition whom all approached with reverence and heard with obedience, and who had the power to extend his edicts to a whole kingdom. "There can be no pleasure," said he, "equal to that of feeling at once the joy of thousands all made happy by wise administration. Yet, since by the law of subordination this sublime delight can be in one nation but the lot of one, it is surely reasonable to think that there is some satisfaction more popular and accessible, and that millions can hardly be subjected to the will of a single man, only to fill his particular breast with incommunicable content."

These thoughts were often in his mind, and he found no solution of the difficulty. But as presents and civilities gained him more familiarity, he found that almost every man who stood high in employment hated all the rest and was hated by them, and that their lives were a continual succession of plots and detections, stratagems and escapes, faction and treachery. Many of those who surrounded the Bassa were sent only to watch and report his conduct: every tongue was muttering censure, and every eye was searching for a fault.

At last the letters of revocation arrived: the Bassa was carried in chains to Constantinople, and his name was mentioned no more.

"What are we now to think of the prerogatives of power," said Rasselas to his sister: "is it without efficacy to good, or is the subordinate degree only dangerous, and the supreme safe and glorious? Is the Sultan the only happy man in his dominions, or is the Sultan himself subject to the torments of suspicion and the dread of enemies?"

In a short time the second Bassa was deposed. The Sultan that had advanced him was murdered by the Janissaries, and his successor had other views or different favourites.

Chapter XXV—The Princess Pursues Her Enquiry with More Diligence Than Success

The princess in the meantime insinuated herself into many families; for there are few doors through which liberality, joined with good humour, cannot find its way. The daughters of many houses were airy and cheerful; but Nekayah had been too long accustomed to the conversation of Imlac and her brother to be much pleased with childish levity and prattle which had no meaning. She found their thoughts narrow, their wishes low, and their merriment often artificial. Their pleasures, poor as they were, could not be preserved pure, but were embittered by petty competitions and worthless emulation. They were always jealous of the beauty of each other, of a quality to which solicitude can add nothing, and from which detraction can take nothing away. Many were in love with triflers like themselves, and many fancied that they were in love when in truth they were only idle. Their affection was seldom fixed on sense or virtue, and therefore seldom ended but in vexation. Their grief, however, like their joy, was transient; everything floated in their mind unconnected with the past or future, so that one desire easily gave way to another, as a second stone, cast into the water, effaces and confounds the circles of the first.

With these girls she played as with inoffensive animals, and found them proud of her countenance and weary of her company.

But her purpose was to examine more deeply, and her affability easily persuaded the hearts that were swelling with sorrow to discharge their secrets in her ear, and those whom hope flattered or prosperity delighted often courted her to partake their pleasure.

The princess and her brother commonly met in the evening in a private summer-house on the bank of the Nile, and related to each other the occurrences of the day. As they were sitting together the princess cast her eyes upon the river that flowed before her. "Answer," said she, "great father of waters, thou that rollest thy floods through eighty nations, to the invocations of the daughter of thy native king. Tell me if thou waterest through all thy course a single habitation from which thou dost not hear the murmurs of complaint."

"You are then," said Rasselas, "not more successful in private houses than I have been in courts." "I have, since the last partition of our provinces," said the princess, "enabled myself to enter familiarly into many families, where there was the fairest show of prosperity and peace, and know not one house that is not haunted by some fury that destroys its quiet.

"I did not seek ease among the poor, because I concluded that there it could not be found. But I saw many poor whom I had supposed to live in affluence. Poverty has in large cities very different appearances. It is often concealed in splendour and often in extravagance. It is the care of a very great part of mankind to conceal their indigence from the rest. They support themselves by temporary expedients, and every day is lost in contriving for the morrow.

"This, however, was an evil which, though frequent, I saw with less pain, because I could relieve it. Yet some have refused my bounties; more offended with my quickness to detect their wants than pleased with my readiness to succour them; and others, whose exigencies compelled them to admit my kindness, have never been able to forgive their benefactress. Many, however, have been sincerely grateful without the ostentation of gratitude or the hope of other favours."

Chapter XXVI—The Princess Continues Her Remarks upon Private Life

Nekayah, perceiving her brother's attention fixed, proceeded in her narrative.

"In families where there is or is not poverty there is commonly discord. If a kingdom be, as Imlac tells us, a great family, a family likewise is a little kingdom, torn with factions and exposed to revolutions. An unpractised observer expects the love of parents and children to be constant and equal. But this kindness seldom continues beyond the years of infancy; in a short time the children become rivals to their parents. Benefits are allayed by reproaches, and gratitude debased by envy.

"Parents and children seldom act in concert; each child endeavours to appropriate the esteem or the fondness of the parents; and the parents, with yet less temptation, betray each other to their children. Thus, some place their confidence in the father and some in the mother, and by degrees the house is filled with artifices and feuds.

"The opinions of children and parents, of the young and the old, are naturally opposite, by the contrary effects of hope and despondence, of expectation and experience, without crime or folly on either side. The colours of life in youth and age appear different, as the face of nature in spring and winter. And how can children credit the assertions of parents which their own eyes show them to be false?

"Few parents act in such a manner as much to enforce their maxims by the credit of their lives. The old man trusts wholly to slow contrivance and gradual progression; the youth expects to force his way by genius, vigour, and precipitance. The old man pays regard to riches, and the youth reverences virtue. The old man deifies prudence; the youth commits himself to magnanimity and chance. The young man, who intends no ill, believes that none is intended, and therefore acts with openness and candour; but his father, having suffered the injuries of fraud, is impelled to suspect and too often allured to practise it. Age looks with anger on the temerity of youth, and youth with contempt on the scrupulosity of age. Thus parents and children for the greatest part live on to love less and less; and if those whom nature has thus closely united are the torments of each other, where shall we look for tenderness and consolation?"

"Surely," said the prince, "you must have been unfortunate in your choice of acquaintance. I am unwilling to believe that the most tender of all relations is thus impeded in its effects by natural necessity."

"Domestic discord," answered she, "is not inevitably and fatally necessary, but yet it is not easily avoided. We seldom see that a whole family is virtuous; the good and the evil cannot well agree, and the evil can yet less agree with one another. Even the virtuous fall sometimes to variance, when their virtues are of different kinds and tending to extremes. In general, those parents have most reverence who most deserve it, for he that lives well cannot be despised.

"Many other evils infest private life. Some are the slaves of servants whom they have trusted with their affairs. Some are kept in continual anxiety to the caprice of rich relations, whom they cannot please and dare not offend. Some husbands are imperious and some wives perverse, and, as it is always more easy to do evil than good, though the wisdom or virtue of one can very rarely make many happy, the folly or vice of one may often make many miserable."

"If such be the general effect of marriage," said the prince, "I shall for the future think it dangerous to connect my interest with that of another, lest I should be unhappy by my partner's fault."[7]

"I have met," said the princess, "with many who live single for that reason, but I never found that their prudence ought to raise envy. They dream away their time without friendship, without fondness, and are driven to rid themselves of the day, for which they have no use, by childish amusements or vicious delights. They act as beings under the constant sense of some known inferiority that fills their minds with rancour and their tongues with censure. They are peevish at home and malevolent abroad, and, as the outlaws of human nature, make it their business and their pleasure to disturb that society which debars them from its privileges. To live without feeling or exciting sympathy, to be fortunate without adding to the felicity of others, or afflicted without tasting the balm of pity, is a state more gloomy than solitude; it is not retreat but exclusion from mankind. Marriage has many pains, but celibacy has no pleasures."

"What then is to be done?" said Rasselas. "The more we inquire the less we can resolve. Surely he is most likely to please himself that has no other inclination to regard."

Chapter XXVII—Disquisition upon Greatness

The conversation had a short pause. The prince, having considered his sister's observations, told her that she had surveyed life with prejudice and supposed misery where she did not find it. "Your narrative," said he, "throws yet a darker gloom upon the prospects of futurity. The predictions of Imlac were but faint sketches of the evils painted by Nekayah. I have been lately convinced that quiet is not the daughter of grandeur or of power; that her presence is not to be bought by wealth nor enforced by conquest. It is evident that as any man acts in a wider compass he must be more exposed to opposition from enmity or miscarriage from chance. Whoever has many to please or to govern must use the ministry of many agents, some of whom will be wicked and some ignorant, by some he will be misled and by others betrayed. If he gratifies one he will offend another; those that are not favoured will think themselves injured, and since favours can be conferred but upon few the greater number will be always discontented."

"The discontent," said the princess, "which is thus unreasonable, I hope that I shall always have spirit to despise and you power to repress."

"Discontent," answered Rasselas, "will not always be without reason under the most just and vigilant administration of public affairs. None, however attentive, can always discover that merit which indigence or faction may happen to obscure, and none, however powerful, can always reward it. Yet he that sees inferior desert advanced above him will naturally impute that preference to partiality or caprice, and indeed it can scarcely be hoped that any man, however magnanimous by nature or exalted by condition, will be able to persist forever in fixed and inexorable justice of distribution; he will sometimes indulge his own affections and sometimes those of his favourites; he will permit some to please him who can never serve him; he will discover in those whom he loves qualities which in reality they do not possess, and to those from whom he receives pleasure he will in his turn endeavour to give it. Thus will recommendations sometimes prevail which were purchased by money or by the more destructive bribery of flattery and servility.

"He that has much to do will do something wrong, and of that wrong must suffer the consequences, and if it were possible that he should always act rightly, yet, when such numbers are to judge of his conduct, the bad will censure and obstruct him by malevolence and the good sometimes by mistake.

"The highest stations cannot therefore hope to be the abodes of happiness, which I would willingly believe to have fled from thrones and palaces to seats of humble privacy and placid obscurity. For what can hinder the satisfaction or intercept the expectations of him whose abilities are adequate to his employments, who sees with his own eyes the whole circuit of his influence, who chooses by his own knowledge all whom he trusts, and whom none are tempted to deceive by hope or fear? Surely he has nothing to do but to love and to be loved, to be virtuous and to be happy."

"Whether perfect happiness would be procured by perfect goodness," said Nekayah, "this world will never afford an opportunity of deciding. But this, at least, may be maintained, that we do not always find visible happiness in proportion to visible virtue. All natural and almost all political evils are incident alike to the bad and good; they are confounded in the misery of a famine, and not much distinguished in the fury of a faction; they sink together in a tempest and are driven together from their country by invaders. All that virtue can afford is quietness of conscience and a steady prospect of a happier state; this may enable us to endure calamity with patience, but remember that patience must suppose pain."

Chapter XXVIII—Rasselas and Nekayah
Continue Their Conversation

"Dear princess," said Rasselas, "you fall into the common errors of exaggeratory declamation, by producing in a familiar disquisition examples of national calamities and scenes of extensive misery which are found in books rather than in the world, and which, as they are horrid, are ordained to be rare. Let us not imagine evils which we do not feel, nor injure life by misrepresentations. I cannot bear that querulous eloquence which threatens every city with a siege like that of Jerusalem, that makes famine attend on every flight of locusts, and suspends pestilence on the wing of every blast that issues from the south.

"On necessary and inevitable evils which overwhelm kingdoms at once all disputation is vain; when they happen they must be endured. But it is evident that these bursts of universal distress are more dreaded than felt; thousands and tens of thousands flourish in youth and wither in age, without the knowledge of any other than domestic evils, and share the same pleasures and vexations, whether their kings are mild or cruel, whether the armies of their country pursue their enemies or retreat before them. While courts are disturbed with intestine competitions and ambassadors are negotiating in foreign countries, the smith still plies his anvil and the husbandman drives his plough forward; the necessaries of life are required and obtained, and the successive business of the season continues to make its wonted revolutions.

"Let us cease to consider what perhaps may never happen, and what, when it shall happen, will laugh at human speculation. We will not endeavour to modify the motions of the elements or to fix the destiny of kingdoms. It is our business to consider what beings like us may perform, each labouring for his own happiness by promoting within his circle, however narrow, the happiness of others.

"Marriage is evidently the dictate of nature; men and women were made to be the companions of each other, and therefore I cannot be persuaded but that marriage is one of the means of happiness."

"I know not," said the princess, "whether marriage be more than one of the innumerable modes of human misery. When I see and reckon the various forms of connubial infelicity, the unexpected causes of lasting discord, the diversities of temper, the oppositions of opinion, the rude collisions of contrary desire where both are urged by violent impulses, the obstinate contest of disagreeing virtues where both are supported by consciousness of good intention, I am sometimes disposed to think, with the severer casuists of most nations, that marriage is rather permitted than approved, and that none, but by the instigation of a passion too much indulged, entangle themselves with indissoluble compact."

"You seem to forget," replied Rasselas, "that you have, even now, represented celibacy as less happy than marriage. Both conditions may be bad, but they cannot both be worse. Thus it happens, when wrong opinions are entertained, that they mutually destroy each other and leave the mind open to truth."

"I did not expect," answered the princess, "to hear that imputed to falsehood which is the consequence only of frailty. To the mind, as to the eye, it is difficult to compare with exactness objects vast in their extent and various in their parts. Where we see or conceive the whole at once, we readily note the discriminations and decide the preference, but of two systems, of which neither can be surveyed by any human being in its full compass of magnitude and multiplicity of complication, where is the wonder that, judging of the whole by parts, I am alternately affected by one and the other as either presses on my memory or fancy? We differ from ourselves just as we differ from each other when we see only part of the question, as in the multifarious relations of politics and morality, but when we perceive the whole at once, as in numerical computations, all agree in one judgment, and none ever varies in his opinion."

"Let us not add," said the prince, "to the other evils of life the bitterness of controversy, nor endeavour to vie with each other in subtleties of argument. We are employed in a search of which both are equally to enjoy the success or suffer by the miscarriage; it is therefore fit that we assist each other. You surely conclude too hastily from the infelicity of marriage against its institution; will not the misery of life prove equally that life cannot be the gift of heaven? The world must be peopled by marriage or peopled without it."

"How the world is to be peopled," returned Nekayah, "is not my care and need not be yours. I see no danger that the present generation should omit to leave successors behind them; we are not now inquiring for the world, but for ourselves."

Chapter XXIX—The Debate on Marriage *(continued)*

"The good of the whole," says Rasselas, "is the same with the good of all its parts. If marriage be best for mankind, it must be evidently best for individuals; or a permanent and necessary duty must be the cause of evil, and some must be inevitably sacrificed to the convenience of others. In the estimate which you have made of the two states, it appears that the incommodities of a single life are in a great measure necessary and certain, but those of the conjugal state accidental and avoidable.

"I cannot forbear to flatter myself that prudence and benevolence will make marriage happy. The general folly of mankind is the cause of general complaint. What can be expected but disappointment and repentance from a choice made in the immaturity of youth, in the ardour of desire, without judgment, without foresight, without inquiry after conformity of opinions, similarity of manners, rectitude of judgment, or purity of sentiment.

"Such is the common process of marriage. A youth and maiden, meeting by chance or brought together by artifice, exchange glances, reciprocate civilities, go home and dream of one another. Having little to divert attention or diversify thought, they find themselves uneasy when they are apart, and therefore conclude that they shall be happy together. They marry, and discover what nothing but voluntary blindness had before concealed; they wear out life in altercations, and charge nature with cruelty.

"From those early marriages proceeds likewise the rivalry of parents and children: the son is eager to enjoy the world before the father is willing to forsake it, and there is hardly room at once for two generations. The daughter begins to bloom before the mother can be content to fade, and neither can forbear to wish for the absence of the other.

"Surely all these evils may be avoided by that deliberation and delay which prudence prescribes to irrevocable choice. In the variety and jollity of youthful pleasures, life may be well enough supported without the help of a partner. Longer time will increase experience, and wider views will allow better opportunities of inquiry and selection; one advantage at least will be certain, the parents will be visibly older than their children."

"What reason cannot collect," said Nekayah, "and what experiment has not yet taught, can be known only from the report of others. I have been told that late marriages are not eminently happy. This is a question too important to be neglected; and I have often proposed it to those whose accuracy of remark and comprehensiveness of knowledge made their suffrages worthy of regard. They have generally determined that it is dangerous for a man and woman to suspend their fate upon each other at a time when opinions are fixed and habits are established, when friendships have been contracted on both sides, when life has been planned into method, and the mind has long enjoyed the contemplation of its own prospects.

"It is scarcely possible that two travelling through the world under the conduct of chance should have been both directed to the same path, and it will not often happen that either will quit the track which custom has made pleasing. When the desultory levity of youth has settled into regularity, it is soon succeeded by pride ashamed to yield, or obstinacy delighting to contend. And even though mutual esteem produces mutual desire to please, time itself, as it modifies unchangeably the external mien, determines likewise the direction of the passions, and gives an inflexible rigidity to the manners. Long customs are not easily broken; he that attempts to change the course of his own life very often labours in vain, and how shall we do that for others which we are seldom able to do for ourselves?"

"But surely," interposed the prince, "you suppose the chief motive of choice forgotten or neglected. Whenever I shall seek a wife, it shall be my first question whether she be willing to be led by reason."

"Thus it is," said Nekayah, "that philosophers are deceived. There are a thousand familiar disputes which reason never can decide; questions that elude investigation, and make logic ridiculous; cases where something must be done, and where little can be said. Consider the state of mankind, and inquire how few can be supposed to act upon any occasions, whether small or great, with all the reasons of action present to their minds. Wretched would be the pair, above all names of wretchedness, who should be doomed to adjust by reason every morning all the minute details of a domestic day.

"Those who marry at an advanced age will probably escape the encroachments of their children, but in the diminution of this advantage they will be likely to leave them, ignorant and helpless, to a guardian's mercy; or if that should not happen, they must at least go out of the world before they see those whom they love best either wise or great.

"From their children, if they have less to fear, they have less also to hope; and they lose without equivalent the joys of early love, and the convenience of uniting with manners pliant and minds susceptible of new impressions, which might wear away their dissimilitudes by long cohabitation, as soft bodies by continual attrition conform their surfaces to each other.

"I believe it will be found that those who marry late are best pleased with their children, and those who marry early with their partners."

"The union of these two affections," said Rasselas, "would produce all that could be wished. Perhaps there is a time when marriage might unite them, a time neither too early for the father nor too late for the husband."

"Every hour," answered the princess, "confirms my prejudice in favour of the position so often uttered by the mouth of Imlac, 'that nature sets her gifts on the right hand and on the left.' Those conditions which flatter hope and attract desire are so constituted that as we approach one we recede from another. There are goods so opposed that we cannot seize both, but by too much prudence may pass between them at too great a distance to reach either. This is often the fate of long consideration; he does nothing who endeavours to do more than is allowed to humanity. Flatter not yourself with contrarieties of pleasure. Of the blessings set before you make your choice, and be content. No man can taste the fruits of autumn while he is delighting his scent with the flowers of the spring; no man can at the same time fill his cup from the source and from the mouth of the Nile."

Chapter XXX—Imlac Enters, and Changes the Conversation

Here Imlac entered, and interrupted them. "Imlac," said Rasselas, "I have been taking from the princess the dismal history of private life, and am almost discouraged from further search."

"It seems to me," said Imlac, "that while you are making the choice of life you neglect to live. You wander about a single city, which, however large and diversified, can now afford few novelties, and forget that you are in a country famous among the earliest monarchies for the power and wisdom of its inhabitants; a country where the sciences first dawned that illuminate the world, and beyond which the arts cannot be traced of civil society or domestic life.

"The old Egyptians have left behind them monuments of industry and power before which all European magnificence is confessed to fade away. The ruins of their architecture are the schools of modern builders; and from the wonders which time has spared we may conjecture, though uncertainly, what it has destroyed."

"My curiosity," said Rasselas, "does not very strongly lead me to survey piles of stone or mounds of earth. My business is with man. I came hither not to measure fragments of temples or trace choked aqueducts, but to look upon the various scenes of the present world."

"The things that are now before us," said the princess, "require attention, and deserve it. What have I to do with the heroes or the monuments of ancient times? with times which can never return, and heroes whose form of life was different from all that the present condition of mankind requires or allows."

"To know anything," returned the poet, "we must know its effects; to see men, we must see their works, that we may learn what reason has dictated or passion has excited, and find what are the most powerful motives of action. To judge rightly of the present, we must oppose it to the past; for all judgment is comparative, and of the future nothing can be known. The truth is that no mind is much employed upon the present; recollection and anticipation fill up almost all our moments. Our passions are joy and grief, love and hatred, hope and fear. Of joy and grief, the past is the object, and the future of hope and fear; even love and hatred respect the past, for the cause must have been before the effect.

"The present state of things is the consequence of the former; and it is natural to inquire what were the sources of the good that we enjoy, or the evils that we suffer. If we act only for ourselves, to neglect the study of history is not prudent. If we are entrusted with the care of others, it is not just. Ignorance, when it is voluntary, is criminal; and he may properly be charged with evil who refused to learn how he might prevent it.

"There is no part of history so generally useful as that which relates the progress of the human mind, the gradual improvement of reason, the successive advances of science, the vicissitudes of learning and ignorance (which are the light and darkness of thinking beings), the extinction and resuscitation of arts, and the revolutions of the intellectual world. If accounts of battles and invasions are peculiarly the business of princes, the useful or elegant arts are not to be neglected; those who have kingdoms to govern have understandings to cultivate.

"Example is always more efficacious than precept. A soldier is formed in war, and a painter must copy pictures. In this, contemplative life has the advantage. Great actions are seldom seen, but the labours of art are always at hand for those who desire to know what art has been able to perform.

"When the eye or the imagination is struck with any uncommon work, the next transition of an active mind is to the means by which it was performed. Here begins the true use of such contemplation. We enlarge our comprehension by new ideas, and perhaps recover some art lost to mankind, or learn what is less perfectly known in our own country. At least we compare our own with former times, and either rejoice at our improvements, or, what is the first motion towards good, discover our defects."

"I am willing," said the prince, "to see all that can deserve my search." "And I," said the princess, "shall rejoice to learn something of the manners of antiquity."

"The most pompous monument of Egyptian greatness, and one of the most bulky works of manual industry," said Imlac, "are the pyramids: fabrics raised before the time of history, and of which the earliest narratives afford us only uncertain traditions. Of these the greatest is still standing, very little injured by time."

"Let us visit them tomorrow," said Nekayah. "I have often heard of the pyramids, and shall not rest till I have seen them, within and without, with my own eyes."

Chapter XXXI—They Visit the Pyramids

The resolution being thus taken, they set out the next day. They laid tents upon their camels, being resolved to stay among the pyramids till their curiosity was fully satisfied. They travelled gently, turned aside to everything remarkable, stopped from time to time and conversed with the inhabitants, and observed the various appearances of towns ruined and inhabited, of wild and cultivated nature.

When they came to the Great Pyramid they were astonished at the extent of the base and the height of the top. Imlac explained to them the principles upon which the pyramidal form was chosen for a fabric intended to co-extend its duration with that of the world: he showed that its gradual diminution gave it such stability as defeated all the common attacks of the elements, and could scarcely be overthrown by earthquakes themselves, the least resistible of natural violence. A concussion that should shatter the pyramid would threaten the dissolution of the continent.

They measured all its dimensions, and pitched their tents at its foot. Next day they prepared to enter its interior apartments, and having hired the common guides, climbed up to the first passage; when the favourite of the princess, looking into the cavity, stepped back and trembled. "Pekuah," said the princess, "of what art thou afraid?" "Of the narrow entrance," answered the lady, "and of the dreadful gloom. I dare not enter a place which must surely be inhabited by unquiet souls. The original possessors of these dreadful vaults will start up before us, and perhaps shut us in for ever." She spoke, and threw her arms round the neck of her mistress.

"If all your fear be of apparitions," said the prince, "I will promise you safety. There is no danger from the dead: he that is once buried will be seen no more."

"That the dead are seen no more," said Imlac, "I will not undertake to maintain against the concurrent and unvaried testimony of all ages and of all nations. There is no people, rude or learned, among whom apparitions of the dead are not related and believed. This opinion, which perhaps prevails as far as human nature is diffused, could become universal only by its truth: those that never heard of one another would not have agreed in a tale which nothing but experience can make credible. That it is doubted by single cavillers can very little weaken the general evidence, and some who deny it with their tongues confess it by their fears.

"Yet I do not mean to add new terrors to those which have already seized upon Pekuah. There can be no reason why spectres should haunt the pyramid more than other places, or why they should have power or will to hurt innocence and purity. Our entrance is no violation of their privileges: we can take nothing from them; how, then, can we offend them?"

"My dear Pekuah," said the princess, "I will always go before you, and Imlac shall follow you. Remember that you are the companion of the Princess of Abyssinia."

"If the princess is pleased that her servant should die," returned the lady, "let her command some death less dreadful than enclosure in this horrid cavern. You know I dare not disobey you: I must go if you command me; but if I once enter, I never shall come back."

The princess saw that her fear was too strong for expostulation or reproof, and, embracing her, told her that she should stay in the tent till their return. Pekuah was not yet satisfied, but entreated the princess not to pursue so dreadful a purpose as that of entering the recesses of the pyramids. "Though I cannot teach courage," said Nekayah, "I must not learn cowardice, nor leave at last undone what I came hither only to do."

Chapter XXXII—They Enter the Pyramid

Pekuah descended to the tents, and the rest entered the pyramid. They passed through the galleries, surveyed the vaults of marble, and examined the chest in which the body of the founder is supposed to have been reposited.[8] They then sat down in one of the most spacious chambers to rest awhile before they attempted to return.

"We have now," said Imlac, "gratified our minds with an exact view of the greatest work of man, except the wall of China.

"Of the wall it is very easy to assign the motives. It secured a wealthy and timorous nation from the incursions of barbarians, whose unskilfulness in the arts made it easier for them to supply their wants by rapine than by industry, and who from time to time poured in upon the inhabitants of peaceful commerce as vultures descend upon domestic fowl. Their celerity and fierceness made the wall necessary, and their ignorance made it efficacious.

"But for the pyramids, no reason has ever been given adequate to the cost and labour of the work. The narrowness of the chambers proves that it could afford no retreat from enemies, and treasures might have been reposited at far less expense with equal security. It seems to have been erected only in compliance with that hunger of imagination which preys incessantly upon life, and must be always appeased by some employment. Those who have already all that they can enjoy must enlarge their desires. He that has built for use till use is supplied must begin to build for vanity, and extend his plan to the utmost power of human performance that he may not be soon reduced to form another wish.

"I consider this mighty structure as a monument of the insufficiency of human enjoyments.[9] A king whose power is unlimited, and whose treasures surmount all real and imaginary wants, is compelled to solace, by the erection of a pyramid, the satiety of dominion and tastelessness of pleasures, and to amuse the tediousness of declining life by seeing thousands labouring without end, and one stone, for no purpose, laid upon another. Whoever thou art that, not content with a moderate condition, imaginest happiness in royal magnificence, and dreamest that command or riches can feed the appetite of novelty with perpetual gratifications, survey the pyramids, and confess thy folly!"

Chapter XXXIII—The Princess Meets with an Unexpected Misfortune

They rose up, and returned through the cavity at which they had entered; and the princess prepared for her favourite a long narrative of dark labyrinths and costly rooms, and of the different impressions which the varieties of the way had made upon her. But when they came to their train, they found every one silent and dejected: the men discovered shame and fear in their countenances, and the women were weeping in their tents.

What had happened they did not try to conjecture, but immediately inquired. "You had scarcely entered into the pyramid," said one of the attendants, "when a troop of Arabs rushed upon us: we were too few to resist them, and too slow to escape. They were about to search the tents, set us on our camels, and drive us along before them, when the approach of some Turkish horsemen put them to flight: but they seized the Lady Pekuah with her two maids, and carried them away: the Turks are now pursuing them by our instigation, but I fear they will not be able to overtake them."

The princess was overpowered with surprise and grief. Rasselas, in the first heat of his resentment, ordered his servants to follow him, and prepared to pursue the robbers with his sabre in his hand. "Sir," said Imlac, "what can you hope from violence or valour? The Arabs are mounted on horses trained to battle and retreat; we have only beasts of burden. By leaving our present station we may lose the princess, but cannot hope to regain Pekuah."

In a short time the Turks returned, having not been able to reach the enemy. The princess burst out into new lamentations, and Rasselas could scarcely forbear to reproach them with cowardice; but Imlac was of opinion that the escape of the Arabs was no addition to their misfortune, for perhaps they would have killed their captives rather than have resigned them.

Chapter XXXIV—They Return to Cairo without Pekuah

There was nothing to be hoped from longer stay. They returned to Cairo, repenting of their curiosity, censuring the negligence of the government, lamenting their own rashness, which had neglected to procure a guard, imagining many expedients by which the loss of Pekuah might have been prevented, and resolving to do something for her recovery, though none could find anything proper to be done.

Nekayah retired to her chamber, where her women attempted to comfort her by telling her that all had their troubles, and that Lady Pekuah had enjoyed much happiness in the world for a long time, and might reasonably expect a change of fortune. They hoped that some good would befall her wheresoever she was, and that their mistress would find another friend who might supply her place.

The princess made them no answer; and they continued the form of condolence, not much grieved in their hearts that the favourite was lost.

Next day the prince presented to the Bassa a memorial of the wrong which he had suffered, and a petition for redress. The Bassa threatened to punish the robbers, but did not attempt to catch them; nor indeed could any account or description be given by which he might direct the pursuit.

It soon appeared that nothing would be done by authority. Governors being accustomed to hear of more crimes than they can punish, and more wrongs than they can redress, set themselves at ease by indiscriminate negligence, and presently forget the request when they lose sight of the petitioner.

Imlac then endeavoured to gain some intelligence by private agents. He found many who pretended to an exact knowledge of all the haunts of the Arabs, and to regular correspondence with their chiefs, and who readily undertook the recovery of Pekuah. Of these, some were furnished with money for their journey, and came back no more; some were liberally paid for accounts which a few days discovered to be false. But the princess would not suffer any means, however improbable, to be left untried. While she was doing something, she kept her hope alive. As one expedient failed, another was suggested; when one messenger returned unsuccessful, another was dispatched to a different quarter.

Two months had now passed, and of Pekuah nothing had been heard; the hopes which they had endeavoured to raise in each other grew more languid; and the princess, when she saw nothing more to be tried, sunk down inconsolable in hopeless dejection. A thousand times she reproached herself with the easy compliance by which she permitted her favourite to stay behind her. "Had not my fondness," said she, "lessened my authority, Pekuah had not dared to talk of her terrors. She ought to have feared me more than spectres. A severe look would have overpowered her; a peremptory command would have compelled obedience. Why did foolish indulgence prevail upon me? Why did I not speak, and refuse to hear?"

"Great Princess," said Imlac, "do not reproach yourself for your virtue, or consider that as blameable by which evil has accidentally been caused. Your tenderness for the timidity of Pekuah was generous and kind. When we act according to our duty, we commit the events to Him by whose laws our actions are governed, and who will suffer none to be finally punished for obedience. When, in prospect of some good, whether natural or moral, we break the rules prescribed us, we withdraw from the direction of superior wisdom, and take all consequences upon ourselves. Man cannot so far know the connection of causes and events as that he may venture to do wrong in order to do right. When we pursue our end by lawful means, we may always console our miscarriage by the hope of future recompense. When we consult only our own policy, and attempt to find a nearer way to good by over leaping the settled boundaries of right and wrong, we cannot be happy even by success, because we cannot escape the consciousness of our fault; but if we miscarry, the disappointment is irremediably embittered. How comfortless is the sorrow of him who feels at once the pangs of guilt and the vexation of calamity which guilt has brought upon him!

"Consider, princess, what would have been your condition if the lady Pekuah had entreated to accompany you, and, being compelled to stay in the tents, had been carried away; or how would you have borne the thought if you had forced her into the pyramid, and she had died before you in agonies of terror."

"Had either happened," said Nekayah, "I could not have endured life till now; I should have been tortured to madness by the remembrance of such cruelty, or must have pined away in abhorrence of myself."

"This, at least," said Imlac, "is the present reward of virtuous conduct, that no unlucky consequence can oblige us to repent it."

Chapter XXXV—The Princess Languishes for Want of Pekuah

Nekayah, being thus reconciled to herself, found that no evil is insupportable but that which is accompanied with consciousness of wrong. She was from that time delivered from the violence of tempestuous sorrow, and sunk into silent pensiveness and gloomy tranquillity. She sat from morning to evening recollecting all that had been done or said by her Pekuah, treasured up with care every trifle on which Pekuah had set an accidental value, and which might recall to mind any little incident or careless conversation. The sentiments of her whom she now expected to see no more were treasured in her memory as rules of life, and she deliberated to no other end than to conjecture on any occasion what would have been the opinion and counsel of Pekuah.

The women by whom she was attended knew nothing of her real condition, and therefore she could not talk to them but with caution and reserve. She began to remit her curiosity, having no great care to collect notions which she had no convenience of uttering. Rasselas endeavoured first to comfort and afterwards to divert her; he hired musicians, to whom she seemed to listen, but did not hear them; and procured masters to instruct her in various arts, whose lectures, when they visited her again, were again to be repeated. She had lost her taste of pleasure and her ambition of excellence; and her mind, though forced into short excursions, always recurred to the image of her friend.

Imlac was every morning earnestly enjoined to renew his inquiries, and was asked every night whether he had yet heard of Pekuah; till, not being able to return the princess the answer that she desired, he was less and less willing to come into her presence. She observed his backwardness, and commanded him to attend her. "You are not," said she, "to confound impatience with resentment, or to suppose that I charge you with negligence because I repine at your unsuccessfulness. I do not much wonder at your absence. I know that the unhappy are never pleasing, and that all naturally avoid the contagion of misery. To hear complaints is wearisome alike to the wretched and the happy; for who would cloud by adventitious grief the short gleams of gaiety which life allows us, or who that is struggling under his own evils will add to them the miseries of another?

"The time is at hand when none shall be disturbed any longer by the sighs of Nekayah: my search after happiness is now at an end. I am resolved to retire from the world, with all its flatteries and deceits, and will hide myself in solitude, without any other care than to compose my thoughts and regulate my hours by a constant succession of innocent occupations, till, with a mind purified from all earthly desires, I shall enter into that state to which all are hastening, and in which I hope again to enjoy the friendship of Pekuah."

"Do not entangle your mind," said Imlac, "by irrevocable determinations, nor increase the burden of life by a voluntary accumulation of misery. The weariness of retirement will continue to increase when the loss of Pekuah is forgotten. That you have been deprived of one pleasure is no very good reason for rejection of the rest."

"Since Pekuah was taken from me," said the princess, "I have no pleasure to reject or to retain. She that has no one to love or trust has little to hope. She wants the radical principle of happiness. We may perhaps allow that what satisfaction this world can afford must arise from the conjunction of wealth, knowledge, and goodness. Wealth is nothing but as it is bestowed, and knowledge nothing but as it is communicated. They must therefore be imparted to others, and to whom could I now delight to impart them? Goodness affords the only comfort which can be enjoyed without a partner, and goodness may be practised in retirement."

"How far solitude may admit goodness or advance it, I shall not," replied Imlac, "dispute at present. Remember the confession of the pious hermit. You will wish to return into the world when the image of your companion has left your thoughts." "That time," said Nekayah, "will never come. The generous frankness, the modest obsequiousness, and the faithful secrecy of my dear Pekuah will always be more missed as I shall live longer to see vice and folly."

"The state of a mind oppressed with a sudden calamity," said Imlac, "is like that of the fabulous inhabitants of the new-created earth, who, when the first night came upon them, supposed that day would never return. When the clouds of sorrow gather over us, we see nothing beyond them, nor can imagine how they will be dispelled; yet a new day succeeded to the night, and sorrow is never long without a dawn of ease. But they who restrain themselves from receiving comfort do as the savages would have done had they put out their eyes when it was dark. Our minds, like our bodies, are in continual flux; something is hourly lost, and something acquired. To lose much at once is inconvenient to either, but while the vital power remains uninjured, nature will find the means of reparation. Distance has the same effect on the mind as on the eye; and while we glide along the stream of time, whatever we leave behind us is always lessening, and that which we approach increasing in magnitude. Do not suffer life to stagnate: it will grow muddy for want of motion; commit yourself again to the current of the world;[10] Pekuah will vanish by degrees; you will meet in your way some other favourite, or learn to diffuse yourself in general conversation."

"At least," said the prince, "do not despair before all remedies have been tried: the inquiry after the unfortunate lady is still continued, and shall be carried on with yet greater diligence, on condition that you will promise to wait a year for the event, without any unalterable resolution."

Nekayah thought this a reasonable demand, and made the promise to her brother, who had been advised by Imlac to require it. Imlac had, indeed, no great hope of regaining Pekuah; but he supposed that if he could secure the interval of a year, the princess would be then in no danger of a cloister.

Chapter XXXVI—Pekuah Is Still Remembered. The Progress of Sorrow

Nekayah, seeing that nothing was omitted for the recovery of her favourite, and having by her promise set her intention of retirement at a distance, began imperceptibly to return to common cares and common pleasures. She rejoiced without her own consent at the suspension of her sorrows, and sometimes caught herself with indignation in the act of turning away her mind from the remembrance of her whom yet she resolved never to forget.

She then appointed a certain hour of the day for meditation on the merits and fondness of Pekuah, and for some weeks retired constantly at the time fixed, and returned with her eyes swollen and her countenance clouded. By degrees she grew less scrupulous, and suffered any important and pressing avocation to delay the tribute of daily tears. She then yielded to less occasions; sometimes forgot what she was indeed afraid to remember, and at last wholly released herself from the duty of periodical affliction.

Her real love of Pekuah was yet not diminished. A thousand occurrences brought her back to memory, and a thousand wants, which nothing but the confidence of friendship can supply, made her frequently regretted. She therefore solicited Imlac never to desist from inquiry, and to leave no art of intelligence untried, that at least she might have the comfort of knowing that she did not suffer by negligence or sluggishness. "Yet what," said she, "is to be expected from our pursuit of happiness, when we find the state of life to be such that happiness itself is the cause of misery? Why should we endeavour to attain that of which the possession cannot be secured? I shall henceforward fear to yield my heart to excellence, however bright, or to fondness, however tender, lest I should lose again what I have lost in Pekuah."

Chapter XXXVII—The Princess Hears News of Pekuah

In seven months one of the messengers who had been sent away upon the day when the promise was drawn from the princess, returned, after many unsuccessful rambles, from the borders of Nubia, with an account that Pekuah was in the hands of an Arab chief, who possessed a castle or fortress on the extremity of Egypt. The Arab, whose revenue was plunder, was willing to restore her, with her two attendants, for two hundred ounces of gold.

The price was no subject of debate. The princess was in ecstasies when she heard that her favourite was alive, and might so cheaply be ransomed. She could not think of delaying for a moment Pekuah's happiness or her own, but entreated her brother to send back the messenger with the sum required. Imlac, being consulted, was not very confident of the veracity of the relater, and was still more doubtful of the Arab's faith, who might, if he were too liberally trusted, detain at once the money and the captives. He thought it dangerous to put themselves in the power of the Arab by going into his district; and could not expect that the rover would so much expose himself as to come into the lower country, where he might be seized by the forces of the Bassa.

It is difficult to negotiate where neither will trust. But Imlac, after some deliberation, directed the messenger to propose that Pekuah should be conducted by ten horsemen to the monastery of St. Anthony, which is situated in the deserts of Upper Egypt, where she should be met by the same number, and her ransom should be paid.

That no time might be lost, as they expected that the proposal would not be refused, they immediately began their journey to the monastery; and when they arrived, Imlac went forward with the former messenger to the Arab's fortress. Rasselas was desirous to go with them; but neither his sister nor Imlac would consent. The Arab, according to the custom of his nation, observed the laws of hospitality with great exactness to those who put themselves into his power, and in a few days brought Pekuah, with her maids, by easy journeys, to the place appointed, where, receiving the stipulated price, he restored her, with great respect, to liberty and her friends, and undertook to conduct them back towards Cairo beyond all danger of robbery or violence.

The princess and her favourite embraced each other with transport too violent to be expressed, and went out together to pour the tears of tenderness in secret, and exchange professions of kindness and gratitude. After a few hours they returned into the refectory of the convent, where, in the presence of the prior and his brethren, the prince required of Pekuah the history of her adventures.

Chapter XXXVIII—The Adventures of the Lady Pekuah

"At what time and in what manner I was forced away," said Pekuah, "your servants have told you. The suddenness of the event struck me with surprise, and I was at first rather stupefied than agitated with any passion of either fear or sorrow. My confusion was increased by the speed and tumult of our flight, while we were followed by the Turks, who, as it seemed, soon despaired to overtake us, or were afraid of those whom they made a show of menacing.

"When the Arabs saw themselves out of danger, they slackened their course; and as I was less harassed by external violence, I began to feel more uneasiness in my mind. After some time we stopped near a spring shaded with trees, in a pleasant meadow, where we were set upon the ground, and offered such refreshments as our masters were partaking. I was suffered to sit with my maids apart from the rest, and none attempted to comfort or insult us. Here I first began to feel the full weight of my misery. The girls sat weeping in silence, and from time to time looked on me for succour. I knew not to what condition we were doomed, nor could conjecture where would be the place of our captivity, or whence to draw any hope of deliverance. I was in the hands of robbers and savages, and had no reason to suppose that their pity was more than their justice, or that they would forbear the gratification of any ardour of desire or caprice of cruelty. I, however, kissed my maids, and endeavoured to pacify them by remarking that we were yet treated with decency, and that since we were now carried beyond pursuit, there was no danger of violence to our lives.

"When we were to be set again on horseback, my maids clung round me, and refused to be parted; but I commanded them not to irritate those who had us in their power. We travelled the remaining part of the day through an unfrequented and pathless country, and came by moonlight to the side of a hill, where the rest of the troop was stationed. Their tents were pitched and their fires kindled, and our chief was welcomed as a man much beloved by his dependents.

"We were received into a large tent, where we found women who had attended their husbands in the expedition. They set before us the supper which they had provided, and I ate it rather to encourage my maids than to comply with any appetite of my own. When the meat was taken away, they spread the carpets for repose. I was weary, and hoped to find in sleep that remission of distress which nature seldom denies. Ordering myself, therefore, to be undressed, I observed that the women looked very earnestly upon me, not expecting, I suppose, to see me so submissively attended. When my upper vest was taken off, they were apparently struck with the splendour of my clothes, and one of them timorously laid her hand upon the embroidery. She then went out, and in a short time came back with another woman, who seemed to be of higher rank and greater authority. She did, at her entrance, the usual act of reverence, and, taking me by the hand placed me in a smaller tent, spread with finer carpets, where I spent the night quietly with my maids.

"In the morning, as I was sitting on the grass, the chief of the troop came towards me. I rose up to receive him, and he bowed with great respect. 'Illustrious lady,' said he, 'my fortune is better than I had presumed to hope: I am told by my women that I have a princess in my camp.' 'Sir,' answered I, 'your women have deceived themselves and you; I am not a princess, but an unhappy stranger who intended soon to have left this country, in which I am now to be imprisoned for ever.' 'Whoever or whencesoever you are,' returned the Arab, 'your dress and that of your servants show your rank to be high and your wealth to be great. Why should you, who can so easily procure your ransom, think yourself in danger of perpetual captivity? The purpose of my incursions is to increase my riches, or, more properly, to gather tribute. The sons of Ishmael are the natural and hereditary lords of this part of the continent, which is usurped by late invaders and low-born tyrants, from whom we are compelled to take by the sword what is denied to justice. The violence of war admits no distinction: the lance that is lifted at guilt and power will sometimes fall on innocence and gentleness.'

"'How little,' said I, 'did I expect that yesterday it should have fallen upon me.'

"'Misfortunes,' answered the Arab, 'should always be expected. If the eye of hostility could learn reverence or pity, excellence like yours had been exempt from injury. But the angels of affliction spread their toils alike for the virtuous and the wicked, for the mighty and the mean. Do not be disconsolate; I am not one of the lawless and cruel rovers of the desert; I know the rules of civil life; I will fix your ransom, give a passport to your messenger, and perform my stipulation with nice punctuality.'

"You will easily believe that I was pleased with his courtesy, and finding that his predominant passion was desire for money, I began now to think my danger less, for I knew that no sum would be thought too great for the release of Pekuah. I told him that he should have no reason to charge me with ingratitude if I was used with kindness, and that any ransom which could be expected for a maid of common rank would be paid, but that he must not persist to rate me as a princess. He said he would consider what he should demand, and then, smiling, bowed and retired.

"Soon after the women came about me, each contending to be more officious than the other, and my maids themselves were served with reverence. We travelled onward by short journeys. On the fourth day the chief told me that my ransom must be two hundred ounces of gold, which I not only promised him, but told him that I would add fifty more if I and my maids were honourably treated.

"I never knew the power of gold before. From that time I was the leader of the troop. The march of every day was longer or shorter as I commanded, and the tents were pitched where I chose to rest. We now had camels and other conveniences for travel; my own women were always at my side, and I amused myself with observing the manners of the vagrant nations, and with viewing remains of ancient edifices, with which these deserted countries appear to have been in some distant age lavishly embellished.

"The chief of the band was a man far from illiterate: he was able to travel by the stars or the compass, and had marked in his erratic expeditions such places as are most worthy the notice of a passenger. He observed to me that buildings are always best preserved in places little frequented and difficult of access; for when once a country declines from its primitive splendour, the more inhabitants are left, the quicker ruin will be made. Walls supply stones more easily than quarries; and palaces and temples will be demolished to make stables of granite and cottages of porphyry."

Chapter XXXIX—The Adventures of Pekuah *(continued)*

"We wandered about in this manner for some weeks, whether, as our chief pretended, for my gratification, or, as I rather suspected, for some convenience of his own. I endeavoured to appear contented where sullenness and resentment would have been of no use, and that endeavour conduced much to the calmness of my mind; but my heart was always with Neka-yah, and the troubles of the night much overbalanced the amusements of the day. My women, who threw all their cares upon their mistress, set their minds at ease from the time when they saw me treated with respect, and gave themselves up to the incidental alleviations of our fatigue without solicitude or sorrow. I was pleased with their pleasure, and animated with their confidence. My condition had lost much of its terror, since I found that the Arab ranged the country merely to get riches. Avarice is a uniform and tractable vice: other intellectual distempers are different in different constitutions of mind; that which soothes the pride of one will offend the pride of another; but to the favour of the covetous there is a ready way, bring money, and nothing is denied.

"At last we came to the dwelling of our chief; a strong and spacious house, built with stone in an island of the Nile, which lies, as I was told, under the tropic. 'Lady,' said the Arab, 'you shall rest after your journey a few weeks in this place, where you are to consider yourself as Sovereign. My occupation is war: I have therefore chosen this obscure residence, from which I can issue unexpected, and to which I can retire unpursued. You may now repose in security: here are few pleasures, but here is no danger.' He then led me into the inner apartments, and seating me on the richest couch, bowed to the ground. His women, who considered me as a rival, looked on me with malignity; but being soon informed that I was a great lady detained only for my ransom, they began to vie with each other in obsequiousness and reverence.

"Being again comforted with new assurances of speedy liberty, I was for some days diverted from impatience by the novelty of the place. The turrets overlooked the country to a great distance, and afforded a view of many windings of the stream. In the day I wandered from one place to another, as the course of the sun varied the splendour of the prospect, and saw many things which I had never seen before. The crocodiles and river-horses are common in this unpeopled region; and I often looked upon them with terror, though I knew they could not hurt me. For some time I expected to see mermaids and tritons, which, as Imlac has told me, the European travellers have stationed in the Nile; but no such beings ever appeared, and the Arab, when I inquired after them, laughed at my credulity.

"At night the Arab always attended me to a tower set apart for celestial observations, where he endeavoured to teach me the names and courses of the stars. I had no great inclination to this study; but an appearance of attention was necessary to please my instructor, who valued himself for his skill, and in a little while I found some employment requisite to beguile the tediousness of time, which was to be passed always amidst the same objects. I was weary of looking in the morning on things from which I had turned away weary in the evening: I therefore was at last willing to observe the stars rather than do nothing, but could not always compose my thoughts, and was very often thinking on Nekayah when others imagined me contemplating the sky. Soon after, the Arab went upon another expedition, and then my only pleasure was to talk with my maids about the accident by which we were carried away, and the happiness we should all enjoy at the end of our captivity."

"There were women in your Arab's fortress," said the princess; "why did you not make them your companions, enjoy their conversation, and partake their diversions? In a place where they found business or amusement, why should you alone sit corroded with idle melancholy? or why could not you bear for a few months that condition to which they were condemned for life?"

"The diversions of the women," answered Pekuah, "were only childish play, by which the mind accustomed to stronger operations could not be kept busy. I could do all which they delighted in doing by powers merely sensitive, while my intellectual faculties were flown to Cairo. They ran from room to room, as a bird hops from wire to wire in his cage. They danced for the sake of motion, as lambs frisk in a meadow. One sometimes pretended to be hurt that the rest might be alarmed, or hid herself that another might seek her. Part of their time passed in watching the progress of light bodies that floated on the river, and part in marking the various forms into which clouds broke in the sky.

"Their business was only needlework, in which I and my maids sometimes helped them; but you know that the mind will easily straggle from the fingers, nor will you suspect that captivity and absence from Nekayah could receive solace from silken flowers.

"Nor was much satisfaction to be hoped from their conversation: for of what could they be expected to talk? They had seen nothing, for they had lived from early youth in that narrow spot: of what they had not seen they could have no knowledge, for they could not read. They had no ideas but of the few things that were within their view, and had hardly names for anything but their clothes and their food. As I bore a superior character, I was often called to terminate their quarrels, which I decided as equitably as I could. If it could have amused me to hear the complaints of each against the rest, I might have been often detained by long stories; but the motives of their animosity were so small that I could not listen without intercepting the tale."

"How," said Rasselas, "can the Arab, whom you represented as a man of more than common accomplishments, take any pleasure in his seraglio, when it is filled only with women like these? Are they exquisitely beautiful?"

"They do not," said Pekuah, "want that unaffecting and ignoble beauty which may subsist without sprightliness or sublimity, without energy of thought or dignity of virtue. But to a man like the Arab such beauty was only a flower casually plucked and carelessly thrown away. Whatever pleasures he might find among them, they were not those of friendship or society. When they were playing about him he looked on them with inattentive superiority; when they vied for his regard he sometimes turned away disgusted. As they had no knowledge, their talk could take nothing from the tediousness of life; as they had no choice, their fondness, or appearance of fondness, excited in him neither pride nor gratitude; he was not exalted in his own esteem by the smiles of a woman who saw no other man, nor was much obliged by that regard of which he could never know the sincerity, and which he might often perceive to be exerted not so much to delight him as to pain a rival. That which he gave, and they received, as love, was only a careless distribution of superfluous time, such love as man can bestow upon that which he despises, such as has neither hope nor fear, neither joy nor sorrow."

"You have reason, lady, to think yourself happy," said Imlac, "that you have been thus easily dismissed. How could a mind, hungry for knowledge, be willing, in an intellectual famine, to lose such a banquet as Pekuah's conversation?"

"I am inclined to believe," answered Pekuah, "that he was for some time in suspense; for, notwithstanding his promise, whenever I proposed to dispatch a messenger to Cairo he found some excuse for delay. While I was detained in his house he made many incursions into the neighbouring countries, and perhaps he would have refused to discharge me had his plunder been equal to his wishes. He returned always courteous, related his adventures, delighted to hear my observations, and endeavoured to advance my acquaintance with the stars. When I importuned him to send away my letters, he soothed me with professions of honour and sincerity; and when I could be no longer decently denied, put his troop again in motion, and left me to govern in his absence. I was much afflicted by this studied procrastination, and was sometimes afraid that I should be forgotten; that you would leave Cairo, and I must end my days in an island of the Nile.

"I grew at last hopeless and dejected, and cared so little to entertain him, that he for a while more frequently talked with my maids. That he should fall in love with them or with me, might have been equally fatal, and I was not much pleased with the growing friendship. My anxiety was not long, for, as I recovered some degree of cheerfulness, he returned to me, and I could not forbear to despise my former uneasiness.

"He still delayed to send for my ransom, and would perhaps never have determined had not your agent found his way to him. The gold, which he would not fetch, he could not reject when it was offered. He hastened to prepare for our journey hither, like a man delivered from the pain of an intestine conflict. I took leave of my companions in the house, who dismissed me with cold indifference."

Nekayah having heard her favourite's relation, rose and embraced her, and Rasselas gave her a hundred ounces of gold, which she presented to the Arab for the fifty that were promised.

Chapter XL—The History of a Man of Learning

They returned to Cairo, and were so well pleased at finding themselves together that none of them went much abroad. The prince began to love learning, and one day declared to Imlac that he intended to devote himself to science and pass the rest of his days in literary solitude.

"Before you make your final choice," answered Imlac, "you ought to examine its hazards, and converse with some of those who are grown old in the company of themselves. I have just left the observatory of one of the most learned astronomers in the world, who has spent forty years in unwearied attention to the motion and appearances of the celestial bodies, and has drawn out his soul in endless calculations. He admits a few friends once a month to hear his deductions and enjoy his discoveries. I was introduced as a man of knowledge worthy of his notice. Men of various ideas and fluent conversation are commonly welcome to those whose thoughts have been long fixed upon a single point, and who find the images of other things stealing away. I delighted him with my remarks. He smiled at the narrative of my travels, and was glad to forget the constellations and descend for a moment into the lower world.

"On the next day of vacation I renewed my visit, and was so fortunate as to please him again. He relaxed from that time the severity of his rule, and permitted me to enter at my own choice. I found him always busy, and always glad to be relieved. As each knew much which the other was desirous of learning, we exchanged our notions with great delight. I perceived that I had every day more of his confidence, and always found new cause of admiration in the profundity of his mind. His comprehension is vast, his memory capacious and retentive, his discourse is methodical, and his expression clear.

"His integrity and benevolence are equal to his learning. His deepest researches and most favourite studies are willingly interrupted for any opportunity of doing good by his counsel or his riches. To his closest retreat, at his most busy moments, all are admitted that want his assistance; 'For though I exclude idleness and pleasure, I will never,' says he, 'bar my doors against charity. To man is permitted the contemplation of the skies, but the practice of virtue is commanded.'"[11]

"Surely," said the princess, "this man is happy."

"I visited him," said Imlac, "with more and more frequency, and was every time more enamoured of his conversation; he was sublime without haughtiness, courteous without formality, and communicative without ostentation. I was at first, great princess, of your opinion, thought him the happiest of mankind, and often congratulated him on the blessing that he enjoyed. He seemed to hear nothing with indifference but the praises of his condition, to which he always returned a general answer, and diverted the conversation to some other topic.

"Amidst this willingness to be pleased and labour to please, I had quickly reason to imagine that some painful sentiment pressed upon his mind. He often looked up earnestly towards the sun, and let his voice fall in the midst of his discourse. He would sometimes, when we were alone, gaze upon me in silence with the air of a man who longed to speak what he was yet resolved to suppress. He would often send for me with vehement injunctions of haste, though when I came to him he had nothing extraordinary to say. And sometimes, when I was leaving him, would call me back, pause a few moments, and then dismiss me."

Chapter XLI—The Astronomer Discovers the Cause of His Uneasiness

"At last the time came when the secret burst his reserve. We were sitting together last night in the turret of his house watching the immersion of a satellite of Jupiter. A sudden tempest clouded the sky and disappointed our observation. We sat awhile silent in the dark, and then he addressed himself to me in these words: 'Imlac, I have long considered thy friendship as the greatest blessing of my life. Integrity without knowledge is weak and useless, and knowledge without integrity is dangerous and dreadful. I have found in thee all the qualities requisite for trust, benevolence, experience, and fortitude. I have long discharged an office which I must soon quit at the call of nature, and shall rejoice in the hour of imbecility and pain to devolve it upon thee.'

"I thought myself honoured by this testimony, and protested that whatever could conduce to his happiness would add likewise to mine.

"'Hear, Imlac, what thou wilt not without difficulty credit. I have possessed for five years the regulation of the weather and the distribution of the seasons. The sun has listened to my dictates, and passed from tropic to tropic by my direction; the clouds at my call have poured their waters, and the Nile has overflowed at my command. I have restrained the rage of the dog-star, and mitigated the fervours of the crab. The winds alone, of all the elemental powers, have hitherto refused my authority, and multitudes have perished by equinoctial tempests which I found myself unable to prohibit or restrain. I have administered this great office with exact justice, and made to the different nations of the earth an impartial dividend of rain and sunshine. What must have been the misery of half the globe if I had limited the clouds to particular regions, or confined the sun to either side of the equator?'"

Chapter XLII—The Opinion of the Astronomer Is Explained and Justified

"I suppose he discovered in me, through the obscurity of the room, some tokens of amazement and doubt, for after a short pause he proceeded thus:

"'Not to be easily credited will neither surprise nor offend me, for I am probably the first of human beings to whom this trust has been imparted. Nor do I know whether to deem this distinction a reward or punishment. Since I have possessed it I have been far less happy than before, and nothing but the consciousness of good intention could have enabled me to support the weariness of unremitted vigilance.'

"'How long, sir,' said I, 'has this great office been in your hands?'

"'About ten years ago,' said he, 'my daily observations of the changes of the sky led me to consider whether, if I had the power of the seasons, I could confer greater plenty upon the inhabitants of the earth. This contemplation fastened on my mind, and I sat days and nights in imaginary dominion, pouring upon this country and that the showers of fertility, and seconding every fall of rain with a due proportion of sunshine. I had yet only the will to do good, and did not imagine that I should ever have the power.

"'One day as I was looking on the fields withering with heat, I felt in my mind a sudden wish that I could send rain on the southern mountains, and raise the Nile to an inundation. In the hurry of my imagination I commanded rain to fall; and by comparing the time of my command with that of the inundation, I found that the clouds had listened to my lips.'

"'Might not some other cause,' said I, 'produce this concurrence? The Nile does not always rise on the same day.'

"'Do not believe,' said he, with impatience, 'that such objections could escape me: I reasoned long against my own conviction, and laboured against truth with the utmost obstinacy. I sometimes suspected myself of madness, and should not have dared to impart this secret but to a man like you, capable of distinguishing the wonderful from the impossible, and the incredible from the false.'

"'Why, sir,' said I, 'do you call that incredible which you know, or think you know, to be true?'

"'Because,' said he, 'I cannot prove it by any external evidence; and I know too well the laws of demonstration to think that my conviction ought to influence another, who cannot, like me, be conscious of its force. I therefore shall not attempt to gain credit by disputation. It is sufficient that I feel this power that I have long possessed, and every day exerted it. But the life of man is short; the infirmities of age increase upon me, and the time will soon come when the regulator of the year must mingle with the dust. The care of appointing a successor has long disturbed me; the night and the day have been spent in comparisons of all the characters which have come to my knowledge, and I have yet found none so worthy as thyself.'"

Chapter XLIII—The Astronomer Leaves Imlac His Directions

"'Hear, therefore, what I shall impart with attention, such as the welfare of a world requires. If the task of a king be considered as difficult, who has the care only of a few millions, to whom he cannot do much good or harm, what must be the anxiety of him on whom depends the action of the elements and the great gifts of light and heat!—Hear me, therefore, with attention.

"'I have diligently considered the position of the earth and sun, and formed innumerable schemes in which I changed their situation. I have sometimes turned aside the axis of the earth, and sometimes varied the ecliptic of the sun, but I have found it impossible to make a disposition by which the world may be advantaged; what one region gains another loses by any imaginable alteration, even without considering the distant parts of the solar system with which we are acquainted. Do not, therefore, in thy administration of the year, indulge thy pride by innovation; do not please thyself with thinking that thou canst make thyself renowned to all future ages by disordering the seasons. The memory of mischief is no desirable fame. Much less will it become thee to let kindness or interest prevail. Never rob other countries of rain to pour it on thine own. For us the Nile is sufficient.'

"I promised that when I possessed the power I would use it with inflexible integrity; and he dismissed me, pressing my hand. 'My heart,' said he, 'will be now at rest, and my benevolence will no more destroy my quiet; I have found a man of wisdom and virtue, to whom I can cheerfully bequeath the inheritance of the sun.'"

The prince heard this narration with very serious regard; but the princess smiled, and Pekuah convulsed herself with laughter. "Ladies," said Imlac, "to mock the heaviest of human afflictions is neither charitable nor wise. Few can attain this man's knowledge and few practise his virtues, but all may suffer his calamity. Of the uncertainties of our present state, the most dreadful and alarming is the uncertain continuance of reason."[12]

The princess was recollected, and the favourite was abashed. Rasselas, more deeply affected, inquired of Imlac whether he thought such maladies of the mind frequent, and how they were contracted.

Chapter XLIV—The Dangerous Prevalence[13] of Imagination

"Disorders of intellect," answered Imlac, "happen much more often than superficial observers will easily believe. Perhaps if we speak with rigorous exactness, no human mind is in its right state. There is no man whose imagination does not sometimes predominate over his reason who can regulate his attention wholly by his will, and whose ideas will come and go at his command. No man will be found in whose mind airy notions do not sometimes tyrannise, and force him to hope or fear beyond the limits of sober probability. All power of fancy over reason is a degree of insanity, but while this power is such as we can control and repress it is not visible to others, nor considered as any deprivation of the mental faculties; it is not pronounced madness but when it comes ungovernable, and apparently influences speech or action.

"To indulge the power of fiction and send imagination out upon the wing is often the sport of those who delight too much in silent speculation. When we are alone we are not always busy; the labour of excogitation is too violent to last long; the ardour of inquiry will sometimes give way to idleness or satiety. He who has nothing external that can divert him must find pleasure in his own thoughts, and must conceive himself what he is not; for who is pleased with what he is? He then expatiates in boundless futurity, and culls from all imaginable conditions that which for the present moment he should most desire, amuses his desires with impossible enjoyments, and confers upon his pride unattainable dominion. The mind dances from scene to scene, unites all pleasures in all combinations, and riots in delights which nature and fortune, with all their bounty, cannot bestow.

"In time some particular train of ideas fixes the attention; all other intellectual gratifications are rejected; the mind, in weariness or leisure, recurs constantly to the favourite conception, and feasts on the luscious falsehood whenever she is offended with the bitterness of truth. By degrees the reign of fancy is confirmed; she grows first imperious and in time despotic. Then fictions begin to operate as realities, false opinions fasten upon the mind, and life passes in dreams of rapture or of anguish.

"This, sir, is one of the dangers of solitude, which the hermit has confessed not always to promote goodness, and the astronomer's misery has proved to be not always propitious to wisdom."

"I will no more," said the favourite, "imagine myself the queen of Abyssinia. I have often spent the hours which the princess gave to my own disposal in adjusting ceremonies and regulating the court; I have repressed the pride of the powerful and granted the petitions of the poor; I have built new palaces in more happy situations, planted groves upon the tops of mountains, and have exulted in the beneficence of royalty, till, when the princess entered, I had almost forgotten to bow down before her."

"And I," said the princess, "will not allow myself anymore to play the shepherdess in my waking dreams. I have often soothed my thoughts with the quiet and innocence of pastoral employments, till I have in my chamber heard the winds whistle and the sheep bleat; sometimes freed the lamb entangled in the thicket, and sometimes with my crook encountered the wolf. I have a dress like that of the village maids, which I put on to help my imagination, and a pipe on which I play softly, and suppose myself followed by my flocks."

"I will confess," said the prince, "an indulgence of fantastic delight more dangerous than yours. I have frequently endeavoured to imagine the possibility of a perfect government, by which all wrong should be restrained, all vice reformed, and all the subjects preserved in tranquillity and innocence. This thought produced innumerable schemes of reformation, and dictated many useful regulations and salutary edicts. This has been the sport and sometimes the labour of my solitude, and I start when I think with how little anguish I once supposed the death of my father and my brothers."

"Such," said Imlac, "are the effects of visionary schemes; when we first form them, we know them to be absurd, but familiarise them by degrees, and in time lose sight of their folly."

Chapter XLV—They Discourse with an Old Man

The evening was now far past, and they rose to return home. As they walked along the banks of the Nile, delighted with the beams of the moon quivering on the water, they saw at a small distance an old man whom the prince had often heard in the assembly of the sages. "Yonder," said he, "is one whose years have calmed his passions, but not clouded his reason. Let us close the disquisitions of the night by inquiring what are his sentiments of his own state, that we may know whether youth alone is to struggle with vexation, and whether any better hope remains for the latter part of life."

Here the sage approached and saluted them. They invited him to join their walk, and prattled awhile as acquaintance that had unexpectedly met one another. The old man was cheerful and talkative, and the way seemed short in his company. He was pleased to find himself not disregarded, accompanied them to their house, and, at the prince's request, entered with them. They placed him in the seat of honour, and set wine and conserves before him.

"Sir," said the princess, "an evening walk must give to a man of learning like you pleasures which ignorance and youth can hardly conceive. You know the qualities and the causes of all that you behold, the laws by which the river flows, the periods in which the planets perform their revolutions. Everything must supply you with contemplation, and renew the consciousness of your own dignity."

"Lady," answered he, "let the gay and the vigorous expect pleasure in their excursions: it is enough that age can attain ease. To me the world has lost its novelty. I look round, and see what I remember to have seen in happier days. I rest against a tree, and consider that in the same shade I once disputed upon the annual overflow of the Nile with a friend who is now silent in the grave. I cast my eyes upwards, fix them on the changing moon, and think with pain on the vicissitudes of life. I have ceased to take much delight in physical truth; for what have I to do with those things which I am soon to leave?"

"You may at least recreate yourself," said Imlac, "with the recollection of an honourable and useful life, and enjoy the praise which all agree to give you."

"Praise," said the sage with a sigh, "is to an old man an empty sound. I have neither mother to be delighted with the reputation of her son, nor wife to partake the honours of her husband. I have outlived my friends and my rivals. Nothing is now of much importance; for I cannot extend my interest beyond myself. Youth is delighted with applause, because it is considered as the earnest of some future good, and because the prospect of life is far extended; but to me, who am now declining to decrepitude, there is little to be feared from the malevolence of men, and yet less to be hoped from their affection or esteem. Something they may yet take away, but they can give me nothing. Riches would now be useless, and high employment would be pain. My retrospect of life recalls to my view many opportunities of good neglected, much time squandered upon trifles, and more lost in idleness and vacancy. I leave many great designs unattempted, and many great attempts unfinished. My mind is burdened with no heavy crime, and therefore I compose myself to tranquillity; endeavour to abstract my thoughts from hopes and cares which, though reason knows them to be vain, still try to keep their old possession of the heart; expect, with serene humility, that hour which nature cannot long delay, and hope to possess in a better state that happiness which here I could not find, and that virtue which here I have not attained."

He rose and went away, leaving his audience not much elated with the hope of long life. The prince consoled himself with remarking that it was not reasonable to be disappointed by this account; for age had never been considered as the season of felicity, and if it was possible to be easy in decline and weakness, it was likely that the days of vigour and alacrity might be happy; that the noon of life might be bright, if the evening could be calm.

The princess suspected that age was querulous and malignant, and delighted to repress the expectations of those who had newly entered the world. She had seen the possessors of estates look with envy on their heirs, and known many who enjoyed pleasures no longer than they could confine it to themselves.

Pekuah conjectured that the man was older than he appeared, and was willing to impute his complaints to delirious dejection; or else supposed that he had been unfortunate, and was therefore discontented. "For nothing," said she, "is more common than to call our own condition the condition of life."

Imlac, who had no desire to see them depressed, smiled at the comforts which they could so readily procure to themselves; and remembered that at the same age he was equally confident of unmingled prosperity, and equally fertile of consolatory expedients. He forbore to force upon them unwelcome knowledge, which time itself would too soon impress. The princess and her lady retired; the madness of the astronomer hung upon their minds; and they desired Imlac to enter upon his office, and delay next morning the rising of the sun.

Chapter XLVI—The Princess and Pekuah Visit the Astronomer

The princess and Pekuah, having talked in private of Imlac's astronomer, thought his character at once so amiable and so strange that they could not be satisfied without a nearer knowledge, and Imlac was requested to find the means of bringing them together.

This was somewhat difficult; the philosopher had never received any visits from women, though he lived in a city that had in it many Europeans, who followed the manners of their own countries, and many from other parts of the world, that lived there with European liberty. The ladies would not be refused, and several schemes were proposed for the accomplishment of their design. It was proposed to introduce them as strangers in distress, to whom the sage was always accessible; but after some deliberation it appeared that by this artifice no acquaintance could be formed, for their conversation would be short, and they could not decently importune him often. "This," said Rasselas, "is true; but I have yet a stronger objection against the misrepresentation of your state. I have always considered it as treason against the great republic of human nature to make any man's virtues the means of deceiving him, whether on great or little occasions. All imposture weakens confidence and chills benevolence. When the sage finds that you are not what you seemed, he will feel the resentment natural to a man who, conscious of great abilities, discovers that he has been tricked by understandings meaner than his own, and perhaps the distrust which he can never afterwards wholly lay aside may stop the voice of counsel and close the hand of charity; and where will you find the power of restoring his benefactions to mankind, or his peace to himself?"

To this no reply was attempted, and Imlac began to hope that their curiosity would subside; but next day Pekuah told him she had now found an honest pretence for a visit to the astronomer, for she would solicit permission to continue under him the studies in which she had been initiated by the Arab, and the princess might go with her, either as a fellow-student, or because a woman could not decently come alone. "I am afraid," said Imlac, "that he will soon be weary of your company. Men advanced far in knowledge do not love to repeat the elements of their art, and I am not certain that even of the elements, as he will deliver them, connected with inferences and mingled with reflections, you are a very capable auditress." "That," said Pekuah, "must be my care: I ask of you only to take me thither. My knowledge is perhaps more than you imagine it, and by concurring always with his opinions I shall make him think it greater than it is."

The astronomer, in pursuance of this resolution, was told that a foreign lady, travelling in search of knowledge, had heard of his reputation, and was desirous to become his scholar. The uncommonness of the proposal raised at once his surprise and curiosity, and when after a short deliberation he consented to admit her, he could not stay without impatience till the next day.

The ladies dressed themselves magnificently, and were attended by Imlac to the astronomer, who was pleased to see himself approached with respect by persons of so splendid an appearance. In the exchange of the first civilities he was timorous and bashful; but when the talk became regular, he recollected his powers, and justified the character which Imlac had given. Inquiring of Pekuah what could have turned her inclination towards astronomy, he received from her a history of her adventure at the pyramid, and of the time passed in the Arab's island. She told her tale with ease and elegance, and her conversation took possession of his heart. The discourse was then turned to astronomy. Pekuah displayed what she knew. He looked upon her as a prodigy of genius, and entreated her not to desist from a study which she had so happily begun.

They came again and again, and were every time more welcome than before. The sage endeavoured to amuse them, that they might prolong their visits, for he found his thoughts grow brighter in their company; the clouds of solitude vanished by degrees as he forced himself to entertain them, and he grieved when he was left, at their departure, to his old employment of regulating the seasons.

The princess and her favourite had now watched his lips for several months, and could not catch a single word from which they could judge whether he continued or not in the opinion of his preternatural commission. They often contrived to bring him to an open declaration; but he easily eluded all their attacks, and, on which side soever they pressed him, escaped from them to some other topic.

As their familiarity increased, they invited him often to the house of Imlac, where they distinguished him by extraordinary respect. He began gradually to delight in sublunary pleasures. He came early and departed late; laboured to recommend himself by assiduity and compliance; excited their curiosity after new arts, that they might still want his assistance; and when they made any excursion of pleasure or inquiry, entreated to attend them.

By long experience of his integrity and wisdom, the prince and his sister were convinced that he might be trusted without danger; and lest he should draw any false hopes from the civilities which he received, discovered to him their condition, with the motives of their journey, and required his opinion on the choice of life.

"Of the various conditions which the world spreads before you which you shall prefer," said the sage, "I am not able to instruct you. I can only tell that I have chosen wrong. I have passed my time in study without experience; in the attainment of sciences which can for the most part be but remotely useful to mankind. I have purchased knowledge at the expense of all the common comforts of life; I have missed the endearing elegance of female friendship, and the happy commerce of domestic tenderness. If I have obtained any prerogatives above other students, they have been accompanied with fear, disquiet, and scrupulosity; but even of these prerogatives, whatever they were, I have, since my thoughts have been diversified by more intercourse with the world, begun to question the reality. When I have been for a few days lost in pleasing dissipation, I am always tempted to think that my inquiries have ended in error, and that I have suffered much, and suffered it in vain."

Imlac was delighted to find that the sage's understanding was breaking through its mists, and resolved to detain him from the planets till he should forget his task of ruling them, and reason should recover its original influence.

From this time the astronomer was received into familiar friendship, and partook of all their projects and pleasures; his respect kept him attentive, and the activity of Rasselas did not leave much time unengaged. Something was always to be done; the day was spent in making observations, which furnished talk for the evening, and the evening was closed with a scheme for the morrow.

The sage confessed to Imlac that since he had mingled in the gay tumults of life, and divided his hours by a succession of amusements, he found the conviction of his authority over the skies fade gradually from his mind, and began to trust less to an opinion which he never could prove to others, and which he now found subject to variation, from causes in which reason had no part. "If I am accidentally left alone for a few hours," said he, "my inveterate persuasion rushes upon my soul, and my thoughts are chained down by some irresistible violence; but they are soon disentangled by the prince's conversation, and instantaneously released at the entrance of Pekuah. I am like a man habitually afraid of spectres, who is set at ease by a lamp, and wonders at the dread which harassed him in the dark; yet, if his lamp be extinguished, feels again the terrors which he knows that when it is light he shall feel no more. But I am sometimes afraid, lest I indulge my quiet by criminal negligence, and voluntarily forget the great charge with which I am entrusted. If I favour myself in a known error, or am determined by my own ease in a doubtful question of this importance, how dreadful is my crime!"

"No disease of the imagination," answered Imlac, "is so difficult of cure as that which is complicated with the dread of guilt; fancy and conscience then act interchangeably upon us, and so often shift their places, that the illusions of one are not distinguished from the dictates of the other. If fancy presents images not moral or religious, the mind drives them away when they give it pain; but when melancholy notions take the form of duty, they lay hold on the faculties without opposition, because we are afraid to exclude or banish them. For this reason the superstitious are often melancholy, and the melancholy almost always superstitious.

"But do not let the suggestions of timidity overpower your better reason; the danger of neglect can be but as the probability of the obligation, which, when you consider it with freedom, you find very little, and that little growing every day less. Open your heart to the influence of the light, which from time to time breaks in upon you; when scruples importune you, which you in your lucid moments know to be vain, do not stand to parley, but fly to business or to Pekuah; and keep this thought always prevalent, that you are only one atom of the mass of humanity, and have neither such virtue nor vice as that you should be singled out for supernatural favours or afflictions."

Chapter XLVII—The Prince Enters and Brings a New Topic

"All this," said the astronomer, "I have often thought; but my reason has been so long subjugated by an uncontrollable and overwhelming idea, that it durst not confide in its own decisions. I now see how fatally I betrayed my quiet, by suffering chimeras to prey upon me in secret; but melancholy shrinks from communication, and I never found a man before to whom I could impart my troubles, though I had been certain of relief. I rejoice to find my own sentiments confirmed by yours, who are not easily deceived, and can have no motive or purpose to deceive. I hope that time and variety will dissipate the gloom that has so long surrounded me, and the latter part of my days will be spent in peace."

"Your learning and virtue," said Imlac, "may justly give you hopes."

Rasselas then entered, with the princess and Pekuah, and inquired whether they had contrived any new diversion for the next day. "Such," said Nekayah, "is the state of life, that none are happy but by the anticipation of change; the change itself is nothing; when we have made it the next wish is to change again. The world is not yet exhausted: let me see something tomorrow which I never saw before."

"Variety," said Rasselas, "is so necessary to content, that even the Happy Valley disgusted me by the recurrence of its luxuries; yet I could not forbear to reproach myself with impatience when I saw the monks of St. Anthony support, without complaint, a life, not of uniform delight, but uniform hardship."

"Those men," answered Imlac, "are less wretched in their silent convent than the Abyssinian princes in their prison of pleasure. Whatever is done by the monks is incited by an adequate and reasonable motive. Their labour supplies them with necessaries; it therefore cannot be omitted, and is certainly rewarded. Their devotion prepares them for another state, and reminds them of its approach while it fits them for it. Their time is regularly distributed; one duty succeeds another, so that they are not left open to the distraction of unguided choice, nor lost in the shades of listless inactivity. There is a certain task to be performed at an appropriated hour, and their toils are cheerful, because they consider them as acts of piety by which they are always advancing towards endless felicity."

"Do you think," said Nekayah, "that the monastic rule is a more holy and less imperfect state than any other? May not he equally hope for future happiness who converses openly with mankind, who succours the distressed by his charity, instructs the ignorant by his learning, and contributes by his industry to the general system of life, even though he should omit some of the mortifications which are practised in the cloister, and allow himself such harmless delights as his condition may place within his reach?"

"This," said Imlac, "is a question which has long divided the wise and perplexed the good. I am afraid to decide on either part. He that lives well in the world is better than he that lives well in a monastery. But perhaps everyone is not able to stem the temptations of public life, and if he cannot conquer he may properly retreat. Some have little power to do good, and have likewise little strength to resist evil. Many are weary of the conflicts with adversity, and are willing to eject those passions which have long busied them in vain. And many are dismissed by age and diseases from the more laborious duties of society. In monasteries the weak and timorous may be happily sheltered, the weary may repose, and the penitent may meditate. Those retreats of prayer and contemplation have something so congenial to the mind of man, that perhaps there is scarcely one that does not purpose to close his life in pious abstraction, with a few associates serious as himself."

"Such," said Pekuah, "has often been my wish, and I have heard the princess declare that she should not willingly die in a crowd."

"The liberty of using harmless pleasures," proceeded Imlac, "will not be disputed, but it is still to be examined what pleasures are harmless. The evil of any pleasure that Nekayah can image is not in the act itself but in its consequences. Pleasure in itself harmless may become mischievous by endearing to us a state which we know to be transient and probatory, and withdrawing our thoughts from that of which every hour brings us nearer to the beginning, and of which no length of time will bring us to the end. Mortification is not virtuous in itself, nor has any other use but that it disengages us from the allurements of sense. In the state of future perfection to which we all aspire there will be pleasure without danger and security without restraint."

The princess was silent, and Rasselas, turning to the astronomer, asked him whether he could not delay her retreat by showing her something which she had not seen before.

"Your curiosity," said the sage, "has been so general, and your pursuit of knowledge so vigorous, that novelties are not now very easily to be found; but what you can no longer procure from the living may be given by the dead. Among the wonders of this country are the catacombs, or the ancient repositories in which the bodies of the earliest generations were lodged, and where, by the virtue of the gums which embalmed them, they yet remain without corruption."

"I know not," said Rasselas, "what pleasure the sight of the catacombs can afford; but, since nothing else is offered, I am resolved to view them, and shall place this with many other things which I have done because I would do something."

They hired a guard of horsemen, and the next day visited the catacombs. When they were about to descend into the sepulchral caves,

"Pekuah," said the princess, "we are now again invading the habitations of the dead; I know that you will stay behind. Let me find you safe when I return." "No, I will not be left," answered Pekuah, "I will go down between you and the prince."

They then all descended, and roved with wonder through the labyrinth of subterraneous passages, where the bodies were laid in rows on either side.

Chapter XLVIII—Imlac Discourses on the Nature of the Soul

"What reason," said the prince, "can be given why the Egyptians should thus expensively preserve those carcasses which some nations consume with fire, others lay to mingle with the earth, and all agree to remove from their sight as soon as decent rites can be performed?"

"The original of ancient customs," said Imlac, "is commonly unknown, for the practice often continues when the cause has ceased; and concerning superstitious ceremonies it is vain to conjecture; for what reason did not dictate, reason cannot explain. I have long believed that the practice of embalming arose only from tenderness to the remains of relations or friends; and to this opinion I am more inclined because it seems impossible that this care should have been general; had all the dead been embalmed, their repositories must in time have been more spacious than the dwellings of the living. I suppose only the rich or honourable were secured from corruption, and the rest left to the course of nature.

"But it is commonly supposed that the Egyptians believed the soul to live as long as the body continued undissolved, and therefore tried this method of eluding death."

"Could the wise Egyptians," said Nekayah, "think so grossly of the soul? If the soul could once survive its separation, what could it afterwards receive or suffer from the body?"

"The Egyptians would doubtless think erroneously," said the astronomer, "in the darkness of heathenism and the first dawn of philosophy. The nature of the soul is still disputed amidst all our opportunities of clearer knowledge; some yet say that it may be material, who, nevertheless, believe it to be immortal."

"Some," answered Imlac, "have indeed said that the soul is material, but I can scarcely believe that any man has thought it who knew how to think; for all the conclusions of reason enforce the immateriality of mind, and all the notices of sense and investigations of science concur to prove the unconsciousness of matter.

"It was never supposed that cogitation is inherent in matter, or that every particle is a thinking being. Yet if any part of matter be devoid of thought, what part can we suppose to think? Matter can differ from matter only in form, density, bulk, motion, and direction of motion; to which of these, however varied or combined, can consciousness be annexed? To be round or square, to be solid or fluid, to be great or little, to be moved slowly or swiftly, one way or another, are modes of material existence all equally alien from the nature of cogitation. If matter be once without thought, it can only be made to think by some new modification; but all the modifications which it can admit are equally unconnected with cogitative powers."

"But the materialists," said the astronomer, "urge that matter may have qualities with which we are unacquainted."

"He who will determine," returned Imlac, "against that which he knows because there may be something which he knows not; he that can set hypothetical possibility against acknowledged certainty, is not to be admitted among reasonable beings. All that we know of matter is, that matter is inert, senseless, and lifeless; and if this conviction cannot he opposed but by referring us to something that we know not, we have all the evidence that human intellect can admit. If that which is known may be overruled by that which is unknown, no being, not omniscient, can arrive at certainty."

"Yet let us not," said the astronomer, "too arrogantly limit the Creator's power."

"It is no limitation of omnipotence," replied the poet, "to suppose that one thing is not consistent with another, that the same proposition cannot be at once true and false, that the same number cannot be even and odd, that cogitation cannot be conferred on that which is created incapable of cogitation."

"I know not," said Nekayah, "any great use of this question. Does that immateriality, which in my opinion you have sufficiently proved, necessarily include eternal duration?"

"Of immateriality," said Imlac, "our ideas are negative, and therefore obscure. Immateriality seems to imply a natural power of perpetual duration as a consequence of exemption from all causes of decay: whatever perishes is destroyed by the solution of its contexture and separation of its parts; nor can we conceive how that which has no parts, and therefore admits no solution, can be naturally corrupted or impaired."

"I know not," said Rasselas, "how to conceive anything without extension: what is extended must have parts, and you allow that whatever has parts may be destroyed."

"Consider your own conceptions," replied Imlac, "and the difficulty will be less. You will find substance without extension. An ideal form is no less real than material bulk; yet an ideal form has no extension. It is no less certain, when you think on a pyramid, that your mind possesses the idea of a pyramid, than that the pyramid itself is standing. What space does the idea of a pyramid occupy more than the idea of a grain of corn? or how can either idea suffer laceration? As is the effect, such is the cause; as thought is, such is the power that thinks, a power impassive and indiscerptible."[14]

"But the Being," said Nekayah, "whom I fear to name, the Being which made the soul, can destroy it."

"He surely can destroy it," answered Imlac, "since, however unperishable, it receives from a superior nature its power of duration. That it will not perish by any inherent cause of decay or principle of corruption, may be shown by philosophy; but philosophy can tell no more. That it will not be annihilated by Him that made it, we must humbly learn from higher authority."

The whole assembly stood awhile silent and collected. "Let us return," said Rasselas, "from this scene of mortality. How gloomy would be these mansions of the dead to him who did not know that he should never die; that what now acts shall continue its agency, and what now thinks shall think on for ever. Those that lie here stretched before us, the wise and the powerful of ancient times, warn us to remember the shortness of our present state; they were perhaps snatched away while they were busy, like us, in the choice of life."

"To me," said the princess, "the choice of life is become less important; I hope hereafter to think only on the choice of eternity."

They then hastened out of the caverns, and under the protection of their guard returned to Cairo.

Chapter XLIX—The Conclusion, in Which Nothing Is Concluded

It was now the time of the inundation of the Nile: a few days after their visit to the catacombs the river began to rise.

They were confined to their house. The whole region being under water, gave them no invitation to any excursions; and being well supplied with materials for talk, they diverted themselves with comparisons of the different forms of life which they had observed, and with various schemes of happiness which each of them had formed.

Pekuah was never so much charmed with any place as the convent of St. Anthony, where the Arab restored her to the princess, and wished only to fill it with pious maidens and to be made prioress of the order. She was weary of expectation and disgust, and would gladly be fixed in some unvariable state.

The princess thought that, of all sublunary things, knowledge was the best. She desired first to learn all sciences, and then proposed to found a college of learned women, in which she would preside, that, by conversing with the old and educating the young, she might divide her time between the acquisition and communication of wisdom, and raise up for the next age models of prudence and patterns of piety.

The prince desired a little kingdom in which he might administer justice in his own person and see all the parts of government with his own eyes; but he could never fix the limits of his dominion, and was always adding to the number of his subjects.

Imlac and the astronomer were contented to be driven along the stream of life without directing their course to any particular port.

Of these wishes that they had formed they well knew that none could be obtained. They deliberated awhile what was to be done, and resolved, when the inundation should cease, to return to Abyssinia.

PART IV

Preface to *The Plays of William Shakespeare* (1765)

That praises are without reason lavished on the dead, and that the honours due only to excellence are paid to antiquity, is a complaint likely to be always continued by those who, being able to add nothing to truth, hope for eminence from the heresies of paradox; or those who, being forced by disappointment upon consolatory expedients, are willing to hope from posterity what the present age refuses, and flatter themselves that the regard which is yet denied by envy, will be at last bestowed by time.

Antiquity, like every other quality that attracts the notice of mankind, has undoubtedly votaries that reverence it, not from reason, but from prejudice. Some seem to admire indiscriminately whatever has been long preserved, without considering that time has sometimes cooperated with chance; all perhaps are more willing to honour past than present excellence; and the mind contemplates genius through the shades of age, as the eye surveys the sun through artificial opacity. The great contention of criticism is to find the faults of the moderns, and the beauties of the ancients. While an author is yet living we estimate his powers by his worst performance, and when he is dead we rate them by his best.

To works, however, of which the excellence is not absolute and definite, but gradual and comparative; to works not raised upon principles demonstrative and scientific, but appealing wholly to observation and experience, no other test can be applied than length of duration and continuance of esteem. What mankind have long possessed they have often examined and compared, and if they persist to value the possession, it is because frequent comparisons have confirmed opinion in its favour. As among the works of nature no man can properly call a river deep or a mountain high, without the knowledge of many mountains and many rivers; so in the productions of genius, nothing can be styled excellent till it has been compared with other works of the same kind. Demonstration immediately displays its power, and has nothing to hope or fear from the flux of years; but works tentative and experimental must be estimated by their proportion to the general and collective ability of man, as it is discovered in a long succession of endeavours. Of the first building that was raised, it might be with certainty determined that it was round or square, but whether it was spacious or lofty must have been referred to time. The Pythagorean scale of numbers was at once discovered to be perfect; but the poems of Homer we yet know not to transcend the common limits of human intelligence, but by remarking, that nation after nation, and century after century, has been able to do little more than transpose his incidents, new name his characters, and paraphrase his sentiments.

The reverence due to writings that have long subsisted arises therefore not from any credulous confidence in the superior wisdom of past ages, or gloomy persuasion of the degeneracy of mankind, but is the consequence of acknowledged and indubitable positions, that what has been longest known has been most considered, and what is most considered is best understood.

The poet, of whose works I have undertaken the revision, may now begin to assume the dignity of an ancient, and claim the privilege of established fame and prescriptive veneration. He has long outlived his century, the term commonly fixed as the test of literary merit. Whatever advantages he might once derive from personal allusions, local customs, or temporary opinions, have for many years been lost; and every topic of merriment or motive of sorrow, which the modes of artificial life afforded him, now only obscure the scenes which they once illuminated. The effects of favour and competition are at an end; the tradition of his friendships and his enmities has perished; his works support no opinion with arguments, nor supply any faction with invectives; they can neither indulge vanity nor gratify malignity, but are read without any other reason than the desire of pleasure, and are therefore praised only as pleasure is obtained; yet, thus unassisted by interest or passion, they have past through variations of taste and changes of manners, and, as they devolved from one generation to another, have received new honours at every transmission.

But because human judgment, though it be gradually gaining upon certainty, never becomes infallible; and approbation, though long continued, may yet be only the approbation of prejudice or fashion; it is proper to inquire by what peculiarities of excellence Shakespeare has gained and kept the favour of his countrymen.

Nothing can please many, and please long, but just representations of general nature. Particular manners can be known to few, and therefore few only can judge how nearly they are copied. The irregular combinations of fanciful invention may delight awhile, by that novelty of which the common satiety of life sends us all in quest; but the pleasures of sudden wonder are soon exhausted, and the mind can only repose on the stability of truth.

Shakespeare is above all writers, at least above all modern writers, the poet of nature; the poet that holds up to his readers a faithful mirror of manners and of life. His characters are not modified by the customs of particular places, unpractised by the rest of the world; by the peculiarities of studies or professions, which can operate but upon small numbers; or by the accidents of transient fashions or temporary opinions: they are the genuine progeny of common humanity, such as the world will always supply and observation will always find. His persons act and speak by the influence of those general passions and principles by which all minds are agitated, and the whole system of life is continued in motion. In the writings of other poets a character is too often an individual; in those of Shakespeare it is commonly a species.

It is from this wide extension of design that so much instruction is derived. It is this which fills the plays of Shakespeare with practical axioms and domestic wisdom. It was said of Euripides, that every verse was a precept; and it may be said of Shakespeare, that from his works may be collected a system of civil and economical prudence. Yet his real power is not shown in the splendour of particular passages, but by the progress of his fable, and the tenor of his dialogue; and he that tries to recommend him by select quotations, will succeed like the pedant in Hierocles, who, when he offered his house to sale, carried a brick in his pocket as a specimen.

It will not easily be imagined how much Shakespeare excels in accommodating his sentiments to real life, but by comparing him with other authors. It was observed of the ancient schools of declamation, that the more diligently they were frequented, the more was the student disqualified for the world, because he found nothing there which he should ever meet in any other place. The same remark may be applied to every stage but that of Shakespeare. The theatre, when it is under any other direction, is peopled by such characters as were never seen, conversing in a language which was never heard, upon topics which will never arise in the commerce of mankind. But the dialogue of this author is often so evidently determined by the incident which produces it, and is pursued with so much ease and simplicity, that it seems scarcely to claim the merit of fiction, but to have been gleaned by diligent selection out of common conversation, and common occurrences.

Upon every other stage the universal agent is love, by whose power all good and evil is distributed, and every action quickened or retarded. To bring a lover, a lady, and a rival into the fable; to entangle them in contradictory obligations, perplex them with oppositions of interest, and harass them with violence of desires inconsistent with each other; to make them meet in rapture and part in agony; to fill their mouths with hyperbolical joy and outrageous sorrow; to distress them as nothing human ever was distressed; to deliver them as nothing human ever was delivered, is the business of a modern dramatist. For this probability is violated, life is misrepresented, and language is depraved. But love is only one of many passions, and as it has no great influence upon the sum of life, it has little operation in the dramas of a poet, who caught his ideas from the living world, and exhibited only what he saw before him. He knew that any other passion, as it was regular or exorbitant, was a cause of happiness or calamity.

Characters thus ample and general were not easily discriminated and preserved, yet perhaps no poet ever kept his personages more distinct from each other. I will not say with Pope, that every speech may be assigned to the proper speaker, because many speeches there are which have nothing characteristical; but, perhaps, though some may be equally adapted to every person, it will be difficult to find any that can be properly transferred from the present possessor to another claimant. The choice is right, when there is reason for choice.

Other dramatists can only gain attention by hyperbolical or aggravated characters, by fabulous and unexampled excellence or depravity, as the writers of barbarous romances invigorated the reader by a giant and a dwarf; and he that should form his expectations of human affairs from the play or from the tale, would be equally deceived. Shakespeare has no heroes; his scenes are occupied only by men, who act and speak as the reader thinks that he should himself have spoken or acted on the same occasion. Even where the agency is supernatural the dialogue is level with life. Other writers disguise the most natural passions and most frequent incidents; so that he who contemplates them in the book will not know them in the world: Shakespeare approximates the remote, and familiarizes the wonderful; the event which he represents will not happen, but if it were possible, its effects would be probably such as he has assigned; and it may be said, that he has not only shown human nature as it acts in real exigencies, but as it would be found in trials to which it cannot be exposed.

This therefore is the praise of Shakespeare, that his drama is the mirror of life; that he who has mazed his imagination, in following the phantoms which other writers raise up before him, may here be cured of his delirious ecstasies, by reading human sentiments in human language; by scenes from which a hermit may estimate the transactions of the world, and a confessor predict the progress of the passions.

His adherence to general nature has exposed him to the censure of critics, who form their judgments upon narrower principles. Dennis and Rhymer think his Romans not sufficiently Roman; and Voltaire censures his kings as not completely royal. Dennis is offended that Menenius, a senator of Rome, should play the buffoon; and Voltaire perhaps thinks decency violated when the Danish usurper is represented as a drunkard. But Shakespeare always makes nature predominate over accident; and if he preserves the essential character, is not very careful of distinctions superinduced and adventitious. His story requires Romans or kings, but he thinks only on men. He knew that Rome, like every other city, had men of all dispositions; and wanting a buffoon, he went into the senate-house for that which the senate-house would certainly have afforded him. He was inclined to show an usurper and a murderer not only odious but despicable, he therefore added drunkenness to his other qualities, knowing that kings love wine like other men, and that wine exerts its natural power upon kings. These are the petty cavils of petty minds; a poet overlooks the casual distinction of country and condition, as a painter, satisfied with the figure, neglects the drapery.

The censure which he has incurred by mixing comic and tragic scenes, as it extends to all his works, deserves more consideration. Let the fact be first stated, and then examined.

Shakespeare's plays are not in the rigorous and critical sense either tragedies or comedies, but compositions of a distinct kind; exhibiting the real state of sublunary nature, which partakes of good and evil, joy and sorrow, mingled with endless variety of proportion and innumerable modes of combination; and expressing the course of the world, in which the loss of one is the gain of another; in which, at the same time, the reveller is hasting to his wine, and the mourner burying his friend; in which the malignity of one is sometimes defeated by the frolic of another; and many mischiefs and many benefits are done and hindered without design.

Out of this chaos of mingled purposes and casualties the ancient poets, according to the laws which custom had prescribed, selected some the crimes of men, and some their absurdities; some the momentous vicissitudes of life, and some the lighter occurrences; some the terrors of distress, and some the gayeties of prosperity. Thus rose the two modes of imitation, known by the names of tragedy and comedy, compositions intended to promote different ends by contrary means, and considered as so little allied, that I do not recollect among the Greeks or Romans a single writer who attempted both.

Shakespeare has united the powers of exciting laughter and sorrow not only in one mind, but in one composition. Almost all his plays are divided between serious and ludicrous characters, and, in the successive evolutions of the design, sometimes produce seriousness and sorrow, and sometimes levity and laughter.

That this is a practice contrary to the rules of criticism will be readily allowed; but there is always an appeal open from criticism to nature. The end of writing is to instruct; the end of poetry is to instruct by pleasing. That the mingled drama may convey all the instruction of tragedy or comedy cannot be denied, because it includes both in its alterations of exhibition, and approaches nearer than either to the appearance of life, by showing how great machinations and slender designs may promote or obviate one another, and the high and the low cooperate in the general system by unavoidable concatenation.

It is objected, that by this change of scenes the passions are interrupted in their progression, and that the principal event, being not advanced by a due gradation of preparatory incidents, wants at last the power to move, which constitutes the perfection of dramatic poetry. This reasoning is so specious, that it is received as true even by those who in daily experience feel it to be false. The interchanges of mingled scenes seldom fail to produce the intended vicissitudes of passion. Fiction cannot move so much, but that the attention may be easily transferred; and though it must be allowed that pleasing melancholy be sometimes interrupted by unwelcome levity, yet let it be considered likewise, that melancholy is often not pleasing, and that the disturbance of one man may be the relief of another; that different auditors have different habitudes; and that, upon the whole, all pleasure consists in variety.

The players, who in their edition divided our author's works into comedies, histories, and tragedies, seem not to have distinguished the three kinds, by any very exact or definite ideas.

An action which ended happily to the principal persons, however serious or distressful through its intermediate incidents, in their opinion constituted a comedy. This idea of a comedy continued long amongst us, and plays were written which, by changing the catastrophe, were tragedies today and comedies tomorrow.

Tragedy was not in those times a poem of more general dignity or elevation than comedy; it required only a calamitous conclusion, with which the common criticism of that age was satisfied, whatever lighter pleasure it afforded in its progress.

History was a series of actions, with no other than chronological succession, independent of each other, and without any tendency to introduce or regulate the conclusion. It is not always very nicely distinguished from tragedy. There is not much nearer approach to unity of action in the tragedy of *Antony and Cleopatra,* than in the history of *Richard the Second.* But a history might be continued through many plays; as it had no plan, it had no limits.

Through all these denominations of the drama, Shakespeare's mode of composition is the same; an interchange of seriousness and merriment, by which the mind is softened at one time, and exhilarated at another. But whatever be his purpose, whether to gladden or depress, or to conduct the story, without vehemence or emotion, through tracts of easy and familiar dialogue, he never fails to attain his purpose; as he commands us, we laugh or mourn, or sit silent with quiet expectation, in tranquillity without indifference.

When Shakespeare's plan is understood, most of the criticisms of Rhymer and Voltaire vanish away. The play of *Hamlet* is opened, without impropriety, by two sentinels; Iago bellows at Brabantio's window, without injury to the scheme of the play, though in terms which a modern audience would not easily endure; the character of Polonius is seasonable and useful; and the gravediggers themselves may be heard with applause.

Shakespeare engaged in dramatic poetry with the world open before him; the rules of the ancients were yet known to few; the public judgment was unformed; he had no example of such fame as might force him upon imitation, nor critics of such authority as might restrain his extravagance. He therefore indulged his natural disposition, and his disposition, as Rhymer has remarked, led him to comedy. In tragedy he often writes with great appearance of toil and study, what is written at last with little felicity; but in his comic scenes, he seems to produce without labour, what no labour can improve. In tragedy he is always struggling after some occasion to be comic, but in comedy he seems to repose, or to luxuriate, as in a mode of thinking congenial to his nature. In his tragic scenes there is always something wanting, but his comedy often surpasses expectation or desire. His comedy pleases by the thoughts and the language, and his tragedy for the greater part by incident and action. His tragedy seems to be skill, his comedy to be instinct.

The force of his comic scenes has suffered little diminution from the changes made by a century and a half, in manners or in words. As his personages act upon principles arising from genuine passion, very little modified by particular forms, their pleasures and vexations are communicable to all times and to all places; they are natural, and therefore durable; the adventitious peculiarities of personal habits are only superficial dyes, bright and pleasing for a little while, yet soon fading to a dim tint, without any remains of former lustre; but the discriminations of true passion are the colours of nature; they pervade the whole mass, and can only perish with the body that exhibits them. The accidental compositions of heterogeneous modes are dissolved by the chance which combined them; but the uniform simplicity of primitive qualities neither admits increase, nor suffers decay. The sand heaped by one flood is scattered by another, but the rock always continues in its place. The stream of time, which is continually washing the dissoluble fabrics of other poets, passes without injury by the adamant of Shakespeare.

If there be, what I believe there is, in every nation, a style which never becomes obsolete, a certain mode of phraseology so consonant and congenial to the analogy and principles of its respective language as to remain settled and unaltered; this style is probably to be sought in the common intercourse of life, among those who speak only to be understood, without ambition of elegance. The polite are always catching modish innovations, and the learned depart from established forms of speech, in hope of finding or making better; those who wish for distinction forsake the vulgar, when the vulgar is right; but there is a conversation above grossness and below refinement, where propriety resides, and where this poet seems to have gathered his comic dialogue. He is therefore more agreeable to the ears of the present age than any other author equally remote, and among his other excellencies deserves to be studied as one of the original masters of our language.

These observations are to be considered not as unexceptionably constant, but as containing general and predominant truth. Shakespeare's familiar dialogue is affirmed to be smooth and clear, yet not wholly without ruggedness or difficulty; as a country may be eminently fruitful, though it has spots unfit for cultivation. His characters are praised as natural, though their sentiments are sometimes forced, and their actions improbable; as the earth upon the whole is spherical, though its surface is varied with protuberances and cavities.

Shakespeare with his excellencies has likewise faults, and faults sufficient to obscure and overwhelm any other merit. I shall show them in the proportion in which they appear to me, without envious malignity or superstitious veneration. No question can be more innocently discussed than a dead poet's pretensions to renown; and little regard is due to that bigotry which sets candour higher than truth.

His first defect is that to which may be imputed most of the evil in books or in men. He sacrifices virtue to convenience, and is so much more careful to please than to instruct, that he seems to write without any moral purpose. From his writings indeed a system of social duty may be selected, for he that thinks reasonably must think morally; but his precepts and axioms drop casually from him; he makes no just distribution of good or evil, nor is always careful to show in the virtuous a disapprobation of the wicked; he carries his persons indifferently through right and wrong, and at the close dismisses them without further care, and leaves their examples to operate by chance. This fault the barbarity of his age cannot extenuate; for it is always a writer's duty to make the world better, and justice is a virtue independent on time or place.

The plots are often so loosely formed, that a very slight consideration may improve them, and so carelessly pursued, that he seems not always fully to comprehend his own design. He omits opportunities of instructing or delighting which the train of his story seems to force upon him, and apparently rejects those exhibitions which would be more affecting, for the sake of those which are more easy.

It may be observed, that in many of his plays the latter part is evidently neglected. When he found himself near the end of his work, and, in view of his reward, he shortened the labour to snatch the profit. He therefore remits his efforts where he should most vigorously exert them, and his catastrophe is improbably produced or imperfectly represented.

He had no regard to distinction of time or place, but gives to one age or nation, without scruple, the customs, institutions, and opinions of another, at the expense not only of likelihood, but of possibility. These faults Pope has endeavoured, with more zeal than judgment, to transfer to his imagined interpolators. We need not wonder to find Hector quoting Aristotle, when we see the loves of Theseus and Hippolyta combined with the Gothic mythology of fairies. Shakespeare, indeed, was not the only violator of chronology, for in the same age Sidney, who wanted not the advantages of learning, has, in his *Arcadia,* confounded the pastoral with the feudal times, the days of innocence, quiet, and security, with those of turbulence, violence, and adventure.

In his comic scenes he is seldom very successful when he engages his characters in reciprocations of smartness and contest of sarcasm; their jests are commonly gross, and their pleasantry licentious; neither his gentlemen nor his ladies have much delicacy, nor are sufficiently distinguished from his clowns by any appearance of refined manners. Whether he represented the real conversation of his time is not easy to determine; the reign of Elizabeth is commonly supposed to have been a time of stateliness, formality, and reserve, yet perhaps the relaxations of that severity were not very elegant. There must, however, have been always some modes of gaiety preferable to others, and a writer ought to choose the best.

In tragedy his performance seems constantly to be worse as his labour is more. The effusions of passion which exigency forces out are for the most part striking and energetic; but whenever he solicits his invention, or strains his faculties, the offspring of his throes is tumour, meanness, tediousness, and obscurity.

In narration he affects a disproportionate pomp of diction and a wearisome train of circumlocution, and tells the incident imperfectly in many words, which might have been more plainly delivered in few. Narration in dramatic poetry is, naturally tedious, as it is unanimated and inactive, and obstructs the progress of the action; it should therefore always be rapid, and enlivened by frequent interruption. Shakespeare found it an encumbrance, and instead of lightening it by brevity, endeavoured to recommend it by dignity and splendour.

His declamations or set speeches are commonly cold and weak, for his power was the power of nature; when he endeavoured, like other tragic writers, to catch opportunities of amplification, and instead of inquiring what the occasion demanded, to show how much his stores of knowledge could supply, he seldom escapes without the pity or resentment of his reader.

It is incident to him to be now and then entangled with an unwieldy sentiment, which he cannot well express, and will not reject; he struggles with it awhile, and if it continues stubborn, comprises it in words such as occur, and leaves it to be disentangled and evolved by those who have more leisure to bestow upon it.

Not that always where the language is intricate the thought is subtle, or the image always great where the line is bulky; the equality of words to things is very often neglected, and trivial sentiments and vulgar ideas disappoint the attention to which they are recommended by sonorous epithets and swelling figures.

But the admirers of this great poet have more reason to complain when he approaches nearest to his highest excellence and seems fully resolved to sink them in dejection, and mollify them with tender emotions by the fall of greatness, the danger of innocence, or the crosses of love. What he does best, he soon ceases to do. He is not long soft and pathetic without some idle conceit, or contemptible equivocation. He no sooner begins to move, than he counteracts himself; and terror and pity, as they are rising in the mind, are checked and blasted by sudden frigidity.

A quibble is to Shakespeare, what luminous vapours are to the traveller; he follows it at all adventures, it is sure to lead him out of his way, and sure to engulf him in the mire. It has some malignant power over his mind, and its fascinations are irresistible. Whatever be the dignity or profundity of his disquisition, whether he be enlarging knowledge or exalting affection, whether he be amusing attention with incidents, or enchaining it in suspense, let but a quibble spring up before him, and he leaves his work unfinished. A quibble is the golden apple for which he will always turn aside from his career, or stoop from his elevation. A quibble, poor and barren as it is, gave him such delight, that he was content to purchase it, by the sacrifice of reason, propriety, and truth. A quibble was to him the fatal Cleopatra for which he lost the world, and was content to lose it.

It will be thought strange that, in enumerating the defects of this writer, I have not yet mentioned his neglect of the unities; his violation of those laws which have been instituted and established by the joint authority of poets and of critics.

For his other deviations from the art of writing, I resign him to critical justice, without making any other demand in his favour, than that which must be indulged to all human excellence; that his virtues be rated with his failings: But, from the censure which this irregularity may bring upon him, I shall, with due reverence to that learning which I must oppose, adventure to try how I can defend him.

His histories, being neither tragedies nor comedies, are not subject to any of their laws; nothing more is necessary to all the praise which they expect, than that the changes of action be so prepared as to be understood, that the incidents be various and affecting, and the characters consistent, natural, and distinct. No other unity is intended, and therefore none is to be sought.

In his other works he has well enough preserved the unity of action. He has not, indeed, an intrigue regularly perplexed and regularly unravelled; he does not endeavour to hide his design only to discover it, for this is seldom the order of real events, and Shakespeare is the poet of nature. But his plan has commonly what Aristotle requires, a beginning, a middle, and an end; one event is concatenated with another, and the conclusion follows by easy consequence. There are perhaps some incidents that might be spared, as in other poets there is much talk that only fills up time upon the stage; but the general system makes gradual advances, and the end of the play is the end of expectation.

To the unities of time and place he has shown no regard, and perhaps a nearer view of the principles on which they stand will diminish their value, and withdraw from them the veneration which, from the time of Corneille, they have very generally received by discovering that they have given more trouble to the poet, than pleasure to the auditor.

The necessity of observing the unities of time and place arises from the supposed necessity of making the drama credible. The critics hold it impossible, that an action of months or years can be possibly believed to pass in three hours; or that the spectator can suppose himself to sit in the theatre, while ambassadors go and return between distant kings, while armies are levied and towns besieged, while an exile wanders and returns, or till he whom they saw courting his mistress, shall lament the untimely fall of his son. The mind revolts from evident falsehood, and fiction loses its force when it departs from the resemblance of reality.

From the narrow limitation of time necessarily arises the contraction of place. The spectator, who knows that he saw the first act at Alexandria, cannot suppose that he sees the next at Rome, at a distance to which not the dragons of Medea could, in so short a time, have transported him; he knows with certainty that he has not changed his place; and he knows that place cannot change itself; that what was a house cannot become a plain; that what was Thebes can never be Persepolis.

Such is the triumphant language with which a critic exults over the misery of an irregular poet, and exults commonly without resistance or reply. It is time therefore to tell him, by the authority of Shakespeare, that he assumes, as an unquestionable principle, a position which, while his breath is forming it into words, his understanding pronounces to be false. It is false, that any representation is mistaken for reality; that any dramatic fable in its materiality was ever credible, or, for a single moment, was ever credited.

The objection arising from the impossibility of passing the first hour at Alexandria, and the next at Rome, supposes, that when the play opens the spectator really imagines himself at Alexandria, and believes that his walk to the theatre has been a voyage to Egypt, and that he lives in the days of Antony and Cleopatra. Surely he that imagines this, may imagine more. He that can take the stage at one time for the palace of the Ptolemies, may take it in half an hour for the promontory of Actium. Delusion, if delusion be admitted, has no certain limitation; if the spectator can be once persuaded that his old acquaintance are Alexander and Caesar, that a room illuminated with candles is the plain of Pharsalia or the bank of Granicus, he is in a state of elevation above the reach of reason, or of truth, and from the heights of empyrean poetry, may despise the circumscriptions of terrestrial nature. There is no reason why a mind thus wandering in ecstasy should count the clock, or why an hour should not be a century in that calenture of the brains that can make the stage a field.

The truth is, that the spectators are always in their senses, and know, from the first act to the last, that the stage is only a stage, and that the players are only players. They come to hear a certain number of lines recited with just gesture and elegant modulation. The lines relate to some action, and an action must be in some place; but the different actions that complete a story may be in places very remote from each other; and where is the absurdity of allowing that space to represent first Athens, and then Sicily, which was always known to be neither Sicily nor Athens, but a modern theatre?

By supposition, as place is introduced, time may be extended; the time required by the fable elapses for the most part between the acts; for, of so much of the action as is represented, the real and poetical duration is the same. If, in the first act, preparations for war against Mithridates are represented to be made in Rome, the event of the war may, without absurdity, be represented, in the catastrophe, as happening in Pontus; we know that there is neither war, nor preparation for war; we know that we are neither in Rome nor Pontus; that neither Mithridates nor Lucullus are before us. The drama exhibits successive imitations of successive actions, and why may not the second imitation represent an action that happened years after the first; if it be so connected with it, that nothing but time can be supposed to intervene? Time is, of all modes of existence, most obsequious to the imagination; a lapse of years is as easily conceived as a passage of hours. In contemplation we easily contract the time of real actions, and therefore willingly permit it to be contracted when we only see their imitation.

It will be asked, how the drama moves, if it is not credited. It is credited with all the credit due to a drama. It is credited, whenever it moves, as a just picture of a real original; as representing to the auditor what he would himself feel, if he were to do or suffer what is there feigned to be suffered or to be done. The reflection that strikes the heart is not that the evils before us are real evils, but that they are evils to which we ourselves may be exposed. If there be any fallacy, it is not that we fancy the players, but that we fancy ourselves unhappy for a moment; but we rather lament the possibility than suppose the presence of misery, as a mother weeps over her babe, when she remembers that death may take it from her. The delight of tragedy proceeds from our consciousness of fiction; if we thought murders and treasons real, they would please no more.

Imitations produce pain or pleasure, not because they are mistaken for realities, but because they bring realities to mind. When the imagination is recreated by a painted landscape, the trees are not supposed capable to give us shade, or the fountains coolness; but we consider, how we should be pleased with such fountains playing beside us, and such woods waving over us. We are agitated in reading the history of *Henry the Fifth,* yet no man takes his book for the field of Agincourt. A dramatic exhibition is a book recited with concomitants that increase or diminish its effect. Familiar comedy is often more powerful on the theatre, than in the page; imperial tragedy is always less. The humour of Petruchio may be heightened by grimace; but what voice or what gesture can hope to add dignity or force to the soliloquy of Cato.

A play read affects the mind like a play acted. It is therefore evident that the action is not supposed to be real, and it follows that between the acts a longer or shorter time may be allowed to pass, and that no more account of space or duration is to be taken by the auditor of a drama, than by the reader of a narrative, before whom may pass in an hour the life of a hero, or the revolutions of an empire.

Whether Shakespeare knew the unities, and rejected them by design, or deviated from them by happy ignorance, it is, I think, impossible to decide, and useless to inquire. We may reasonably suppose that, when he rose to notice, he did not want the counsels and admonitions of scholars and critics, and that he at last deliberately persisted in a practice which he might have begun by chance. As nothing is essential to the fable but unity of action, and as the unities of time and place arise evidently from false assumptions, and, by circumscribing the extent of the drama, lessen its variety, I cannot think it much to be lamented that they were not known by him, or not observed. Nor, if such another poet could arise, should I very vehemently reproach him, that his first act passed at Venice, and his next in Cyprus. Such violations of rules merely positive become the comprehensive genius of Shakespeare, and such censures are suitable to the minute and slender criticism of Voltaire:

> *Non usque adeo permiscuit imis*
> *Longus summa dies, ut non, si voce Metelli*
> *Serventur leges, malint a Caesare tolli.*
> Lucan, *Pharsalia,* III. 138–140

> *Nor time, nor chance breed such confusions yet,*
> *Nor are the mean so rais'd, nor sunk the great;*
> *But laws themselves would rather chuse to be*
> *Suppress'd by Caesar, than preserved by thee.*
> transl. Nicholas Rowe

Yet when I speak thus slightly of dramatic rules, I cannot but recollect how much wit and learning may be produced against me; before such authorities I am afraid to stand, not that I think the present question one of those that are to be decided by mere authority, but because it is to be suspected that these precepts have not been so easily received but for better reasons than I have yet been able to find. The result of my enquiries, in which it would be ludicrous to boast of impartiality, is, that the unities of time and place are not essential to a just drama, that though they may sometimes conduce to pleasure, they are always to be sacrificed to the nobler beauties of variety and instruction; and that a play, written with nice observation of critical rules, is to be contemplated as an elaborate curiosity, as the product of superfluous and ostentatious art, by which is shown rather what is possible, than what is necessary.

He that, without diminution of any other excellence, shall preserve all the unities unbroken, deserves the like applause with the architect, who shall display all the orders of architecture in a citadel, without any deduction from its strength; but the principal beauty of a citadel is to exclude the enemy; and the greatest graces of a play, are to copy nature and instruct life.

Perhaps, what I have here not dogmatically but deliberately written, may recall the principles of the drama to a new examination. I am almost frightened at my own temerity; and when I estimate the fame and the strength of those that maintain the contrary opinion, am ready to sink down in reverential silence; as Aeneas withdrew from the defence of Troy, when he saw Neptune shaking the wall, and Juno heading the besiegers.

Those whom my arguments cannot persuade to give their approbation to the judgment of Shakespeare, will easily, if they consider the condition of his life, make some allowance for his ignorance.

Every man's performances, to be rightly estimated, must be compared with the state of the age in which he lived, and with his own particular opportunities; and though to the reader a book be not worse or better for the circumstances of the author, yet as there is always a silent reference of human works to human abilities, and as the enquiry, how far man may extend his designs, or how high he may rate his native force, is of far greater dignity than in what rank we shall place any particular performance, curiosity is always busy to discover the instruments, as well as to survey the workmanship, to know how much is to be ascribed to original powers, and how much to casual and adventitious help. The palaces of Peru or Mexico were certainly mean and incommodious habitations, if compared to the houses of European monarchs; yet who could forbear to view them with astonishment, who remembered that they were built without the use of iron?

The English nation, in the time of Shakespeare, was yet struggling to emerge from barbarity. The philology of Italy had been transplanted hither in the reign of Henry the Eighth; and the learned languages had been successfully cultivated by Lily, Linacre, and More; by Pole, Cheke, and Gardiner; and afterwards by Smith, Clerk, Haddon, and Ascham.[1] Greek was now taught to boys in the principal schools; and those who united elegance with learning, read, with great diligence, the Italian and Spanish poets. But literature was yet confined to professed scholars, or to men and women of high rank. The public was gross and dark; and to be able to read and write was an accomplishment still valued for its rarity.

Nations, like individuals, have their infancy. A people newly awakened to literary curiosity, being yet unacquainted with the true state of things, knows not how to judge of that which is proposed as its resemblance. Whatever is remote from common appearances is always welcome to vulgar, as to childish credulity; and of a country unenlightened by learning, the whole people is the vulgar. The study of those who then aspired to plebeian learning was laid out upon adventures, giants, dragons, and enchantments. [Sir Thomas Malory's] *The Death of Arthur* was the favourite volume.

The mind which has feasted on the luxurious wonders of fiction has no taste of the insipidity of truth. A play which imitated only the common occurrences of the world, would, upon the admirers of *Palmerin*[2] and *Guy of Warwick*, have made little impression; he that wrote for such an audience was under the necessity of looking round for strange events and fabulous transactions, and that incredibility, by which maturer knowledge is offended, was the chief recommendation of writings, to unskilful curiosity.

Our author's plots are generally borrowed from novels, and it is reasonable to suppose that he chose the most popular, such as were read by many, and related by more; for his audience could not have followed him through the intricacies of the drama, had they not held the thread of the story in their hands.

The stories, which we now find only in remoter authors, were in his

time accessible and familiar. The fable of *As You Like It,* which is supposed to be copied from Chaucer's *Gamelyn,* was a little pamphlet of
those times; and old Mr. Cibber remembered the tale of Hamlet in plain
English prose, which the critics have now to seek in Saxo Grammaticus.

His English histories he took from English chronicles and English bal-
lads; and as the ancient writers were made known to his countrymen
by versions, they supplied him with new subjects; he dilated some of Plu-
tarch's lives into plays, when they had been translated by [Sir Thomas]
North.

His plots, whether historical or fabulous, are always crowded with incidents, by which the attention of a rude people was more easily caught
than by sentiment or argumentation; and such is the power of the marvellous even over those who despise it, that every man finds his mind more
strongly seized by the tragedies of Shakespeare than of any other writer;
others please us by particular speeches, but he always makes us anxious
for the event, and has perhaps excelled all but Homer in securing the first
purpose of a writer, by exciting restless and unquenchable curiosity, and
compelling him that reads his work to read it through.

The shows and bustle with which his plays abound have the same
original. As knowledge advances, pleasure passes from the eye to the ear,
but returns, as it declines, from the ear to the eye. Those to whom our
author's labours were exhibited had more skill in pomps or processions
than in poetical language, and perhaps wanted some visible and discriminated events, as comments on the dialogue. He knew how he should most
please; and whether his practice is more agreeable to nature, or whether
his example has prejudiced the nation, we still find that on our stage
something must be done as well as said, and inactive declamation is very
coldly heard, however musical or elegant, passionate or sublime.

Voltaire expresses his wonder, that our author's extravagances are endured by a nation, which has seen the tragedy of *Cato.* Let him be answered, that Addison speaks the language of poets, and Shakespeare, of
men. We find in *Cato* innumerable beauties which enamour us of its author, but we see nothing that acquaints us with human sentiments or human actions; we place it with the fairest and the noblest progeny which
judgment propagates by conjunction with learning, but *Othello* is the vigorous and vivacious offspring of observation impregnated by genius. *Cato*

affords a splendid exhibition of artificial and fictitious manners, and delivers just and noble sentiments, in diction easy, elevated, and harmonious, but its hopes and fears communicate no vibration to the heart; the composition refers us only to the writer; we pronounce the name of *Cato,* but we think on Addison.

The work of a correct and regular writer is a garden accurately formed and diligently planted, varied with shades, and scented with flowers; the composition of Shakespeare is a forest, in which oaks extend their branches, and pines tower in the air, interspersed sometimes with weeds and brambles, and sometimes giving shelter to myrtles and to roses; filling the eye with awful pomp, and gratifying the mind with endless diversity. Other poets display cabinets of precious rarities, minutely finished, wrought into shape, and polished into brightness. Shakespeare opens a mine which contains gold and diamonds in inexhaustible plenty, though clouded by incrustations, debased by impurities, and mingled with a mass of meaner minerals.

It has been much disputed, whether Shakespeare owed his excellence to his own native force, or whether he had the common helps of scholastic education, the precepts of critical science, and the examples of ancient authors.

There has always prevailed a tradition, that Shakespeare wanted learning, that he had no regular education, nor much skill in the dead languages. Jonson, his friend, affirms that *he had small Latin and less Greek;* who, besides that he had no imaginable temptation to falsehood, wrote at a time when the character and acquisitions of Shakespeare were known to multitudes. His evidence ought therefore to decide the controversy, unless some testimony of equal force could be opposed.

Some have imagined that they have discovered deep learning in many imitations of old writers; but the examples which I have known urged, were drawn from books translated in his time; or were such easy coincidences of thought as will happen to all who consider the same subjects; or such remarks on life or axioms of morality as float in conversation, and are transmitted through the world in proverbial sentences.

I have found it remarked that, in this important sentence, "Go before, I'll follow," we read a translation of *I prae, sequar.* I have been told, that when Caliban, after a pleasing dream, says, "I cry'd to sleep again," the author imitates Anacreon, who had, like every other man, the same wish on the same occasion.

There are a few passages which may pass for imitations, but so few, that the exception only confirms the rule; he obtained them from accidental quotations, or by oral communication, and as he used what he had, would have used more if he had obtained it.

The *Comedy of Errors* is confessedly taken from the *Menaechmi* of Plautus; from the only play of Plautus which was then in English. What can be more probable than that he who copied that, would have copied more; but that those which were not translated were inaccessible?

Whether he knew the modern languages is uncertain. That his plays have some French scenes proves but little; he might easily procure them to be written, and probably, even though he had known the language in the common degree, he could not have written it without assistance. In the story of *Romeo and Juliet* he is observed to have followed the English translation, where it deviates from the Italian; but this on the other part proves nothing against his knowledge of the original. He was to copy, not what he knew himself, but what was known to his audience.

It is most likely that he had learned Latin sufficiently to make him acquainted with construction, but that he never advanced to an easy perusal of the Roman authors. Concerning his skill in modern languages, I can find no sufficient ground of determination; but as no imitations of French or Italian authors have been discovered, though the Italian poetry was then high in esteem, I am inclined to believe that he read little more than English, and chose for his fables only such tales as he found translated.

That much knowledge is scattered over his works is very justly observed by Pope, but it is often such knowledge as books did not supply. He that will understand Shakespeare, must not be content to study him in the closet, he must look for his meaning sometimes among the sports of the field, and sometimes among the manufactures of the shop.

There is however proof enough that he was a very diligent reader, nor was our language then so indigent of books, but that he might very liberally indulge his curiosity without excursion into foreign literature. Many of the Roman authors were translated, and some of the Greek; the Reformation had filled the kingdom with theological learning; most of the topics of human disquisition had found English writers; and poetry had been cultivated, not only with diligence, but success. This was a stock of knowledge sufficient for a mind so capable of appropriating and improving it.

But the greater part of his excellence was the product of his own genius. He found the English stage in a state of the utmost rudeness; no essays either in tragedy or comedy had appeared, from which it could be discovered to what degree of delight either one or other might be carried. Neither character nor dialogue were yet understood. Shakespeare may be truly said to have introduced them both amongst us, and in some of his happier scenes to have carried them both to the utmost height.

By what gradations of improvement he proceeded, is not easily known; for the chronology of his works is yet unsettled. Rowe is of opinion, that "perhaps we are not to look for his beginning, like those of other writers, in his least perfect works; art had so little, and nature so large a share in what he did, that for ought I know," says he, "the performances of his youth, as they were the most vigorous, were the best." But the power of nature is only the power of using to any certain purpose the materials which diligence procures, or opportunity supplies. Nature gives no man knowledge, and when images are collected by study and experience, can only assist in combining or applying them. Shakespeare, however favoured by nature, could impart only what he had learned; and as he must increase his ideas, like other mortals, by gradual acquisition, he, like them, grew wiser as he grew older, could display life better, as he knew it more, and instruct with more efficacy, as he was himself more amply instructed.

There is a vigilance of observation and accuracy of distinction which books and precepts cannot confer; from this almost all original and native excellence proceeds. Shakespeare must have looked upon mankind with perspicacity, in the highest degree curious and attentive. Other writers borrow their characters from preceding writers, and diversify them only by the accidental appendages of present manners; the dress is a little varied, but the body is the same. Our author had both matter and form to provide; for except the characters of Chaucer, to whom I think he is not much indebted, there were no writers in English, and perhaps not many in other modern languages, which showed life in its native colours.

The contest about the original benevolence or malignity of man had not yet commenced. Speculation had not yet attempted to analyse the

mind, to trace the passions to their sources, to unfold the seminal principles of vice and virtue, or sound the depths of the heart for the motives of
action. All those enquiries which from that time that human nature became the fashionable study have been made sometimes with nice discernment, but often with idle subtlety, were yet unattempted. The tales,
with which the infancy of learning was satisfied, exhibited only the superficial appearances of action, related the events but omitted the causes, and
were formed for such as delighted in wonders rather than in truth. Mankind was not then to be studied in the closet; he that would know the
world, was under the necessity of gleaning his own remarks, by mingling
as he could in its business and amusements.

Boyle congratulated himself upon his high birth, because it favoured
his curiosity by facilitating his access. Shakespeare had no such advantage; he came to London a needy adventurer, and lived for a time by very
mean employments. Many works of genius and learning have been performed in states of life that appear very little favourable to thought or to
enquiry; so many, that he who considers them is inclined to think that he
sees enterprise and perseverance predominating over all external agency,
and bidding help and hindrance vanish before them. The genius of
Shakespeare was not to be depressed by the weight of poverty, nor limited
by the narrow conversation to which men in want are inevitably condemned; the encumbrances of his fortune were shaken from his mind, "as
dewdrops from a lion's mane."[3]

Though he had so many difficulties to encounter, and so little assistance to surmount them, he has been able to obtain an exact knowledge
of many modes of life, and many casts of native dispositions; to vary
them with great multiplicity; to mark them by nice distinctions; and to
show them in full view by proper combinations. In this part of his performances he had none to imitate, but has himself been imitated by all succeeding writers; and it may be doubted, whether from all his successors
more maxims of theoretical knowledge, or more rules of practical prudence, can be collected, than he alone has given to his country.

Nor was his attention confined to the actions of men; he was an exact
surveyor of the inanimate world; his descriptions have always some peculiarities, gathered by contemplating things as they really exist. It may be
observed, that the oldest poets of many nations preserve their reputa-

tion, and that the following generations of wit, after a short celebrity, sink into oblivion. The first, whoever they be, must take their sentiments and descriptions immediately from knowledge; the resemblance is therefore just, their descriptions are verified by every eye, and their sentiments acknowledged by every breast. Those whom their fame invites to the same studies, copy partly them, and partly nature, till the books of one age gain such authority as to stand in the place of nature to another, and imitation, always deviating a little, becomes at last capricious and casual. Shakespeare, whether life or nature be his subject, shows plainly that he has seen with his own eyes; he gives the image which he receives, not weakened or distorted by the intervention of any other mind; the ignorant feel his representations to be just, and the learned see that they are complete.

Perhaps it would not be easy to find any author, except Homer, who invented so much as Shakespeare, who so much advanced the studies which he cultivated, or effused so much novelty upon his age or country. The form, the characters, the language, and the shows of the English drama are his. "He seems," says Dennis, "to have been the very original of our English tragical harmony, that is, the harmony of blank verse, diversified often by disyllable and trisyllable terminations. For the diversity distinguishes it from heroic harmony, and by bringing it nearer to common use makes it more proper to gain attention, and more fit for action and dialogue. Such verse we make when we are writing prose; we make such verse in common conversation."

I know not whether this praise is rigorously just. The disyllable termination, which the critic rightly appropriates to the drama, is to be found, though, I think, not in *Gorboduc,* which is confessedly before our author; yet in *Hieronimo* [Thomas Kyd's *Spanish Tragedy*], of which the date is not certain, but which there is reason to believe at least as old as his earliest plays. This however is certain, that he is the first who taught either tragedy or comedy to please, there being no theatrical piece of any older writer, of which the name is known, except to antiquaries and collectors of books, which are sought because they are scarce, and would not have been scarce, had they been much esteemed.

To him we must ascribe the praise, unless Spenser may divide it with him, of having first discovered to how much smoothness and harmony the English language could be softened. He has speeches, perhaps sometimes scenes, which have all the delicacy of Rowe, without his effeminacy. He endeavours indeed commonly to strike by the force and vigour of his dialogue, but he never executes his purpose better than when he tries to sooth by softness.

Yet it must be at last confessed, that as we owe everything to him, he owes something to us; that, if much of his praise is paid by perception and judgment, much is likewise given by custom and veneration. We fix our eyes upon his graces, and turn them from his deformities, and endure in him what we should in another loath or despise. If we endured without praising, respect for the father of our drama might excuse us; but I have seen, in the book of some modern critic, a collection of anomalies which show that he has corrupted language by every mode of depravation, but which his admirer has accumulated as a monument of honour.

He has scenes of undoubted and perpetual excellence, but perhaps not one play which, if it were now exhibited as the work of a contemporary writer, would be heard to the conclusion. I am indeed far from thinking that his works were wrought to his own ideas of perfection; when they were such as would satisfy the audience, they satisfied the writer. It is seldom that authors, though more studious of fame than Shakespeare, rise much above the standard of their own age; to add a little of what is best will always be sufficient for present praise, and those who find themselves exalted into fame, are willing to credit their encomiasts, and to spare the labour of contending with themselves.

It does not appear that Shakespeare thought his works worthy of posterity, that he levied any ideal tribute upon future times, or had any further prospect, than of present popularity and present profit. When his plays had been acted, his hope was at an end; he solicited no addition of honour from the reader. He therefore made no scruple to repeat the same jests in many dialogues, or to entangle different plots by the same knot of perplexity, which may be at least forgiven him, by those who recollect, that of Congreve's four comedies, two are concluded by a marriage in a mask, by a deception, which perhaps never happened, and which, whether likely or not, he did not invent.

So careless was this great poet of future fame that, though he retired to ease and plenty, while he was yet little "declined into the vale of years," before he could be disgusted with fatigue or disabled by infirmity, he made no collection of his works, nor desired to rescue those that had been already published from the depravations that obscured them, or secure to the rest a better destiny by giving them to the world in their genuine state.

Of the plays which bear the name of Shakespeare in the late editions, the greater part were not published till about seven years after his death, and the few which appeared in his life are apparently thrust into the world without the care of the author, and therefore probably without his knowledge.

Of all the publishers, clandestine or professed, their negligence and unskilfulness has by the late revisers [editors] been sufficiently shown. The faults of all are indeed numerous and gross, and have not only corrupted many passages perhaps beyond recovery, but have brought others into suspicion, which are only obscured by obsolete phraseology, or by the writer's unskilfulness and affectation. To alter is more easy than to explain, and temerity is a more common quality than diligence. Those who saw that they must employ conjecture to a certain degree, were willing to indulge it a little further. Had the author published his own works, we should have sat quietly down to disentangle his intricacies, and clear his obscurities; but now we tear what we cannot loose, and eject what we happen not to understand.

The faults are more than could have happened without the concurrence of many causes. The style of Shakespeare was in itself ungrammatical, perplexed, and obscure; his works were transcribed for the players by those who may be supposed to have seldom understood them; they were transmitted by copiers equally unskilful, who still multiplied errors; they were perhaps sometimes mutilated by the actors, for the sake of shortening the speeches; and were at last printed without correction of the press.

In this state they remained, not as Dr. Warburton supposes, because they were unregarded, but because the editor's art was not yet applied to modern languages, and our ancestors were accustomed to so much negligence of English printers, that they could very patiently endure it. At last an edition was undertaken by Rowe; not because a poet was to be published by a poet, for Rowe seems to have thought very little on correction or explanation, but that our author's works might appear like those of his fraternity, with the appendages of a life and recommendatory preface.

Rowe has been clamorously blamed for not performing what he did not undertake, and it is time that justice be done him, by confessing that though he seems to have had no thought of corruption beyond the printer's errors, yet he has made many emendations, if they were not made before, which his successors have received without acknowledgment, and which, if they had produced them, would have filled pages and pages with censures of the stupidity by which the faults were committed, with displays of the absurdities which they involved, with ostentatious exposition of the new reading, and self congratulations on the happiness of discovering it.

As of the other editors, I have preserved the prefaces, I have likewise borrowed the author's life from Rowe, though not written with much elegance or spirit; it relates however what is now to be known, and therefore deserves to pass through all succeeding publications.

The nation had been for many years content enough with Mr. Rowe's performance, when Mr. Pope made them acquainted with the true state of Shakespeare's text, showed that it was extremely corrupt, and gave reason to hope that there were means of reforming it. He collated the old copies, which none had thought to examine before, and restored many lines to their integrity; but, by a very compendious criticism, he rejected whatever he disliked, and thought more of amputation than of cure.

I know not why he is commended by Dr. Warburton for distinguishing the genuine from the spurious plays. In this choice he exerted no judgment of his own; the plays which he received were given by Heminges and Condell, the first editors; and those which he rejected, though, according to the licentiousness of the press in those times, they were printed during Shakespeare's life, with his name, had been omitted by his friends, and were never added to his works before the edition of 1664, from which they were copied by the later printers.

This was a work which Pope seems to have thought unworthy of his abilities, being not able to suppress his contempt of "the dull duty of an editor." He understood but half his undertaking. The duty of a collator is indeed dull, yet, like other tedious tasks, is very necessary; but an emendatory critic would ill discharge his duty, without qualities very different from dullness. In perusing a corrupted piece, he must have before him all possibilities of meaning, with all possibilities of expression. Such must be his comprehension of thought, and such his copiousness of language. Out of many readings possible, he must be able to select that which best suits with the state, opinions, and modes of language prevailing in every age, and with his author's particular cast of thought, and turn of expression. Such must be his knowledge, and such his taste. Conjectural criticism demands more than humanity possesses, and he that exercises it with most praise has very frequent need of indulgence. Let us now be told no more of the dull duty of an editor.

Confidence is the common consequence of success. They whose excellence of any kind has been loudly celebrated are ready to conclude that their powers are universal. Pope's edition fell below his own expectations, and he was so much offended, when he was found to have left any thing for others to do, that he passed the latter part of his life in a state of hostility with verbal criticism.

I have retained all his notes, that no fragment of so great a writer may be lost; his preface, valuable alike for elegance of composition and justness of remark, and containing a general criticism on his author, so extensive that little can be added, and so exact, that little can be disputed, every editor has an interest to suppress, but that every reader would demand its insertion.

Pope was succeeded by [Lewis] Theobald, a man of narrow comprehension and small acquisitions, with no native and intrinsic splendour of genius, with little of the artificial light of learning, but zealous for minute accuracy, and not negligent in pursuing it. He collated the ancient copies, and rectified many errors. A man so anxiously scrupulous might have been expected to do more, but what little he did was commonly right.

In his report of copies and editions he is not to be trusted, without examination. He speaks sometimes indefinitely of copies, when he has only one. In his enumeration of editions, he mentions the two first folios as of high, and the third folio as of middle authority; but the truth is, that the first is equivalent to all others, and that the rest only deviate from it by the printer's negligence. Whoever has any of the folios has all, excepting those diversities which mere reiteration of editions will produce. I collated them all at the beginning, but afterwards used only the first.

Of his notes I have generally retained those which he retained himself in his second edition, except when they were confuted by subsequent annotators, or were too minute to merit preservation. I have sometimes adopted his restoration of a comma, without inserting the panegyric in which he celebrated himself for his achievement. The exuberant excrescence of diction I have often lopped, his triumphant exultations over Pope and Rowe I have sometimes suppressed, and his contemptible ostentation I have frequently concealed; but I have in some places shown him, as he would have shown himself, for the reader's diversion, that the inflated emptiness of some notes may justify or excuse the contraction of the rest.

Theobald, thus weak and ignorant, thus mean and faithless, thus petulant and ostentatious, by the good luck of having Pope for his enemy, has escaped, and escaped alone, with reputation, from this undertaking. So willingly does the world support those who solicit favour, against those who command reverence; and so easily is he praised, whom no man can envy.

Our author fell then into the hands of Sir Thomas Hanmer, the Oxford editor, a man, in my opinion, eminently qualified by nature for such studies. He had what is the first requisite to emendatory criticism, that intuition by which the poet's intention is immediately discovered, and that dexterity of intellect which dispatches its work by the easiest means. He had undoubtedly read much; his acquaintance with customs, opinions, and traditions, seems to have been large; and he is often learned without show. He seldom passes what he does not understand, without an attempt to find or to make a meaning, and sometimes hastily makes what a little more attention would have found. He is solicitous to reduce to grammar what he could not be sure that his author intended to be grammatical. Shakespeare regarded more the series of ideas, than of words; and his language, not being designed for the reader's desk, was all that he desired it to be, if it conveyed his meaning to the audience.

Hanmer's care of the metre has been too violently censured. He found the measures reformed in so many passages, by the silent labours of some editors, with the silent acquiescence of the rest, that he thought himself allowed to extend a little further the license, which had already been carried so far without reprehension; and of his corrections in general, it must be confessed, that they are often just, and made commonly with the least possible violation of the text.

But, by inserting his emendations, whether invented or borrowed, into the page, without any notice of varying copies, he has appropriated the labour of his predecessors, and made his own edition of little authority. His confidence indeed, both in himself and others, was too great; he supposes all to be right that was done by Pope and Theobald; he seems not to suspect a critic of fallibility, and it was but reasonable that he should claim what he so liberally granted.

As he never writes without careful enquiry and diligent consideration, I have received all his notes, and believe that every reader will wish for more.

Of the last editor [William Warburton] it is more difficult to speak. Respect is due to high place, tenderness to living reputation, and veneration to genius and learning; but he cannot be justly offended at that liberty of which he has himself so frequently given an example, nor very solicitous what is thought of notes, which he ought never to have considered as part of his serious employments, and which, I suppose, since the ardour of composition is remitted, he no longer numbers among his happy effusions.

The original and predominant error of his commentary, is acquiescence in his first thoughts; that precipitation which is produced by consciousness of quick discernment; and that confidence which presumes to do, by surveying the surface, what labour only can perform, by penetrating the bottom. His notes exhibit sometimes perverse interpretations, and sometimes improbable conjectures; he at one time gives the author more profundity of meaning than the sentence admits, and at another discovers absurdities, where the sense is plain to every other reader. But his emendations are likewise often happy and just; and his interpretation of obscure passages learned and sagacious.

Of his notes, I have commonly rejected those against which the general voice of the public has exclaimed, or which their own incongruity immediately condemns, and which, I suppose, the author himself would desire to be forgotten. Of the rest, to part I have given the highest approbation, by inserting the offered reading in the text; part I have left to the judgment of the reader, as doubtful, though specious; and part I have censured without reserve, but I am sure without bitterness of malice, and, I hope, without wantonness of insult.

It is no pleasure to me, in revising my volumes, to observe how much paper is wasted in confutation. Whoever considers the revolutions of learning, and the various questions of greater or less importance, upon which wit and reason have exercised their powers, must lament the unsuccessfulness of enquiry, and the slow advances of truth, when he reflects, that great part of the labour of every writer is only the destruction of those that went before him. The first care of the builder of a new system, is to demolish the fabrics which are standing. The chief desire of him that comments an author, is to show how much other commentators have corrupted and obscured him. The opinions prevalent in one age, as truths above the reach of controversy, are confuted and rejected in another, and rise again to reception in remoter times. Thus the human mind is kept in motion without progress. Thus sometimes truth and error, and sometimes contrarieties of error, take each other's place by reciprocal invasion. The tide of seeming knowledge which is poured over one generation, retires and leaves another naked and barren; the sudden meteors of intelligence which for a while appear to shoot their beams into the regions of obscurity, on a sudden withdraw their lustre, and leave mortals again to grope their way.

These elevations and depressions of renown, and the contradictions to which all improvers of knowledge must for ever be exposed, since they are not escaped by the highest and brightest of mankind, may surely be endured with patience by critics and annotators, who can rank themselves but as the satellites of their authors. How canst thou beg for life, says Achilles to his captive, when thou knowest that thou art now to suffer only what must another day be suffered by Achilles?

Dr. Warburton had a name sufficient to confer celebrity on those who could exalt themselves into antagonists, and his notes have raised a clamour too loud to be distinct. His chief assailants are the authors of *The Canons of Criticism* [Thomas Edwards] and of the *Review of Shakespeare's Text* [Benjamin Heath]; of whom one ridicules his errors with airy petulance, suitable enough to the levity of the controversy; the other attacks them with gloomy malignity, as if he were dragging to justice an assassin or incendiary. The one stings like a fly, sucks a little blood, takes a gay flutter, and returns for more; the other bites like a viper, and would be glad to leave inflammations and gangrene behind him. When I think on one, with his confederates, I remember the danger of Coriolanus, who was afraid that "girls with spits, and boys with stones, should slay him in puny battle [IV.iv. 5–6];" when the other crosses my imagination, I remember the prodigy in *Macbeth*,

> *A falcon tow'ring in his pride of place,*
> *Was by a mousing owl hawk'd at and kill'd.*
>
> II.iv. 12–13

Let me however do them justice. One is a wit, and one a scholar. They have both shown acuteness sufficient in the discovery of faults, and have both advanced some probable interpretations of obscure passages; but when they aspire to conjecture and emendation, it appears how falsely we all estimate our own abilities, and the little which they have been able to perform might have taught them more candour to the endeavours of others.

Before Dr. Warburton's edition, *Critical Observations on Shakespeare* had been published by Mr. [John] Upton, a man skilled in languages and acquainted with books, but who seems to have had no great vigour of genius or nicety of taste. Many of his explanations are curious and useful, but he likewise, though he professed to oppose the licentious confidence of editors and adhere to the old copies, is unable to restrain the rage of emendation, though his ardour is ill seconded by his skill. Every cold empiric, when his heart is expanded by a successful experiment, swells into a theorist, and the laborious collator some unlucky moment frolics in conjecture.

Critical, Historical and Explanatory Notes have been likewise published upon Shakespeare by Dr. [Zachary] Grey, whose diligent perusal of the old English writers has enabled him to make some useful observations. What he undertook he has well enough performed, but as he neither attempts judicial nor emendatory criticism, he employs rather his memory than his sagacity. It were to be wished that all would endeavour to imitate his modesty who have not been able to surpass his knowledge.

I can say with great sincerity of all my predecessors, what I hope will hereafter be said of me, that not one has left Shakespeare without improvement, nor is there one to whom I have not been indebted for assistance and information. Whatever I have taken from them it was my intention to refer to its original author, and it is certain, that what I have not given to another, I believed when I wrote it to be my own. In some perhaps I have been anticipated; but if I am ever found to encroach upon the remarks of any other commentator, I am willing that the honour, be it more or less, should be transferred to the first claimant, for his right, and his alone, stands above dispute; the second can prove his pretensions only to himself, nor can himself always distinguish invention, with sufficient certainty, from recollection.

They have all been treated by me with candour, which they have not been careful of observing to one another. It is not easy to discover from what cause the acrimony of a scholiast can naturally proceed. The subjects to be discussed by him are of very small importance; they involve neither property nor liberty; nor favour the interest of sect or party. The various readings of copies, and different interpretations of a passage, seem to be questions that might exercise the wit, without engaging the passions. But, whether it be that "small things make mean men proud," and vanity catches small occasions; or that all contrariety of opinion, even in those that can defend it no longer, makes proud men angry; there is often found in commentaries a spontaneous strain of invective and contempt, more eager and venomous than is vented by the most furious controvertist in politics against those whom he is hired to defame.

Perhaps the lightness of the matter may conduce to the vehemence of the agency; when the truth to be investigated is so near to inexistence as to escape attention, its bulk is to be enlarged by rage and exclamation: that to which all would be indifferent in its original state, may attract notice when the fate of a name is appended to it. A commentator has indeed great temptations to supply by turbulence what he wants of dignity, to beat his little gold to a spacious surface, to work that to foam which no art or diligence can exalt to spirit.

The notes which I have borrowed or written are either illustrative, by which difficulties are explained; or judicial, by which faults and beauties are remarked; or emendatory, by which depravations are corrected.

The explanations transcribed from others, if I do not subjoin any other interpretation, I suppose commonly to be right, at least I intend by acquiescence to confess, that I have nothing better to propose.

After the labours of all the editors, I found many passages which appeared to me likely to obstruct the greater number of readers, and thought it my duty to facilitate their passage. It is impossible for an expositor not to write too little for some, and too much for others. He can only judge what is necessary by his own experience; and how long soever he may deliberate, will at last explain many lines which the learned will think impossible to be mistaken, and omit many for which the ignorant will want his help. These are censures merely relative and must be quietly endured. I have endeavoured to be neither superfluously copious, nor scrupulously reserved, and hope that I have made my author's meaning accessible to many who before were freighted from perusing him, and contributed something to the public, by diffusing innocent and rational pleasure.

The complete explanation of an author not systematic and consequential, but desultory and vagrant, abounding in casual allusions and light hints, is not to be expected from any single scholiast. All personal reflections, when names are suppressed, must be in a few years irrecoverably obliterated; and customs, too minute to attract the notice of law, such as mode of dress, formalities of conversation, rules of visits, disposition of furniture, and practices of ceremony, which naturally find places in familiar dialogue, are so fugitive and unsubstantial that they are not easily retained or recovered. What can be known, will be collected by chance, from the recesses of obscure and obsolete papers, perused commonly with some other view. Of this knowledge every man has some, and none has much; but when an author has engaged the public attention, those who can add anything to his illustration, communicate their discoveries, and time produces what had eluded diligence.

To time I have been obliged to resign many passages, which, though I did not understand them, will perhaps hereafter be explained, having, I hope, illustrated some, which others have neglected or mistaken, sometimes by short remarks or marginal directions, such as every editor has added at his will, and often by comments more laborious than the matter will seem to deserve; but that which is most difficult is not always most important, and to an editor nothing is a trifle by which his author is obscured.

The poetical beauties or defects I have not been very diligent to observe. Some plays have more, and some fewer judicial observations, not in proportion to their difference of merit, but because I gave this part of my design to chance and to caprice. The reader, I believe, is seldom pleased to find his opinion anticipated; it is natural to delight more in what we find or make, than in what we receive. Judgment, like other faculties, is improved by practice, and its advancement is hindered by submission to dictatorial decisions, as the memory grows torpid by the use of a table book. Some initiation is however necessary; of all skill, part is infused by precept, and part is obtained by habit; I have therefore shown so much as may enable the candidate of criticism to discover the rest.

To the end of most plays, I have added short strictures, containing a general censure of faults, or praise of excellence; in which I know not how much I have concurred with the current opinion; but I have not, by any affectation of singularity, deviated from it. Nothing is minutely and particularly examined, and therefore it is to be supposed, that in the plays which are condemned there is much to be praised, and in these which are praised much to be condemned.

The part of criticism in which the whole succession of editors has laboured with the greatest diligence, which has occasioned the most arrogant ostentation, and excited the keenest acrimony, is the emendation of corrupted passages, to which the public attention having been first drawn by the violence of contention between Pope and Theobald, has been continued by the persecution which, with a kind of conspiracy, has been since raised against all the publishers of Shakespeare.

That many passages have passed in a state of depravation through all the editions is indubitably certain; of these the restoration is only to be attempted by collation of copies or sagacity of conjecture. The collator's province is safe and easy, the conjecturer's perilous and difficult. Yet as the greater part of the plays are extant only in one copy, the peril must not be avoided, nor the difficulty refused.

Of the readings which this emulation of amendment has hitherto produced, some from the labours of every publisher have advanced into the text; those are to be considered as in my opinion sufficiently supported; some I have rejected without mention, as evidently erroneous; some I have left in the notes without censure or approbation, as resting in equipoise between objection and defence; and some, which seemed specious but not right, I have inserted with a subsequent animadversion.

Having classed the observations of others, I was at last to try what I could substitute for their mistakes, and how I could supply their omissions. I collated such copies as I could procure, and wished for more, but have not found the collectors of these rarities very communicative.[4] Of the editions which chance or kindness put into my hands I have given an enumeration, that I may not be blamed for neglecting what I had not the power to do.

By examining the old copies, I soon found that the late publishers, with all their boasts of diligence, suffered many passages to stand unauthorised, and contented themselves with Rowe's regulation of the text, even where they knew it to be arbitrary, and with a little consideration might have found it to be wrong. Some of these alterations are only the ejection of a word for one that appeared to him more elegant or more intelligible. These corruptions I have often silently rectified; for the history of our language, and the true force of our words, can only be preserved by keeping the text of authors free from adulteration. Others, and those very frequent, smoothed the cadence, or regulated the measure; on these I have not exercised the same rigour; if only a word was transposed, or a particle inserted or omitted, I have sometimes suffered the line to stand; for the inconstancy of the copies is such, as that some liberties may be easily permitted. But this practice I have not suffered to proceed far, having restored the primitive diction wherever it could for any reason be preferred.

The emendations, which comparison of copies supplied, I have inserted in the text; sometimes where the improvement was slight, without notice, and sometimes with an account of the reasons of the change.

Conjecture, though it be sometimes unavoidable, I have not wantonly nor licentiously indulged. It has been my settled principle, that the reading of the ancient books is probably true, and therefore is not to be disturbed for the sake of elegance, perspicuity, or mere improvement of the sense. For though much credit is not due to the fidelity, nor any to the judgment of the first publishers, yet they who had the copy before their eyes were more likely to read it right than we who read it only by imagination. But it is evident that they have often made strange mistakes by ignorance or negligence, and that therefore something may be properly attempted by criticism, keeping the middle way between presumption and timidity.

Such criticism I have attempted to practise, and where any passage appeared inextricably perplexed, have endeavoured to discover how it may be recalled to sense with least violence. But my first labour is, always to turn the old text on every side, and try if there be any interstice, through which light can find its way; nor would Huetius[5] himself condemn me, as refusing the trouble of research, for the ambition of alteration. In this modest industry I have not been unsuccessful. I have rescued many lines from the violations of temerity, and secured many scenes from the inroads of correction. I have adopted the Roman sentiment, that it is more honourable to save a citizen, than to kill an enemy, and have been more careful to protect than to attack.

I have preserved the common distribution of the plays into acts, though I believe it to be in almost all the plays void of authority. Some of those which are divided in the later editions have no division in the first folio, and some that are divided in the folio have no division in the preceding copies. The settled mode of the theatre requires four intervals in the play, but few, if any, of our author's compositions can be properly distributed in that manner. An act is so much of the drama as passes without intervention of time or change of place. A pause makes a new act. In every real, and therefore in every imitative action, the intervals may be more or fewer, the restriction of five acts being accidental and arbitrary. This Shakespeare knew, and this he practised; his plays were written, and at first printed in one unbroken continuity, and ought now to be exhibited with short pauses, interposed as often as the scene is changed, or any considerable time is required to pass. This method would at once quell a thousand absurdities.

In restoring the author's works to their integrity, I have considered the punctuation as wholly in my power; for what could be their care of colons and commas, who corrupted words and sentences. Whatever could be done by adjusting points is therefore silently performed, in some plays with much diligence, in others with less; it is hard to keep a busy eye steadily fixed upon evanescent atoms, or a discursive mind upon evanescent truth.

The same liberty has been taken with a few particles, or other words of slight effect. I have sometimes inserted or omitted them without notice. I have done that sometimes, which the other editors have done always, and which indeed the state of the text may sufficiently justify.

The greater part of readers, instead of blaming us for passing trifles, will wonder that on mere trifles so much labour is expended, with such importance of debate, and such solemnity of diction. To these I answer with confidence, that they are judging of an art which they do not understand; yet cannot much reproach them with their ignorance, nor promise that they would become in general, by learning criticism, more useful, happier, or wiser.

As I practised conjecture more, I learned to trust it less; and after I had printed a few plays, resolved to insert none of my own readings in the text. Upon this caution I now congratulate myself, for every day increases my doubt of my emendations.

Since I have confined my imagination to the margin, it must not be considered as very reprehensible, if I have suffered it to play some freaks in its own dominion. There is no danger in conjecture, if it be proposed as conjecture; and while the text remains uninjured, those changes may be safely offered, which are not considered even by him that offers them as necessary or safe.

If my readings are of little value, they have not been ostentatiously displayed or importunately obtruded. I could have written longer notes, for the art of writing notes is not of difficult attainment. The work is performed, first by railing at the stupidity, negligence, ignorance, and asinine tastelessness of the former editors, and showing, from all that goes before and all that follows, the inelegance and absurdity of the old reading; then by proposing something, which to superficial readers would seem specious, but which the editor rejects with indignation; then by producing the true reading, with a long paraphrase, and concluding with loud acclamations on the discovery, and a sober wish for the advancement and prosperity of genuine criticism.

All this may be done, and perhaps done sometimes without impropriety. But I have always suspected that the reading is right, which requires many words to prove it wrong; and the emendation wrong, that cannot without so much labour appear to be right. The justness of a happy restoration strikes at once, and the moral precept may be well applied to criticism, "quod dubitas ne feceris."

To dread the shore which he sees spread with wrecks, is natural to the sailor. I had before my eye, so many critical adventures ended in miscarriage, that caution was forced upon me. I encountered in every page wit struggling with its own sophistry, and learning confused by the multiplicity of its views. I was forced to censure those whom I admired, and could not but reflect, while I was dispossessing their emendations, how soon the same fate might happen to my own, and how many of the readings which I have corrected may be by some other editor defended and established.

> *Criticks I saw, that other's names efface,*
> *And fix their own, with labour, in the place;*
> *Their own, like others, soon their place resign'd,*
> *Or disappear'd, and left the first behind.*
> Pope, *Temple of Fame,* ll. 37–40

That a conjectural critic should often be mistaken, cannot be wonderful, either to others or himself, if it be considered that in his art there is no system, no principal and axiomatical truth that regulates subordinate positions. His chance of error is renewed at every attempt; an oblique view of the passage, a slight misapprehension of a phrase, a casual inattention to the parts connected, is sufficient to make him not only fail but fail ridiculously; and when he succeeds best, he produces perhaps but one reading of many probable, and he that suggests another will always be able to dispute his claims.

It is an unhappy state, in which danger is hid under pleasure. The allurements of emendation are scarcely resistible. Conjecture has all the joy and all the pride of invention, and he that has once started a happy change, is too much delighted to consider what objections may rise against it.

Yet conjectural criticism has been of great use in the learned world; nor is it my intention to depreciate a study that has exercised so many mighty minds, from the revival of learning to our own age, from the Bishop of Aleria to English Bentley.[6] The critics on ancient authors have, in the exercise of their sagacity, many assistances, which the editor of Shakespeare is condemned to want. They are employed upon grammatical and settled languages, whose construction contributes so much to perspicuity, that Homer has fewer passages unintelligible than Chaucer. The words have not only a known regimen, but invariable quantities, which direct and confine the choice. There are commonly more manuscripts than one; and they do not often conspire in the same mistakes. Yet Scaliger could confess to Salmasius how little satisfaction his emendations gave him. *Illudunt nobis conjecturae nostrae, quarum nos pudet, posteaquam in meliores codices incidimus.*[7] And Lipsius could complain that critics were making faults, by trying to remove them, *Ut olim vitiis, ita nunc remediis laboratur.* And indeed, where mere conjecture is to be used, the emendations of Scaliger and Lipsius, notwithstanding their wonderful sagacity and erudition, are often vague and disputable, like mine or Theobald's.

Perhaps I may not be more censured for doing wrong, than for doing little; for raising in the public expectations, which at last I have not answered. The expectation of ignorance is indefinite, and that of knowledge is often tyrannical. It is hard to satisfy those who know not what to demand, or those who demand by design what they think impossible to be done. I have indeed disappointed no opinion more than my own; yet I have endeavoured to perform my task with no slight solicitude. Not a single passage in the whole work has appeared to me corrupt, which I have not attempted to restore; or obscure, which I have not endeavoured to illustrate. In many I have failed like others; and from many, after all my efforts, I have retreated, and confessed the repulse. I have not passed over, with affected superiority, what is equally difficult to the reader and to myself, but where I could not instruct him, have owned my ignorance. I might easily have accumulated a mass of seeming learning upon easy scenes; but it ought not to be imputed to negligence that, where nothing was necessary, nothing has been done, or that, where others have said enough, I have said no more.

Notes are often necessary, but they are necessary evils. Let him, that is yet unacquainted with the powers of Shakespeare, and who desires to feel the highest pleasure that the drama can give, read every play from the first scene to the last, with utter negligence of all his commentators. When his fancy is once on the wing, let it not stoop at correction or explanation. When his attention is strongly engaged, let it disdain alike to turn aside to the name of Theobald and Pope. Let him read on through brightness and obscurity, through integrity and corruption; let him preserve his comprehension of the dialogue and his interest in the fable. And when the pleasures of novelty have ceased, let him attempt exactness; and read the commentators.

Particular passages are cleared by notes, but the general effect of the work is weakened. The mind is refrigerated by interruption; the thoughts are diverted from the principal subject; the reader is weary, he suspects not why; and at last throws away the book, which he has too diligently studied.

Parts are not to be examined till the whole has been surveyed; there is a kind of intellectual remoteness necessary for the comprehension of any great work in its full design and its true proportions; a close approach shows the smaller niceties, but the beauty of the whole is discerned no longer.

It is not very grateful to consider how little the succession of editors has added to this author's power of pleasing. He was read, admired, studied, and imitated, while he was yet deformed with all the improprieties which ignorance and neglect could accumulate upon him; while the reading was yet not rectified, nor his allusions understood; yet then did Dryden pronounce "that Shakespeare was the man, who, of all modern and perhaps ancient poets, had the largest and most comprehensive soul. All the images of nature were still present to him, and he drew them not laboriously, but luckily: When he describes any thing, you more than see it, you feel it too. Those who accuse him to have wanted learning, give him the greater commendation: he was naturally learned: he needed not the spectacles of books to read nature; he looked inwards, and found her there. I cannot say he is every where alike; were he so, I should do him injury to compare him with the greatest of mankind. He is many times flat and insipid; his comic wit degenerating into clenches, his serious swelling into bombast. But he is always great, when some great occasion is presented to him: No man can say, he ever had a fit subject for his wit, and did not then raise himself as high above the rest of poets, 'Quantum lenta solent inter viburna cupressi.'"[8]

It is to be lamented that such a writer should want a commentary; that his language should become obsolete, or his sentiments obscure. But it is vain to carry wishes beyond the condition of human things; that which must happen to all, has happened to Shakespeare, by accident and time; and more than has been suffered by any other writer since the use of types, has been suffered by him through his own negligence of fame, or perhaps by that superiority of mind, which despised its own performances, when it compared them with its powers, and judged those works unworthy to be preserved, which the critics of following ages were to contend for the fame of restoring and explaining.

Among these candidates of inferior fame, I am now to stand the judgment of the public; and wish that I could confidently produce my commentary as equal to the encouragement which I have had the honour of receiving. Every work of this kind is by its nature deficient, and I should feel little solicitude about the sentence, were it to be pronounced only by the skilful and the learned.

PART V

Excerpts from *Lives of the Poets*

Cowley

Cowley, like other poets who have written with narrow views, and, instead of tracing intellectual pleasure to its natural sources in the minds of men, paid their court to temporary prejudices, has been at one time too much praised, and too much neglected at another.

Wit, like all other things subject by their nature to the choice of man, has its changes and fashions, and at different times takes different forms. About the beginning of the seventeenth century appeared a race of writers that may be termed the metaphysical poets; of whom, in a criticism on the works of Cowley, it is not improper to give some account.

The metaphysical poets were men of learning, and to show their learning was their whole endeavour; but, unluckily resolving to show it in rhyme, instead of writing poetry they only wrote verses, and very often such verses as stood the trial of the finger better than of the ear; for the modulation was so imperfect, that they were only found to be verses by counting the syllables.

If the father of criticism[1] had rightly denominated poetry . . . *an imitative art,* these writers will, without great wrong, lose their right to the name of poets; for they cannot be said to have imitated anything; they neither copied nature nor life, neither painted the forms of matter, nor represented the operations of intellect.

Those however who deny them to be poets allow them to be wits. Dryden confesses of himself and his contemporaries that they fall below Donne in wit, but maintains that they surpass him in poetry.[2]

If wit be well described by Pope, as being "that which has been often thought, but was never before so well expressed,"[3] they certainly never attained, nor ever sought it; for they endeavoured to be singular in their thoughts and were careless of their diction. But Pope's account of wit is undoubtedly erroneous; he depresses it below its natural dignity and reduces it from strength of thought to happiness of language.

If by a more noble and more adequate conception that be considered as wit which is at once natural and new, that which, though not obvious, is upon its first production acknowledged to be just; if it be that which he that never found it, wonders how he missed; to wit of this kind the metaphysical poets have seldom risen. Their thoughts are often new but seldom natural; they are not obvious, but neither are they just; and the reader, far from wondering that he missed them, wonders more frequently by what perverseness of industry they were ever found.

But wit, abstracted from its effects upon the hearer, may be more rigorously and philosophically considered as a kind of *discordia concors;*[4] a combination of dissimilar images or discovery of occult resemblances in things apparently unlike. Of wit thus defined they have more than enough. The most heterogeneous ideas are yoked by violence together; nature and art are ransacked for illustrations, comparisons, and allusions; their learning instructs and their subtlety surprises; but the reader commonly thinks his improvement dearly bought, and though he sometimes admires, is seldom pleased.

From this account of their compositions it will be readily inferred that they were not successful in representing or moving the affections. As they were wholly employed on something unexpected and surprising, they had no regard to that uniformity of sentiment which enables us to conceive and to excite the pains and the pleasure of other minds: they never inquired what, on any occasion, they should have said or done; but wrote rather as beholders than partakers of human nature; as beings looking upon good and evil, impassive and at leisure, as Epicurean deities making remarks on the actions of men and the vicissitudes of life without interest and without emotion. Their courtship was void of fondness, and their lamentation of sorrow. Their wish was only to say what they hoped had been never said before.

Nor was the sublime more within their reach than the pathetic, for they never attempted that comprehension and expanse of thought which at once fills the whole mind, and of which the first effect is sudden astonishment and the second rational admiration. Sublimity is produced by aggregation, and littleness by dispersion. Great thoughts are always general and consist in positions not limited by exceptions, and in descriptions not descending to minuteness. It is with great propriety that subtlety, which in its original import means exility of particles, is taken in its metaphorical meaning for nicety of distinction. Those writers who lay on the watch for novelty could have little hope of greatness; for great things cannot have escaped former observation. Their attempts were always analytic; they broke every image into fragments and could no more represent, by their slender conceits and laboured particularities, the prospects of nature, or the scenes of life, than he who dissects a sunbeam with a prism can exhibit the wide effulgence of a summer noon.

What they wanted however of the sublime they endeavoured to supply by hyperbole; their amplifications had no limits; they left not only reason but fancy behind them and produced combinations of confused magnificence, that not only could not be credited but could not be imagined.

Yet great labour, directed by great abilities, is never wholly lost; if they frequently threw away their wit upon false conceits, they likewise sometimes struck out unexpected truth; if their conceits were far fetched, they were often worth the carriage. To write on their plan, it was at least necessary to read and think. No man could be born a metaphysical poet, nor assume the dignity of a writer, by descriptions copied from descriptions, by imitations borrowed from imitations, by traditional imagery and hereditary similes, by readiness of rhyme, and volubility of syllables.

In perusing the works of this race of authors, the mind is exercised either by recollection or inquiry; either something already learned is to be retrieved, or something new is to be examined. If their greatness seldom elevates, their acuteness often surprises; if the imagination is not always gratified, at least the powers of reflection and comparison are employed; and in the mass of materials which ingenious absurdity has thrown together, genuine wit and useful knowledge may be sometimes found buried perhaps in grossness of expression, but useful to those who know their value; and such as, when they are expanded to perspicuity and polished to elegance, may give lustre to works which have more propriety though less copiousness of sentiment.

This kind of writing, which was, I believe, borrowed from Marino and his followers, had been recommended by the example of Donne, a man of very extensive and various knowledge, and by Jonson, whose manner resembled that of Donne more in the ruggedness of his lines than in the cast of his sentiments.

When their reputation was high they had undoubtedly more imitators than time has left behind. Their immediate successors, of whom any remembrance can be said to remain, were Suckling, Waller, Denham, Cowley, Cleveland, and Milton. Denham and Waller sought another way to fame, by improving the harmony of our numbers. Milton tried the metaphysic style only in his lines upon Hobson the carrier. Cowley adopted it, and excelled his predecessors, having as much sentiment and more music. Suckling neither improved versification nor abounded in conceits. The fashionable style remained chiefly with Cowley: Suckling could not reach it, and Milton disdained it.

Critical remarks are not easily understood without examples, and I have therefore collected instances of the modes of writing by which this species of poets (for poets they were called by themselves and their admirers) was eminently distinguished.

As the authors of this race were perhaps more desirous of being admired than understood, they sometimes drew their conceits from recesses of learning not very much frequented by common readers of poetry. Thus Cowley on *Knowledge:*

> *The sacred tree midst the fair orchard grew;*
> *The phoenix Truth did on it rest,*
> *And built his perfum'd nest,*
> *That right Porphyrian tree which did true logick shew.*
> *Each leaf did learned notions give,*
> *And th' apples were demonstrative:*
> *So clear their colour and divine,*
> *The very shade they cast did other lights outshine.*

On Anacreon continuing a lover in his old age:

Love was with thy life entwin'd,
Close as heat with fire is join'd;
A powerful brand prescrib'd the date
Of thine, like Meleager's fate.
Th' antiperistasis of age
More enflam'd thy amorous rage.

In the following verses we have an allusion to a Rabbinical opinion concerning manna:

Variety I ask not: give me one
To live perpetually upon.
The person Love does to us fit,
Like manna, has the taste of all in it.

Thus Donne shows his medicinal knowledge in some encomiastic verses:

In every thing there naturally grows
A balsamum to keep it fresh and new,
    If 'twere not injur'd by extrinsique blows:
Your youth and beauty are this balm in you.
    But you, of learning and religion,
And virtue and such ingredients, have made
    A mithridate, whose operation
Keeps off or cures what can be done or said.

[...]

Of thoughts so far-fetched as to be not only unexpected but unnatural, all their books are full.

To a lady, who wrote posies for rings:

They, who above do various circles find,
Say, like a ring, th' equator heaven does bind

When heaven shall be adorn'd by thee,
(Which then more heaven than 'tis, will be)
'Tis thou must write the poesy there,
For it wanteth one as yet,
Then the sun pass through't twice a year,
The sun, which is esteem'd the god of wit.

COWLEY.

The tears of lovers are always of great poetical account, but Donne has extended them into worlds. If the lines are not easily understood, they may be read again:

On a round ball
A workman, that hath copies by, can lay
An Europe, Afric, and an Asia,
And quickly make that, which was nothing, all.
  So doth each tear,
  Which thee doth wear,
A globe, yea world, by that impression grow,
Till thy tears mixt with mine do overflow
This world, by waters sent from thee my heaven dissolved so.

On reading the following lines, the reader may perhaps cry out "Confusion worse confounded."

Here lies a she sun, and a he moon here,
  She gives the best light to his sphere,
  Or each is both, and all, and so,
They unto one another nothing owe.

DONNE.

Who but Donne would have thought that a good man is a telescope?

Though God be our true glass, through which we see
All, since the being of all things is he,
Yet are the trunks, which do to us derive

Things in proportion fit, by perspective,
Deeds of good men; for by their living here,
Virtues, indeed remote, seem to be near.

[. . .]

Of enormous and disgusting hyperboles these may be examples:

By every wind, that comes this way,
Send me at least a sigh or two,
Such and so many I'll repay
As shall themselves make winds to get to you.

COWLEY.

In tears I'll waste these eyes,
By Love so vainly fed:
So lust of old the Deluge punished.

COWLEY.

All arm'd in brass, the richest dress of war
(A dismal glorious sight!) he shone afar.
The sun himself started with sudden fright,
To see his beams return so dismal bright.

COWLEY.

[. . .]

Their fictions were often violent and unnatural.
Of his mistress bathing:

The fish around her crowded, as they do
To the false light that treacherous fishers show,
And all with as much ease might taken be,
   As she at first took me:
   For ne'er did light so clear
   Among the waves appear,
Though every night the sun himself set there.

COWLEY.

The poetical effect of a lover's name upon glass:

> *My name engrav'd herein*
> *Doth contribute my firmness to this glass;*
>   *Which, ever since that charm, hath been*
> *As hard as that which grav'd it was.*

DONNE.

Their conceits were sometimes slight and trifling.
On an inconstant woman:

> *He enjoys thy calmy sunshine now,*
>   *And no breath stirring hears;*
> *In the clear heaven of thy brow,*
>   *No smallest cloud appears.*
> *He sees thee gentle, fair and gay,*
> *And trusts the faithless April of thy May.*

COWLEY.

Upon a paper written with the juice of lemon, and read by the fire:

> *Nothing yet in thee is seen;*
>   *But when a genial heat warms thee within,*
> *A new-born wood of various lines there grows;*
>   *Hers buds an L, and there a B,*
>   *Here sprouts a V, and there a T,*
> *And all the flourishing letters stand in rows.*

COWLEY.

As they sought only for novelty, they did not much inquire whether their allusions were to things high or low, elegant or gross; whether they compared the little to the great, or the great to the little.

Physic and chirurgery[5] for a lover:

> *Gently, ah gently, madam, touch*
>   *The wound, which you yourself have made;*

That pain must needs be very much
Which makes me of your hand afraid.
Cordials of pity give me now,
For I too weak of purgings grow.

COWLEY.

The world and a clock:

Mahol th' inferior world's fantastic face
Through all the turns of matter's maze did trace;
Great Nature's well-set clock in pieces took;
On all the springs and smallest wheels did look
Of life and motion; and with equal art
Made up again the whole of every part.

COWLEY.

A coal-pit has not often found its poet; but, that it may not want its due honour, Cleveland has paralleled it with the sun:

The moderate value of our guiltless ore
Makes no man atheist, and no woman whore;
Yet why should hallow'd vestal's sacred shrine
Deserve more honour than a flaming mine?
These pregnant wombs of heat would fitter be
Than a few embers, for a deity.
    Had he our pits, the Persian would admire
No sun, but warm's devotion at our fire:
He'd leave the trotting whipster, and prefer
Our profound Vulcan 'bove that waggoner.
For wants he heat, or light? or would have store
Of both? 'tis here: and what can suns give more?
Nay, what's the sun but, in a different name,
A coal-pit rampant, or a mine on flame!
Then let this truth reciprocally run,
The sun's heaven's coalery, and coals our sun.

[. . .]

Their thoughts and expressions were sometimes grossly absurd, and such as no figures or licence can reconcile to the understanding.

A lover neither dead nor alive:

> *Then down I laid my head,*
> *Down on cold earth; and for a while was dead,*
> *And my freed soul to a strange somewhere fled:*
>   *Ah, sottish soul, said I,*
>   *When back to its cage again I saw it fly;*
>   *Fool to resume her broken chain,*
>   *And row her galley here again!*
>   *Fool, to that body to return*
> *Where it condemn'd and destin'd is to burn!*
>   *Once dead, how can it be,*
> *Death should a thing so pleasant seem to thee,*
> *That thou should'st come to live it o'er again in me?*
>
>   COWLEY.

[...]

They were sometimes indelicate and disgusting. Cowley thus apostrophises beauty:

> *Thou tyrant which leav'st no man free!*
> *Thou subtle thief, from whom nought safe can be!*
> *Thou murtherer, which has kill'd, and devil, which would'st damn*
>   *me!*

[...]

Thus he represents the meditations of a lover:

> *Though in thy thoughts scarce any tracts have been*
>   *So much as of original sin,*
> *Such charms thy beauty wears as might*
> *Desires in dying confest saints excite.*
>   *Thou with strange adultery*
> *Dost in each breast a brothel keep;*

Awake all men do lust for thee,
And some enjoy thee when they sleep.

The true taste of tears:

Hither with crystal vials, lovers, come,
And take my tears, which are Love's wine,
And try your mistress' tears at home;
For all are false that taste not just like mine.

DONNE.

This is yet more indelicate:

As the sweet sweat of roses in a still,
As that which from chaf'd musk-cat's pores doth trill,
As the almighty balm of th' early East,
Such are the sweat-drops of my mistress' breast.
And on her neck her skin such lustre sets,
They seem no sweat drops, but pearl coronets:
Rank sweaty froth thy mistress' brow defiles.

DONNE.

Their expressions sometimes raise horror, when they intend perhaps to be pathetic:

As men in hell are from diseases free,
So from all other ills am I,
Free from their known formality:
But all pains eminently lie in thee.

COWLEY.

They were not always strictly curious, whether the opinions from which they drew their illustrations were true; it was enough that they were popular. Bacon remarks that some falsehoods are continued by tradition because they supply commodious allusions.

It gave a piteous groan, and so it broke;
In vain it something would have spoke:
The love within too strong for 't was,
Like poison put into a Venice-glass.

COWLEY.

[. . .]

It must be however confessed of these writers that if they are upon common subjects often unnecessarily and unpoetically subtle, yet where scholastic speculation can be properly admitted, their copiousness and acuteness may justly be admired. What Cowley has written upon hope shows an unequalled fertility of invention:

Hope, whose weak being ruin'd is,
    Alike if it succeed and if it miss;
Whom good or ill does equally confound,
And both the horns of Fate's dilemma wound;
    Vain shadow, which dost vanish quite,
    Both at full noon and perfect night!
The stars have not a possibility
    Of blessing thee;
If things then from their end we happy call,
'Tis Hope is the most hopeless thing of all.
    Hope, thou bold tester of delight,
Who, whilst thou should'st but taste, devour'st it quite!
Thou bring'st us an estate, yet leav'st us poor,
By clogging it with legacies before!
    The joys, which we entire should wed,
    Come deflowr'd virgins to our bed;
Good fortunes without gain imported be,
    Such mighty custom's paid to thee:
For joy, like wine, kept close, does better taste
If it take air before its spirits waste.

To the following comparison of a man that travels and his wife that stays at home, with a pair of compasses, it may be doubted whether absurdity or ingenuity has the better claim:

Our two souls, therefore, which are one,
  Though I must go, endure not yet
A breach, but an expansion,
  Like gold to airy thinness beat.

If they be two, they are two so
  As stiff twin-compasses are two:
Thy soul, the fixt foot, makes no show
  To move, but doth, if th' other do.

And, though it in the centre sit,
  Yet when the other far doth roam,
It leans, and hearkens after it,
  And grows erect, as that comes home.

Such wilt thou be to me, who must
  Like th' other foot obliquely run;
Thy firmness makes my circle just,
  And makes me end where I begun.

                                        DONNE.

    In all these examples it is apparent that whatever is improper or vicious is produced by a voluntary deviation from nature in pursuit of something new and strange; and that the writers fail to give delight by their desire of exciting admiration.

    Having thus endeavoured to exhibit a general representation of the style and sentiments of the metaphysical poets, it is now proper to examine particularly the works of Cowley, who was almost the last of that race and undoubtedly the best. . . .

    In his poem on the death of Hervey, there is much praise, but little passion; a very just and ample delineation of such virtues as a studious privacy admits, and such intellectual excellence as a mind not yet called forth to action can display. He knew how to distinguish, and how to commend, the qualities of his companion; but, when he wishes to make us weep, he forgets to weep himself, and diverts his sorrow by imagining how his crown of bays, if he had it, would *crackle* in the *fire*. It is the odd fate of this thought to be the worse for being true. The bay-leaf crackles remarkably as it burns; as therefore this property was not assigned it by chance, the mind must be thought sufficiently at ease that could attend to such minuteness of physiology. But the power of Cowley is not so much to move the affections, as to exercise the understanding.

[...]

The next class of his poems is called *The Mistress*, of which it is not necessary to select any particular pieces for praise or censure. They have all the same beauties and faults, and nearly in the same proportion. They are written with exuberance of wit, and with copiousness of learning; and it is truly asserted by Sprat, that the plenitude of the writer's knowledge flows in upon his page, so that the reader is commonly surprised into some improvement. But, considered as the verses of a lover, no man that has ever loved will much commend them. They are neither courtly nor pathetic, have neither gallantry nor fondness. His praises are too far sought, and too hyperbolical, either to express love or to excite it; every stanza is crowded with darts and flames, with wounds and death, with mingled souls and with broken hearts.

... Love is by Cowley, as by other poets, expressed metaphorically by flame and fire; and that which is true of real fire is said of love, or figurative fire, the same word in the same sentence retaining both significations. Thus "observing the cold regard of his mistress's eyes, and at the same time their power of producing love in him, he considers them as burning-glasses made of ice. Finding himself able to live in the greatest extremities of love, he concludes the torrid zone to be habitable. Upon the dying of a tree, on which he had cut his loves, he observes that his flames had burnt up and withered the tree."

These conceits Addison calls mixed wit; that is, wit which consists of thoughts true in one sense of the expression, and false in the other. Addison's representation is sufficiently indulgent: that confusion of images may entertain for a moment; but being unnatural it soon grows wearisome. Cowley delighted in it, as much as if he had invented it; but, not to mention the ancients, he might have found it full-blown in modern Italy. ...

One of the severe theologians of that time censured him as having published "a book of profane and lascivious verses." From the charge of profaneness, the constant tenor of his life, which seems to have been eminently virtuous, and the general tendency of his opinions, which discover no irreverence of religion, must defend him; but that the accusation of lasciviousness is unjust, the perusal of his works will sufficiently evince.

Cowley's *Mistress* has no power of seduction: she "plays round the head, but comes not at the heart." Her beauty and absence, her kindness and cruelty, her disdain and inconstancy, produce no correspondence of emotion. His poetical accounts of the virtues of plants and colours of flowers, is not perused with more sluggish frigidity. The compositions are such as might have been written for penance by a hermit, or for hire by a philosophical rhymer who had only heard of another sex; for they turn the mind only on the writer, whom, without thinking on a woman but as the subject for his task, we sometimes esteem as learned and sometimes despise as trifling, always admire as ingenious, and always condemn as unnatural. . . .

The fault of Cowley, and perhaps of all the writers of the metaphysical race, is that of pursuing his thoughts to their last ramifications, by which he loses the grandeur of generality, for of the greatest things the parts are little; what is little can be but pretty, and by claiming dignity becomes ridiculous. Thus all the power of description is destroyed by a scrupulous enumeration; and the force of metaphors is lost when the mind by the mention of particulars is turned more upon the original than the secondary sense, more upon that from which the illustration is drawn than that to which it is applied.

Of this we have a very eminent example in the ode entitled *The Muse,* who goes to "take the air" in an intellectual chariot, to which he harnesses Fancy and Judgment, Wit and Eloquence, Memory and Invention: how he distinguished Wit from Fancy, or how Memory could properly contribute to Motion, he has not explained; we are however content to suppose that he could have justified his own fiction, and wish to see the Muse begin her career; but there is yet more to be done.

> *Let the* postilion *Nature mount, and let*
> *The* coachman *Art be set;*
> *And let the airy* footmen, *running all beside,*
> *Make a long row of goodly pride;*
> *Figures, conceits, raptures, and sentences,*

In a well-worded dress,
And innocent loves, and pleasant truths, and useful lies,
In all their gaudy liveries.

Every mind is now disgusted with this cumber of magnificence; yet I cannot refuse myself the four next lines:

Mount, glorious queen, thy travelling throne,
And bid it to put on;
For long though cheerful is the way,
And life alas! allows but one ill winter's day.

In the same ode, celebrating the power of the Muse, he gives her prescience or, in poetical language, the foresight of events hatching in futurity; but having once an egg in his mind, he cannot forbear to show us that he knows what an egg contains:

Thou into the close nests of Time dost peep,
And there with piercing eye
Through the firm shell and the thick white dost spy
Years to come a-forming lie,
Close in their sacred fecundine asleep.

[...]

If the Pindaric style be what Cowley thinks it, "the highest and noblest kind of writing in verse," it can be adapted only to high and noble subjects; and it will not be easy to reconcile the poet with the critic, or to conceive how that can be the highest kind of writing in verse which, according to Sprat, "is chiefly to be preferred for its near affinity to prose."

This lax and lawless versification so much concealed the deficiencies of the barren, and flattered the laziness of the idle, that it immediately overspread our books of poetry; all the boys and girls caught the pleasing fashion, and they that could do nothing else could write like Pindar. The rights of antiquity were invaded, and disorder tried to break into the Latin: a poem on the Sheldonian Theatre, in which all kinds of verse are shaken together, is unhappily inserted in the *Musae Anglicanae.* Pindarism prevailed about half a century, but at last died gradually away, and other imitations supply its place.

The *Pindarique Odes* have so long enjoyed the highest degree of poetical reputation that I am not willing to dismiss them with unabated censure; and surely though the mode of their composition be erroneous, yet many parts deserve at least that admiration which is due to great comprehension of knowledge, and great fertility of fancy. The thoughts are often new, and often striking; but the greatness of one part is disgraced by the littleness of another; and total negligence of language gives the noblest conceptions the appearance of a fabric august in the plan, but mean in the materials. Yet surely those verses are not without a just claim to praise of which it may be said with truth that no man but Cowley could have written them.

The *Davideis* now remains to be considered; a poem which the author designed to have extended to twelve books, merely, as he makes no scruple of declaring, because the *AEneid* had that number; but he had leisure or perseverance only to write the third part. Epic poems have been left unfinished by Virgil, Statius, Spenser, and Cowley. That we have not the whole *Davideis* is, however, not much to be regretted, for in this undertaking Cowley is, tacitly at least, confessed to have miscarried. There are not many examples of so great a work produced by an author generally read, and generally praised, that has crept through a century with so little regard. Whatever is said of Cowley is meant of his other works. Of the *Davideis* no mention is made: it never appears in books, nor emerges in conversation. By the *Spectator* it has been once quoted; by Rymer it has once been praised; and by Dryden, in *Mac Flecknoe,* it has once been imitated; nor do I recollect much other notice from its publication till now in the whole succession of English literature.

Of this silence and neglect, if the reason be inquired, it will be found partly in the choice of the subject, and partly in the performance of the work.

Sacred history has been always read with submissive reverence and an imagination overawed and controlled. We have been accustomed to acquiesce in the nakedness and simplicity of the authentic narrative, and to repose on its veracity with such humble confidence as suppresses curiosity. We go with the historian as he goes, and stop with him when he stops.

All amplification is frivolous and vain: all addition to that which is already sufficient for the purposes of religion seems not only useless, but in some degree profane.

Such events as were produced by the visible interposition of Divine Power are above the power of human genius to dignify. The miracle of Creation, however it may teem with images, is best described with little diffusion of language: "He spake the word, and they were made."

[. . .]

It is not only when the events are confessedly miraculous that fancy and fiction lose their effect; the whole system of life, while the theocracy was yet visible, has an appearance so different from all other scenes of human action that the reader of the sacred volume habitually considers it as the peculiar mode of existence of a distinct species of mankind, that lived and acted with manners uncommunicable; so that it is difficult even for imagination to place us in the state of them whose story is related, and by consequence their joys and griefs are not easily adopted, nor can the attention be often interested in anything that befalls them.

To the subject thus originally indisposed to the reception of poetical embellishments, the writer brought little that could reconcile impatience or attract curiosity. Nothing can be more disgusting than a narrative spangled with conceits; and conceits are all that the *Davideis* supplies.

One of the great sources of poetical delight is description, or the power of presenting pictures to the mind. Cowley gives inferences instead of images, and shows not what may be supposed to have been seen but what thoughts the sight might have suggested. . . .

[. . .]

In the perusal of the *Davideis,* as of all Cowley's works, we find wit and learning unprofitably squandered. Attention has no relief: the affections are never moved; we are sometimes surprised, but never delighted; and find much to admire, but little to approve. Still, however, it is the work of Cowley, of a mind capacious by nature, and replenished by study.

In the general review of Cowley's poetry it will be found that he wrote with abundant fertility but negligent or unskilful selection; with much thought, but with little imagery; that he is never pathetic, and rarely sublime; but always either ingenious or learned, either acute or profound.

[...]

His character of writing was indeed not his own; he unhappily adopted that which was predominant. He saw a certain way to present praise; and, not sufficiently inquiring by what means the ancients have continued to delight through all the changes of human manners, he contented himself with a deciduous laurel, of which the verdure in its spring was bright and gay, but which time has been continually stealing from his brows.

[...]

His diction was in his own time censured as negligent. He seems not to have known, or not to have considered, that words being arbitrary must owe their power to association, and have the influence, and that only, which custom has given them. Language is the dress of thought; and as the noblest mien, or most graceful action, would' be degraded and obscured by a garb appropriated to the gross employments of rustics or mechanics; so the most heroic sentiments will lose their efficacy, and the most splendid ideas drop their magnificence, if they are conveyed by words used commonly upon low and trivial occasions, debased by vulgar mouths, and contaminated by inelegant applications.

Truth indeed is always truth, and reason is always reason; they have an intrinsic and unalterable value and constitute that intellectual gold which defies destruction; but gold may be so concealed in baser matter that only a chemist can recover it; sense may be so hidden in unrefined and plebeian words that none but philosophers can distinguish it; and both may be so buried in impurities as not to pay the cost of their extraction.

The diction, being the vehicle of the thoughts, first presents itself to the intellectual eye; and if the first appearance offends, a further knowledge is not often sought. Whatever professes to benefit by pleasing, must please at once. The pleasures of the mind imply something sudden and unexpected; that which elevates must always surprise. What is perceived by slow degrees may gratify us with the consciousness of improvement, but will never strike with the sense of pleasure.

Of all this Cowley appears to have been without knowledge or without care. He makes no selection of words, nor seeks any neatness of phrase; he has no elegances either lucky or elaborate: as his endeavours were rather to impress sentences upon the understanding than images on the fancy he has few epithets, and those scattered without peculiar propriety or nice adaptation. It seems to follow from the necessity of the subject, rather than the care of the writer, that the diction of his heroic poem is less familiar than that of his slightest writings. . . .

His versification seems to have had very little of his care; and if what he thinks be true, that his numbers are unmusical only when they are ill-read, the art of reading them is at present lost; for they are commonly harsh to modern ears. He has indeed many noble lines, such as the feeble care of Waller never could produce. The bulk of his thoughts sometimes swelled his verse to unexpected and inevitable grandeur; but his excellence of this kind is merely fortuitous; he sinks willingly down to his general careless-ness, and avoids with very little care either meanness or asperity.

[...]

It may be affirmed, without any encomiastic fervour that he brought to his poetic labours a mind replete with learning, and that his pages are embellished with all the ornaments which books could supply; that he was the first who imparted to English numbers the enthusiasm of the greater ode, and the gaiety of the less; that he was equally qualified for sprightly sallies, and for lofty flights; that he was among those who freed translation from servility, and, instead of following his author at a dis-tance, walked by his side; and that, if he left versification yet improvable, he left likewise from time to time such specimens of excellence as enabled succeeding poets to improve it.

Milton

Milton has the reputation of having been in his youth eminently beautiful, so as to have been called the Lady of his college. His hair, which was of a light brown, parted at the foretop and hung down upon his shoulders, according to the picture which he has given of Adam. He was, however, not of the heroic stature, but rather below the middle size, according to Mr. Richardson, who mentions him as having narrowly escaped from being "short and thick."[1] He was vigorous and active, and delighted in the exercise of the sword, in which he is related to have been eminently skilful. His weapon was, I believe, not the rapier, but the backsword, of which he recommends the use in his book on education.

His eyes are said never to have been bright; but, if he was a dexterous fencer, they must have been once quick.

His domestic habits, so far as they are known, were those of a severe student. He drank little strong drink of any kind, and fed without excess in quantity, and in his earlier years without delicacy of choice. In his youth he studied late at night; but afterwards changed his hours, and rested in bed from nine to four in the summer and five in winter. The course of his day was best known after he was blind. When he first rose, he heard a chapter in the Hebrew Bible, and then studied till twelve; then took some exercise for an hour; then dined, then played on the organ, and sang, or heard another sing, then studied to six; then entertained his visitors till eight; then supped, and, after a pipe of tobacco and a glass of water, went to bed.

So is his life described; but this even tenour appears attainable only in colleges. He that lives in the world will sometimes have the succession of his practice broken and confused. Visitors, of whom Milton is represented to have had great numbers, will come and stay unseasonably; business, of which every man has some, must be done when others will do it.

When he did not care to rise early, he had something read to him by his bedside; perhaps at this time his daughters were employed. He composed much in the morning, and dictated in the day, sitting obliquely in an elbow-chair, with his leg thrown over the arm.

Fortune appears not to have had much of his care. In the civil wars, he lent his personal estate to the Parliament; but when, after the contest was decided, he solicited repayment, he met not only with neglect but "sharp rebuke"; and, having tired both himself and his friends, was given up to poverty and hopeless indignation, till he showed how able he was to do greater service. He was then made Latin Secretary, with two hundred pounds a year; and had a thousand pounds for his *Defence of the People.* His widow, who after his death retired to Nantwich, in Cheshire, and died about 1729, is said to have reported that he lost two thousand pounds by entrusting it to a scrivener; and that, in the general depredation upon the Church, he had grasped an estate of about sixty pounds a year belonging to Westminster Abbey, which, like other sharers of the plunder of rebellion, he was afterwards obliged to return. Two thousand pounds which he had placed in the Excise Office were also lost. There is yet no reason to believe that he was ever reduced to indigence. His wants, being few, were competently supplied. He sold his library before his death, and left his family fifteen hundred pounds, on which his widow laid hold, and only gave one hundred to each of his daughters.

His literature was unquestionably great. He read all the languages which are considered either as learned or polite: Hebrew, with its two dialects, Greek, Latin, Italian, French, and Spanish. In Latin his skill was such as places him in the first rank of writers and critics; and he appears to have cultivated Italian with uncommon diligence. The books in which his daughter, who used to read to him, represented him as most delighting, after Homer, which he could almost repeat, were Ovid's *Metamorphoses* and Euripides. His Euripides is, by Mr. Cradock's kindness, now in my hands: the margin is sometimes noted; but I have found nothing remarkable.

Of the English poets he set most value upon Spenser, Shakespeare, and Cowley. Spenser was apparently his favourite; Shakespeare he may easily be supposed to like, with every other skilful reader; but I should not have expected that Cowley, whose ideas of excellence were different from his own, would have had much of his approbation. His character of Dryden, who sometimes visited him, was that he was a good rhymist, but no poet.

His theological opinions are said to have been first Calvinistical; and afterwards, perhaps when he began to hate the Presbyterians, to have tended towards Arminianism. In the mixed questions of theology and government, he never thinks that he can recede far enough from popery, or prelacy; but what Baudius says of Erasmus seems applicable to him, "Magis habuit quod fugeret, quam quod sequeretur." He had determined rather what to condemn than what to approve. He has not associated himself with any denomination of Protestants: we know rather what he was not than what he was. He was not of the Church of Rome; he was not of the Church of England.

To be of no church is dangerous. Religion, of which the rewards are distant, and which is animated only by faith and hope, will glide by degrees out of the mind unless it be invigorated and reimpressed by external ordinances, by stated calls to worship, and the salutary influence of example. Milton, who appears to have had a full conviction of the truth of Christianity, and to have regarded the Holy Scriptures with the profoundest veneration, to have been untainted by any heretical peculiarity of opinion, and to have lived in a confirmed belief of the immediate and occasional agency of Providence, yet grew old without any visible worship. In the distribution of his hours, there was no hour of prayer, either solitary or with his household; omitting public prayers, he omitted all.

Of this omission the reason has been sought upon a supposition which ought never to be made, that men live with their own approbation, and justify their conduct to themselves. Prayer certainly was not thought superfluous by him, who represents our first parents as praying acceptably in the state of innocence, and efficaciously after their fall. That he lived without prayer can hardly be affirmed; his studies and meditations were an habitual prayer. The neglect of it in his family was probably a fault for which he condemned himself, and which he intended to correct; but that death, as too often happens, intercepted his reformation.

His political notions were those of an acrimonious and surly republican, for which it is not known that he gave any better reason than that "a popular government was the most frugal; for the trappings of a monarchy would set up an ordinary commonwealth."[2] It is surely very shallow policy that supposes money to be the chief good; and even this, without considering that the support and expense of a court is, for the most part, only a particular kind of traffic, for which money is circulated without any national impoverishment.

Milton's republicanism was, I am afraid, founded in an envious hatred of greatness, and a sullen desire of independence; in petulance impatient of control, and pride disdainful of superiority. He hated monarchs in the state, and prelates in the church; for he hated all whom he was required to obey. It is to be suspected that his predominant desire was to destroy rather than establish, and that he felt not so much the love of liberty as repugnance to authority.

It has been observed that they who most loudly clamour for liberty do not most liberally grant it. What we know of Milton's character in domestic relations is that he was severe and arbitrary. His family consisted of women; and there appears in his books something like a Turkish contempt of females, as subordinate and inferior beings. That his own daughters might not break the ranks, he suffered them to be depressed by a mean and penurious education. He thought woman made only for obedience, and man only for rebellion.

[...]

In the examination of Milton's poetical works, I shall pay so much regard to time as to begin with his juvenile productions. For his early pieces he seems to have had a degree of fondness not very laudable; what he has once written he resolves to preserve, and gives to the public an unfinished poem which he broke off because he was "nothing satisfied with what he had done," supposing his readers less nice than himself. These preludes to his future labours are in Italian, Latin, and English. Of the Italian I cannot pretend to speak as a critic; but I have heard them commended by a man well qualified to decide their merit. The Latin pieces are lusciously elegant: but the delight which they afford is rather by the exquisite imitation of the ancient writers, by the purity of the diction, and the harmony of the numbers, than by any power of invention or vigour of sentiment. They are not all of equal value; the elegies excel the odes; and some of the exercises on Gunpowder Treason might have been spared.

The English poems, though they make no promises of *Paradise Lost,* have this evidence of genius, that they have a cast original and unborrowed. But their peculiarity is not excellence; if they differ from the verses of others, they differ for the worse; for they are too often distinguished by repulsive harshness; the combinations of words are new, but they are not pleasing; the rhymes and epithets seem to be laboriously sought, and violently applied.

That in the early parts of his life he wrote with much care appears from his manuscripts, happily preserved at Cambridge, in which many of his smaller works are found as they were first written, with the subsequent corrections. Such relics show how excellence is acquired; what we hope ever to do with ease, we must learn first to do with diligence.

Those who admire the beauties of this great poet sometimes force their own judgment into false approbation of his little pieces, and prevail upon themselves to think that admirable which is only singular. All that short compositions can commonly attain is neatness and elegance. Milton never learned the art of doing little things with grace; he overlooked the milder excellence of suavity and softness; he was a "Lion" that had no skill in "dandling the Kid."

One of the poems on which much praise has been bestowed is *Lycidas;* of which the diction is harsh, the rhymes uncertain, and the numbers unpleasing. What beauty there is we must therefore seek in the sentiments and images. It is not to be considered as the effusion of real passion; for passion runs not after remote allusions and obscure opinions. Passion plucks no berries from the myrtle and ivy, nor calls upon Arethuse and Mincius, nor tells of rough "satyrs" and "fauns with cloven heel." Where there is leisure for fiction,[3] there is little grief.

In this poem there is no nature, for there is no truth; there is no art, for there is nothing new. Its form is that of a pastoral; easy, vulgar, and therefore disgusting; whatever images it can supply are long ago exhausted; and its inherent improbability always forces dissatisfaction on the mind. When Cowley tells of Hervey, that they studied together, it is easy to suppose how much he must miss the companion of his labours, and the partner of his discoveries; but what image of tenderness can be excited by these lines!

> *We drove afield, and both together heard*
> *What time the grey fly winds her sultry horn,*
> *Battening our flocks with the fresh dews of night.*

We know that they never drove afield, and that they had no flocks to batten; and though it be allowed that the representation may be allegorical, the true meaning is so uncertain and remote, that it is never sought, because it cannot be known when it is found.

Among the flocks, and copses, and flowers, appear the heathen deities; Jove and Phoebus, Neptune and Æolus, with a long train of mythological imagery, such as a college easily supplies. Nothing can less display knowledge, or less exercise invention, than to tell how a shepherd has lost his companion, and must now feed his flocks alone, without any judge of his skill in piping; and how one god asks another god what is become of Lycidas, and how neither god can tell. He who thus grieves will excite no sympathy; he who thus praises will confer no honour.

This poem has yet a grosser fault. With these trifling fictions are mingled the most awful and sacred truths, such as ought never to be polluted with such irreverent combinations. The shepherd likewise is now a feeder of sheep, and afterwards an ecclesiastical pastor, a superintendent of a Christian flock. Such equivocations are always unskilful; but here they are indecent, and at least approach to impiety, of which, however, I believe the writer not to have been conscious.

Such is the power of reputation justly acquired, that its blaze drives away the eye from nice examination. Surely no man could have fancied that he read *Lycidas* with pleasure, had he not known the author.

Of the two pieces *L'Allegro* and *Il Penseroso,* I believe, opinion is uniform; every man that reads them, reads them with pleasure. The author's design is not, what Theobald has remarked, merely to show how objects derive their colours from the mind, by representing the operation of the same things upon the gay and the melancholy temper, or upon the same man as he is differently disposed; but rather how, among the successive variety of appearances, every disposition of mind takes hold on those by which it may be gratified.

The *cheerful* man hears the lark in the morning; the *pensive* man hears the nightingale in the evening. The *cheerful* man sees the cock strut, and hears the horn and hounds echo in the wood; then walks "not unseen" to observe the glory of the rising sun, or listen to the singing milk-maid, and view the labours of the ploughman and the mower; then casts his eyes about him over scenes of smiling plenty, and looks up to the distant tower, the residence of some fair inhabitant; thus he pursues real gaiety through a day of labour or of play, and delights himself at night with the fanciful narratives of superstitious ignorance.

The *pensive* man at one time walks "unseen" to muse at midnight, and at another hears the sullen curfew. If the weather drives him home, he sits in a room lighted only by "glowing embers"; or by a lonely lamp out-watches the North Star, to discover the habitation of separate souls, and varies the shades of meditation by contemplating the magnificent or pathetic scenes of tragic and epic poetry. When the morning comes, a morning gloomy with rain and wind—he walks into the dark, trackless woods, falls asleep by some murmuring water, and with melancholy enthusiasm expects some dream of prognostication, or some music played by aerial performers.

Both Mirth and Melancholy are solitary, silent inhabitants of the breast, that neither receive nor transmit communication; no mention is therefore made of a philosophical friend, or a pleasant companion. The seriousness does not arise from any participation of calamity, nor the gaiety from the pleasures of the bottle.

The man of *cheerfulness* having exhausted the country tries what "towered cities" will afford, and mingles with scenes of splendour, gay assemblies, and nuptial festivities; but he mingles a mere spectator, as when the learned comedies of Jonson, or the wild dramas of Shakespeare, are exhibited, he attends the theatre.

The *pensive* man never loses himself in crowds, but walks the cloister, or frequents the cathedral. Milton probably had not yet forsaken the Church.

[...]

The greatest of his juvenile performances is the *Mask of Comus,* in which may very plainly be discovered the dawn or twilight of *Paradise Lost.* Milton appears to have formed very early that system of diction and mode of verse which his maturer judgment approved, and from which he never endeavoured nor desired to deviate.

Nor does *Comus* afford only a specimen of his language; it exhibits likewise his power of description and his vigour of sentiment, employed in the praise and defence of virtue. A work more truly poetical is rarely found; allusions, images, and descriptive epithets, embellish almost every period with lavish decoration. As a series of lines, therefore, it may be considered as worthy of all the admiration with which the votaries have received it.

As a drama it is deficient. The action is not probable. A Masque, in those parts where supernatural intervention is admitted, must indeed be given up to all the freaks of imagination, but so far as the action is merely human, it ought to be reasonable, which can hardly be said of the conduct of the two brothers; who, when their sister sinks with fatigue in a pathless wilderness, wander both away together in search of berries too far to find their way back, and leave a helpless Lady to all the sadness and danger of solitude. This, however, is a defect over-balanced by its convenience.

What deserves more reprehension is that the prologue spoken in the wild wood by the attendant Spirit is addressed to the audience; a mode of communication so contrary to the nature of dramatic representation that no precedents can support it.

The discourse of the Spirit is too long, an objection that may be made to almost all the following speeches; they have not the sprightliness of a dialogue animated by reciprocal contention, but seem rather declamations deliberately composed, and formally repeated, on a moral question. The auditor therefore listens as to a lecture, without passion, without anxiety.

The song of Comus has airiness and jollity; but, what may recommend Milton's morals as well as his poetry, the invitations to pleasure are so general that they excite no distinct images of corrupt enjoyment, and take no dangerous hold on the fancy.

The following soliloquies of Comus and the Lady are elegant, but tedious. The song must owe much to the voice, if it ever can delight. At last the Brothers enter with too much tranquillity; and when they have feared lest their sister should be in danger, and hoped that she is not in danger, the Elder makes a speech in praise of chastity, and the Younger finds how fine it is to be a philosopher.

Then descends the Spirit in form of a shepherd; and the Brother, instead of being in haste to ask his help, praises his singing, and inquires his business in that place. It is remarkable that at this interview the Brother is taken with a short fit of rhyming. The Spirit relates that the Lady is in the power of Comus; the Brother moralises again; and the Spirit makes a long narration, of no use because it is false, and therefore unsuitable to a good Being.

In all these parts the language is poetical and the sentiments are generous but there is something wanting to allure attention.

The dispute between the Lady and Comus is the most animated and affecting scene of the drama, and wants nothing but a brisker reciprocation of objections and replies to invite attention and detain it.

The songs are vigorous and full of imagery; but they are harsh in their diction, and not very musical in their numbers.

Throughout the whole the figures are too bold and the language too luxuriant for dialogue. It is a drama in the epic style, inelegantly splendid, and tediously instructive.

[...]

Those little pieces may be despatched without much anxiety; a greater work calls for greater care. I am now to examine *Paradise Lost,* a poem which, considered with respect to design, may claim the first place, and with respect to performance the second, among the productions of the human mind.

By the general consent of critics the first praise of genius is due to the writer of an epic poem, as it requires an assemblage of all the powers which are singly sufficient for other compositions. Poetry is the art of uniting pleasure with truth, by calling imagination to the help of reason.

Epic poetry undertakes to teach the most important truths by the most pleasing precepts, and therefore relates some great event in the most affecting manner. History must supply the writer with the rudiments of narration, which he must improve and exalt by a nobler art, must animate by dramatic energy, and diversify by retrospection and anticipation; morality must teach him the exact bounds, and different shades, of vice and virtue; from policy, and the practice of life, he has to learn the discriminations of character, and the tendency of the passions, either single or combined; and physiology must supply him with illustrations and images. To put these materials to poetical use is required an imagination capable of painting nature and realising fiction. Nor is he yet a poet till he has attained the whole extension of his language, distinguished all the delicacies of phrase, and all the colours of words, and learned to adjust their different sounds to all the varieties of metrical modulation.

. . . the moral of other poems is incidental and consequent; in Milton's only it is essential and intrinsic. His purpose was the most useful and the most arduous: "to vindicate the ways of God to man"; to show the reasonableness of religion, and the necessity of obedience to the Divine Law.

To convey this moral there must be a *fable,* a narration artfully constructed, so as to excite curiosity and surprise expectation. In this part of his work Milton must be confessed to have equalled every other poet. He has involved in his account of the Fall of Man the events which preceded, and those that were to follow it: he has interwoven the whole system of theology with such propriety, that every part appears to be necessary; and scarcely any recital is wished shorter for the sake of quickening the progress of the main action.

The subject of an epic poem is naturally an event of great importance. That of Milton is not the destruction of a city, the conduct of a colony, or the foundation of an empire. His subject is the fate of worlds, the revolutions of heaven and of earth; rebellion against the Supreme King raised by the highest order of created beings; the overthrow of their host and the punishment of their crime; the creation of a new race of reasonable creatures; their original happiness and innocence, their forfeiture of immortality, and their restoration to hope and peace.

Great events can be hastened or retarded only by persons of elevated dignity. Before the greatness displayed in Milton's poem, all other greatness shrinks away. The weakest of his agents are the highest and noblest of human beings, the original parents of mankind; with whose actions the elements consented; on whose rectitude or deviation of will, depended the state of terrestrial nature, and the condition of all the future inhabitants of the globe.

Of the other agents in the poem, the chief are such as it is irreverence to name on slight occasions. The rest were lower powers;

> *of which the least could wield*
> *Those elements, and arm him with the force*
> *Of all their regions;*

powers which only the control of Omnipotence restrains from laying creation waste, and filling the vast expanse of space with ruin and confusion. To display the motives and actions of beings thus superior, so far as human reason can examine them, or human imagination represent them, is the task which this mighty poet has undertaken and performed.

In the examination of epic poems much speculation is commonly employed upon the *characters*. The characters in the *Paradise Lost* which admit of examination are those of angels and of man; of angels good and evil, of man in his innocent and sinful state.

Among the angels, the virtue of Raphael is mild and placid, of easy condescension and free communication; that of Michael is regal and lofty, and, as may seem, attentive to the dignity of his own nature. Abdiel and Gabriel appear occasionally, and act as every incident requires; the solitary fidelity of Abdiel is very amiably painted.

Of the evil angels the characters are more diversified. To Satan, as Addison observes, such sentiments are given as suit "the most exalted and most depraved being."[4] . . . To make Satan speak as a rebel, without any such expression as might taint the reader's imagination, was indeed one of the great difficulties in Milton's undertaking, and I cannot but think that he has extricated himself with great happiness. There is in Satan's speeches little that can give pain to a pious ear. The language of rebellion cannot be the same with that of obedience. The malignity of Satan foams in haughtiness and obstinacy; but his expressions are commonly general, and no otherwise offensive than as they are wicked.

[...]

To Adam and to Eve are given during their innocence such sentiments as innocence can generate and utter. Their love is pure benevolence and mutual veneration; their repasts are without luxury and their diligence without toil. Their addresses to their Maker have little more than the voice of admiration and gratitude. Fruition left them nothing to ask and innocence left them nothing to fear.

But with guilt enter distrust and discord, mutual accusation, and stubborn self-defence; they regard each other with alienated minds, and dread their Creator as the avenger of their transgression. At last they seek shelter in His mercy, soften to repentance, and melt in supplication. Both before and after the Fall the superiority of Adam is diligently sustained.

Of the *probable* and the *marvellous,* two parts of a vulgar epic poem which immerge the critic in deep consideration, the *Paradise Lost* requires little to be said. It contains the history of a miracle, of Creation and Redemption; it displays the power and the mercy of the Supreme Being; the probable therefore is marvellous, and the marvellous is probable. The substance of the narrative is truth; and as truth allows no choice, it is, like necessity, superior to rule. To the accidental or adventitious parts, as to everything human, some slight exceptions may be made. But the main fabric is immovably supported.

It is justly remarked by Addison that this poem has, by the nature of its subject, the advantage above all others, that it is universally and perpetually interesting.[5] All mankind will, through all ages, bear the same relation to Adam and to Eve, and must partake of that good and evil which extend to themselves.

[...]

To the completeness or *integrity* of the design nothing can be objected; it has distinctly and clearly what Aristotle requires, a beginning, a middle, and an end. There is perhaps no poem of the same length from which so little can be taken without apparent mutilation. Here are no funeral games, nor is there any long description of a shield. The short digressions at the beginning of the third, seventh, and ninth books might doubtless be spared, but superfluities so beautiful who would take away? Or who does not wish that the author of the *Iliad* had gratified succeeding ages with a little knowledge of himself? Perhaps no passages are more frequently or more attentively read than those extrinsic paragraphs; and, since the end of poetry is pleasure, that cannot be unpoetical with which all are pleased.

The questions whether the action of the poem be strictly *one,* whether the poem can be properly termed *heroic,* and who is the hero, are raised by such readers as draw their principles of judgment rather from books than from reason. Milton, though he entitled *Paradise Lost* only a "poem," yet calls it himself "heroic song." Dryden, petulantly and indecently, denies the heroism of Adam, because he was overcome; but there is no reason why the hero should not be unfortunate except established practice, since success and virtue do not go necessarily together. Cato is the hero of Lucan, but Lucan's authority will not be suffered by Quintilian to decide. However, if success be necessary, Adam's deceiver was at last crushed; Adam was restored to his Maker's favour, and therefore may securely resume his human rank.

After the scheme and fabric of the poem must be considered its component parts, the sentiments and the diction.

The *sentiments,* as expressive of manners, or appropriated to characters, are, for the greater part unexceptionably just.

Splendid passages containing lessons of morality or precepts of prudence occur seldom. Such is the original formation of this poem, that, as it admits no human manners till the Fall, it can give little assistance to human conduct. Its end is to raise the thoughts above sublunary cares or pleasures. Yet the praise of that fortitude, with which Abdiel maintained his singularity of virtue against the scorn of multitudes, may be accommodated to all times; and Raphael's reproof of Adam's curiosity after the planetary motions, with the answer returned by Adam, may be confidently opposed to any rule of life which any poet has delivered.

The thoughts which are occasionally called forth in the progress are such as could only be produced by an imagination in the highest degree fervid and active, to which materials were supplied by incessant study and unlimited curiosity. The heat of Milton's mind may be said to sublimate his learning, to throw off into his work the spirit of science, unmingled with its grosser parts.

He had considered creation in its whole extent, and his descriptions are therefore learned. He had accustomed his imagination to unrestrained indulgence, and his conceptions therefore were extensive. The characteristic quality of his poem is sublimity. He sometimes descends to the elegant, but his element is the great. He can occasionally invest himself with grace; but his natural port is gigantic loftiness. He can please when pleasure is required; but it is his peculiar power to astonish.

He seems to have been well acquainted with his own genius, and to know what it was that Nature had bestowed upon him more bountifully than upon others; the power of displaying the vast, illuminating the splendid, enforcing the awful, darkening the gloomy, and aggravating the dreadful: he therefore chose a subject on which too much could not be said, on which he might tire his fancy without the censure of extravagance.

The appearances of nature and the occurrences of life did not satiate his appetite of greatness. To paint things as they are requires a minute attention, and employs the memory rather than the fancy. Milton's delight was to sport in the wide regions of possibility; reality was a scene too narrow for his mind. He sent his faculties out upon discovery, into worlds where only imagination can travel, and delighted to form new modes of existence, and furnish sentiment and action to superior beings, to trace the counsels of hell, or accompany the choirs of heaven.

But he could not be always in other worlds; he must sometimes revisit earth, and tell of things visible and known. When he cannot raise wonder by the sublimity of his mind, he gives delight by its fertility.

Whatever be his subject he never fails to fill the imagination. But his images and descriptions of the scenes or operations of nature do not seem to be always copied from original form, nor to have the freshness, raciness, and energy of immediate observation. He saw nature, as Dryden expresses it, "through the spectacles of books";[6] and on most occasions calls learning to his assistance. The garden of Eden brings to his mind the vale of Enna, where Proserpine was gathering flowers. Satan makes his way through fighting elements, like Argo between the Cyanean rocks, or

Ulysses between the two *Sicilian* whirlpools, when he shunned Charybdis "on the larboard."[7] The mythological allusions have been justly censured, as not being always used with notice of their vanity; but they contribute variety to the narration, and produce an alternate exercise of the memory and the fancy.

His similes are less numerous and more various than those of his predecessors. But he does not confine himself within the limits of rigorous comparison: his great excellence is amplitude, and he expands the adventitious image beyond the dimensions which the occasion required. Thus, comparing the shield of Satan to the orb of the moon, he crowds the imagination with the discovery of the telescope, and all the wonders which the telescope discovers.

Of his moral sentiments it is hardly praise to affirm that they excel those of all other poets; for this superiority he was indebted to his acquaintance with the sacred writings. The ancient epic poets, wanting the light of Revelation, were very unskilful teachers of virtue; their principal characters may be great, but they are not amiable. The reader may rise from their works with a greater degree of active or passive fortitude, and sometimes of prudence; but he will be able to carry away few precepts of justice, and none of mercy.

[. . .]

In Milton every line breathes sanctity of thought and purity of manners, except when the train of the narration requires the introduction of the rebellious spirits; and even they are compelled to acknowledge their subjection to God in such a manner as excites reverence and confirms piety.

Of human beings there are but two; but those two are the parents of mankind, venerable before their fall for dignity and innocence, and amiable after it for repentance and submission. In the first state their affection is tender without weakness, and their piety sublime without presumption. When they have sinned they show how discord begins in mutual frailty, and how it ought to cease in mutual forbearance; how confidence of the Divine favour is forfeited by sin, and how hope of pardon may be obtained by penitence and prayer. A state of innocence we can only conceive, if indeed, in our present misery, it be possible to conceive it; but the sentiments and worship proper to a fallen and offending being, we have all to learn, as we have all to practise.

The poet, whatever be done, is always great. Our progenitors in their first state conversed with angels; even when folly and sin had degraded them, they had not in their humiliation "the port of mean suitors"; and they rise again to reverential regard when we find that their prayers were heard.

As human passions did not enter the world before the Fall, there is in the *Paradise Lost* little opportunity for the pathetic; but what little there is has not been lost. That passion which is peculiar to rational nature, the anguish arising from the consciousness of transgression, and the horrors attending the sense of the Divine Displeasure, are very justly described and forcibly impressed. But the passions are moved only on one occasion; sublimity is the general and prevailing quality in this poem—sublimity variously modified, sometimes descriptive, sometimes argumentative.

The defects and faults of *Paradise Lost,* for faults and defects every work of man must have, it is the business of impartial criticism to discover. As in displaying the excellence of Milton I have not made long quotations, because of selecting beauties there had been no end, I shall in the same general manner mention that which seems to deserve censure; for what Englishman can take delight in transcribing passages which, if they lessen the reputation of Milton, diminish in some degree the honour of our country?

[...]

The plan of *Paradise Lost* has this inconvenience, that it comprises neither human actions nor human manners. The man and woman who act and suffer are in a state which no other man or woman can ever know. The reader finds no transaction in which he can be engaged, beholds no condition in which he can by any effort of imagination place himself; he has, therefore, little natural curiosity or sympathy.

We all, indeed, feel the effects of Adam's disobedience; we all sin like Adam, and like him must all bewail our offences; we have restless and insidious enemies in the fallen angels, and in the blessed spirits we have guardians and friends; in the Redemption of mankind we hope to be included: in the description of heaven and hell we are surely interested, as we are all to reside hereafter either in the regions of horror or bliss.

But these truths are too important to be new; they have been taught to our infancy; they have mingled with our solitary thoughts and familiar conversations, and are habitually interwoven with the whole texture of life. Being therefore not new, they raise no unaccustomed emotion in the mind; what we knew before we cannot learn; what is not unexpected cannot surprise.

[...]

Pleasure and terror are indeed the genuine sources of poetry; but poetical pleasure must be such as human imagination can at least conceive, and poetical terror such as human strength and fortitude may combat. The good and evil of Eternity are too ponderous for the wings of wit; the mind sinks under them in passive helplessness, content with calm belief and humble adoration.

Known truths however may take a different appearance and be conveyed to the mind by a new train of intermediate images. This Milton has undertaken and performed with pregnancy and vigour of mind peculiar to himself. Whoever considers the few radical positions which the Scriptures afforded him will wonder by what energetic operation he expanded them to such extent and ramified them to so much variety, restrained as he was by religious reverence from licentiousness of fiction.

Here is a full display of the united force of study and genius; of a great accumulation of materials, with judgment to digest and fancy to combine them: Milton was able to select from nature or from story, from an ancient fable or from modern science, whatever could illustrate or adorn his thoughts. An accumulation of knowledge impregnated his mind, fermented by study and exalted by imagination.

[...]

But original deficiency cannot be supplied. The want of human interest is always felt. *Paradise Lost* is one of the books which the reader admires and lays down, and forgets to take up again. None ever wished it longer than it is. Its perusal is a duty rather than a pleasure. We read Milton for instruction, retire harassed and overburdened, and look elsewhere for recreation; we desert our master, and seek for companions.

Another inconvenience of Milton's design is that it requires the description of what cannot be described, the agency of spirits. He saw that immateriality supplied no images, and that he could not show angels acting but by instruments of action; he therefore invested them with form and matter. This being necessary was therefore defensible; and he should have secured the consistency of his system by keeping immateriality out of sight and enticing his reader to drop it from his thoughts. But he has unhappily perplexed his poetry with his philosophy. His infernal and celestial powers are sometimes pure spirit, and sometimes animated body. When Satan walks with his lance upon the "burning marl," he has a body; when in his passage between hell and the new world he is in danger of sinking in the vacuity, and is supported by a gust of rising vapours, he has a body; when he animates the toad, he seems to be mere spirit that can penetrate matter at pleasure; when he "starts up in his own shape," he has at least a determined form; and when he is brought before Gabriel, he has "a spear and a shield," which he had the power of hiding in the toad, though the arms of the contending angels are evidently material.

[...]

After the operation of immaterial agents which cannot be explained may be considered that of allegorical persons which have no real existence. To exalt causes into agents, to invest abstract ideas with form, and animate them with activity, has always been the right of poetry. But such airy beings are for the most part suffered only to do their natural office, and retire. Thus Fame tells a tale and Victory hovers over a general or perches on a standard; but Fame and Victory can do no more. To give them any real employment, or ascribe to them any material agency, is to make them allegorical no longer, but to shock the mind by ascribing effects to non-entity. In the *Prometheus* of Æschylus, we see Violence and Strength, and in the *Alcestis* of Euripides we see Death, brought upon the stage, all as active persons of the drama; but no precedents can justify absurdity.

Milton's allegory of Sin and Death is undoubtedly faulty. Sin is indeed the mother of Death, and may be allowed to be the portress of hell; but when they stop the journey of Satan, a journey described as real, and when Death offers him battle, the allegory is broken. That Sin and Death should have shown the way to hell might have been allowed; but they cannot facilitate the passage by building a bridge because the difficulty of Satan's passage is described as real and sensible, and the bridge ought to be only figurative. The hell assigned to the rebellious spirits is described as not less local than the residence of man. It is placed in some distant part of space, separated from the regions of harmony and order by a chaotic waste and an unoccupied vacuity; but Sin and Death worked up a "mole of aggravated soil" cemented with asphaltus, a work too bulky for ideal architects.

This unskilful allegory appears to me one of the greatest faults of the poem; and to this there was no temptation but the author's opinion of its beauty.

[...]

To find sentiments for the state of innocence was very difficult; and something of anticipation perhaps is now and then discovered. Adam's discourse of dreams seems not to be the speculation of a new-created being. I know not whether his answer to the angel's reproof for curiosity does not want something of propriety; it is the speech of a man acquainted with many other men. Some philosophical notions, especially when the philosophy is false, might have been better omitted. The angel, in a comparison, speaks of "timorous deer," before deer were yet timorous, and before Adam could understand the comparison.

Dryden remarks that Milton has some flats among his elevations.[8] This is only to say that all the parts are not equal. In every work, one part must be for the sake of others; a palace must have passages; a poem must have transitions. It is no more to be required that wit should always be blazing than that the sun should always stand at noon. In a great work there is a vicissitude of luminous and opaque parts, as there is in the world a succession of day and night. Milton, when he has expatiated in the sky, may be allowed sometimes to revisit earth; for what other author ever soared so high or sustained his flight so long?

[...]

Such are the faults of that wonderful performance *Paradise Lost;* which he who can put in balance with its beauties must be considered not as nice but as dull, as less to be censured for want of candour than pitied for want of sensibility.

Of *Paradise Regained,* the general judgment seems now to be right, that it is in many parts elegant, and everywhere instructive. It was not to be supposed that the writer of *Paradise Lost* could ever write without great effusions of fancy and exalted precepts of wisdom. The basis of *Paradise Regained* is narrow; a dialogue without action can never please like a union of the narrative and dramatic powers. Had this poem been written not by Milton, but by some imitator, it would have claimed and received universal praise.

If *Paradise Regained* has been too much depreciated, *Samson Agonistes* has, in requital, been too much admired. It could only be by long prejudice and the bigotry of learning that Milton could prefer the ancient tragedies with their encumbrance of a chorus to the exhibitions of the French and English stages; and it is only by a blind confidence in the reputation of Milton that a drama can be praised in which the intermediate parts have neither cause nor consequence, neither hasten nor retard the catastrophe.

In this tragedy are however many particular beauties, many just sentiments and striking lines; but it wants that power of attracting the attention which a well connected plan produces.

Milton would not have excelled in dramatic writing; he knew human nature only in the gross, and had never studied the shades of character, nor the combinations of concurring or the perplexity of contending passions. He had read much and knew what books could teach; but had mingled little in the world and was deficient in the knowledge which experience must confer.

Through all his greater works there prevails a uniform peculiarity of *diction,* a mode and cast of expression which bears little resemblance to that of any former writer, and which is so far removed from common use that an unlearned reader when he first opens his book finds himself surprised by a new language.

This novelty has been, by those who can find nothing wrong in Milton, imputed to his laborious endeavours after words suitable to the grandeur of his ideas. "Our language," says Addison, "sunk under him." But the truth is that, both in prose and verse, he had formed his style by a perverse and pedantic principle. He was desirous to use English words with a foreign idiom. This in all his prose is discovered and condemned, for there judgment operates freely, neither softened by the beauty nor awed by the dignity of his thoughts; but such is the power of his poetry that his call is obeyed without resistance, the reader feels himself in captivity to a higher and a nobler mind, and criticism sinks in admiration.

[...]

Whatever be the faults of his diction, he cannot want the praise of copiousness and variety. He was master of his language in its full extent and has selected the melodious words with such diligence that from his book alone the art of English poetry might be learned.

After his diction something must be said of his versification. "The measure," he says, "is the English heroic verse without rhyme." Of this mode he had many examples among the Italians, and some in his own country. The Earl of Surrey is said to have translated one of Virgil's books without rhyme; and, beside our tragedies, a few short poems had appeared in blank verse, particularly one tending to reconcile the nation to Raleigh's wild attempt upon Guiana, and probably written by Raleigh himself. These petty performances cannot be supposed to have much influenced Milton, who more probably took his hint from Trissino's *Italia Liberata;* and, finding blank verse easier than rhyme, was desirous of persuading himself that it is better.

"Rhyme," he says, and says truly, "is no necessary adjunct of true poetry." But, perhaps of poetry as a mental operation metre or music is no necessary adjunct; it is however by the music of metre that poetry has been discriminated in all languages, and in languages melodiously constructed with a due proportion of long and short syllables, metre is sufficient. But one language cannot communicate its rules to another; where metre is scanty and imperfect some help is necessary. The music of the English heroic lines strikes the ear so faintly that it is easily lost unless all the syllables of every line cooperate together; this cooperation can only be obtained by the preservation of every verse unmingled with another as a distinct system of sounds, and this distinctness is obtained and preserved by the artifice of rhyme. The variety of pauses so much boasted by the lovers of blank verse changes the measures of an English poet to the periods of a declaimer; and there are only a few skilful and happy readers of Milton who enable their audience to perceive where the lines end or begin. "Blank verse," said an ingenious critic,[9] "seems to be verse only to the eye."

Poetry may subsist without rhyme, but English poetry will not often please; nor can rhyme ever be safely spared but where the subject is able to support itself. Blank verse makes some approach to that which is called the "lapidary style"; has neither the easiness of prose, nor the melody of numbers, and therefore tires by long continuance. Of the Italian writers without rhyme, whom Milton alleges as precedents, not one is popular; what reason could urge in its defence has been confuted by the ear.

But whatever be the advantages of rhyme I cannot prevail on myself to wish that Milton had been a rhymer; for I cannot wish his work to be other than it is; yet like other heroes, he is to be admired rather than imitated. He that thinks himself capable of astonishing may write blank verse, but those that hope only to please must condescend to rhyme.

The highest praise of genius is original invention. Milton cannot be said to have contrived the structure of an epic poem, and therefore owes reverence to that vigour and amplitude of mind to which all generations must be indebted for the art of poetical narration, for the texture of the fable, the variation of incidents, the interposition of dialogue, and all the stratagems that surprise and enchain attention. But, of all the borrowers from Homer, Milton is perhaps the least indebted. He was naturally a thinker for himself, confident of his own abilities and disdainful of help or hindrance; he did not refuse admission to the thoughts or images of his predecessors, but he did not seek them. From his contemporaries he neither courted nor received support; there is in his writings nothing by which the pride of other authors might be gratified or favour gained; no exchange of praise, nor solicitation of support. His great works were performed under discountenance and in blindness, but difficulties vanished at his touch; he was born for whatever is arduous; and his work is not the greatest of heroic poems, only because it is not the first.

Pope

The person of Pope is well known not to have been formed by the nicest model. He has, in his account of the "Little Club,"[1] compared himself to a spider, and by another is described as protuberant behind and before. He is said to have been beautiful in his infancy, but he was of a constitution originally feeble and weak; and, as bodies of a tender frame are easily distorted, his deformity was probably in part the effect of his application. His stature was so low that, to bring him to a level with common tables, it was necessary to raise his seat. But his face was not displeasing, and his eyes were animated and vivid.

By natural deformity or accidental distortion his vital functions were so much disordered that his life was "a long disease." His most frequent assailant was the headache, which he used to relieve by inhaling the steam of coffee, which he very frequently required.

Most of what can be told concerning his petty peculiarities was communicated by a female domestic of the Earl of Oxford, who knew him perhaps after the middle of life. He was then so weak as to stand in perpetual need of female attendance; extremely sensible of cold, so that he wore a kind of fur doublet under a shirt of a very coarse warm linen with fine sleeves. When he rose, he was invested in bodice made of stiff canvas, being scarcely able to hold himself erect till they were laced, and he then put on a flannel waistcoat. One side was contracted. His legs were so slender that he enlarged their bulk with three pairs of stockings, which were drawn on and off by the maid, for he was not able to dress or undress himself, and neither went to bed nor rose without help. His weakness made it very difficult for him to be clean.

His hair had fallen almost all away, and he used to dine sometimes with Lord Oxford, privately, in a velvet cap. His dress of ceremony was black, with a tie-wig and a little sword.

The indulgence and accommodation which his sickness required had taught him all the unpleasing and unsocial qualities of a valetudinary man. He expected that everything should give way to his ease or humour, as a child whose parents will not hear her cry has an unresisted dominion in the nursery.

> *C'est que l'enfant toujours est homme,*
> *C'est que l'homme est toujours enfant.*

When he wanted to sleep he "nodded in company," and once slumbered at his own table while the Prince of Wales was talking of poetry.

The reputation which his friendship gave procured him many invitations, but he was a very troublesome inmate. He brought no servant, and had so many wants that a numerous attendance was scarcely able to supply them. Wherever he was he left no room for another because he exacted the attention and employed the activity of the whole family. His errands were so frequent and frivolous that the footmen in time avoided and neglected him, and the Earl of Oxford discharged some of his servants for their resolute refusal of his messages. The maids, when they had neglected their business, alleged that they had been employed by Mr. Pope. One of his constant demands was of coffee in the night, and to the woman that waited on him in his chamber he was very burdensome; but he was careful to recompense her want of sleep, and Lord Oxford's servant declared that in the house where her business was to answer his call she would not ask for wages.

He had another fault, easily incident to those who suffering much pain think themselves entitled to what pleasures they can snatch. He was too indulgent to his appetite: he loved meat highly seasoned and of strong taste; and, at the intervals of the table, amused himself with biscuits and dry conserves. If he sat down to a variety of dishes, he would oppress his stomach with repletion; and though he seemed angry when a dram was offered him, did not forbear to drink it. His friends, who knew the avenues to his heart, pampered him with presents of luxury, which he did not suffer to stand neglected. The death of great men is not always proportioned to the lustre of their lives. Hannibal, says Juvenal, did not perish by the javelin or the sword; the slaughters of Cannæ were revenged by a ring. The death of Pope was imputed by some of his friends to a silver saucepan, in which it was his delight to eat potted heat lampreys.

That he loved too well to eat is certain; but that his sensuality shortened his life will not be hastily concluded when it is remembered that a conformation so irregular lasted six-and-fifty years, notwithstanding such pertinacious diligence of study and meditation. In all his intercourse with mankind he had great delight in artifice, and endeavoured to attain all his purposes by indirect and unsuspected methods. "He hardly drank tea without a stratagem." If at the house of friends he wanted any accommodation, he was not willing to ask for it in plain terms, but would mention it remotely as something convenient; though when it was procured, he soon made it appear for whose sake it had been recommended. Thus he teased Lord Orrery till he obtained a screen. He practised his arts on such small occasions that Lady Bolingbroke used to say, in a French phrase, that "he played the politician about cabbages and turnips." His unjustifiable impression[2] of the *Patriot King*, as it can be attributed to no particular motive, must have proceeded from his general habit of secrecy and cunning; he caught an opportunity of a sly trick, and pleased himself with the thought of outwitting Bolingbroke.

In familiar or convivial conversation, it does not appear that he excelled. He may be said to have resembled Dryden as being not one that was distinguished by vivacity in company. It is remarkable that, so near his time, so much should be known of what he has written, and so little of what he has said: traditional memory retains no sallies of raillery, nor sentences of observation; nothing either pointed or solid, either wise or merry. One apophthegm only stands upon record. When an objection raised against his inscription for Shakespeare was defended by the authority of Patrick, he replied,—*horresco referens*—that "he would allow the publisher of a Dictionary to know the meaning of a single word, but not of two words put together."[3]

He was fretful and easily displeased, and allowed himself to be capriciously resentful. He would sometimes leave Lord Oxford silently, no one could tell why, and was to be courted back by more letters and messages than the footmen were willing to carry. The table was indeed infested by Lady Mary Wortley, who was the friend of Lady Oxford, and who, knowing his peevishness, could by no entreaties be restrained from contradicting him, till their disputes were sharpened to such asperity that one or the other quitted the house.

He sometimes condescended to be jocular with servants or inferiors; but by no merriment, either of others or his own, was he ever seen excited to laughter.

Of his domestic character, frugality was a part eminently remarkable. Having determined not to be dependent, he determined not to be in want, and therefore wisely and magnanimously rejected all temptations to expense unsuitable to his fortune. This general care must be universally approved; but it sometimes appeared in petty artifices of parsimony, such as the practice of writing his compositions on the back of letters, as may be seen in the remaining copy of the *Iliad,* by which perhaps in five years five shillings were saved; or in a niggardly reception of his friends, and scantiness of entertainment, as when he had two guests in his house he would set at supper a single pint upon the table, and having himself taken two small glasses would retire and say, "Gentlemen, I leave you to your wine." Yet he tells his friends that "he has a heart for all, a house for all, and whatever they may think, a fortune for all."

He sometimes, however, made a splendid dinner, and is said to have wanted no part of the skill or elegance which such performances require. That this magnificence should be often displayed, that obstinate prudence with which he conducted his affairs would not permit; for his revenue, certain and casual, amounted only to about eight hundred pounds a year, of which, however, he declares himself able to assign one hundred to charity.

Of this fortune, which, as it arose from public approbation was very honourably obtained, his imagination seems to have been too full: it would be hard to find a man so well entitled to notice by his wit, that ever delighted so much in talking of his money. In his letters and in his poems, his garden and his grotto, his quincunx and his vines, or some hints of his opulence, are always to be found. The great topic of his ridicule is poverty; the crimes with which he reproaches his antagonists are their debts, their habitation in the Mint, and their want of a dinner. He seems to be of an opinion not very uncommon in the world, that to want money is to want everything.

Next to the pleasure of contemplating his possessions seems to be that of enumerating the men of high rank with whom he was acquainted, and whose notice he loudly proclaims not to have been obtained by any practices of meanness or servility; a boast which was never denied to be true, and to which very few poets have ever aspired. Pope never set genius to sale; he never flattered those whom he did not love, nor praised those whom he did not esteem. Savage, however, remarked that he began a little to relax his dignity when he wrote a distich for "his Highness's dog."

His admiration of the great seems to have increased in the advance of life. He passed over peers and statesmen to inscribe his *Iliad* to Congreve, with a magnanimity of which the praise had been complete had his friend's virtue been equal to his wit. Why he was chosen for so great an honour it is not now possible to know; there is no trace in literary history of any particular intimacy between them. The name of Congreve appears in the letters among those of his other friends, but without any observable distinction or consequence.

To his latter works, however, he took care to annex names dignified with titles, but was not very happy in his choice; for, except Lord Bathurst, none of his noble friends were such as that a good man would wish to have his intimacy with them known to posterity: he can derive little honour from the notice of Cobham, Burlington, or Bolingbroke.

Of his social qualities, if an estimate be made from his letters, an opinion too favourable cannot easily be formed; they exhibit a perpetual and unclouded effulgence of general benevolence and particular fondness. There is nothing but liberality, gratitude, constancy, and tenderness. It has been so long said as to be commonly believed that the true characters of men may be found in their letters, and that he who writes to his friend lays his heart open before him. But the truth is that such were the simple friendships of the *Golden Age,* and are now the friendships only of children. Very few can boast of hearts which they dare lay open to themselves, and of which, by whatever accident exposed, they do not shun a distinct and continued view; and certainly what we hide from ourselves we do not show to our friends. There is, indeed, no transaction which offers stronger temptations to fallacy and sophistication than epistolary intercourse. In the eagerness of conversation the first emotions of the mind often burst out before they are considered; in the tumult of business, interest and passion have their genuine effect; but a friendly letter is a calm and deliberate performance in the cool of leisure, in the stillness of solitude, and surely no man sits down to depreciate by design his own character.

Friendship has no tendency to secure veracity; for by whom can a man so much wish to be thought better than he is, as by him whose kindness he desires to gain or keep? Even in writing to the world there is less constraint; the author is not confronted with his reader, and takes his chance of approbation among the different dispositions of mankind; but a letter is addressed to a single mind, of which the prejudices and partialities are known; and must therefore please, if not by favouring them, by forbearing to oppose them. To charge those favourable representations, which men give of their own minds, with the guilt of hypocritical falsehood, would show more severity than knowledge. The writer commonly believes himself. Almost every man's thoughts, while they are general, are right; and most hearts are pure while temptation is away. It is easy to awaken generous sentiments in privacy; to despise death when there is no danger; to glow with benevolence when there is nothing to be given. While such ideas are formed they are felt; and self-love does not suspect the gleam of virtue to be the meteor of fancy.

If the letters of Pope are considered merely as compositions, they seem to be premeditated and artificial. It is one thing to write because there is something which the mind wishes to discharge, and another to solicit the imagination because ceremony or vanity requires something to be written. Pope confesses his early letters to be vitiated with "affectation and ambition": to know whether he disentangled himself from these perverters of epistolary integrity his book and his life must be set in comparison.

One of his favourite topics is contempt of his own poetry. For this, if it had been real, he would deserve no commendation; and in this he was certainly not sincere, for his high value of himself was sufficiently observed; and of what could he be proud but of his poetry? He writes, he says, when "he has just nothing else to do"; yet Swift complains that he was never at leisure for conversation because he "had always some poetical scheme in his head."[4] It was punctually required that his writing-box should be set upon his bed before he rose; and Lord Oxford's domestic related that, in the dreadful winter of Forty, she was called from her bed by him four times in one night to supply him with paper, lest he should lose a thought.

He pretends insensibility to censure and criticism, though it was observed by all who knew him that every pamphlet disturbed his quiet, and that his extreme irritability laid him open to perpetual vexation; but he wished to despise his critics, and therefore hoped that he did despise them.

As he happened to live in two reigns when the court paid little attention to poetry, he nursed in his mind a foolish disesteem of kings, and proclaims that "he never sees courts." Yet a little regard shown him by the Prince of Wales melted his obduracy, and he had not much to say when he was asked by his Royal Highness, "How he could love a Prince while he disliked kings?"

He very frequently professes contempt of the world, and represents himself as looking on mankind, sometimes with gay indifference, as on emmets of a hillock below his serious attention; and sometimes with gloomy indignation, as on monsters more worthy of hatred than pity. These were dispositions apparently counterfeited. How could he despise those whom he lived by pleasing, and on whose approbation his esteem of himself was superstructed? Why should he hate those to whose favour he owed his honour and his ease? Of things that terminate in human life, the world is the proper judge: to despise its sentence, if it were possible, is not just; and if it were just, is not possible. Pope was far enough from this unreasonable temper; he was sufficiently "a fool to Fame," and his fault was that he pretended to neglect it. His levity and his sullenness were only in his letters; he passed through common life, sometimes vexed and sometimes pleased, with the natural emotions of common men.

His scorn of the great is repeated too often to be real; no man thinks much of that which he despises; and as falsehood is always in danger of inconsistency, he makes it his boast at another time that he lives among them.

It is evident that his own importance swells often in his mind. He is afraid of writing lest the clerks of the Post-office should know his secrets; he has many enemies; he considers himself as surrounded by universal jealousy: "After many deaths, and many dispersions, two or three of us," says he, "may still be brought together, not to plot, but to divert ourselves, and the world too, if it pleases"; and they can live together, and "show what friends wits may be, in spite of all the fools in the world." All this while it was likely that the clerks did not know his hand; he certainly had no more enemies than a public character like his inevitably excites; and with what degree of friendship the wits might live, very few were so much fools as ever to inquire.

Some part of this pretended discontent he learned from Swift, and expresses it, I think, most frequently in his correspondence with him. Swift's resentment was unreasonable, but it was sincere; Pope's was the mere mimicry of his friend, a fictitious part which he began to play before it became him. When he was only twenty-five years old, he related that "a glut of study and retirement had thrown him on the world," and that there was danger lest "a glut of the world should throw him back upon study and retirement." To this Swift answered with great propriety that Pope had not yet acted or suffered enough in the world to have become weary of it. And, indeed, it must have been some very powerful reason that can drive back to solitude him who has once enjoyed the pleasures of society.

In the letters both of Swift and Pope there appears such narrowness of mind as makes them insensible of any excellence that has not some affinity with their own, and confines their esteem and approbation to so small a number that whoever should form his opinion of their age from their representation, would suppose them to have lived amidst ignorance and barbarity, unable to find among their contemporaries either virtue or intelligence, and persecuted by those that could not understand them.

When Pope murmurs at the world, when he professes contempt of fame, when he speaks of riches and poverty, of success and disappointment, with negligent indifference, he certainly does not express his habitual and settled sentiments, but either wilfully disguises his own character, or, what is more likely, invests himself with temporary qualities, and sallies out in the colours of the present moment. His hopes and fears, his joys and sorrows, acted strongly upon his mind, and if he differed from others it was not by carelessness. He was irritable and resentful; his malignity to Philips, whom he had first made ridiculous and then hated for being angry, continued too long. Of his vain desire to make Bentley[5] contemptible, I never heard any adequate reason. He was sometimes wanton in his attacks, and before Chandos, Lady Wortley, and Hill was mean in his retreat.

The virtues which seem to have had most of his affection were liberality and fidelity of friendship, in which it does not appear that he was other than he describes himself. His fortune did not suffer his charity to be splendid and conspicuous, but he assisted Dodsley with a hundred pounds that he might open a shop, and of the subscription of forty pounds a year that he raised for Savage twenty were paid by himself. He was accused of loving money, but his love was eagerness to gain, not solicitude to keep it.

In the duties of friendship he was zealous and constant: his early maturity of mind commonly united him with men older than himself, and therefore, without attaining any considerable length of life, he saw many companions of his youth sink into the grave; but it does not appear that he lost a single friend by coldness or by injury: those who loved him once continued their kindness. His ungrateful mention of Allen in his will was the effect of his adherence to one whom he had known much longer, and whom he naturally loved with greater fondness. His violation of the trust reposed in him by Bolingbroke could have no motive inconsistent with the warmest affection; he either thought the action so near to indifferent that he forgot it, or so laudable that he expected his friend to approve it.

It was reported with such confidence as almost to enforce belief, that in the papers entrusted to his executors was found a defamatory *Life of Swift,* which he had prepared as an instrument of vengeance to be used if any provocation should be ever given. About this I inquired of the Earl of Marchmont, who assured me that no such piece was among his remains.

The religion in which he lived and died was that of the Church of Rome, to which in his correspondence with Racine he professes himself a sincere adherent. That he was not scrupulously pious in some part of his life is known by many idle and indecent applications of sentences taken from the Scriptures; a mode of merriment which a good man dreads for its profaneness, and a witty man disdains for its easiness and vulgarity. But to whatever levities he has been betrayed, it does not appear that his principles were ever corrupted, or that he ever lost his belief of revelation. The positions which he transmitted from Bolingbroke he seems not to have understood, and was pleased with an interpretation that made them orthodox.

A man of such exalted superiority and so little moderation would naturally have all his delinquencies observed and aggravated; those who could not deny that he was excellent would rejoice to find that he was not perfect.

Perhaps it may be imputed to the unwillingness with which the same man is allowed to possess many advantages that his learning has been depreciated. He certainly was in his early life a man of great literary curiosity, and when he wrote his *Essay on Criticism* had for his age a very wide acquaintance with books. When he entered into the living world it seems to have happened to him, as to many others, that he was less attentive to dead masters: he studied in the academy of Paracelsus, and made the universe his favourite volume. He gathered his notions fresh from reality, not from the copies of authors, but the originals of Nature. Yet there is no reason to believe that literature ever lost his esteem; he always professed to love reading, and Dobson, who spent some time at his house translating his *Essay on Man,* when I asked him what learning he found him to possess, answered, "More than I expected." His frequent references to history, his allusions to various kinds of knowledge, and his images selected from art and nature, with his observations on the operations of the mind and the modes of life, show an intelligence perpetually on the wing, excursive, vigorous, and diligent, eager to pursue knowledge, and attentive to retain it.

From this curiosity arose the desire of travelling, to which he alludes in his verses to Jervas, and which, though he never found an opportunity to gratify it, did not leave him till his life declined.

Of his intellectual character, the constituent and fundamental principle was good sense, a prompt and intuitive perception of consonance and propriety. He saw immediately of his own conceptions what was to be chosen and what to be rejected, and, in the works of others, what was to be shunned and what was to be copied.

But good sense alone is a sedate and quiescent quality, which manages its possessions well, but does not increase them; it collects few materials for its own operations, and preserves safety, but never gains supremacy. Pope had likewise genius; a mind active, ambitious, and adventurous, always investigating, always aspiring; in its widest searches still longing to go forward, in its highest flights still wishing to be higher, always imagining some thing greater than it knows, always endeavouring more than it can do.

To assist these powers he is said to have had great strength and exactness of memory. That which he had heard or read was not easily lost, and he had before him not only what his own meditations suggested, but what he had found in other writers that might be accommodated to his present purpose.

These benefits of nature he improved by incessant and unwearied diligence; he had recourse to every source of intelligence, and lost no opportunity of information; he consulted the living as well as the dead; he read his compositions to his friends, and was never content with mediocrity when excellence could be attained. He considered poetry as the business of his life, and however he might seem to lament his occupation he followed it with constancy: to make verses was his first labour, and to mend them was his last.

From his attention to poetry he was never diverted. If conversation offered anything that could be improved, he committed it to paper; if a thought, or perhaps an expression, more happy than was common, rose to his mind, he was careful to write it; an independent distich was preserved for an opportunity of insertion, and some little fragments have been found containing lines, or parts of lines, to be wrought upon at some other time.

He was one of those few whose labour is their pleasure; he was never elevated to negligence nor wearied to impatience; he never passed a fault unamended by indifference, nor quitted it by despair. He laboured his works first to gain reputation, and afterwards to keep it.

Of composition there are different methods. Some employ at once memory and invention, and, with little intermediate use of the pen, form and polish large masses by continued meditation, and write their productions only when, in their own opinion, they have completed them. It is related of Virgil that his custom was to pour out a great number of verses in the morning and pass the day in retrenching exuberances and correcting inaccuracies. The method of Pope, as may be collected from his translation, was to write his first thoughts in his first words, and gradually to amplify, decorate, rectify, and refine them.

With such faculties and such dispositions he excelled every other writer in *poetical prudence;* he wrote in such a manner as might expose him to few hazards. He used almost always the same fabric of verse, and, indeed, by those few essays which he made of any other, he did not enlarge his reputation. Of this uniformity the certain consequence was readiness and dexterity. By perpetual practice language had, in his mind, a systematical arrangement; having always the same use for words, he had words so selected and combined as to be ready at his call. This increase of facility he confessed himself to have perceived in the progress of his translation.

But what was yet of more importance, his effusions were always voluntary, and his subjects chosen by himself. His independence secured him from drudging at a task, and labouring upon a barren topic; he never exchanged praise for money, nor opened a shop of condolence or congratulation. His poems, therefore, were scarcely ever temporary. He suffered coronations and royal marriages to pass without a song, and derived no opportunities from recent events, nor any popularity from the accidental disposition of his readers. He was never reduced to the necessity of soliciting the sun to shine upon a birthday, of calling the graces and virtues to a wedding, or of saying what multitudes have said before him. When he could produce nothing new he was at liberty to be silent.

His publications were for the same reason never hasty. He is said to have sent nothing to the press till it had lain two years under his inspection: it is at least certain that he ventured nothing without nice examination. He suffered the tumult of imagination to subside, and the novelties of invention to grow familiar. He knew that the mind is always enamoured of its own productions, and did not trust his first fondness. He consulted his friends, and listened with great willingness to criticism; and, what was of more importance, he consulted himself, and let nothing pass against his own judgment.

He professed to have learned his poetry from Dryden, whom, whenever an opportunity was presented, he praised through his whole life with unvaried liberality; and perhaps his character may receive some illustration if he be compared with his master.

Integrity of understanding and nicety of discernment were not allotted in a less proportion to Dryden than to Pope. The rectitude of Dryden's mind was sufficiently shown by the dismission of his poetical prejudices, and the rejection of unnatural thoughts and rugged numbers. But Dryden never desired to apply all the judgment that he had. He wrote, and professed to write, merely for the people; and when he pleased others, he contented himself. He spent no time in struggles to rouse latent powers: he never attempted to make that better which was already good, nor often to mend what he must have known to be faulty. He wrote, as he tells us, with very little consideration; when occasion or necessity called upon him, he poured out what the present moment happened to supply, and, when once it had passed the press, ejected it from his mind; for when he had no pecuniary interest, he had no further solicitude.

Pope was not content to satisfy; he desired to excel, and therefore always endeavoured to do his best: he did not court the candour, but dared the judgment of his reader, and, expecting no indulgence from others, he showed none to himself. He examined lines and words with minute and punctilious observation, and retouched every part with indefatigable diligence, till he had left nothing to be forgiven.

For this reason he kept his pieces very long in his hands, while he considered and reconsidered them. The only poems which can be supposed to have been written with such regard to the times as might hasten their publication were the two satires of *Thirty-eight;* of which Dodsley told me that they were brought to him by the author that they might be fairly copied. "Almost every line," he said, "was then written twice over; I gave him a clean transcript, which he sent some time afterwards to me for the press, with almost every line written twice over a second time."

His declaration that his care for his works ceased at their publication was not strictly true. His parental attention never abandoned them; what he found amiss in the first edition, he silently corrected in those that followed. He appears to have revised the *Iliad,* and freed it from some of its imperfections; and the *Essay on Criticism* received many improvements after its first appearance. It will seldom be found that he altered without adding clearness, elegance, or vigour. Pope had perhaps the judgment of Dryden; but Dryden certainly wanted the diligence of Pope.

In acquired knowledge, the superiority must be allowed to Dryden, whose education was more scholastic, and who before he became an author had been allowed more time for study, with better means of information. His mind has a larger range, and he collects his images and illustrations from a more extensive circumference of science. Dryden knew more of man in his general nature, and Pope in his local manners. The notions of Dryden were formed by comprehensive speculation, and those of Pope by minute attention. There is more dignity in the knowledge of Dryden, and more certainty in that of Pope.

Poetry was not the sole praise of either, for both excelled likewise in prose; but Pope did not borrow his prose from his predecessor. The style of Dryden is capricious and varied; that of Pope is cautious and uniform. Dryden obeys the motions of his own mind; Pope constrains his mind to his own rules of composition. Dryden is sometimes vehement and rapid; Pope is always smooth, uniform, and gentle. Dryden's page is a natural field, rising into inequalities, and diversified by the varied exuberance of abundant vegetation; Pope's is a velvet lawn, shaven by the scythe, and levelled by the roller.

Of genius, that power which constitutes a poet; that quality without which judgment is cold, and knowledge is inert; that energy which collects, combines, amplifies, and animates; the superiority must, with some hesitation, be allowed to Dryden. It is not to be inferred that of this poetical vigour Pope had only a little, because Dryden had more; for every other writer since Milton must give place to Pope; and even of Dryden it must be said that, if he has brighter paragraphs, he has not better poems. Dryden's performances were always hasty, either excited by some external occasion, or extorted by domestic necessity; he composed without consideration, and published without correction. What his mind could supply at call, or gather in one excursion, was all that he sought, and all that he gave. The dilatory caution of Pope enabled him to condense his sentiments, to multiply his images, and to accumulate all that study might produce or chance might supply. If the flights of Dryden therefore are higher, Pope continues longer on the wing. If of Dryden's fire the blaze is brighter, of Pope's the heat is more regular and constant. Dryden often surpasses expectation, and Pope never falls below it. Dryden is read with frequent astonishment, and Pope with perpetual delight.

This parallel will, I hope, when it is well considered, be found just; and if the reader should suspect me, as I suspect myself, of some partial fondness for the memory of Dryden, let him not too hastily condemn me; for meditation and inquiry may, perhaps, show him the reasonableness of my determination.

The works of Pope are now to be distinctly examined, not so much with attention to slight faults or petty beauties, as to the general character and effect of each performance.

It seems natural for a young poet to initiate himself by pastorals, which, not professing to imitate real life, require no experience; and, exhibiting only the simple operation of unmingled passions, admit no subtle reasoning or deep inquiry. Pope's *Pastorals* are not however composed but with close thought; they have reference to the times of the day, the seasons of the year, and the periods of human life. The last, that which turns the attention upon age and death, was the author's favourite. To tell of disappointment and misery, to thicken the darkness of futurity and perplex the labyrinth of uncertainty, has been always a delicious employment of the poets. His preference was probably just. I wish, however, that his fondness had not overlooked a line in which the "Zephyrs" are made to "lament in silence."

To charge these *Pastorals* with want of invention is to require what was never intended. The imitations are so ambitiously frequent that the writer evidently means rather to show his literature than his wit. It is surely sufficient for an author of sixteen not only to be able to copy the poems of antiquity with judicious selection, but to have obtained sufficient power of language and skill in metre to exhibit a series of versification which had in English poetry no precedent, nor has since had an imitation.

The design of *Windsor Forest* is evidently derived from *Cooper's Hill*, with some attention to Waller's poem on *The Park;* but Pope cannot be denied to excel his masters in variety and elegance, and the art of interchanging description, narrative, and morality. The objection made by Dennis is the want of plan, of a regular subordination of parts terminating in the principal and original design.[6] There is this want in most descriptive poems because as the scenes, which they must exhibit successively, are all subsisting at the same time, the order in which they are shown must by necessity be arbitrary, and more is not to be expected from the last part than from the first. The attention, therefore, which cannot be detained by suspense, must be excited by diversity, such as this poem offers to its reader.

But the desire of diversity may be too much indulged; the parts of *Windsor Forest* which deserve least praise are those which were added to enliven the stillness of the scene, the appearance of Father Thames, and the transformation of Lodona. Addison had in his *Campaign* derided the "Rivers" that "rise from their oozy beds" to tell stories of heroes, and it is therefore strange that Pope should adopt a fiction not only unnatural but lately censured. The story of Lodona is told with sweetness; but a new metamorphosis is a ready and puerile expedient; nothing is easier than to tell how a flower was once a blooming virgin, or a rock an obdurate tyrant.

The Temple of Fame has, as Steele warmly declared, "a thousand beauties." Every part is splendid; there is great luxuriance of ornaments; the original vision of Chaucer was never denied to be much improved; the allegory is very skilfully continued, the imagery is properly selected, and learnedly displayed; yet, with all this comprehension of excellence, as its scene is laid in remote ages, and its sentiments, if the concluding paragraph be excepted, have little relation to general manners or common life, it never obtained much notice, but is turned silently over, and seldom quoted or mentioned with either praise or blame.

That the *The Messiah* excels the *Pollio*[7] is no great praise, if it be considered from what original[8] the improvements are derived.

The *Verses on the Unfortunate Lady* have drawn much attention by the illaudable singularity of treating suicide with respect; and they must be allowed to be written in some parts with vigorous animation, and in others with gentle tenderness; nor has Pope produced any poem in which the sense predominates more over the diction. But the tale is not skilfully told: it is not easy to discover the character of either the lady or her guardian. History relates that she was about to disparage herself by a marriage with an inferior; Pope praises her for the dignity of ambition, and yet condemns the uncle to detestation for his pride: the ambitious love of a niece may be opposed by the interest, malice, or envy of an uncle, but never by his pride. On such an occasion a poet may be allowed to be obscure, but inconsistency never can be right.

The *Ode for St. Cecilia's Day* was undertaken at the desire of Steele: in this the author is generally confessed to have miscarried, yet he has miscarried only as compared with Dryden; for he has far outgone other competitors. Dryden's plan is better chosen; history will always take stronger hold of the attention than fable: the passions excited by Dryden are the pleasures and pains of real life, the scene of Pope is laid in imaginary existence; Pope is read with calm acquiescence, Dryden with turbulent delight; Pope hangs upon the ear, and Dryden finds the passes of the mind.

Both the odes want the essential constituent of metrical compositions, the stated recurrence of settled numbers. It may be alleged that Pindar is said by Horace to have written *numeris lege solutis;*[9] but as no such lax performances have been transmitted to us, the meaning of that expression cannot be fixed; and perhaps the like return might properly be made to a modern Pindarist, as Mr. Cobb[10] received from Bentley, who, when he found his criticisms upon a Greek exercise, which Cobb had presented, refuted one after another by Pindar's authority, cried out at last, "Pindar was a bold fellow, but thou art an impudent one."

If Pope's ode be particularly inspected it will be found that the first stanza consists of sounds well chosen indeed, but only sounds.

The second consists of hyperbolical commonplaces, easily to be found, and perhaps without much difficulty to be as well expressed.

In the third, however, there are numbers, images, harmony, and vigour, not unworthy the antagonist of Dryden. Had all been like this—but every part cannot be the best.

The next stanzas place and detain us in the dark and dismal regions of mythology, where neither hope nor fear, neither joy nor sorrow can be found: the poet however faithfully attends us; we have all that can be performed by elegance of diction or sweetness of versification; but what can form avail without better matter?

The last stanza recurs again to commonplaces. The conclusion is too evidently modelled by that of Dryden; and it may be remarked that both end with the same fault, the comparison of each is literal on one side and metaphorical on the other.

Poets do not always express their own thoughts; Pope, with all this labour in the praise of music, was ignorant of its principles and insensible of its effects.

One of his greatest though of his earliest works is the *Essay on Criticism,* which if he had written nothing else would have placed him among the first critics and the first poets, as it exhibits every mode of excellence that can embellish or dignify didactic composition, selection of matter, novelty of arrangement, justness of precept, splendour of illustration, and propriety of digression. I know not whether it be pleasing to consider that he produced this piece at twenty, and never afterwards excelled it: he that delights himself with observing that such powers may be soon attained cannot but grieve to think that life was ever after at a stand.

To mention the particular beauties of the *Essay* would be unprofitably tedious; but I cannot forbear to observe that the comparison of a student's progress in the sciences with the journey of a traveller in the Alps is perhaps the best that English poetry can show. A simile, to be perfect, must both illustrate and ennoble the subject; must show it to the understanding in a clearer view, and display it to the fancy with greater dignity; but either of these qualities may be sufficient to recommend it. In didactic poetry, of which the great purpose is instruction, a simile may be praised which illustrates, though it does not ennoble; in heroics, that may be admitted which ennobles, though it does not illustrate. That it may be complete, it is required to exhibit, independently of its references, a pleasing image; for a simile is said to be a short episode. To this antiquity was so attentive that circumstances were sometimes added which, having no parallels, served only to fill the imagination, and produced what Perrault ludicrously called "comparisons with a long tail." In their similes the greatest writers have sometimes failed: the ship-race, compared with the chariot-race, is neither illustrated nor aggrandised;[11] land and water make all the difference: when Apollo, running after Daphne, is likened to a greyhound chasing a hare;[12] there is nothing gained; the ideas of pursuit and flight are too plain to be made plainer; and a god and the daughter of a god are not represented much to their advantage by a hare and dog. The simile of the Alps has no useless parts, yet affords a striking picture by itself; it makes the foregoing position better understood, and enables it to take faster hold on the attention; it assists the apprehension and elevates the fancy.

Let me likewise dwell a little on the celebrated paragraph in which it is directed that "the sound should seem an echo to the sense"; a precept which Pope is allowed to have observed beyond any other English poet.

This notion of representative metre, and the desire of discovering frequent adaptations of the sound to the sense, have produced, in my opinion, many wild conceits and imaginary beauties. All that can furnish this representation are the sounds of the words considered singly and the time in which they are pronounced. Every language has some words framed to exhibit the noises which they express, as *thump, rattle, growl, hiss.* These, however, are but few, and the poet cannot make them more, nor can they be of any use but when sound is to be mentioned. The time of pronunciation was in the dactylic measures of the learned languages capable of considerable variety; but that variety could be accommodated only to motion or duration, and different degrees of motion were perhaps expressed by verses rapid or slow, without much attention of the writer, when the image had full possession of his fancy: but our language having little flexibility, our verses can differ very little in their cadence. The fancied resemblances, I fear, arise sometimes merely from the ambiguity of words; there is supposed to be some relation between a *soft* line and *soft* couch, or between *hard* syllables and *hard* fortune.

Motion, however, may be in some sort exemplified; and yet it may be suspected that in such resemblances the mind often governs the ear, and the sounds are estimated by their meaning. One of their most successful attempts has been to describe the labour of Sisyphus:

> *With many a weary step, and many a groan,*
> *Up a high hill he heaves a huge round stone;*
> *The huge round stone, resulting with a bound,*
> *Thunders impetuous down, and smokes along the ground.*

Who does not perceive the stone to move slowly upward, and roll violently back? But set the same numbers to another sense:

> *While many a merry tale, and many a song,*
> *Cheer'd the rough road, we wish'd the rough road long.*

> *The rough road then, returning in a round,*
> *Mock'd our impatient steps, for all was fairy ground.*

We have now surely lost much of the delay and much of the rapidity.

But to show how little the greatest master of numbers can fix the principles of representative harmony, it will be sufficient to remark that the poet who tells us that

> *When Ajax strives some rock's vast weight to throw,*
> *The line too labours and the words move slow:*
> *Not so when swift Camilla scours the plain,*
> *Flies o'er th' unbending corn, and skims along the main;*

when he had enjoyed for about thirty years the praise of Camilla's lightness of foot, tried another experiment upon *sound* and *time*, and produced this memorable triplet:

> *Waller was smooth; but Dryden taught to join*
> *The varying verse, the full resounding line,*
> *The long majestic march, and energy divine.*

Here are the swiftness of the rapid race and the march of slow-paced majesty exhibited by the same poet in the same sequence of syllables, except that the exact prosodist will find the line of *swiftness* by one time longer than that of *tardiness*.

Beauties of this kind are commonly fancied; and when real are technical and nugatory, not to be rejected and not to be solicited.

To the praises which have been accumulated on *The Rape of the Lock* by readers of every class, from the critic to the waiting-maid, it is difficult to make any addition. Of that which is universally allowed to be the most attractive of all ludicrous compositions, let it rather be now inquired from what sources the power of pleasing is derived.

Dr. Warburton, who excelled in critical perspicacity, has remarked that the preternatural agents are very happily adapted to the purposes of the poem. The heathen deities can no longer gain attention: we should have turned away from a contest between Venus and Diana. The employment of allegorical persons always excites conviction of its own absurdity; they may produce effects but cannot conduct actions; when the phantom is put in motion, it dissolves; thus discord may raise a mutiny, but discord cannot conduct a march, nor besiege a town. Pope brought into view a new race of beings, with powers and passions proportionate to their operation. The sylphs and gnomes act at the toilet and the tea-table what more terrific and more powerful phantoms perform on the stormy ocean or the field of battle: they give their proper help and do their proper mischief.

Pope is said by an objector not to have been the inventor of this petty nation; a charge which might with more justice have been brought against the author of the *Iliad,* who doubtless adopted the religious system of his country; for what is there but the names of his agents which Pope has not invented? Has he not assigned them characters and operations never heard of before? Has he not, at least, given them their first poetical existence? If this is not sufficient to denominate his work original, nothing original ever can be written.

In this work are exhibited in a very high degree the two most engaging powers of an author: new things are made familiar, and familiar things are made new. A race of aerial people never heard of before is presented to us in a manner so clear and easy that the reader seeks for no further information, but immediately mingles with his new acquaintance, adopts their interests, and attends their pursuits, loves a sylph, and detests a gnome.

That familiar things are made new every paragraph will prove. The subject of the poem is an event below the common incidents of common life; nothing real is introduced that is not seen so often as to be no longer regarded; yet the whole detail of a female-day is here brought before us, invested with so much art of decoration that, though nothing is disguised, everything is striking, and we feel all the appetite of curiosity for that from which we have a thousand times turned fastidiously away.

The purpose of the poet is, as he tells us, to laugh at "the little unguarded follies of the female sex." It is therefore without justice that Dennis charges *The Rape of the Lock* with the want of a moral,[13] and for that reason sets it below *The Lutrin,* which exposes the pride and discord of the clergy. Perhaps neither Pope nor Boileau has made the world much better than he found it; but if they had both succeeded, it were easy to tell who would have deserved most from public gratitude. The freaks, and humours, and spleen, and vanity of women as they embroil families in discord, and fill houses with disquiet, do more to obstruct the happiness of life in a year than the ambition of the clergy in many centuries. It has been well observed that the misery of man proceeds not from any single crush of overwhelming evil, but from small vexatious continually repeated.

It is remarked by Dennis likewise that the machinery is superfluous; that by all the bustle of preternatural operation the main event is neither hastened nor retarded.[14] To this charge an efficacious answer is not easily made. The sylphs cannot be said to help or to oppose, and it must be allowed to imply some want of art that their power has not been sufficiently intermingled with the action. Other parts may likewise be charged with want of connection; the game at *ombre* might be spared, but if the lady had lost her hair while she was intent upon her cards it might have been inferred that those who are too fond of play will be in danger of neglecting more important interests. Those perhaps are faults; but what are such faults to so much excellence!

The *Epistle of Eloise to Abelard* is one of the most happy productions of human wit; the subject is so judiciously chosen that it would be difficult in turning over the annals of the world to find another which so many circumstances concur to recommend. We regularly interest ourselves most in the fortune of those who most deserve our notice. Abelard and Eloise were conspicuous in their days for eminence of merit. The heart naturally loves truth. The adventures and misfortunes of this illustrious pair are known from undisputed history. Their fate does not leave the mind in hopeless dejection, for they both found quiet and consolation in retirement and piety. So new and so affecting is their story that it supersedes invention, and imagination ranges at full liberty without straggling into scenes of fable.

The story thus skilfully adopted has been diligently improved. Pope has left nothing behind him which seems more the effect of studious perseverance and laborious revisal. Here is particularly observable the *curiosa felicitas*,[15] a fruitful soil and careful cultivation. Here is no crudeness of sense nor asperity of language. The sources from which sentiments which have so much vigour and efficacy have been drawn are shown to be the mystic writers by the learned author of the *Essay on the Life and Writings of Pope,*[16] a book which teaches how the brow of criticism may be smoothed, and how she may be enabled, with all her severity, to attract and to delight.

The train of my disquisition has now conducted me to that poetical wonder, the translation of the *Iliad,* a performance which no age or nation can pretend to equal. To the Greeks translation was almost unknown; it was totally unknown to the inhabitants of Greece. They had no recourse to the barbarians for poetical beauties, but sought for everything in Homer, where, indeed, there is but little which they might not find. The Italians have been very diligent translators, but I can hear of no version, unless perhaps Anguillara's *Ovid* may be excepted, which is read with eagerness. The *Iliad* of Salvini [1723] every reader may discover to be punctiliously exact; but it seems to be the work of a linguist skilfully pedantic, and his countrymen, the proper judges of its power to please, reject it with disgust.

Their predecessors the Romans have left some specimens of translation behind them, and that employment must have had some credit in which Tully and Germanicus engaged; but unless we suppose, what is perhaps true, that the plays of Terence were versions of Menander, nothing translated seems ever to have risen to high reputation. The French in the meridian hour of their learning were very laudably industrious to enrich their own language with the wisdom of the ancients; but found themselves reduced by whatever necessity to turn the Greek and Roman poetry into prose. Whoever could read an author could translate him. From such rivals little can be feared.

The chief help of Pope in this arduous undertaking was drawn from the versions of Dryden. Virgil had borrowed much of his imagery from Homer; and part of the debt was now paid by his translator. Pope searched the pages of Dryden for happy combinations of heroic diction, but it will not be denied that he added much to what he found. He cultivated our language with so much diligence and art that he has left in his *Homer* a treasure of poetical elegances to posterity. His version may be said to have tuned the English tongue; for since its appearance no writer, however deficient in other powers, has wanted melody. Such a series of lines, so elaborately corrected, and so sweetly modulated, took possession of the public ear; the vulgar was enamoured of the poem, and the learned wondered at the translation.

But in the most general applause discordant voices will always be heard. It has been objected by some who wish to be numbered among the sons of learning that Pope's version of Homer is not Homerical; that it exhibits no resemblance of the original and characteristic manner of the Father of Poetry, as it wants his awful simplicity, his artless grandeur, his unaffected majesty. This cannot be totally denied; but it must be remembered that *necessitas quod cogit defendit,* that may be lawfully done which cannot be forborne. Time and place will always enforce regard. In estimating this translation, consideration must be had of the nature of our language, the form of our metre, and, above all, of the change which two thousand years have made in the modes of life and the habits of thought. Virgil wrote in a language of the same general fabric with that of Homer, in verses of the same measure, and in an age nearer to Homer's time by eighteen hundred years; yet he found even then the state of the world so much altered, and the demand for elegance so much increased, that mere nature would be endured no longer; and, perhaps, in the multitude of borrowed passages, very few can be shown which he has not embellished.

There is a time when nations emerging from barbarity, and falling into regular subordination, gain leisure to grow wise, and feel the shame of ignorance and the craving pain of unsatisfied curiosity. To this hunger of the mind plain sense is grateful; that which fills the void removes uneasiness, and to be free from pain for a while is pleasure; but repletion generates fastidiousness; a saturated intellect soon becomes luxurious, and knowledge finds no willing reception till it is recommended by artificial diction. Thus it will be found in the progress of learning that in all nations the first writers are simple, and that every age improves in elegance. One refinement always makes way for another, and what was expedient to Virgil was necessary to Pope.

I suppose many readers of the English *Iliad,* when they have been touched with some unexpected beauty of the lighter kind, have tried to enjoy it in the original, where, alas! it was not to be found. Homer doubtless owes to his translator many Ovidian graces not exactly suitable to his character; but to have added can be no great crime if nothing be taken away. Elegance is surely to be desired if it be not gained at the expense of dignity. A hero would wish to be loved, as well as to be reverenced.

To a thousand cavils one answer is sufficient: the purpose of a writer is to be read, and the criticism which would destroy the power of pleasing must be blown aside. Pope wrote for his own age and his own nation: he knew that it was necessary to colour the images and point the sentiments of his author; he therefore made him graceful, but lost him some of his sublimity.

The copious notes with which the version is accompanied, and by which it is recommended to many readers, though they were undoubtedly written to swell the volumes, ought not to pass without praise: commentaries which attract the reader by the pleasure of perusal have not often appeared; the notes of others are read to clear difficulties, those of Pope to vary entertainment.

It has, however, been objected, with sufficient reason, that there is in the commentary too much of unseasonable levity and affected gaiety; that too many appeals are made to the ladies, and the ease which is so carefully preserved is sometimes the ease of a trifler. Every art has its terms, and every kind of instruction its proper style; the gravity of common critics may be tedious, but is less despicable than childish merriment.

Of the *Odyssey* nothing remains to be observed; the same general praise may be given to both translations, and a particular examination of either would require a large volume. The notes were written by Broome, who endeavoured, not unsuccessfully, to imitate his master.

Of *The Dunciad* the hint is confessedly taken from Dryden's *Mac Flecknoe,* but the plan is so enlarged and diversified as justly to claim the praise of an original, and affords the best specimen that has yet appeared of personal satire ludicrously pompous.

That the design was moral, whatever the author might tell either his readers or himself, I am not convinced. The first motive was the desire of revenging the contempt with which Theobald had treated his *Shakespeare,* and regaining the honour which he had lost, by crushing his opponent. Theobald was not of bulk enough to fill a poem, and therefore it was necessary to find other enemies with other names, at whose expense he might divert the public.

In this design there was petulance and malignity enough; but I cannot think it very criminal. An author places himself uncalled before the tribunal of criticism, and solicits fame at the hazard of disgrace. Dulness or deformity are not culpable in themselves, but may be very justly reproached when they pretend to the honour of wit or the influence of beauty. If bad writers were to pass without reprehension, what should restrain them? . . . The satire which brought Theobald and Moore into contempt dropped impotent from Bentley, like the javelin of Priam.

All truth is valuable, and satirical criticism may be considered as useful when it rectifies error and improves judgment; he that refines the public taste is a public benefactor.

The beauties of this poem are well known; its chief fault is the grossness of its images. Pope and Swift had an unnatural delight in ideas physically impure, such as every other tongue utters with unwillingness, and of which every ear shrinks from the mention.

But even this fault, offensive as it is, may be forgiven for the excellence of other passages; such as the formation and dissolution of Moore, the account of the Traveller, the misfortune of the Florist, and the crowded thoughts and stately numbers which dignify the concluding paragraph.

The alterations which have been made in *The Dunciad,* not always for the better, require that it should be published, as in the last collection, with all its variations.

The *Essay on Man* was a work of great labour and long consideration, but certainly not the happiest of Pope's performances. The subject is perhaps not very proper for poetry, and the poet was not sufficiently master of his subject; metaphysical morality was to him a new study, he was proud of his acquisitions, and, supposing himself master of great secrets, was in haste to teach what he had not learned. Thus he tells us, in the first Epistle, that from the nature of the Supreme Being may be deduced an order of beings such as mankind because Infinite Excellence can do only what is best. He finds out that these beings must be "somewhere," and that "all the question is, whether man be in a wrong place." Surely if, according to the poet's Leibnitian reasoning, we may infer that man ought to be only because he is, we may allow that his place is the right place, because he has it. Supreme Wisdom is not less infallible in disposing than in creating. But what is meant by "somewhere" and "place" and "wrong place," it has been in vain to ask Pope, who probably had never asked himself.

Having exalted himself into the chair of wisdom, he tells us much that every man knows, and much that he does not know himself; that we see but little, and that the order of the universe is beyond our comprehension, an opinion not very uncommon; and that there is a chain of subordinate beings "from infinite to nothing," of which himself and his readers are equally ignorant. But he gives us one comfort which, without his help he supposes unattainable, in the position "that though we are fools, yet God is wise."

This *Essay* affords an egregious instance of the predominance of genius, the dazzling splendour of imagery, and the seductive powers of eloquence. Never was penury of knowledge and vulgarity of sentiment so happily disguised. The reader feels his mind full, though he learns nothing; and, when he meets it in its new array, no longer knows the talk of his mother and his nurse. When these wonder-working sounds sink into sense and the doctrine of the *Essay,* disrobed of its ornaments, is left to the powers of its naked excellence, what shall we discover? That we are, in comparison with our Creator, very weak and ignorant; that we do not uphold the chain of existence; and that we could not make one another with more skill than we are made. We may learn yet more: that the arts of human life were copied from the instinctive operations of other animals; that if the world be made for man, it may be said that man was made for geese. To these profound principles of natural knowledge are added some moral instructions equally new: that self-interest, well understood, will produce social concord; that men are mutual gainers by mutual benefits; that evil is sometimes balanced by good; that human advantages are unstable and fallacious, of uncertain duration and doubtful effect; that our true honour is not to have a great part, but to act it well; that virtue only is our own; and that happiness is always in our power.

Surely a man of no very comprehensive search may venture to say that he has heard all this before, but it was never till now recommended by such a blaze of embellishments, or such sweetness of melody. The vigorous contraction of some thoughts, the luxuriant amplification of others, the incidental illustrations, and sometimes the dignity, sometimes the softness of the verses, enchain philosophy, suspend criticism, and oppress judgment by overpowering pleasure.

This is true of many paragraphs; yet, if I had undertaken to exemplify Pope's felicity of composition before a rigid critic, I should not select the *Essay on Man;* for it contains more lines unsuccessfully laboured, more harshness of diction, and more thoughts imperfectly expressed, more levity without elegance, and more heaviness without strength, than will easily be found in all his other works.

The *Characters of Men and Women* are the product of diligent speculation upon human life; much labour has been bestowed upon them, and Pope very seldom laboured in vain. That his excellence may be properly estimated, I recommend a comparison of his *Characters of Women* with Boileau's *Satire;* it will then be seen with how much more perspicacity female nature is investigated, and female excellence selected; and he surely is no mean writer to whom Boileau should be found inferior. The *Characters of Men,* however, are written with more, if not with deeper, thought, and exhibit many passages exquisitely beautiful. The "Gem and the Flower" will not easily be equalled. In the women's part are some defects; the character of Atossa is not so neatly finished as that of Clodio, and some of the female characters may be found perhaps more frequently among men; what is said of Philomede was true of Prior.

In the *Epistle to Lord Bathurst* and *Lord Burlington,* Dr. Warburton has endeavoured to find a train of thought which was never in the writer's head, and, to support his hypothesis, has printed that first which was published last. In one the most valuable passage is perhaps the elegy on *Good Sense,* and in the other the *End of the Duke of Buckingham.*

The *Epistle to Arbuthnot,* now arbitrarily called the *Prologue to the Satires,* is a performance consisting, as it seems, of many fragments wrought into one design, which, by this union of scattered beauties, contains more striking paragraphs than could probably have been brought together into an occasional work. As there is no stronger motive to exertion than self-defence, no part has more elegance, spirit, or dignity than the poet's vindication of his own character. The meanest passage is the satire upon Sporus.

Of the two poems which derived their names from the year, and which are called the *Epilogue to the Satires,* it was very justly remarked by Savage that the second was in the whole more strongly conceived and more equally supported, but that it had no single passages equal to the contention in the first for the dignity of vice and the celebration of the triumph of corruption.

The *Imitations of Horace* seem to have been written as relaxations of his genius. This employment became his favourite by its facility; the plan was ready to his hand, and nothing was required but to accommodate as he could the sentiments of an old author to recent facts or familiar images; but what is easy is seldom excellent: such imitations cannot give pleasure to common readers. The man of learning may be sometimes surprised and delighted by an unexpected parallel, but the comparison requires knowledge of the original, which will likewise often detect strained applications. Between Roman images and English manners there will be an irreconcilable dissimilitude, and the works will be generally uncouth and party-coloured; neither original nor translated, neither ancient nor modern.

Pope had, in proportions very nicely adjusted to each other, all the qualities that constitute genius. He had invention, by which new trains of events are formed and new scenes of imagery displayed, as in *The Rape of the Lock,* and by which extrinsic and adventitious embellishments and illustrations are connected with a known subject, as in the *Essay on Criticism;* he had imagination, which strongly impresses on the writer's mind and enables him to convey to the reader the various forms of nature, incidents of life, and energies of passion, as in his *Eloisa, Windsor Forest,* and the *Ethic Epistles.* He had judgment, which selects from life or nature what the present purpose requires, and, by separating the essence of things from its concomitants, often makes the representation more powerful than the reality; and he had colours of language always before him ready to decorate his matter with every grace of elegant expression, as when he accommodates his diction to the wonderful multiplicity of Homer's sentiments and descriptions.

Poetical expression includes sound as well as meaning. "Music," says Dryden, "is inarticulate poetry";[17] among the excellences of Pope, therefore, must be mentioned the melody of his metre. By perusing the works of Dryden, he discovered the most perfect fabric of English verse, and habituated himself to that only which he found the best; in consequence of which restraint his poetry has been censured as too uniformly musical, and as glutting the ear with unvaried sweetness. I suspect this objection to be the cant of those who judge by principles rather than perception, and who would even themselves have less pleasure in his works if he had tried to relieve attention by studied discords, or affected to break his lines and vary his pauses.

But though he was thus careful of his versification he did not oppress his powers with superfluous rigour. He seems to have thought with Boileau that the practice of writing might be refined till the difficulty should overbalance the advantage. The construction of the language is not always strictly grammatical; with those rhymes which prescription had conjoined he contented himself, without regard to Swift's remonstrances, though there was no striking consonance, nor was he very careful to vary his terminations or to refuse admission, at a small distance, to the same rhymes.

To Swift's edict for the exclusion of alexandrines and triplets he paid little regard; he admitted them, but, in the opinion of Fenton, too rarely; he uses them more liberally in his translation than his poems.

He has a few double rhymes, and always, I think, unsuccessfully, except once in *The Rape of the Lock*.

Expletives he very early ejected from his verses; but he now and then admits an epithet rather commodious than important. Each of the six first lines of the *Iliad* might lose two syllables with very little diminution of the meaning; and sometimes, after all his art and labour, one verse seems to be made for the sake of another. In his latter productions the diction is sometimes vitiated by French idioms, with which Bolingbroke had perhaps infected him.

I have been told that the couplet by which he declared his own ear to be most gratified was this:

> *Lo, where Maeotis sleeps, and hardly flows*
> *The freezing Tanais thro' a waste of snows.*

But the reason of this preference I cannot discover.

It is remarked by Watts that there is scarcely a happy combination of words, or a phrase poetically elegant in the English language, which Pope has not inserted into his version of Homer.[18] How he obtained possession of so many beauties of speech it were desirable to know. That he gleaned from authors, obscure as well as eminent, what he thought brilliant or useful, and preserved it all in a regular collection, is not unlikely. When, in his last years, Hall's *Satires* were shown him he wished that he had seen them sooner.

New sentiments and new images others may produce, but to attempt any further improvement of versification will be dangerous. Art and diligence have now done their best, and what shall be added will be the effort of tedious toil and needless curiosity.

After all this it is surely superfluous to answer the question that has once been asked, whether Pope was a poet otherwise than by asking in return, if Pope be not a poet, where is poetry to be found? To circumscribe poetry by a definition will only show the narrowness of the definer, though a definition which shall exclude Pope will not easily be made. Let us look round upon the present time and back upon the past; let us inquire to whom the voice of mankind has decreed the wreath of poetry; let their productions be examined and their claims stated, and the pretensions of Pope will be no more disputed. Had he given the world only his version the name of poet must have been allowed him: if the writer of the *Iliad* were to class his successors he would assign a very high place to his translator, without requiring any other evidence of genius.

Collins

William Collins was born at Chichester on the twenty-fifth of December, about 1720. His father was a hatter of good reputation. He was in 1733, as Dr. Warton has kindly informed me, admitted scholar of Winchester College, where he was educated by Dr. Burton. His English exercises were better than his Latin.

He first courted the notice of the public by some verses *To a Lady Weeping*, published in the *Gentleman's Magazine*.

In 1740 he stood first in the list of the scholars to be received in succession at New College, but unhappily there was no vacancy. This was the original misfortune of his life. He became a Commoner of Queen's College, probably with a scanty maintenance; but was in about half a year elected a *Demy* of Magdalen College, where he continued till he had taken a Bachelor's degree, and then suddenly left the university; for what reason I know not that he told.

He now (about 1744) came to London a literary adventurer, with many projects in his head, and very little money in his pocket. He designed many works, but his great fault was irresolution, or the frequent calls of immediate necessity broke his schemes, and suffered him to pursue no settled purpose. A man doubtful of his dinner, or trembling at a creditor, is not much disposed to abstracted meditation or remote inquiries. He published proposals for a *History of the Revival of Learning;* and I have heard him speak with great kindness of Leo the Tenth, and with keen resentment of his tasteless successor. But probably not a page of his history was ever written. He planned several tragedies, but he only planned them. He wrote now and then odes and other poems, and did something, however little. About this time I fell into his company. His appearance was decent and manly; his knowledge considerable, his views extensive, his conversation elegant, and his disposition cheerful. By degrees I gained his confidence; and one day was admitted to him when he was immured by a bailiff that was prowling in the street. On this occasion recourse was had to the booksellers, who, on the credit of a translation of Aristotle's *Poetics,* which he engaged to write with a large commentary, advanced as much money as enabled him to escape into the country. He showed me the guineas safe in his hand. Soon afterwards his uncle, Mr. Martin, a lieutenant-colonel, left him about two thousand pounds; a sum which Collins could scarcely think exhaustible, and which he did not live to exhaust. The guineas were then repaid, and the translation neglected. But man is not born for happiness. Collins, who, while he "studied to live," felt no evil but poverty, no sooner lived to study than his life was assailed by more dreadful calamities, disease, and insanity.

Having formerly written his character,[1] while perhaps it was yet more distinctly impressed upon my memory, I shall insert it here.

Mr. Collins was a man of extensive literature, and of vigorous faculties. He was acquainted not only with the learned tongues, but with the Italian, French, and Spanish languages. He had employed his mind chiefly on works upon fiction and subjects of fancy; and by indulging some peculiar habits of thought was eminently delighted with those flights of imagination which pass the bounds of nature, and to which the mind is reconciled only by a passive acquiescence in popular traditions. He loved fairies, genii, giants, and monsters; he delighted to rove through the meanders of enchantment, to gaze on the magnificence of golden palaces, to repose by the waterfalls of Elysian gardens.

This was however the character rather of his inclination than his genius; the grandeur of wildness and the novelty of extravagance were always desired by him, but not always attained. Yet as diligence is never wholly lost, if his efforts sometimes caused harshness and obscurity, they likewise produced in happier moments sublimity and splendour. This idea which he had formed of excellence led him to oriental fictions and allegorical imagery, and, perhaps, while he was intent upon description, he did not sufficiently cultivate sentiment. His poems are the productions of a mind not deficient in fire, nor unfurnished with knowledge either of books or life, but somewhat obstructed in its progress by deviation in quest of mistaken beauties.

His morals were pure and his opinions pious; in a long continuance of poverty and long habits of dissipation, it cannot be expected that any character should be exactly uniform. There is a degree of want by which the freedom of agency is almost destroyed; and long association with fortuitous companions will at last relax the strictness of truth and abate the fervour of sincerity. That this man, wise and virtuous as he was, passed always unentangled through the snares of life, it would be prejudice and temerity to affirm; but it may be said that at least he preserved the source of action unpolluted, that his principles were never shaken, that his distinctions of right and wrong were never confounded, and that his faults had nothing of malignity or design, but proceeded from some unexpected pressure, or casual temptation.

The latter part of his life cannot be remembered but with pity and sadness. He languished some years under that depression of mind which enchains the faculties without destroying them, and leaves reason the knowledge of right without the power of pursuing it. These clouds which he perceived gathering on his intellect he endeavoured to disperse by travel, and passed into France; but found himself constrained to yield to his malady, and returned. He was for some time confined in a house of lunatics, and afterwards retired to the care of his sister in Chichester, where death in 1756 came to his relief.

After his return from France the writer of this character paid him a visit at Islington, where he was waiting for his sister, whom he had directed to meet him. There was then nothing of disorder discernible in his mind by any but himself, but he had withdrawn from study, and travelled with no other book than an English Testament, such as children carry to the school. When his friend took it into his hand, out of curiosity to see what companion a Man of Letters had chosen, "I have but one book," said Collins, "but that is the best."

Such was the fate of Collins, with whom I once delighted to converse, and whom I yet remember with tenderness.

He was visited at Chichester in his last illness by his learned friends Dr. Warton and his brother, to whom he spoke with disapprobation of his *Oriental Eclogues,* as not sufficiently expressive of Asiatic manners, and called them his "Irish Eclogues." He showed them at the same time an ode inscribed to Mr. John Hume on the superstitions of the Highlands, which they thought superior to his other works, but which no search has yet found.

His disorder was not alienation of mind, but general laxity and feebleness, a deficiency rather of his vital than his intellectual powers. What he spoke wanted neither judgment nor spirit; but a few minutes exhausted him, so that he was forced to rest upon the couch, till a short cessation restored his powers, and he was again able to talk with his former vigour.

The approaches of this dreadful malady he began to feel soon after his uncle's death, and, with the usual weakness of men so diseased, eagerly snatched that temporary relief with which the table and the bottle flatter and seduce. But his health continually declined, and he grew more and more burdensome to himself.

To what I have formerly said of his writings may be added that his diction was often harsh, unskilfully laboured, and injudiciously selected. He affected the obsolete when it was not worthy of revival; and he puts his words out of the common order, seeming to think, with some later candidates for fame, that not to write prose is certainly to write poetry. His lines commonly are of slow motion, clogged and impeded with clusters of consonants. As men are often esteemed who cannot be loved, so the poetry of Collins may sometimes extort praise when it gives little pleasure.

Savage

It has been observed in all ages that the advantages of nature or of fortune have contributed very little to the promotion of happiness; and that those whom the splendour of their rank or the extent of their capacity have placed upon the summits of human life, have not often given any just occasion to envy in those who look up to them from a lower station: whether it be that apparent superiority incites great designs, and great designs are naturally liable to fatal miscarriages; or that the general lot of mankind is misery, and the misfortunes of those whose eminence drew upon them an universal attention have been more carefully recorded, because they were more generally observed, and have in reality been only more conspicuous than those of others, not more frequent, or more severe.

That affluence and power, advantages extrinsic and adventitious, and therefore easily separable from those by whom they are possessed, should very often flatter the mind with expectations of felicity which they cannot give, raises no astonishment: but it seems rational to hope that intellectual greatness should produce better effects; that minds qualified for great attainments should first endeavour their own benefit; and that they who are most able to teach others the way to happiness should with most certainty follow it themselves.

But this expectation, however plausible, has been very frequently disappointed. The heroes of literary as well as civil history have been very often no less remarkable for what [they have suffered than for what] they have achieved; and volumes have been written only to enumerate the miseries of the learned, and relate their unhappy lives and untimely deaths.

To these mournful narratives I am about to add the *Life of Richard Savage,* a man whose writings entitle him to an eminent rank in the classes of learning, and whose misfortunes claim a degree of compassion not always due to the unhappy, as they were often the consequences of the crimes of others rather than his own.

In the year 1697 Anne Countess of Macclesfield, having lived for some time upon very uneasy terms with her husband, thought a public confession of adultery the most obvious and expeditious method of obtaining her liberty, and therefore declared that the child with which she was then great was begotten by the Earl Rivers. This, as may be imagined, made her husband no less desirous of a separation than herself, and he prosecuted his design in the most effectual manner; for he applied not to the ecclesiastical courts for a divorce, but to the parliament for an act by which his marriage might be dissolved, the nuptial contract totally annulled, and the children of his wife illegitimated. This act, after the usual deliberation, he obtained, though without the approbation of some, who considered marriage as an affair only cognizable by ecclesiastical judges; and on March 3d was separated from his wife, whose fortune, which was very great, was repaid her, and who having, as well as her husband, the liberty of making another choice, was in a short time married to Colonel Brett.

While the Earl of Macclesfield was prosecuting this affair his wife was, on the 10th of January, 1697–8, delivered of a son, and the Earl Rivers, by appearing to consider him as his own, left none any reason to doubt of the sincerity of her declaration; for he was his godfather, and gave him his own name, which was by his direction inserted in the register of St. Andrew's parish in Holborn, but unfortunately left him to the care of his mother, whom, as she was now set free from her husband, he probably imagined likely to treat with great tenderness the child that had contributed to so pleasing an event. It is not indeed easy to discover what motives could be found to overbalance that natural affection of a parent, or what interest could be promoted by neglect or cruelty. The dread of shame or of poverty, by which some wretches have been incited to abandon or to murder their children, cannot be supposed to have affected a woman who had proclaimed her crimes and solicited reproach, and on whom the clemency of the legislature had undeservedly bestowed a fortune, which would have been very little diminished by the expenses which the care of her child could have brought upon her. It was therefore not likely that she would be wicked without temptation, that she would look upon her son from his birth with a kind of resentment and abhorrence, and, instead of supporting, assisting, and defending him, delight to see him struggling with misery; or that she would take every opportunity of aggravating his misfortunes and obstructing his resources, and with an implacable and restless cruelty continue her persecution from the first hour of his life to the last.

But whatever were her motives, no sooner was her son born than she discovered a resolution of disowning him; and in a very short time removed him from her sight by committing him to the care of a poor woman, whom she directed to educate him as her own, and enjoined never to inform him of his true parents.

Such was the beginning of the life of Richard Savage. Born with a legal claim to honour and to affluence he was in two months illegitimated by the parliament and disowned by his mother, doomed to poverty and obscurity, and launched upon the ocean of life only that he might be swallowed by its quicksands or dashed upon its rocks.

His mother could not indeed infect others with the same cruelty. As it was impossible to avoid the inquiries which the curiosity or tenderness of her relations made after her child, she was obliged to give some account of the measures that she had taken; and her mother, the Lady Mason, whether in approbation of her design or to prevent more criminal contrivances, engaged to transact with the nurse, to pay her for her care, and to superintend the education of the child.

In this charitable office she was assisted by his godmother Mrs. Lloyd, who, while she lived, always looked upon him with that tenderness which the barbarity of his mother made peculiarly necessary; but her death, which happened in his tenth year, was another of the misfortunes of his childhood: for though she kindly endeavoured to alleviate his loss by a legacy of three hundred pounds, yet, as he had none to prosecute his claim, to shelter him from oppression, or call in law to the assistance of justice, her will was eluded by the executors, and no part of the money was ever paid.

He was, however, not yet wholly abandoned. The Lady Mason still continued her care, and directed him to be placed at a small grammar-school near St. Alban's, where he was called by the name of his nurse, without the least intimation that he had a claim to any other.

Here he was initiated in literature, and passed through several of the classes, with what rapidity or what applause cannot now be known. As he always spoke with respect of his master, it is probable that the mean rank, in which he then appeared, did not hinder his genius from being distinguished, or his industry from being rewarded; and if in so low a state he obtained distinction and rewards, it is not likely that they were gained but by genius and industry.

It is very reasonable to conjecture that his application was equal to his abilities, because his improvement was more than proportioned to the opportunities which he enjoyed; nor can it be doubted that if his earliest productions had been preserved like those of happier students, we might in some have found vigorous sallies of that sprightly humour which distinguishes *The Author to Be Let,* and in others strong touches of that ardent imagination which painted the solemn scenes of *The Wanderer.*

While he was thus cultivating his genius, his father, the Earl Rivers, was seized with a distemper, which in a short time put an end to his life. He had frequently inquired after his son, and had always been amused with fallacious and evasive answers but, being now in his own opinion on his death-bed, he thought it his duty to provide for him among his other natural children and therefore demanded a positive account of him, with an importunity not to be diverted or denied. His mother, who could no longer refuse an answer, determined at least to give such as should cut him off for ever from that happiness which competence affords, and therefore declared that he was dead; which is perhaps the first instance of a lie invented by a mother to deprive her son of a provision which was designed him by another, and which she could not expect herself, though he should lose it.

This was therefore an act of wickedness which could not be defeated, because it could not be suspected: the Earl did not imagine that there could exist in a human form a mother that would ruin her son without enriching herself; and therefore bestowed upon some other person six thousand pounds, which he had in his will bequeathed to Savage.

[...]

He lodged as much by accident as he dined, and passed the night sometimes in mean houses, which are set open at night to any casual wanderers, sometimes in cellars, among the riot and filth of the meanest and most profligate of the rabble; and sometimes, when he had not money to support even the expenses of these receptacles, walked about the streets till he was weary, and lay down in the summer upon a bulk, or in the winter, with his associates in poverty, among the ashes of a glass-house.

In this manner were passed those days and those nights which nature had enabled him to have employed in elevated speculations, useful studies, or pleasing conversation. On a bulk, in a cellar, or in a glass-house among thieves and beggars, was to be found the author of *The Wanderer,* the man of exalted sentiments, extensive views, and curious observations; the man whose remarks on life might have assisted the statesman, whose ideas of virtue might have enlightened the moralist, whose eloquence might have influenced senates, and whose delicacy might have polished courts.

[...]

Whoever was acquainted with him was certain to be solicited for small sums, which the frequency of the request made in time considerable, and he was therefore quickly shunned by those who were become familiar enough to be trusted with his necessities; but his rambling manner of life, and constant appearance at houses of public resort, always procured him a new succession of friends, whose kindness had not been exhausted by repeated requests; so that he was seldom absolutely without resources, but had in his utmost exigencies this comfort, that he always imagined himself sure of speedy relief.

It was observed that he always asked favours of this kind without the least submission or apparent consciousness of dependence, and that he did not seem to look upon a compliance with his request as an obligation that deserved any extraordinary acknowledgements; but a refusal was resented by him as an affront, or complained of as an injury: nor did he readily reconcile himself to those who either denied to lend, or gave him afterwards any intimation that they expected to be repaid.

He was sometimes so far compassionated by those who knew both his merit and distresses that they received him into their families, but they soon discovered him to be a very incommodious inmate; for, being always accustomed to an irregular manner of life, he could not confine himself to any stated hours, or pay any regard to the rules of a family, but would prolong his conversation till midnight, without considering that business might require his friend's application in the morning; and, when he had persuaded himself to retire to bed, was not, without equal difficulty, called up to dinner: it was therefore impossible to pay him any distinction without the entire subversion of all economy, a kind of establishment which, wherever he went, he always appeared ambitious to overthrow.

It must therefore be acknowledged, in justification of mankind, that it was not always by the negligence or coldness of his friends that Savage was distressed, but because it was in reality very difficult to preserve him long in a state of ease. To supply him with money was a hopeless attempt, for no sooner did he see himself master of a sum sufficient to set him free from care for a day, than he became profuse and luxurious. When once he had entered a tavern, or engaged in a scheme of pleasure, he never retired till want of money obliged him to some new expedient. If he was entertained in a family nothing was any longer to be regarded there but amusements and jollity: wherever Savage entered he immediately expected that order and business should fly before him, that all should thenceforward be left to hazard, and that no dull principle of domestic management should be opposed to his inclination, or intrude upon his gaiety.

His distresses, however afflictive, never dejected him; in his lowest state he wanted not spirit to assert the natural dignity of wit, and was always ready to repress that insolence which superiority of fortune incited, and to trample on that reputation which rose upon any other basis than that of merit: he never admitted any gross familiarities, or submitted to be treated otherwise than as an equal. Once, when he was without lodging, meat, or clothes, one of his friends, a man not indeed remarkable for moderation in his prosperity, left a message that he desired to see him about nine in the morning. Savage knew that his intention was to assist him; but was very much disgusted that he should presume to prescribe the hour of his attendance, and, I believe, refused to visit him, and rejected his kindness.

[...]

After many alterations and delays, a subscription was at length raised, which did not amount to fifty pounds a year, though twenty were paid by one gentleman: such was the generosity of mankind, that what had been done by a player without solicitation could not now be effected by application and interest; and Savage had a great number to court and to obey for a pension less than that which Mrs. Oldfield paid him without exacting any servilities.

Mr. Savage, however, was satisfied and willing to retire, and was convinced that the allowance, though scanty, would be more than sufficient for him, being now determined to commence a rigid economist, and to live according to the exactest rules of frugality; for nothing was in his opinion more contemptible than a man who, when he knew his income, exceeded it; and yet he confessed that instances of such folly were too common, and lamented that some men were not to be trusted with their own money.

Full of these salutary resolutions he left London in July, 1739, having taken leave with great tenderness of his friends, and parted from the author of this narrative with tears in his eyes. He was furnished with fifteen guineas, and informed that they would be sufficient not only for the expense of his journey, but for his support in Wales for some time, and that there remained but little more of the first collection. He promised a strict adherence to his maxims of parsimony, and went away in the stage-coach; nor did his friends expect to hear from him till he informed them of his arrival at Swansea.

But when they least expected arrived a letter dated the fourteenth day after his departure, in which he sent them word that he was yet upon the road, and without money, and that he therefore could not proceed without a remittance. They then sent him the money that was in their hands, with which he was enabled to reach Bristol, from whence he was to go to Swansea by water.

At Bristol he found an embargo laid upon the shipping, so that he could not immediately obtain a passage; and being therefore obliged to stay there some time he, with his usual felicity, ingratiated himself with many of the principal inhabitants, was invited to their houses, distinguished at their public feasts, and treated with a regard that gratified his vanity, and therefore easily engaged his affection.

He began very early after his retirement to complain of the conduct of his friends in London, and irritated many of them so much by his letters that they withdrew, however honourably, their contributions; and it is believed that little more was paid him than the twenty pounds a year, which were allowed him by the gentleman who proposed the subscription.

[...]

Thus Mr. Savage, after the curiosity of the inhabitants was gratified, found the number of his friends daily decreasing, perhaps without suspecting for what reason their conduct was altered; for he still continued to harass with his nocturnal intrusions those that yet countenanced him and admitted him to their houses.

But he did not spend all the time of his residence at Bristol in visits or at taverns, for he sometimes returned to his studies, and began several considerable designs. When he felt an inclination to write he always retired from the knowledge of his friends, and lay hid in an obscure part of the suburbs till he found himself again desirous of company, to which it is likely that intervals of absence made him more welcome.

He was always full of his design of returning to London to bring his tragedy upon the stage; but, having neglected to depart with the money that was raised for him, he could not afterwards procure a sum sufficient to defray the expenses of his journey: nor perhaps would a fresh supply have had any other effect than, by putting immediate pleasures in his power, to have driven the thoughts of his journey out of his mind.

While he was thus spending the day in contriving a scheme for the morrow, distress stole upon him by imperceptible degrees. His conduct had already wearied some of those who were at first enamoured of his conversation; but he might, perhaps, still have devolved to others, whom he might have entertained with equal success, had not the decay of his clothes made it no longer consistent with their vanity to admit him to their tables or to associate with him in public places. He now began to find every man from home at whose house he called; and was therefore no longer able to procure the necessaries of life, but wandered about the town, slighted and neglected, in quest of a dinner, which he did not always obtain.

To complete his misery he was pursued by the officers for small debts which he had contracted; and was therefore obliged to withdraw from the small number of friends from whom he had still reason to hope for favours. His custom was to lie in bed the greatest part of the day and to go out in the dark with the utmost privacy, and after having paid his visit return again before morning to his lodging, which was in the garret of an obscure inn.

Being thus excluded on one hand, and confined on the other, he suffered the utmost extremities of poverty, and often fasted so long that he was seized with faintness, and had lost his appetite, not being able to bear the smell of meat till the action of his stomach was restored by a cordial.

In this distress he received a remittance of five pounds from London, with which he provided himself a decent coat, and determined to go to London, but unhappily spent his money at a favourite tavern. Thus was he again confined to Bristol, where he was every day hunted by bailiffs. In this exigence he once more found a friend, who sheltered him in his house, though at the usual inconveniences with which his company was attended; for he could neither be persuaded to go to bed in the night nor to rise in the day.

It is observable that in these various scenes of misery he was always disengaged and cheerful: he at some times pursued his studies, and at others continued or enlarged his epistolary correspondence; nor was he ever so far dejected as to endeavour to procure an increase of his allowance by any other methods than accusations and reproaches.

He had now no longer any hopes of assistance from his friends at Bristol, who as merchants, and by consequence sufficiently studious of profit, cannot be supposed to have looked with much compassion upon negligence and extravagance, or to think any excellence equivalent to a fault of such consequence as neglect of economy. It is natural to imagine that many of those who would have relieved his real wants were discouraged from the exertion of their benevolence by observation of the use which was made of their favours, and conviction that relief would only be momentary, and that the same necessity would quickly return.

At last he quitted the house of his friend, and returned to his lodging at the inn, still intending to set out in a few days for London; but on the 10th of January, 1742-3, having been at supper with two of his friends, he was at his return to his lodgings arrested for a debt of about eight pounds, which he owed at a coffee-house, and conducted to the house of a sheriff's officer. . . .

[. . .]

Surely the fortitude of this man deserves, at least, to be mentioned with applause; and, whatever faults may be imputed to him, the virtue of suffering well cannot be denied him. The two powers which, in the opinion of Epictetus, constituted a wise man are those of bearing and forbearing, which cannot indeed be affirmed to have been equally possessed by Savage; and indeed the want of one obliged him very frequently to practise the other.

He was treated by Mr. Dagg, the keeper of the prison, with great humanity; was supported by him at his own table without any certainty of recompense; had a room to himself, to which he could at any time retire from all disturbance; was allowed to stand at the door of the prison, and sometimes taken out into the fields: so that he suffered fewer hardships in prison than he had been accustomed to undergo in the greatest part of his life.

The keeper did not confine his benevolence to a gentle execution of his office, but made some overtures to the creditor for his release, though without effect; and continued, during the whole time of his imprisonment, to treat him with the utmost tenderness and civility.

[. . .]

His time was spent in the prison for the most part in study, or in receiving visits, but sometimes he descended to lower amusements, and diverted himself in the kitchen with the conversation of the criminals; for it was not pleasing to him to be much without company, and though he was very capable of a judicious choice he was often contented with the first that offered: for this he was sometimes reproved by his friends, who found him surrounded with felons; but the reproof was on that, as on other occasions, thrown away: he continued to gratify himself, and to set very little value on the opinion of others.

But here, as in every other scene of his life, he made use of such opportunities as occurred of benefiting those who were more miserable than himself, and was always ready to perform any office of humanity to his fellow-prisoners.

He had now ceased from corresponding with any of his subscribers except one, who yet continued to remit him the twenty pounds a year which he had promised him, and by whom it was expected that he would have been in a very short time enlarged, because he had directed the keeper to enquire after the state of his debts.

However, he took care to enter his name according to the forms of the court, that the creditor might be obliged to make him some allowance if he was continued a prisoner, and when on that occasion he appeared in the hall was treated with very unusual respect.

But the resentment of the city was afterwards raised by some accounts that had been spread of the satire, and he was informed that some of the merchants intended to pay the allowance which the law required, and to detain him a prisoner at their own expense. This he treated as an empty menace; and perhaps might have hastened the publication, only to show how much he was superior to their insults, had not all his schemes been suddenly destroyed.

When he had been six months in prison he received from one of his friends, in whose kindness he had the greatest confidence and on whose assistance he chiefly depended, a letter that contained a charge of very atrocious ingratitude, drawn up in such terms as sudden resentment dictated. Henley, in one of his advertisements, had mentioned "Pope's treatment of Savage." This was supposed by Pope to be the consequence of a complaint made by Savage to Henley, and was therefore mentioned by him with much resentment. Mr. Savage returned a very solemn protestation of his innocence, but, however, appeared much disturbed at the accusation. Some days afterwards he was seized with a pain in his back and side, which, as it was not violent, was not suspected to be dangerous; but growing daily more languid and dejected on the 25th of July he confined himself to his room, and a fever seized his spirits. The symptoms grew every day more formidable, but his condition did not enable him to procure any assistance. The last time that the keeper saw him was on July the 31st, 1743, when Savage, seeing him at his bedside, said, with an uncommon earnestness, "I have something to say to you, Sir," but, after a pause, moved his hand in a melancholy manner, and, finding himself unable to recollect what he was going to communicate, said, "'Tis gone!" The keeper soon after left him; and the next morning he died. He was buried in the churchyard of St. Peter, at the expense of the keeper.

Such were the life and death of Richard Savage, a man equally distinguished by his virtues and vices; and at once remarkable for his weaknesses and abilities.

He was of a middle stature, of a thin habit of body, a long visage, coarse features, and melancholy aspect; of a grave and manly deportment, a solemn dignity of mien, but which, upon a nearer acquaintance, softened into an engaging easiness of manners. His walk was slow, and his voice tremulous and mournful. He was easily excited to smiles, but very seldom provoked to laughter.

His mind was in an uncommon degree vigorous and active. His judgment was accurate, his apprehension quick, and his memory so tenacious that he was frequently observed to know what he had learned from others in a short time, better than those by whom he was informed; and could frequently recollect incidents with all their combination of circumstances, which few would have regarded at the present time, but which the quickness of his apprehension impressed upon him. He had the peculiar felicity that his attention never deserted him: he was present to every object, and regardful of the most trifling occurrences. He had the art of escaping from his own reflections, and accommodating himself to every new scene.

To this quality is to be imputed the extent of his knowledge, compared with the small time which he spent in visible endeavours to acquire it. He mingled in cursory conversation with the same steadiness of attention as others apply to a lecture; and, amidst the appearance of thoughtless gaiety, lost no new idea that was started, nor any hint that could be improved. He had therefore made in coffee-houses the same proficiency as others in their closets; and it is remarkable that the writings of a man of little education and little reading have an air of learning scarcely to be found in any other performances, but which perhaps as often obscures as embellishes them.

His judgment was eminently exact both with regard to writings and to men. The knowledge of life was indeed his chief attainment; and it is not without some satisfaction that I can produce the suffrage of Savage in favour of human nature, of which he never appeared to entertain such odious ideas as some, who perhaps had neither his judgment nor experience, have published, either in ostentation of their sagacity, vindication of their crimes, or gratification of their malice.

His method of life particularly qualified him for conversation, of which he knew how to practise all the graces. He was never vehement or loud, but at once modest and easy, open and respectful; his language was vivacious and elegant, and equally happy upon grave or humourous subjects. He was generally censured for not knowing when to retire, but that was not the defect of his judgment, but of his fortune; when he left his company he was frequently to spend the remaining part of the night in the street, or at least was abandoned to gloomy reflections, which it is not strange that he delayed as long as he could; and sometimes forgot that he gave others pain to avoid it himself.

It cannot be said that he made use of his abilities for the direction of his own conduct: an irregular and dissipated manner of life had made him the slave of every passion that happened to be excited by the presence of its object, and that slavery to his passions reciprocally produced a life irregular and dissipated. He was not master of his own motions, nor could promise anything for the next day.

With regard to his economy nothing can be added to the relation of his life. He appeared to think himself born to be supported by others, and dispensed from all necessity of providing for himself; he therefore never prosecuted any scheme of advantage, nor endeavoured even to secure the profits which his writings might have afforded him. His temper was, in consequence of the dominion of his passions, uncertain and capricious: he was easily engaged, and easily disgusted; but he is accused of retaining his hatred more tenaciously than his benevolence.

He was compassionate both by nature and principle, and always ready to perform offices of humanity; but when he was provoked (and very small offences were sufficient to provoke him), he would prosecute his revenge with the utmost acrimony till his passion had subsided.

His friendship was therefore of little value; for though he was zealous in the support or vindication of those whom he loved, yet it was always dangerous to trust him, because he considered himself as discharged by the first quarrel from all ties of honour or gratitude, and would betray those secrets which, in the warmth of confidence, had been imparted to him. This practice drew upon him an universal accusation of ingratitude: nor can it be denied that he was very ready to set himself free from the load of an obligation, for he could not bear to conceive himself in a state of dependence; his pride being equally powerful with his other passions, and appearing in the form of insolence at one time, and of vanity at another. Vanity, the most innocent species of pride, was most frequently predominant: he could not easily leave off when he had once begun to mention himself or his works; nor ever read his verses without stealing his eyes from the page, to discover, in the faces of his audience, how they were affected with any favourite passage.

A kinder name than that of vanity ought to be given to the delicacy with which he was always careful to separate his own merit from every other man's, and to reject that praise to which he had no claim. He did not forget, in mentioning his performances, to mark every line that had been suggested or amended; and was so accurate as to relate that he owed *three words* in *The Wanderer* to the advice of his friends.

His veracity was questioned, but with little reason; his accounts, though not indeed always the same, were generally consistent. When he loved any man he suppressed all his faults; and, when he had been offended by him, concealed all his virtues: but his characters were generally true, so far as he proceeded; though it cannot be denied that his partiality might have sometimes the effect of falsehood.

In cases indifferent he was zealous for virtue, truth, and justice: he knew very well the necessity of goodness to the present and future happiness of mankind; nor is there perhaps any writer who has less endeavoured to please by flattering the appetites or perverting the judgment.

As an author therefore, and he now ceases to influence mankind in any other character, if one piece which he had resolved to suppress be excepted, he has very little to fear from the strictest moral or religious censure. And though he may not be altogether secure against the objections of the critic, it must, however, be acknowledged that his works are the productions of a genius truly poetical, and, what many writers who have been more lavishly applauded cannot boast, that they have an original air, which has no resemblance of any foregoing work; that the versification and sentiments have a cast peculiar to themselves, which no man can imitate with success, because what was nature in Savage would in another be affectation. It must be confessed that his descriptions are striking, his images animated, his fictions justly imagined, and his allegories artfully pursued; that his diction is elevated, though sometimes forced, and his numbers sonorous and majestic, though frequently sluggish and encumbered. Of his style, the general fault is harshness, and its general excellence is dignity; of his sentiments, the prevailing beauty is sublimity, and uniformity the prevailing defect.

For his life or for his writings none who candidly consider his fortune will think an apology either necessary or difficult. If he was not always sufficiently instructed in his subject, his knowledge was at least greater than could have been attained by others in the same state. If his works were sometimes unfinished, accuracy cannot reasonably be exacted from a man oppressed with want, which he has no hope of relieving but by a speedy publication. The insolence and resentment of which he is accused were not easily to be avoided by a great mind, irritated by perpetual hardships, and constrained hourly to return the spurns of contempt and repress the insolence of prosperity; and vanity may surely readily be pardoned in him, to whom life afforded no other comforts than barren praises, and the consciousness of deserving them.

Those are no proper judges of his conduct who have slumbered away their time on the down of plenty, nor will any wise man presume to say, "Had I been in Savage's condition, I should have lived or written better than Savage."

This relation will not be wholly without its use if those who languish under any part of his sufferings shall be enabled to fortify their patience by reflecting that they feel only those afflictions from which the abilities of Savage did not exempt him; or those who, in confidence of superior capacities or attainments, disregard the common maxims of life, shall be reminded that nothing will supply the want of prudence, and that negligence and irregularity long continued will make knowledge useless, wit ridiculous, and genius contemptible.

Notes

Bibliography

Notes

INTRODUCTION

1. Walter Jackson Bate.
2. *Boswell's Life of Johnson* (1791), Ed. G. B. Hill, revd and enlarged by L. F. Powell (6 vols, 1934; rpt 1979), I: 210; Catherine Talbot, *A Series of Letters between Mrs Elizabeth Carter and Miss Catherine Talbot, from the Year 1741 to 1770,* ed. Revd Montagu Pennington, I: 229–230.
3. John Ruskin, *Praeterita and Dilecta* (Everyman, 2005), pp. 198–200; Beckett, as cited by Deirdre Blair, *Samuel Beckett: A Biography* (1978), p. 257; Bloom, *Shakespeare: The Invention of the Human,* p. 227, and *Genius: A Mosaic of One Hundred Exemplary Creative Minds* (2002), p. 169.
4. Harold Bloom, Introduction, *Dr. Samuel Johnson and James Boswell* (Modern Critical Views), edited by Harold Bloom (1986), pp. 1–2.
5. *Correspondence of Samuel Richardson,* ed. Anna Letitia Barbauld (1804), I: 169, 164–165.
6. William Shaw, *Memoirs of the Life and Writings of the Late Dr Samuel Johnson* (1785), p. 34.
7. *Letters between Mrs Elizabeth Carter and Miss Catherine Talbot,* I: 320.
8. *Diaries, Prayers, and Annals,* ed. E. L. McAdam, Jr., with Donald and Mary Hyde (1958), Yale Edition of the Works of Samuel Johnson, I (1958): 48.
9. For a convenient and fuller introduction to the *Dictionary,* the reader may turn to Jack Lynch's edition of selections from it, *Samuel Johnson's Dictionary* (2002).
10. Henry Hitchings, *Dr. Johnson's Dictionary: The Extraordinary Story of the Book that Defined the World* (2005), p. 1.
11. *Boswell's Life of Johnson,* I: 330–331.
12. *Memoirs of the Life and Writings of the Late Dr Samuel Johnson* (1785), p. 39.

MORALITY, BEHAVIOR, AND PSYCHOLOGY

1. *Don Quixote,* Pt. I, chs. 7, 15, 21.
2. "Lasting but a moment" (Johnson, *Dictionary*).

3. *Rambler* no. 24.

4. Bacon, *Of Friendship.*

5. Psalms iv. 4.

6. "Act of sending away" (Johnson, *Dictionary*).

7. *The Worthy Communicant,* ch. 2, section 3.

8. *Solomon,* I. 236.

9. I.e., erasure.

10. "To lay up; to lodge as in a place of safety" (Johnson, *Dictionary*).

11. Claudius Aelianus, *Varia Historia,* I, par. 10.

12. *De Constantia,* II. 20–26.

13. *Works and Days,* l. 40.

14. Diodorus Siculus, *Bibliotheca historica,* I. 58.2.

15. *Aeneid,* VI. 277.

16. Lucretius, *De Rerum Natura,* II. 1–4.

17. *Hebrews,* xi. 38.

18. "A female guardian of a gate" (Johnson, *Dictionary*).

19. *Ars Poetica,* l. 172.

20. "Continued; not interrupted" (Johnson, *Dictionary*).

21. Lucretius, V. 200–209.

22. Erasmus, *Stultitiae Laus, Praefatio Thomas More Suo* (1515).

23. "To lay up; to lodge as in a place of safety" (Johnson, *Dictionary*).

24. *Macbeth,* V.iii, 43.

SOCIETY AND MANNERS

1. See *Rambler* nos. 18 and 115.

2. *Satires,* I.1. 4–12.

3. *Paradise Lost,* XI. 546.

4. *Henry IV,* Pt. I, V. iv.

5. "Of Education."

6. *Politics,* I.2. 21.

7. *Paradise Lost,* XII. 645.

8. *Odyssey,* XX. 302.

9. Diogenes Laertius, *Lives,* "Socrates," IX.

BIOGRAPHY AND AUTOBIOGRAPHY

1. *Epistles,* III.1.

2. *Historiarum Sui Temporis* (1733), VII, Pt. IV, p. 3.

3. *De Coniuratione Catilinae,* XV.5.

4. Joachim Camerarius, *Vita Melanchthonis* (1777), p. 62.

5. Sir William Temple, "Essay on the Cure of Gout," *Works* (1770), III. 244.

6. Preface, Addison, *Works* (1721), I.xvi.

7. Gilbert Burnet, *Life and Death of Sir Matthew Hale, Kt.* (1682), p. 35.
8. Radicate: "to root; to plant deeply and firmly" (Johnson, *Dictionary*).
9. *Tusculum Disputations,* V. 23. 64.
10. *Domesday* Book.
11. *Satires,* XIII. 159–160.
12. *Odyssey,* XI. 582–592.
13. On a man's disappointment in later life when he returns to his native place or hometown, see also *Idler* nos. 43 and 58.
14. *The Courtier,* II. 11.
15. *Paradise Lost,* V. 38–39.
16. *Paradise Lost,* V. 43.
17. Madeleine de Scudéry, *Clélie* (1654–1661).
18. Pope, *Essay on Criticism,* l. 357.
19. *Sylvae,* V.4.
20. *Sex Libri Plantarum,* IV. 49–60.
21. *Religio Medici,* II. 12.
22. Samuel Butler, *Hudibras,* II.1. 905–908.
23. Edward Young, *Busiris,* I. l. 13.
24. *Paradise Lost,* IV. 37.

LITERATURE AND AUTHORSHIP

1. *Epistles,* II. 1. 170.
2. Pliny, *Natural History,* XXXV. 36. 85.
3. *Epistles,* I. 20.
4. "The lappet of a head which flies loose; a pinmaker" (Johnson, *Dictionary*).
5. One who will "meditate," "contemplate," or "take a view of any thing with the mind" (Johnson, *Dictionary*).
6. *Luke,* xii. 48.
7. *Of the Conduct of the Understanding,* par. 28.
8. Paraphrase from "Of Studies."
9. *Peri Hupsous,* IX. 13.
10. Horace, *Ars Poetica,* l. 192.
11. *2 Henry IV,* III.2. 339.

DEATH

1. *Paradise Lost,* XI. 461–465.
2. *Visions,* tr. Sir Roger L'Estrange (1702), pp. 173–174 (Vision VI).
3. *De senectute,* VII. 24.
4. *Luke,* xv.10.
5. *II Timothy,* i. 10.

POLITICS

1. The British were victorious at Dettingen in 1743, the French at Fontenoy in 1745; *Victory* was sunk in 1744; a fire broke out in 1745 and destroyed over one hundred houses in Cornhill; Westminster Bridge was opened at last in 1750, and the road to the north was completed in June 1761.
2. Admiral Byng was shot in Portsmouth in March 1757 for removing the English fleet from Minorca.
3. The Congress of the United States passed a law in 1824 abolishing arrest and imprisonment for debt.
4. Quebec fell in September 1759.
5. "I love the University of Salamanca," Johnson remarked, "for when the Spaniards were in doubt as to the lawfulness of their conquering America, the University of Salamanca gave it as their opinion that it was not lawful" (James Boswell, *Life of Johnson*, I. 455).

FROM THE PREFACE TO THE *DICTIONARY*

1. Horace, *Epistles*, II. ii. 212.
2. Henry Hammond (1605–1660), author of *Paraphrase and Annotations on the New Testament.*
3. Richard Hooker (1554–1600), author of *The Laws of Ecclesiastical Polity.*
4. Nathan Bailey (d. 1742), lexicographer; Robert Ainsworth (1660–1743), lexicographer and author of *Thesaurus Linguæ Latinæ Compendiarius;* Edward Phillips (1630–c.1696), lexicographer and author of *The New World of Words.*
5. To "detort" is "to wrest from the original import" (Johnson, *Dictionary*).
6. "Dryness; aridity; want of moisture" (Johnson, *Dictionary*).
7. "The act of lopping or cutting" (Johnson, *Dictionary*).
8. Robert Boyle (1627–1691), author of *The Sceptical Chymist.*

RASSELAS, PRINCE OF ABYSSINIA

1. "Thinness" (Johnson, *Dictionary*).
2. "Flying; passing through the air" (Johnson, *Dictionary*).
3. Imlac's dissertation on poetry has been variously interpreted as an exposition of Johnson's own theories about poetry and as contradictory to them.
4. This famous sentiment is articulated by Johnson in many places, but see especially *Rambler* no. 165.
5. Early on, Johnson had thoughts of including the phrase "choice of life" in the title of *Rasselas.* See also chapter XVI.
6. "Disputant" (Johnson, *Dictionary*).
7. On marriage as both the happiest and unhappiest of states, see *Rambler* nos. 18, 39, 45, and 115; see also chapter XXIX below.
8. Reposite: "To lay up; to lodge as in a place of safety" (Johnson, *Dictionary*).

9. In *Rambler* no. 207, Johnson writes of "the emptiness of human enjoyment."
10. Johnson's warnings against stagnation, especially in a state of grief and sorrow, are diverse and urgent. See, for example, *Rambler* no. 47.
11. The astronomer's character and assertions often have been likened to Johnson's. See *Rambler* no. 180.
12. The foregoing conversations with the astronomer, climaxing in chapter XLI on the "dangerous prevalence of imagination," or overindulgence in imagination, and in chapter XLVI, highlight Johnson's lifelong fear of insanity and his urgent preoccupation with what constitutes madness and "disease of the imagination."
13. "Influence; predominance" (Johnson, *Dictionary*).
14. "Not to be separated; incapable of being broken or destroyed by dissolution of parts" (Johnson, *Dictionary*).

PREFACE TO *SHAKESPEARE*

1. William Lily, Thomas Linacre, Sir Thomas More, Reginald Pole, Sir John Cheke, Stephen Gardiner, Sir Thomas Smith, Walter Haddon, Roger Ascham.
2. *Il Palmerino d'Inghilterra.*
3. *Troilus and Cressida,* III. iii. 224.
4. It is generally accepted that Johnson directed this rebuke against his good friend the actor David Garrick, who confessed his surprise since he maintained he had made his collection of old Shakespeare editions available to Johnson.
5. Pierre Daniel Huet.
6. The great editor Dr. Richard Bentley.
7. Joseph Scaliger, *Epistolae:* "Our conjectures make fools of us, putting us to shame, when later we hit upon better MSS."
8. Virgil, *Eclogue,* I. 25, transl. Dryden, *Essay on Dramatic Poesy,* I. 79–80: "as are wont the cypresses among the bending osiers."

COWLEY

1. Aristotle, in the *Poetics.*
2. *Essays,* ed. W. P. Ker (1926), II, 102.
3. Pope, *Essay on Criticism,* l. 298.
4. Harmonious disharmony.
5. "The art of curing by external applications" (Johnson, *Dictionary*).

MILTON

1. Jonathan Richardson, *Explanatory Notes and Remarks on Paradise Lost* (1734), p. 2.
2. John Toland, *Life of Milton,* p. 139

3. Pagan mythology.
4. *Spectator* no. 303.
5. *Spectator* no. 273.
6. *Essays,* ed. W. P. Ker (1926), I. 80.
7. *Spectator* no. 297.
8. Preface to *Sylvae,* in *Essays,* ed. W. P. Ker, I. 268.
9. William Locke.

POPE

1. The *Guardian* no. 92.
2. A publication that was not authorized.
3. Samuel Patrick was a publisher of classical dictionaries.
4. *Works of Jonathan Swift,* ed. Sir Walter Scott (1814), XVIII. 138.
5. Richard Bentley, classical scholar satirized by both Pope and Swift and notorious for his "slashing" editing of Milton and others.
6. John Dennis, "Remarks on Pope's Homer," *Critical Works* (1939), ed. Hooker, II. 136.
7. Virgil, *Eclogue* IV.
8. *The Book of Isaiah.*
9. Horace, *Odes,* iv. 2: free verse.
10. The poet Samuel Cobb.
11. *Aeneid,* V. 144–147.
12. Ovid, *Metamorphoses,* I. 533–538.
13. Dennis, *Critical Works,* ed. Hooker, II. 330–331.
14. Dennis, *Critical Works,* ed. Hooker, II. 328.
15. Painstaking felicity.
16. Joseph Warton, Johnson's friend and headmaster of Winchester College, in *An Essay on the Genius and Writings of Pope,* I. 1756.
17. Preface to *Tyrannical Love.*
18. *The Improvement of the Mind* (1741).

COLLINS

1. First printed in *The Poetical Calendar* (1763).

Bibliography

PRIMARY SOURCES

Johnson's Works

The Yale Edition of the Works of Samuel Johnson, presently 15 vols, not consecutive (New Haven: Yale University Press, 1958 onwards):

Diaries, Prayers, and Annals, ed. E. L. McAdam, Jr, with Donald and Mary Hyde, vol. I (1958)

The Idler and The Adventurer (ed. W. J. Bate, John M. Bullitt, and L. F. Powell), in *Works,* vol. II (1963)

The Rambler, ed. W. J. Bate and Albrecht B. Strauss, vols III–V (1969)

Poems, ed. E. L. McAdam, Jr, with George Milne, vol. VI (1964)

Johnson on Shakespeare, ed. Arthur Sherbo (with an introduction by Bertrand A. Bronson), vols VII and VIII (1968)

A Journey to the Western Islands of Scotland, ed. Mary Lascelles, vol. IX (1971)

Political Writings, ed. Donald Greene, vol. X (1977)

Sermons, ed. Jean Hagstrum and James Gray, vol. XIV (1978)

Voyage to Abyssinia, ed. Joel J. Gold, vol. XV (1985)

Rasselas and Other Tales, ed. Gwin J. Kolb, vol. XVI (1990)

Johnson on the English Language, ed. Gwin J. Kolb and Robert DeMaria, Jr, vol. XVIII (1990)

A Commentary on Mr Pope's Principles of Morality, or Essay on Man (a Translation from the French), ed. O. M. Brack, vol. XVII (2005)

The Works of Samuel Johnson, LL.D. (with life), ed. John Hawkins (15 vols, 1787–1789)

The Dictionary of the English Language (1st edn 1755)

The Dictionary of the English Language (4th edn 1773)

Lynch, Jack (ed.), *Samuel Johnson's Dictionary* (2002)

Crystal, David (ed.), *Dr Johnson's Dictionary* (2005)

Hazen, A. T. (ed.), *Samuel Johnson's Prefaces and Dedications* (1937)

Fleeman, J. D. (ed.), *The Complete English Poems* (1971)

Fleeman, J. D. (ed.), *Journey to the Western Islands of Scotland* (1985)

Chapman, R. W. (ed.), *The Letters of Samuel Johnson* (3 vols, 1952)

Redford, Bruce (ed.), *The Letters of Samuel Johnson* (5 vols, 1992–1994)

BIOGRAPHIES, EDITIONS, AND CRITICAL WORKS

This is a selective list of editions and writings.

Abbott, J. L., *John Hawkesworth* (1982)

Adam, E. L., and L. F. Powell, *Dr Johnson and the English Law* (6 vols, 1934–1950; vols. V and VI, 2d ed., 1964)

Adam, R. B., *Facsimile of Boswell's Notebook* (1919)

Baker, Peter et al. (eds), *The Correspondence of James Boswell with David Garrick, Edmund Burke, and Edmond Malone* (1986)

Balderston, K. C. (ed.), *Thraliana: The Diary of Mrs Hester Lynch Thrale* (2 vols, 1942)

Balderston, Katherine, "Johnson's Vile Melancholy," in *The Age of Johnson,* ed. F. W. Hilles and W. S. Lewis (1949), pp. 3–14

Barbauld, Anna Laetitia (ed.) *Correspondence of Samuel Richardson* (6 vols, 1804)

Basker, James G., "Johnson, Boswell, and the Abolition of Slavery," *The New Rambler* (2000–2001), pp. 36–48

—— "Samuel Johnson and the African-American Reader," *The New Rambler* (1994–1995)

Bate, Walter Jackson, *Samuel Johnson* (1977)

—— *The Achievement of Samuel Johnson* (1955)

Bloch, Marc, *The Royal Touch: Sacred Monarchy and Scrofula in England and France* (1973)

Bloom, E. A. and L. D. Bloom (eds), *Piozzi Letters* (2 vols, 1989)

Bloom, E. A., *Samuel Johnson in Grub Street* (1957)

Bloom, Edward A. and Lillian D. Bloom (eds), *The Journals and Letters of Fanny Burney* (Madame D'Arblay) (12 vols, 1978)

Bloom, Harold, *Shakespeare: The Invention of the Human* (1998)

Bond, William H., *Eighteenth-Century Studies in Honor of Donald F. Hyde* (1970)

Boswell, James, *Journals: The Yale Editions of the Private Papers of James Boswell* (listed chronologically):

Boswell's London Journal 1762–1765, ed. Frederick A. Pottle (1951)

Boswell in Search of a Wife 1766–1769, ed. Frank Brady and Frederick A. Pottle (1956)

Boswell for the Defence 1769–1774, ed. William K. Wimsatt, Jr. and Frederick A. Pottle (1960)

Boswell's Journal of a Tour to the Hebrides with Samuel Johnson, LL.D., 1773, ed. Frederick A. Pottle and Charles H. Bennett (1961)

Boswell: The Ominous Years 1774–1776, ed. Charles Ryskamp and Frederick A. Pottle (1963)

Boswell in Extremes 1776–1778, ed. Charles McC. Weis and Frederick A. Pottle (1970)

Boswell: Laird of Auchinleck 1778–1782, ed. Joseph W. Reed and Frederick A. Pottle (1977; rpt Edinburgh, 1993)

Boswell: The Applause of the Jury 1782–1785, ed. Irma S. Lustig and Frederick A. Pottle (1981)

—— *Notebook,* ed. R. B. Adam (1919)

Boswell Papers, Beinecke Rare Book and Manuscript Library, Yale University

Boswell's Life of Johnson, Together with Boswell's Journal of a Tour to the Hebrides and Johnson's Diary of a Journey into North Wales, ed. G. B. Hill, revd and enlarged by L. F. Powell (6 vols, 1934; rpt 1979)

Boulton, James T., *Johnson: The Critical Heritage* (1971)

Brack, O. M. and R. E. Kelley, *The Early Biographies of Samuel Johnson* (1974)

——— (eds), *The Shorter Prose Writings of Samuel Johnson* (1987)

Brady, Frank, *James Boswell: The Later Years 1769–1795* (1984)

Broadley, A. M., *Doctor Johnson and Mrs Thrale* (1910)

Bronson, Bertrand H., *Johnson Agonistes and Other Essays* (1965)

Brooke, John, "The Library of King George III," *Yale University Library Gazette* 52 (1977)

Brooks, Cleanth (ed.), *Correspondence of Thomas Percy and William Shenstone* (1977)

Brownell, Morris, *Samuel Johnson's Attitude to the Arts* (1989)

Burney, Fanny, *The Early Diary of Fanny Burney,* ed. A. R. Ellis. (1889)

Burney, Frances, *The Early Journals and Letters of Fanny Burney* (vol III: part I, 1778–1779), ed. Lars E. Troide and Stewart J. Cooke (1994)

——— *The Early Journals and Letters of Fanny Burney* (vol. IV: part II, 1780–1781), ed. Betty Rizzo (2003)

Chambers, Robert, *A Course of Lectures on the English Law,* ed. Thomas M. Curley (1986)

Chapin, C. F., *The Religious Thought of Samuel Johnson* (1968)

Chapman, R. W. (ed.), *The Letters of Samuel Johnson* (3 vols, 1952)

Clark, J. C. D., *Samuel Johnson: Literature, Religion and English Cultural Politics from the Restoration to Romanticism* (1994)

Clifford, James L. (ed.), *Dr [Thomas] Campbell's Diary* (1947)

——— "Johnson's Trip to Devon in 1762," in *Eighteenth-Century Studies in Honor of Donald F. Hyde* (1970)

——— *Dictionary Johnson* (1979)

——— *Hester Lynch Piozzi* (1941, 1952)

——— *Young Sam Johnson* (1955)

Clingham, Greg (ed.), *The Cambridge Companion to Samuel Johnson* (1997)

Cochrane, J. A., *Dr Johnson's Printer: The Life of William Strahan* (1964)

Copeland, T. W. et al. (eds.), *The Correspondence of Edmund Burke* (1958–1970)

Crystal, David (ed.), *Dr Johnson's Dictionary* (2005)

Curley, Thomas M., *Samuel Johnson and the Age of Travel* (1976)

——— *Sir Robert Chambers: Law, Literature and Empire in the Age of Johnson*

——— (ed.), *A Course of Lectures on the English Law* (1986)

D'Arblay, Madame Frances, *Diary and Letters of Madame d'Arblay* (edited by her niece, 1842)

Davies, Thomas, *Memoirs of the Life of David Garrick* (1808)

——— *Miscellaneous and Fugitive Pieces* (1773)

Davis, Bertram H., "Johnson's Visit to Percy," in *Johnson After Two Hundred Years,* ed. P. J. Korshin (1986)

——— *The Life of Samuel Johnson, LL.D. by Sir John Hawkins* (1961)

——— *Thomas Percy: A Scholar-Cleric in the Age of Johnson* (1989)

DeMaria, Robert, Jr, *The Life of Samuel Johnson* (1993)

——— *Samuel Johnson and the Life of Reading* (1997)

——— *Johnson's Dictionary and the Language of Learning* (1986)

Dobson, Austin, *The Diary and Letters of Madame D'Arblay* (1904)

Eaves, T. C. D., "Dr Johnson's Letters to Richardson," *PMLA,* 75 (1960)

Eaves, T. C. D. and B. D. Kimpel, *Samuel Richardson* (1971)

Fairer, David, "Oxford and the Literary World" in *The History of the University of Oxford*, vol. 5 *(The Eighteenth Century)*, ed. L. S. Sutherland and L. G. Mitchell (1986)

—— "Authorship Problems in *The Adventurer*," *Review of English Studies*, 25 (1974)

Fifer, C. N. (ed.), *The Correspondence of James Boswell with Certain Members of The Club* (1976)

Fleeman, J. D., *A Bibliography of the Works of Samuel Johnson* (2000)

—— *A Preliminary Handlist of Documents and Manuscripts of Samuel Johnson* (1967)

—— "Some Notes on Johnson's Prayers and Meditations," *Review of English Studies*, n.s. 29 (May 1968), 172–179 [Corrections of Yale ed., vol. I]

—— (ed.), *Samuel Johnson: A Journey to the Western Islands of Scotland* (1985)

—— (ed.), *Early Biographical Writings of Samuel Johnson* (1973)

—— (ed.), *Samuel Johnson: The Complete English Poems* (1971)

Folkenflik, Robert, *Samuel Johnson: Biographer* (1978)

—— "The Politics of Johnson's *Dictionary* Revisited," *Age of Johnson*, vol. 18 (2007), pp. 1–17

—— "Johnson's Politics," in *The Cambridge Companion to Samuel Johnson* (1977), pp. 102–113

Forbes, Margaret, *James Beattie and His Friends* (1904)

The Gentleman's Magazine (1731–1907)

Gray, James, "*Arras! Hellas!*, A Fresh Look at Samuel Johnson's French," in *Johnson After Two Hundred Years*, ed. Paul Korshin (1986), pp. 85–86

Greene, Donald, *Samuel Johnson's Library* (1975)

—— "Dr Johnson's 'Late Conversion': A Reconsideration," *Johnsonian Studies*, ed. Magdi Wahba (1962)

—— *The Politics of Samuel Johnson* (1960, 2nd edn 1990)

Grundy, Isobel, *Samuel Johnson and the Scale of Greatness* (1986)

Guppy, H. and M. Tyson (eds), *The French Journals of Mrs Thrale and Doctor Johnson* (1932)

Hagstrum, Jean, *Samuel Johnson's Literary Criticism* (rev. edn 1967)

Hanley, Brian, *Samuel Johnson as Book Reviewer* (2001)

Harwood, Thomas, *History and Antiquities of Lichfield* (1806)

Hawkins, Sir John, *The Life of Samuel Johnson, LL.D.* (2nd edn 1787)

Hazen, Allen T., *Samuel Johnson's Prefaces and Dedications* (1937)

Hemlow, Joyce, *The History of Fanny Burney* (1958)

Hill, G. Birkbeck (ed.), *Johnsonian Miscellanies* (2 vols, 1897)

—— and L. F. Powell (eds), *Boswell's Life of Johnson* (5 vols, 1934; reprinted 1979)

Hilles, Frederick W. (ed.), *New Light on Dr Johnson* (1959)

Hitchings, Henry, *Dr Johnson's Dictionary: The Extraordinary Story of the Book That Defined the World* (2005)

Holmes, Richard, *Dr Johnson and Mr Savage* (1993)

Hopkins, M. A., *Dr Johnson's Lichfield* (1952)

Hyde, Mary, *The Impossible Friendship: Boswell and Mrs Thrale* (1972)

—— *The Thrales of Streatham Park* (1977)

—— "The Library Portraits at Streatham Park," *The New Rambler* (1979), pp. 10–24

Isles, Duncan, "The Lennox Collection," *Harvard Library Bulletin* 19 (1971)

Jackson, John, *History of the City and Cathedral of Lichfield* (1805)

Jackson, Stanley W., *Melancholia and Depression: From Hippocratic Times to Modern Times* (1986)

Johnson, Boswell and Their Circle: 1965. *Essays Presented to L. F. Powell* (1965) by Mary M. Lascelles, James L. Clifford, J. D. Fleeman, and John P. Hardy

Jonard, Norbert, *Giuseppe Baretti* (1963)

Kaminski, Thomas, *The Early Career of Samuel Johnson* (1987)

Kernan, Alvin, *Samuel Johnson and the Impact of Print* (1989)

Knight, Ellis Cordelia, *The Autobiography of Miss Knight,* ed. Roger Fulford (1960)

Kolb, G. J., "Johnson's 'Little Pompadour': A Textual Crux and a Hypothesis," in *Restoration and Eighteenth-Century Literature,* ed. Carroll Camden (1963)

Korshin, Paul J., "Johnson and the Earl of Orrery," *Eighteenth-Century Studies in Honor of Donald F. Hyde* (1970)

—— (ed.), *Johnson After Two Hundred Years* (1986)

Larsen, Lyle, *Dr Johnson's Household* (1985)

Leslie, C. R. and Tom Taylor, *Life and Times of Sir Joshua Reynolds* (1865)

Lewis, W. S., *The Yale Edition of Horace Walpole's Correspondence,* ed. W. S. Lewis et al. (1937–1983)

Liebert, H. W., "Portraits of the Author: Lifetime Likenesses of Samuel Johnson," in *English Portraits of the Seventeenth and Eighteenth Centuries* (1974)

Lillywhite, Bryant, *London Coffee Houses* (1963)

Lipking, Lawrence, *Samuel Johnson: The Life of an Author* (1998)

Little, D. M. and G. M. Kahrl (eds), *The Letters of David Garrick* (3 vols, 1963)

Lonsdale, Roger (ed.), *Samuel Johnson: The Lives of the Poets* (4 vols, 2006)

—— *Dr Charles Burney* (1965)

Lustig, Irma S., "The Myth of Johnson's Misogyny in the *Life of Johnson:* Another View," in *Boswell in Scotland and Beyond,* ed. Thomas Crawford (1997), pp. 71–88

—— "'My Dear Enemy': Margaret Montgomerie Boswell in the *Life of Johnson,*" in *Boswell: Citizen of the World, Man of Letters,* ed. Irma S. Lustig (1995)

Lynch, Jack and Anne McDermott (eds), *Anniversary Essays on Johnson's* Dictionary (2005)

Lynch, Jack (ed.), *Samuel Johnson's Dictionary* (2002)

Lynn, Steven, "Locke's Eye, Adam's Tongue and Johnson's Word: Language, Marriage and the Choice of Life," *Age of Johnson,* 3 (1990), 35–61

Martin, Peter, *A Life of James Boswell* (1999, 2000)

—— *Edmond Malone, Shakespeare Scholar: A Literary Biography* (1995)

—— *Samuel Johnson: A Biography* (2008)

Mathias, Peter, *The Brewing Industry in England, 1700–1830* (1959)

Maxted, Ian, *The London Book Trades, 1775–1800* (1977)

McGuffie, H. L., *Samuel Johnson in the British Press, 1749–1784* (1971)

McHenry, Lawrence, "Samuel Johnson's Tics and Gesticulations," *Journal of the History of Medicine and Allied Sciences,* 22 (1967), pp. 152–168

McIntyre, Ian, *Garrick* (1999)

Menninger, Roy W., "Johnson's Psychic Turmoil and the Women in His Life," *The Age of Johnson,* 5 (1992), pp. 179–200

Midgley, Graham, *University Life in Eighteenth-Century Oxford* (1996)

Morgan, Lee, *Dr Johnson's "Own Dear Master": The Life of Henry Thrale* (1998)

Murphy, Arthur, *An Essay on the Life and Genius of Samuel Johnson* (1792) in *Johnsonian Miscellanies*, vol. I

Namier, Sir Lewis and John Brooke, *The House of Commons, 1754–1790* (3 vols, 1964)

Nicholls, Graham, "'The Race with Death': Samuel Johnson and Holy Dying," *The New Rambler* (2005–2006), pp. 11–21

Nichols, John, *Literary Anecdotes of the Eighteenth Century* (9 vols, 1812–1815)

Northcote, James, *Life of Sir Joshua Reynolds* (1818)

Pennington, Revd Montagu (ed.), *A Series of Letters between Mrs Elizabeth Carter and Miss Catherine Talbot 1741–1770* (2 vols, 1809)

Percy, Thomas, "Diary," BL Add. MS. 32, 332–336, 337 (begins 17 June 1753)

Piozzi, Hester Lynch, *Anecdotes of the Late Samuel Johnson, During the Last Twenty Years of his Life* (1786)

—— *Letters To and From the Late Samuel Johnson, LL.D.* (2 vols, 1788)

Porter, Roy, *Enlightenment: Britain and the Creation of the Modern World* (2000)

—— *London: A Social History* (1994)

—— *Mind-Forg'd Manacles: A History of Madness in England from the Restoration to the Regency* (1987)

Pottle, Frederick A., *James Boswell: The Earlier Years, 1740–1769* (1966)

—— *The Literary Career of James Boswell, Esq.* (1929)

Reade, A. L., *Johnsonian Gleanings* (11 vols, 1909–1952; reprinted 1968)

Reddick, Allen, *The Making of Johnson's Dictionary, 1746–1773* (1990, 1996)

Redford, Bruce (ed.), *The Letters of Samuel Johnson* (5 vols, 1992)

—— *James Boswell's Life of Johnson,* The Yale Editions of the Private Papers of James Boswell: Research Edition, vol. 2: 1766–1776 (1998)

Roberts, William (ed.), *Memoirs of the Life and Correspondence of Mrs Hannah More* (2 vols, 1834)

Rogers, Pat, *The Samuel Johnson Encyclopedia* (1996)

Rudé, George, *Wilkes and Liberty* (1962)

Sachs, Arieh, *Passionate Intelligence: Imagination and Reason in the Work of Samuel Johnson* (1967)

Schwartz, R. B., *Samuel Johnson and the New Science* (1971)

Seward, Anna, *The Swan of Litchfield: Correspondence of Anna Seward,* ed. Hesketh Pearson (1936)

Shaw, William, *Memoirs of the Life and Writings of the Late Dr Samuel Johnson* (1785)

Sherbo, Arthur (ed.), *Hester Lynch Piozzi: Anecdotes of the late Samuel Johnson, LL.D. during the Last Twenty Years of His Life* (1974)

—— (ed.), William Shaw, *Memoirs of the Life and Writings of the Late Dr Samuel Johnson* (1785, 1974)

—— *Samuel Johnson, Editor of Shakespeare* (1956)

Sledd, J. H. and G. J. Kolb, *Dr Johnson's Dictionary* (1955)

Small, M. R., *Charlotte Ramsay Lennox* (1935)

Smallwood, P. J., *Johnson's Preface to Shakespeare* (1985)

Thrale, Hester Lynch, *Thraliana: The Diary of Mrs Hester Lynch Thrale, 1776–1809,* ed. Katharine C. Balderston (2 vols, 2nd edn 1951)

Tomarken, Edward, *A History of the Commentary on Selected Writings of Samuel Johnson* (1994)

Tracy, Clarence, *The Artificial Bastard: A Biography of Richard Savage* (1953)

Twining, the Revd Thomas, *Recreations and Studies of a Country Clergyman of the Eighteenth Century* (1882)

Tyson, Moses and Henry Guppy (eds), *The French Journals of Mrs Thrale and Doctor Johnson* (1932)

Vance, John A., *Samuel Johnson and the Sense of History* (1984)

Wain, John, *Johnson on Johnson* (1976)

—— *Samuel Johnson: A Biography* (1974)

Waingrow, Marshall (ed.), *The Correspondence and Other Papers of James Boswell Relating to the Making of the 'Life of Johnson'* (1969), The Yale Edition of the Private Papers of James Boswell: Research Edition, Boswell's Correspondence, vol. 2

—— (ed.), *James Boswell's Life of Johnson,* The Yale Editions of the Private Papers of James Boswell: Research Edition, vol. 1: 1709–1765 (1994)

—— (ed.), *James Boswell's Life of Johnson,* The Yale Editions of the Private Papers of James Boswell: Research Edition, vol. 2: 1766–1776 (1998)

Weinbrot, Howard D., "Johnson, Jacobitism and the Historiography of Nostalgia," in *The Age of Johnson,* vol. 7 (1996), pp. 163 ff.

—— "Johnson and Jacobitism Redux: Evidence, Interpretation and Intellectual History," in *The Age of Johnson,* vol. 8 (1997), pp. 89–125

—— "Meeting the Monarch: Johnson, Boswell and the Anatomy of a Genre," in *The Age of Johnson,* vol. 18 (2007), pp. 131–150

Wendorf, Richard and Charles Ryskamp, "A Bluestocking Friendship: The Letters of Elizabeth Montagu and Frances Reynolds in the Princeton Collection," *Princeton University Chronicle,* 41 (1979–1980), pp. 173–207

Wendorf, Richard, *Sir Joshua Reynolds: The Painter in Society* (1996)

—— *The Elements of Life: Biography and Portrait-Painting in Stuart and Georgian England* (1990)

Wheatley, Henry B., *London Past and Present: Its History, Associations, and Tradition* (3 vols, 1891)

Wiltshire, John, *Samuel Johnson in the Medical World* (1991)

Wimsatt, William K., *The Prose Style of Samuel Johnson* (1941)

Windham, William, *The Diary of the Right Hon. William Windham 1784–1810,* ed. Mrs Henry Baring (1866)

Wooll, John, *Biographical Memoir of the Late Rev. Joseph Warton* (1806)

Woolman, Thomas, *A Preface to Samuel Johnson* (1993)

Wright, J. D., "Unpublished Letters of Dr Johnson," *Bulletin of the John Rylands Library* 16 (1932)

Yung, K. K., *Samuel Johnson, 1709–1784: A Bicentenary Exhibition* (1984)